WIDOWS IN WHITE: MIGRATION AND THE TRANSFORMATION OF RURAL ITALIAN WOMEN, SICILY, 1880–1920

The transnational migrations of the early twentieth century had a profound impact on the lives of many people, not least those who were left behind. In this lively interdisciplinary study, Linda Reeder examines how the lives of rural Sicilian women changed as a result of male migration to the United States.

Reeder uses a wide variety of primary sources, including birth and death records, government documents, novels, and newspapers, to trace the changing notions of female and male in rural Sicily, and to explore the impact of industrialization on motherhood, family, wage work, and female civic identity. She also shows how the processes of migration, globalization, and nation formation are deeply gendered. Reeder uses the methods and theories of social history, women's history, anthropology, and cultural studies to explain how migration altered women's identities. The choices these women made regarding family, work, schooling, and material wealth redefined the boundaries of community and nation and helped them claim a central place in the rapidly expanding global economy.

LINDA REEDER is an assistant professor in the Department of History at the University of Missouri, Columbia.

STUDIES IN GENDER AND HISTORY
General editors: Franca Iacovetta and Karen Dubinsky

Widows in White

Migration and the Transformation of Rural Italian Women, Sicily, 1880–1920

LINDA REEDER

UNIVERSITY OF TORONTO PRESS
Toronto Buffalo London

Toronto Buffalo London

ISBN 0-8020-3731-3 (cloth)
ISBN 0-8020-8525-3 (paper)

National Library of Canada Cataloguing in Publication

Reeder, Linda
Widows in white : migration and the transformation of rural Italian women, Sicily, 1880–1920 / Linda Reeder.

(Studies in gender and history)
Includes bibliographical references and index.
ISBN 0-8020-3731-3 (bound) ISBN 0-8020-8525-3 (pbk.)

1. Rural women – Italy – Sicily – Social conditions. 2. Sicily (Italy) – Rural conditions. 3. Sicily (Italy) – Emigration and immigration – History. I. Title. II. Series.

HQ1644.S5R44 2003 305.42'09458'091734 C2002-903138-9

University of Toronto Press acknowledges the financial assistance to its publishing program of the Canada Council for the Arts and the Ontario Arts Council.

University of Toronto Press acknowledges the financial support for its publishing activities of the Government of Canada through the Book Publishing Industry Development Program (BDIDP).

To David and Ana Ruth

Contents

List of Tables and Figures

Tables

Figures

Acknowledgments

This work owes a great deal to the intellectual, financial, and emotional support of many institutions and people on both sides of the Atlantic. Rutgers University and the Fondazione Giovanni Agnelli in Torino provided financial support at the initial stages. The Research Board and Research Council of the University of Missouri generously financed additional research.

Gero Difrancesco, librarian, archivist, and historian of Sutera, offered invaluable assistance. He guided me not only through the municipal and provincial archives, but also through the intricacies of local politics and the history of Sutera. Dottore Claudio Torrisi, the director of the State Archive of Caltanissetta, enthusiastically supported my work and helped me sift through property records. I am also deeply indebted to the staffs of the provincial archives in Caltanissetta, Palermo, and the Archivio Centrale in Rome.

Over the years I have worked on this project I have benefited from the encouragement and criticism of a great many people. I wish to thank Rudolph Bell, my advisor at Rutgers University, who has given me help and support at every stage of this project, and who taught me that one should always follow one's heart, even in academia. I would also like to thank Patrizia Audenino, Sam Baily, Peter D'Agostino, Donna Gabaccia, Franca Iacovetta, Theodore Koditschek, Kerby Miller, Mary Neth, Marlou Shrover, Maddalena Tirabassi, and Virginia Yans for their suggestions and comments during various stages of the project. I also wish to thank LeeAnn Whites for challenging me to think about my material in different ways. Her friendship has improved my work and my life enormously.

The hospitality and generosity of Sicilians have left me indebted to many people on the island. I owe an enormous debt of gratitude to all the people in Sutera who shared their world and their stories with a stranger. To everyone who worked at the *municipio,* including Dr Mario Difrancesco, Avv. Caltagirone, and Angelo Ferlisi, thank you for making my work a pleasure. I would also like to thank Fru Pardi, Angelo Montalto, Andrea Montalto, Marta Montalto, Carmela Pardi, Juan Esperanza, Emiliano Esperanza, and Daniele Esperanza, who opened their homes and hearts to us. In Palermo, I wish to thank Giuseppe Gagliano, Lelia Collura, Rosella Gagliano, Guglielmo Gagliano, Ester Gagliano, Valentina Gagliano, and Gianfranco Salatiello for making that city feel like home.

Many thanks go to my friends who listen to my laments, help keep my priorities in order, and keep me entertained: Lisa Baron, Michelle Brattain, Michael Davidovits, Ingrid Guiter, Grace Elizabeth Hale, Anna Lingo, Andrew Milne, Chris Padgett, Roberto Romano. I am especially grateful to Carol Hendrickson and Marco Giametti for introducing me to Sutera and for their Roman hospitality.

This book owes its existence to family. The support and faith of Florence Tager, Miriam Tager and Robin Givens helped me through many difficult times. Julie and Jim Montgomery provided sanctuary at critical moments. Don and Carol Reeder introduced me to Italy and generously supported many years of study and travel. I dedicate this book to David Tager and Ana Ruth Reeder Tager. David's love, editorial skills, and willingness to travel to Sutera and beyond truly made this book possible. To Ana Ruth, who makes everything worthwhile.

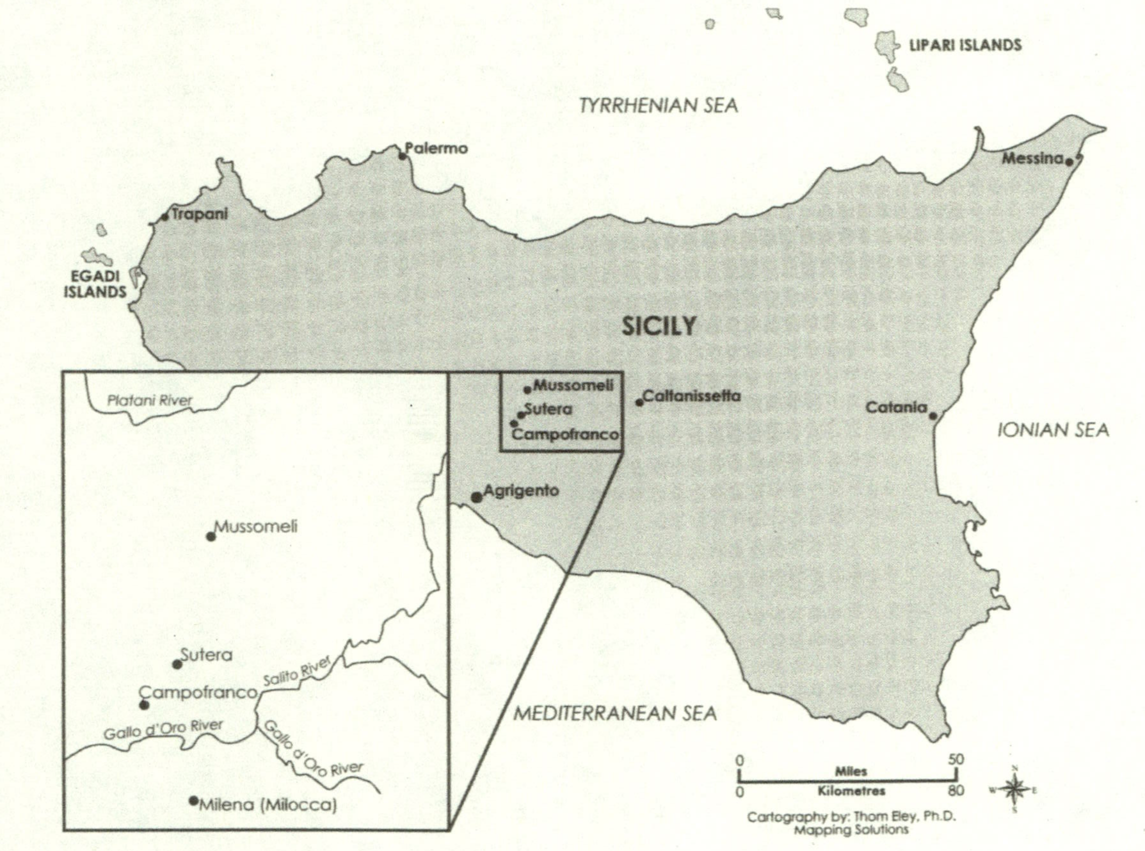
LIPARI ISLANDS
TYRRHENIAN SEA
Palermo
Messina
Trapani
EGADI ISLANDS
SICILY
Mussomeli
Sutera
Campofranco
Caltanissetta
Catania
IONIAN SEA
Agrigento
Platani River
Mussomeli
Sutera
Salito River
Campofranco
Gallo d'Oro River
Gallo d'Oro River
Milena (Milocca)
MEDITERRANEAN SEA
0
Miles
50
0
Kilometres
80
Cartography by: Thom Eley, Ph.D.
Mapping Solutions

WIDOWS IN WHITE:
MIGRATION AND THE TRANSFORMATION OF RURAL ITALIAN WOMEN, SICILY, 1880–1920

Introduction: The Women of the South

Sutera, a small town in central-western Sicily, clings to the side of Mount San Paolino, a squat, flat-topped mountain. From the main square, bounded by the church and the city hall, the wrinkled hills, scarred by centuries of erosion, seem to stretch out to the edge of the earth. Amidst this vast expanse of land and sky, the houses are built one top of another as if seeking comfort in numbers; they crowd in on the narrow streets and turn their backs on the surrounding countryside. As you stroll through the town in the silence of a late summer afternoon, broken only by an occasional shout or passing mule, Sutera seems lost in the past. This sense of entering a fast-disappearing world is reinforced by the fleeting glimpses of women dressed in black scuttling down side streets or peering out from behind shuttered windows, and by the men returning home from the fields, their hoes slung over their shoulders. With the sudden thunder of a motorcycle, the twenty-first century comes roaring back. As you wander into the main square and see young women and men dressed in the latest Milan fashions crowding into the coffee bar to watch new music videos, you are reminded sharply that this town is not frozen in the past. The beeping sounds of video games and the digital rhythms of Euro-rock bear witness to rapid change from one generation to the next. The older residents seem to live lives shaped by a world long since vanished, when men and women worked in separate spaces and life moved slowly. The town's youth live lives that seem to defy traditional Sicilian gender roles and wholeheartedly embrace the current faith in rapid change, technology, and modern culture. Yet a closer look suggests that the women now dressed in black, who are so closely identified with tradition and the past, also lived through a time of profound social, economic, and political transformation. By the 1920s, the expand-global economy and the power of nation-states had redefined the relationship between rural Europe and the industrialized world and, in the process, changed women's economic, civic, and communal roles. Although few women born at the end of the nineteenth century ever left Sutera, they, like their great-granddaughters today, experienced a break with the past. In their lives, notions of marriage, work, and mothering, and even the very sense of being Suteran and Italian, took on new meanings.

In this book I look at how the lives of Sicilian women changed between 1880 and 1920 and explore how these transformations reflect the gendered nature of work, family, and citizenship in the twentieth century. Looking at the social, economic, political, and cultural transformations that accompanied the rise of the Italian state and the expansion of global capitalism, I argue that mass male migration radically altered the lives of rural women, changing their ideas about motherhood, work, and national belonging. At the centre of these transformations stood the *vedove bianche* (white widows), women whose husbands were alive but absent. As these women struggled to realize their personal and familial dreams of social success and upward mobility, they moved into new personal and public roles. Within families, female roles shifted as education claimed a more prominent place in defining status and wealth. Mothering took on new meanings as rural women shouldered greater responsibility for the moral character and behaviour of their children. Rural women carved out new economic opportunities for themselves, using remittances sent home by migrant men. Migration created a demand for consumer goods in a world of dwindling wage-earning opportunities, and women moved into these economic spaces, which were characterized by dry-goods stores, catalogues, and real estate transactions. Women's new economic and domestic roles translated into new civic relations. By 1910 a distinctly female image of national belonging had emerged in rural Italy. Transoceanic migration repositioned rural European women in their communities, in the nation-state, and in the rapidly expanding global economy. In the lives of these women we see how fundamental gender is to the formation of social and political identities.

The experiences of Suteresi at the beginning of the last century illustrate the impact that the expanding capitalist world economy had on rural European men and women. The rocky, arid, and heartbreakingly beautiful hills surrounding Sutera are constant reminders of just how difficult it has been to earn a living from this land. By the late nineteenth century, falling farm prices, competition from American wheat, and the enactment of protectionist legislation had created a crisis in the Sicilian economy. Sharecroppers, tenant farmers, and wage workers watched as their livelihoods disappeared. There were no factories in the neighbouring cities to absorb the growing ranks of landless unemployed. The political sympathies, economic interests, and cultural stereotypes that shaped the newly formed Italian state ensured that capital investment would be directed toward northern industries. The decline of local wage-earning opportunities, combined with the lack of new industry, drove rural southern Italian men to seek their fortunes elsewhere. Many left for the Americas, where unskilled jobs were plentiful and the pay was higher.[1] By the early twentieth century, families were finding it more lucrative to send men overseas to work in the mills and factories of the Americas than to keep them home to seek work for low wages on the surrounding estates. Like most rural Sicilians, Suteresi were not anxious to leave their homes; however, Sicily's rapidly changing position in the world economy made transoceanic migration an economic opportunity that few could ignore altogether.

In the early twentieth century, deep gender divisions marked transnational migration. Throughout Mediterranean Europe, migration was predominantly a male experience. Over three-quarters of Sicilians who immigrated to the Americas between 1880 and 1914 were male. Suteresi began to join the rapidly rising wave of Sicilian migrants after 1900, and men comprised 86 per cent of these migrants. Most of these men were married and had left their wives and children at home. Women and children accounted for less than 15 percent of all migrants who left prior to the First World War. Sicilian women sailed overseas in greater numbers than women from Calabria, Greece, or Spain, but even they never made up more than one-third of the emigrants who left before 1925.[2]

The characteristic sex ratios reflect the different ways that rural men and women responded to an industrializing world. As global capitalism intensified the transformation of rural Sicilian men into itinerant wage labourers, it hastened the expulsion of women from paid work. By the end of the nineteenth century, fewer women were appearing as industrial or agricultural wage workers in the national census.[3] The disappearance of women from paid labour coincided with the decline of cottage textile industries. Unable to compete with the cheaper, mass-produced cloth from the north, Sicilian women stopped weaving cloth for market. Unlike in northern Europe, where factory work accompanied the decline of agriculture and rural men and women moved to cities to join the growing ranks of urban wage workers, Sicilian women did not leave their homes to seek work in urban centres. Rather, in rural Sicily, industrialization brought transoceanic migration for men and the elimination of paid labour for women.

As scholars, writers, and film makers translated the migrant experience into tales of struggle, loss, and salvation, they strengthened these gender divisions by identifying migration with men and the homeland with women. These stories contrast the peaceful rural worlds the migrants left behind with the difficulties of forging new lives in modern cities. For the men who succeeded in the New World, the rewards were enormous. After a few difficult years marked by deprivation and hard work, the successful were able to buy houses, open their own businesses, and send their children to school to earn professional degrees. They became 'Italian American.' Those who settled in the new communities saw their birthplaces as the fount of their values, faith, and beliefs, but not as a place for a man to make a life in the modern world.[4] The homeland was the repository of the past, of individual and collective histories, a place tinged with failure. Those who never left – mostly women – were perceived as abandoned; those men who returned sick and disheartened were considered weak and ineffectual. In these descriptions the backward homelands became increasingly feminized, identified in terms of abandoned women, infirm men, and illegitimate children. Echoing the descriptions of nineteenth-century writers, women appeared as mute bystanders who clutched their children to their breasts, weeping uncontrollably as their husbands boarded the train to the nearest port. In these descriptions, rural women suffered as a consequence of their husbands' selfish dreams of wealth and adventure.[5] The world of men had moved to the other side of the Atlantic. Italy, like the women who remained behind, became the hapless victim of transatlantic migration.

This story, identifying the migrant experience almost exclusively in terms of male emigrants and their new lives, became the principal framework for understanding the modern Italian migrant experience. Early models of migration that focused on the immigrant experience obscured the influence of the homelands and the women who remained behind. Until relatively recently, scholars generally agreed that migration began the moment an individual arrived in a new world, clutching a small suitcase and a dream. His survival depended on his talents, ambitions, and willingness to work. These models rested on two assumptions:

that men migrated, and that they bought one-way tickets. The success of an immigrant could be measured by his assimilation into mainstream society and by his rejection of Old World values and of traditional social and cultural institutions.[6]

Over the past decades, scholars have significantly revised these models by questioning the links between success and assimilation. Their work has challenged the notion that the male experience constituted the history of migration and that emigrants did not go home again. In the last few decades scholars have argued that the migrant experience cannot be fully understood in terms of individuals who rushed to abandon old customs as they sought to meet the demands of life in the modern industrial world.[7] These scholars have shown that emigrants who set sail for the Americas were neither uprooted nor transplanted from their homelands: they remained tied to their villages, linked by blood and community. In these studies, migrants appear as central figures in the creation of transnational social and economic networks. The constant back-and-forth exchange of people, goods, and services built complex webs binding two or more regions together.[8] The emphasis on community and kinship networks in the migration process highlighted the role of the family and placed women on centre stage. Recent works telling the story of female migration have made it clear that women commonly experienced migration and settlement in markedly different ways than their male compatriots. With a few notable exceptions, European women emigrated as members of families rather than as wage workers, and played crucial roles in creating communities and shaping notions of ethnicity in the new lands.[9]

These recent works also show that free migration in the late nineteenth and early twentieth centuries did not move in just one direction. This is especially evident in the high repatriation rates that characterized Sicilian labour migration. Few families viewed the separation as a permanent one, or as a first step to moving to the United States. Like most migrants from southern Italy, these men intended to work for a few years to earn enough money to purchase the material trappings of success and wealth back home. When the men earned enough money to buy a two-storey house, a small plot of land, or a business back home, they returned to their families.[10] Although time spent in the Americas changed the dreams of some migrants, who called for their families and permanently settled overseas, many returned home. Nearly three-quarters of the men from Sutera who migrated eventually repatriated. Though the history of migration from this town is marked by local peculiarities –

its late start, its concentrated sex ratios, and its high repatriation rates – the overall pattern is not unique. Throughout the southern and island provinces of Italy, nearly half the men who emigrated eventually returned.[11] No longer can repatriation be considered evidence of a migrant's failure: returning home was often a sign of success.

Though historians of women and migration have radically altered our understanding of the process of transnational migration, the migrant has remained the privileged subject of study. Although these new studies show that migration was not one person's quest for a new life, but a group decision involving the migrant and his or her wider family, few scholars have chosen to study the role that family members in the homeland, especially women, played in the process. In this study, by writing the history of migration from the perspective of the women who remained home, I seek to deepen our understanding of patterns of migration, of how transnational networks reconfigured relations between local, national, and global communities, and of the significance of gender in the process.[12] We cannot understand transoceanic migration without recognizing the role that wives and mothers played in it. Although most migrants were men, rural women influenced the transatlantic flow of people and capital. The women who remained behind acted as linchpins in the emerging transnational capitalist economy that was rapidly refiguring local, global, and national relations.

In Sicily, the decision to migrate usually reflected a family's dream of improving life back home. It was hoped that by working in the Americas for a few years, a man could earn enough money to purchase enough land, buy a larger house, or open a small business in Italy. He left in order to improve his family's fortunes. All members of the family invested their individual and collective dreams of upward social mobility in the project. Some rural women actively encouraged their husbands to leave, and all women played crucial roles in realizing the emigrant dream. The women of Sutera helped their husbands finance and arrange their passage overseas; they even organized male migrant groups. These women, like the men who migrated, saw transoceanic migration as a means to improve their social and economic position in Sutera. The money earned overseas offered rural women the possibility of acquiring the cultural and material trappings that distinguished the elite from the rest of the population. These women invested the remittances their husbands wired home, looked after the family interests, and sent their children to school. If all went well, their children became doctors or lawyers and left the land behind.

Among the most visible symbols of success were large families and two-storey houses. The ability to provide for large families was traditionally a sign of status in Sicily, and migration provided the resources necessary to continue to have as many children as the family could support. Family reconstructions in Sutera show that women married to emigrants chose to have more children than their counterparts whose husbands remained home. Only in the 1920s, when smaller families became associated with wealth and success, did these women and their husbands decide to limit family size. Housing was also important for social legitimation. Two-storey houses not only separated people from animals, but also distinguished the *civili* (gentry) from the *contadini* (agricultural workers). While these measures alone probably did not lead to acceptance by the local gentry, they created the possibility for the next generation to acquire the resources and power that marked social status. They also worked to undermine existing forms of social and economic organization. The demographic effects of transnational migration merged with changing notions of family and ideas of mothering that seeped into rural life at the turn of the century.

The history of the women of Sutera shows that although greater integration into the industrial world's economy did not transform rural women into wage workers, it did create new economic opportunities for them. Women who were married to migrants, and who chose to remain behind, generally avoided the few paid work opportunities that were available. Except in a few prescribed circumstances (in widowhood, abandonment, or extreme poverty), respectable women did not work in the fields, the only wage work readily available. Women whose husbands migrated had little incentive to break these cultural taboos and undermine the family's attempt to acquire status and respect. However, the economic growth that accompanied migration, especially in the construction industry and in real estate, provided women with new ways of participating in commerce and trade. As women moved into their larger homes with the attendant social responsibilities, they required furniture, rugs, mirrors, and kitchens. Rural women became consumers. Cash from the Americas also offered women the means to enter the entrepreneurial world. Women used the remittances to open small businesses and to enter the real estate market. Access to greater disposable income encouraged rural women and their husbands to invest in bigger houses and larger families and to start new businesses.

Rural women also began going to school. Male migration provided the personal incentive for many women to learn to read and write.

Women flocked to the schools, and female literacy rates began to rise. After nearly fifty years of state efforts to encourage elementary school attendance among Italians, rural Sicilians began to go to school only when the men began to migrate. Throughout the nineteenth century, government educational reforms had been directed mainly at males. As potential voters and soldiers, their education was considered more urgent than that of girls. Officials believed that lessons in Italian, history, and civics could create a loyal, patriotic, and obedient (male) citizenry who could be trusted to vote responsibly and not be seduced by the illusory promises of socialism. Though the government required elementary classes for girls, local city councils saw female education as a low priority. Funding shortfalls often meant the cancellation of classes for females. Echoing institutional attitudes, most families did not consider a daughter's education to be as important as a son's. Only when faced with the absence of men, the exigencies of transoceanic communication, and the real possibility of improving the family's economic and social condition did adult women and young girls readily attend school.

Through book learning and their increased access to cash, rural women repositioned themselves in the nation-state, and this fostered a new sense of national belonging. Reading and writing introduced these women to a national literature. By the early twentieth century, regional newspapers were carrying serialized novels, usually romances, directed at female readers and designed to boost circulation. Although many of the stories, especially the historical romances, reflected regional differences, embedded in these plots were clear descriptions of the good and bad Italian woman. Through these images and advertisements, literacy offered women unmediated access to a distinctly female national community. For the first time, rural women were able read news items, serialized stories, and advertisements in the regional newspapers without turning to their fathers, husbands, or brothers. Flush with cash from overseas, these women could then use their new skills to actively participate in the growing consumer economy by purchasing furniture, fashionable dresses, cosmetics, sewing machines, and the other accoutrements of modern life advertised in local newspapers. Literacy and consumerism offered these women a new route into the 'imagined community' of the nation.[13]

Transnational migration redefined the personal and collective lives of these women, just as it did for their men. Sicilians, like most rural Europeans, historically defined themselves through kin and community.[14] Family fastened each person into the social hierarchy and into the historical record. Occupation and personal accomplishments had little importance in describing a person's identity. The strength of family and of town in defining personal and group identities shaped the migration process itself, affecting decisions about destinations and repatriation. Transnational migration redefined the nineteenth-century physical and mental boundaries that defined the village, but it did not diminish the significance of the local community in people's lives. Even now the only acceptable answer to the inevitable question, *ma chi sei?* (who are you?) is an explanation of your relationship to a particular family through blood or friendship. Nationality, occupation, and personal background are all interesting details, but they are also ultimately irrelevant in placing you in the Suteran social order. If you are merely passing through, unconnected to anyone, you are dismissed as a stranger and are invisible. Suteresi still define themselves as distinct, through language and history, from residents in a neighbouring town a mere two or three kilometres away. What is true today was even more pronounced a hundred years ago, before the automobile, the telephone, and radio and television made their appearance. Yet, through careful study, it is possible to see that this fierce sense of loyalty has not remained static. Between 1880 and 1920 the sense of identity among rural Europeans was changing.

With transoceanic migration came multiple identities; self-identification varied according to sex, place, and situation. When a young man, newly married, left Sutera to seek work in Alabama accompanied by his brother-in-law and a cousin, he surely continued to define himself by blood, just as his father and grandfather had done before him. To the outside world, however, he was an Italian. As soon as he boarded the British ship docked in Palermo, clutching his newly minted Italian passport, his national identity took precedence. In the mining camps and mill towns of Alabama, his identity constantly shifted; to non-Italians he was Italian, to other Italians he was Sicilian, and to other Sicilians he was a Suteresi. Scholars have begun to look at the complex social, political, and cultural forces that shape ethnicity, recognizing that migration created multiple identities within migrant communities.[15] However, few scholars have considered how this process affected those family members – women in the case of rural Sicily – who anchored the migration network in the homelands. From the experiences of the women of Sutera, it is possible to see how transoceanic migration worked to build a new sense of being an Italian woman, as well as being a Suterese, a wife, and a mother.

As family ties stretched across oceans, husbands and wives turned to the national government to facilitate communication, seek redress from unscrupulous shipping agencies, demand benefits from overseas employers, and untangle the bureaucratic difficulties involved in wiring money overseas. Those women who remained behind exploited the increasing female presence in official family matters (births and deaths) in order to claim the right to engage in financial transactions and take on new civic responsibilities. Wives of migrants were temporarily responsible for registering children for school and paying taxes. Their new duties forged close physical ties with the *Municipio.* The practical necessities of migration encouraged women to view state agencies as means to realize familial dreams of social advancement. The act of turning to government bureaucracies offered the possibility of creating an independent relationship between rural women and the Italian state for the first time since unification.

Besides strengthening a sense of national belonging among the women who remained behind (as well as among the migrants themselves), transoceanic migration created a new global community that incorporated residents from rural Europe. Though transnational migration failed to create a global proletariat separate from all national ties, it did create an international labour force. The women who remained behind were part of the process, actively reproducing and maintaining this labour force. The familial ties that linked the Old World with the new created a global community that transcended the formal boundaries of nation-states. As Henri Lefebvre wrote: 'No space disappears in the course of growth and development: the worldwide does not abolish the local.'[16] As the history of women and migration from Sutera illustrates, global, national, and local communities seemed to develop simultaneously in the rural worlds of western Europe.

To begin to see the complicated intersections that have long linked global and local communities we must focus our attention on the smallest unit: the village. Although village-based studies have often been criticized as too specific, as inhibiting the ability of historians to draw broad conclusions, they are invaluable in writing a certain kind of history. They offer the only means of uncovering the different ways that men and women, city folk and country dwellers, experienced the major economic, social, and cultural changes that redefined European life over the last two centuries. It is difficult to trace the experiences of rural women through the historical record. At the turn of the last century nearly 80 per cent of Sicilian women were illiterate.[17] Few women left written records attesting to their daily lives, their role in the family, or their private aspirations. To see how rural women experienced transoceanic migration, we must focus sharply on the history of a specific place where both quantitative and qualitative sources can be examined. Sutera provided an excellent window onto the world of southern Europe at the turn of the last century and onto the migration experience. By reconstructing the histories of more than 1,500 Suteran families using passport registers, passenger logs from steamships, official correspondence from the mayor's office, vital registers, and land records, I have traced migration, patterns and the demographic and economic changes that accompanied transoceanic migration. Descriptions of daily life, of migration, and of women, in newspapers, government reports, travellers' accounts, schoolbooks, and novels, complement the quantitative sources. This approach seeks to avoid the pitfalls of relying solely on one kind of evidence, and to recognize that material conditions and cultural constructions are intimately entwined.

In recent years, local studies of southern Italy have played an important role in challenging accepted understandings of the history of modern Italy. Since unification, historians and theorists from both the left and the right have generally accepted the idea that a backwards, corrupt, and immobile South was born out of the creation of Italy itself. As Lucy Riall writes: 'In the modern period, the history of the South has been almost entirely a history of the Southern Question, a failure of modernization and an analysis of whom or what to blame for Southern difference.'[18] Only since the 1980s have scholars started to write a different kind of history, one that does not accept the idea of southern difference as a basic assumption, but rather begins from the premise that a variety of economic, social, and cultural experiences characterize the history of southern regions. A number of local and regional studies have shown that there is no single South. Burrowing through estate records, city hall meeting minutes, and electoral lists, scholars have uncovered a South where a vibrant commercial economy coexisted with subsistence agriculture, where the state had a more active role in shaping political and social relations, and where a new agrarian middle-class was plainly challenging the power of the nobility.

The significance of this new research is immense. It has challenged the primacy of the Risorgimento as the crucial force of economic, social, and cultural change in the South and on the peninsula generally. It has also strengthened the idea that there were multiple paths leading into the expanding capitalist world market that transformed European social relations by the end of the nineteenth century. Without going too deeply into the controversies surrounding the ability of these new histories to explain the conditions of the South, it is enough to point out that these works have shown that the southern societies were not peripheral to international and national events. The problems of the South cannot be grounded in the history of unification; they must be located in broader economic, social, and political systems. While the work of these historians has transformed the fields of southern Italian history and modern Italian history, few studies have explicitly recognized the differing ways that men and women shaped their economic, political, and social conditions. By looking at one aspect of the transformation of the South (migration) through the lens of gender, this history of the women from Sutera furthers our understanding of the multiple worlds that make up the *Mezzogiorno*.[19]

Finally, this study of women and mass migration contributes to a growing body of literature that has rewritten the history of rural women in the modern age. In the past few decades, historians have sought to recover women's historical experiences in order to show how women, like men, acted as historical subjects, participating in political, economic, cultural, and social change. With few exceptions, studies of European women in the workplace, in politics, and in the global economy have assumed the physical integration of women into the industrial world. Their subjects are the factory girls, the shopping clerks, the political activists, and the writers who settled in the cities. Since rural women did not move to the cities to seek work as domestics or wage labourers, they did not seem to participate directly in this process of industrialization. Only in recent years have scholars begun to write the history of rural women in periods of capital expansion.[20] While most of the women of Sutera never travelled beyond the provincial borders, industrialization and the nation-state impinged on their lives as surely as it did on their northern counterparts who sought work in the cities of Milano and Torino, or who immigrated to France or the Americas. The same transportation, commercial, and industrial forces that encouraged so many of their husbands, fathers, and sons to search for work overseas, gave these women the necessary cash to open small businesses, or purchase land and store-bought goods. In short, these forces gave rural women the means to participate in the fast-growing national and international consumer economy that transfigured the lives of urban women in metropolitan Europe and North America.

The history of the women of Sutera, like other stories of reclamation, is also significant in that it forces historians to rethink a number of widely held assumptions. As social historians uncovered women's roles in the Renaissance, the French Revolution, and the Industrial Revolution, their arguments often challenged the accepted wisdom about progress and regress. Their works showed how European women experienced periods of radical change (commonly considered moments of 'liberation' or 'emancipation' in the male experience) in terms of loss of prestige, power, and access to resources.[21] The recognition that women had their own history also undermined assumptions about historical narrative. In writing the history of women, historians challenged the notion of a genderless universal narrative. The histories of class formation, industrialization, nation formation, and migration are all gendered. Living and working together, men and women experienced and participated in these processes in different ways because of their sex. In recent years these insights have led historians to see gender not only as a characteristic of class, but also as an analytical tool in its own right. Their studies show how gender informs the shape and functions of social, political, cultural, and economic systems.[22] The story of these women from Sutera shows how a study seeking to reclaim the history of a particular group of rural women reveals the deeply gendered nature of transnational migration and nation formation, and thus complicates our understanding of the relationship between public and private worlds.

However, we must be cautious. While the history of Suteran women tells a story of profound economic and social transformation that marked important changes in the meaning of women's public and private roles, these changes did not necessarily translate into greater equality for women. Remittances from overseas provided women with new commercial opportunities as entrepreneurs and consumers, but greater access to cash also reinforced their exclusion from wage work and their roles as mothers and wives. Rural women, like their urban counterparts, responded creatively to industrialization and global capitalism, finding new opportunities for improving their families' social and economic conditions. However, we cannot assume that these new possibilities undermined the patriarchal codes that defined southern Italian gender relations. Society and the state acted to limit the revolutionary potential of these new roles by controlling the meanings of wage work, capital, and motherhood. Even so, the lives of these women testify to the complicated nature of patriarchal relations in southern Italy, and point to the ways Sicilian women carved out some degree of moral and economic power within the family. Analyzing how mass male migration altered women's work, family structure, and civic relations in Sicily, along with the public debates surrounding the meaning of these changes, sheds light on the ways industrialization, nation building, and global capitalism reconstructed female subordination. The story of these rural women, like that of all women, cannot be told simply in terms of loss or gain.

Today, the oldest generations of women from the South are identified with a mythical rural past when women lived in the shadows of their fathers and husbands. In sharp contrast to the modern generation of miniskirted, college-educated professional women, the older women draped in black are seen as extraneous to historical change. A close examination of the lives of these older women reveals another story. In this tale, these women appear at the centre of the great social, economic, and political changes that transformed rural life at the beginning of the twentieth century. Although these women of Sutera did not leave the countryside to join the growing female wage labour force, or emigrate overseas to seek their fortunes in America, they participated in the changes that transformed rural Europe at the end of the nineteenth century. As mothers, wives, and workers, they played an active role in the establishing the transnational migrant networks that characterized the changing face of global capitalism. In turn, mass male migration repositioned these women within the family, the local community, and the nation. The lives of these women speak directly to our twenty-first-century concerns about nationalism, ethnicity, and gender in the context of the heightened mobility of capital and labour around the world. Their stories serve as important reminders that even the most invisible of people have a history.

PART I

Rural Women and Transnational Migration

Chapter One

Blood, Honour, and Belonging: The World of Rural Sicilians

In the harsh June sunlight, in 1889, nineteen-year-old Antonia A. and twenty-six-year-old Giovanni S. celebrated their marriage in the old stone church of S. Agata, overlooking the main square of Sutera, a small village in western Sicily.[1] Their wedding was more than a celebration of love or testimony to the power of parental will. When the priest finished his sermon and the newlyweds walked into the main square as man and wife, surrounded by their parents, sisters, brothers, aunts, uncles, cousins, and godparents, they were stepping into the adult world with all its attendant responsibilities and privileges. They were also announcing to the wider community the presence of a new family. Their marriage altered the social and economic relations of every member of their extended families. Constituted through blood and ritual, family was the basis of personal status, reputation, and power within the social hierarchy of the village. In nineteenth-century Sicily, family was the source of individual identity and bound each person to the myths, legends, and histories that constituted the community.

Family created continuity, connecting people to the past and to the future. Each generation physically and symbolically incorporated aspects of past families into its own. Parents passed family names, occupations, and houses on to their children. Antonia and Giuseppe, named after dead relatives, passed on ancestors' names – Paolino, Virciglio, and Concetta – to their children. Antonia learned how to clean, cook, weave, and sew by watching her mother as a small child. As an adult she spent her days making the family's clothes, caring for her children, and raising chickens and pigs, much as her grandmother had done before her. Giuseppe, like his father and grandfather, worked the wheatfields surrounding the village. In Sutera, as in most rural communities, blood defined individual identity and linked each person to the community's history. Families passed on from parents to children the myths and legends recounting the town's origins. While ancestry fixed individuals in the community's past, it also expressed faith in its future. Each marriage in Sutera publicly affirmed the continuation of bloodlines and of the village itself, for at least one more generation.[2]

Kinship ties located Giovanni and Antonia within the community, and shaped their daily activities and their friendships just as blood shaped their parents' lives. Yet family was not a static construct; though a conservative institution, it was not immune to change. The economic and social opportunities available to this young couple differed significantly from those available to their mothers and fathers. When Giovanni and Antonia wed, the world around them was in a state of flux. In the last decades of the nineteenth century the local economy was beginning to show signs of decline. Changing commercial markets were transforming local labour markets and work opportunities. Giovanni's father worked the surrounding estates as a sharecropper; in contrast, Giovanni sold his labour for wages and eventually left the land altogether. Giovanni twice crossed the Atlantic to work in the coal mines of Birmingham, Alabama. Antonia also took on economic and social responsibilities.

In this chapter Sutera is used as a window onto rural Sicily to describe the economic, political, and social conditions of that island at the turn of the century. Peering into this corner of the world, it is immediately apparent that family and community are powerful forces in defining a person's sense of self. It is also clear that the boundaries of blood and place are far more flexible than is generally imagined. An overview of the political and economic history of Sutera provides the necessary historical context for understanding the choices rural Sicilians made at the beginning of the twentieth century, and illustrates the permeable boundaries that separated the public lives of work and politics with the private life of family. Struggles over land and work that swept across the island at the end of the nineteenth century – consequences of national and global economic and political changes – shaped a family's decision to send a father or son to the Americas, a daughter to school, a son into a profession.

Men and women both experienced political and economic change, but in different ways. Gender not only shaped daily life, determining people's contributions to the family's well-being, but also informed social relations between families. The Sicilian family marked its social position, and that of all its members, in terms of reputation and honour.

And the community measured honour by a family's ability to control female sexuality. A good name did more than provide a family with a sense of moral correctness; it also carried concrete economic benefits. Respected families could negotiate the best land contracts and marriages. The power of sex to locate a person within the family and the wider community meant that political, economic, and cultural transformations, including transoceanic migration, held different meanings for husbands, wives, sons, and daughters. Sharply gendered kinship networks tied individuals to the local economy and society.

If the family located men and women within the community, it was local myths and legends that offered a collective definition of what it meant to be Suteresi. Stories passed from one generation to the next, celebrating the virtues of Suteresi, created a sense of communal distinction and underscored the notion that people from Sutera were different. This fierce sense of local pride, held equally by men and women, informed relations with the government in Rome and influenced the effects of mass male migration on notions of individual and collective identity. This overview of the economic, political, and social conditions of life in rural Sicily uncovers a world in transformation, and provides a framework for understanding how rural women experienced mass migration and its effects on family, work, and national belonging.

Rural Life in Nineteenth-Century Sicily

Sutera is in central-western Sicily in the province of Caltanissetta, on the highway connecting Palermo on the north coast with Agrigento on the south. It sits near the top of Mount San Paolino, 615 metres above sea level, overlooking the valley of the Platani River. Behind the last house in the village is a path leading to the top of the mountain, 200 metres above the main square. If you climb to the very top of San Paolino and stand by the bell tower, you can look out across the island. Small gardens and orchards, where families grow their olives and vegetables, surround the village. In summer a swath of bright green encircles the houses as if to protect them from the burnt-yellow wheatfields that stretch out toward every horizon. In physical terms, Sutera is typical of many hill towns in Sicily's mountainous interior – a small, nuclear village surrounded by uninhabited countryside. In 1876, Sidney Sonnino, a senator from Rome, rode across Sicily gathering information on social and economic conditions. He tells of days he travelled for five or six hours from one town to another and never saw a tree or a bush: 'Valley after valley; the scene is always the same, silence everywhere and a desolation that wrings your heart.'[3]

At the end of the nineteenth century, Sutera sat in splendid isolation on its mountain. No direct road linked the village to the provincial capital of Caltanissetta only twenty miles away. To go the five miles from Milocca, a *frazione* of Sutera, to the main square in Sutera was a long walk along a dirt path and could take up to half a day.[4] In the rainy winter months the narrow, winding roads were often impassible, washed out by the mud. As late as 1907, no direct road connected Sutera to its own railway station in the valley. It took more than two hours on a mule to climb the winding mountain path from the station to Sutera's main square.[5] Campofranco was Sutera's nearest neighbour, about a mile down the mountain. To buy any item not produced locally, a resident had to travel to market in Mussomeli about ten miles to the west, or as far as Agrigento, thirty miles to the south. Transportation and communication difficulties strengthened residents' allegiance to the town.

At the end of the nineteenth century, the *comune* of Sutera included the town itself and a cluster of houses and a church that constituted the hamlet of Milocca. The total territory of Sutera extended over 4802 hectares.[6] The village was divided into three neighbourhoods, each boasting a small square and at least one church: Rabato and Rabatello on the north side of the mountain, and Giardinello spread out along the southeastern side. The houses were built close together along very steep, narrow streets that encircled the base of the mountain. Most of the buildings had two stories, with one or two rooms per storey, and each room had at least one window to let in air and light. The houses were bright white, covered in gypsum.[7]

Even in the nineteenth century the outward appearance of most Sicilian villages, including Sutera, was surprisingly urban. There were no barnyards or small gardens attached to the homes, as there were in the villages of northern Europe.[8] Common walls connected houses to one another, just as in Palermo or Rome. Sicilian agricultural villages tended to be densely populated. Sutera, one of the smaller villages in the province, had more than five thousand inhabitants by the end of the nineteenth century, and there were three piazzas, five schools, and four churches. The state was represented by local health officials and teachers.[9] Despite its size, it is difficult to compare Sutera to villages of a similar size in northern Europe. As with German hamlets and English rural villages, the vast majority of Suteresi were peasants, not tradesmen or artisans. Social relationships and political loyalties were based on

A current view of Sutera nestled in the hill. (David Tager)

A contemporary street scene in Sutera. (David Tager)

bloodlines rather than class. The architectural, geographical, economic, and social characteristics of Sutera are typical of the classic Sicilian agricultural village, a large community of agricultural workers.[10]

The origins of Sicilian agrotowns lie in the turbulent history of the island. Historians have argued that people chose to live above the valleys to protect themselves from the malaria that was endemic to the lowlands, as well as from the countless invading armies and robber bands. In the early twentieth century, critics were still citing the dangers associated with bandits and outlaws as one of the main reasons for the uneven population distribution in Sicily.[11] Poor roads combined with heat and dust made travelling difficult and at times quite dangerous. Bandits seized or murdered barons on the way to their country estates, and noblemen rarely travelled without an armed escort.[12] Few peasants chose to live in the isolated countryside, preferring the safety of the village to the convenience of living close to the fields. Aside from these threats, daily life outside the village was more difficult. Water was scarce, and generally found far from the nearest houses; roads were usually impassible; and doctors and midwives were unavailable. The land tenure system that placed vast amounts of land under the control of one owner also discouraged people from settling in the country.

The development of the agrotowns is linked to the latifundium system.[13] Latifundia – large landed estates under the control of one person or family – were introduced to Sicily by the Romans and became the basis for land tenure throughout most of the island's interior. Under Byzantine rule the church gained control of huge tracts of land, further consolidating property in the hands of a few.[14] The arrival of the Muslims in the ninth century slowed the expansion of the great estates, although the latifundia did not disappear completely. The Arabs built small settlements, *casali*, amidst the wheatfields and pasturelands, and each family worked a small plot of land; it seems that even local peasants were able to acquire land.[15] In the eleventh century, when the Normans began forcibly removing the Moslems, many smaller settlements disappeared. The Norman invasion brought Sicily back from the African coast and firmly tied the island to Europe's shores. Feudalism replaced the less centralized Arabic government. A baronial class was created as the Norman kings granted huge tracts of land in exchange for the loyalty and the military assistance of the local nobility.[16]

Over the following centuries the barons enclosed still more land to provide pasturage for their growing flocks of sheep and to increase wheat production. Rural residents had little possibility of acquiring their own small plots, as arable lands remained under the tight control of local barons or the church. Most people had access to the land through use rights on common lands, these rights being defined by custom and tradition. However, the evolution of latifundia combined with the privatization of feudal lands threatened these customary rights. Eventually, long-term leases became the only means to gain access to land. This system of emphyteusis replaced military and personal service with one fixed rent. Whether land was held by feudal right or leased, its ownership remained concentrated in the hands of the few, and this prevented rural residents from settling in the countryside.[17] The *latifondo* was by no means a static, unchanging system. By the nineteenth century, the *latifondo* system had evolved into a flexible and profitable system. Centuries of centralization resulted in a potentially modern enterprise: one administrative body could oversee a variety of economic activities and shift production and labour according to market forces.[18]

The fate of Sutera, like that of most agrotowns, was closely tied to the island's changing political economy. In Sutera, the concentration of land in baronial hands under Norman and then Spanish rule coincided with a sharp rise in population. The resident population rose more than one-third between the fifteenth and sixteenth centuries, from 2,339 to 3,432.[19] Suteresi built new houses, extending the town's boundaries for the first time since Arab rule. In the fifteenth century, residents built new houses to form the district of Giardinello, next door to the neighbourhoods of Rabato and Rabatello, both built under Muslim rule in the ninth century and still referred to today as the Arab quarter. The Catholic Church expanded its presence to meet the needs of the growing population. In 1185, under the Norman king William II, the Carmelites established the first permanent religious community in the area, building a monastery a half-mile outside the town and a church in Rabatello. In 1664 the order moved into a new monastery attached to its church in town to meet the spiritual needs of the growing community. Shortly after that, a group of Capuchin friars settled into what once had been the Carmelite monastery. As well, the diocese authorized the building of a new church, S. Agata, to serve the growing population of Giardinello. In Milocca, the Benedictine order owned San Martino, the only church in Milocca, along with a great deal of the surrounding land.[20]

The population of Sutera began to decline in the seventeenth century in the wake of Spanish land reforms. Beginning in the sixteenth century, the ruling viceroys made a concerted effort to improve the quality and quantity of the island's agricultural production. A number of charters were issued promising noble rank to anyone who built a new community on unused land and convinced peasants to settle there. Local elite desperate for a title rushed to establish new towns, building over one hundred communities between 1570 and 1650. Several small villages sprang up outside Sutera, attracting local residents. Most of the settlers came from the ranks of the wealthy but titleless, who were tempted by the possibility of joining the landed aristocracy. Campofranco was settled in 1573, followed by Casteltermini in 1629, Buompensiere in 1631, and Aquaviva-Platani in 1635. Suteresi also settled in Milocca, one of the few remaining *casali* in the district. Because of its particular status, Milocca fell under the political, judicial, and economic administration of Sutera.[21] Some of these charter communities managed to survive; many did not. Underfinanced, built on marginal lands with low yields, and unable to compete with agricultural products imported from more efficient estates in England and northern Europe, many of these towns stopped growing. Some were abandoned completely, while others became little more than seasonal shelters for harvest workers.[22]

Sutera, unlike many of its neighbours, was a vassal city for only fifty years and was spared the worst abuses of baronial rule. In 1398 the Spanish king declared Sutera a *città demaniale*, or a royal demesne under the direct control of the king, in order to punish the upstart barons who were challenging his reign.[23] The noblemen who governed Sutera during this time were inevitably drawn into the bloody power struggles between the local barons, who had amassed a great deal of political and economic strength during the thirteenth century, and the Spanish king, who was attempting to regain control of the island. The last two barons of Sutera, Vicario Andrea Chiaramonte and Raimondo Moncado, were stripped of all their possessions and executed when they attempted to resist the authority of the Spanish crown.[24]

After 1398, a few wealthy Suteresi controlled the local government and most of the land. Their power was so great that in 1535, when Charles V decided to sell the village to a nobleman in order to raise money to go to war, the ruling families petitioned the king for permission to buy it themselves. They banded together to raise 18,000 florins to buy back their freedom and prevent their community from being sold to the highest bidder. A new grist tax and increased excise taxes on all wine, tobacco, salami, cheese, and cloth that entered Sutera provided the necessary funds. Their petition to the king was welcomed, and they were offering enough money, and in 1560 a royal decree was issued reinstating Sutera as a royal demesne. According to the decree, the royal family would not be able to buy, sell, or alienate the village under any circumstances; in exchange, Sutera would obey all royal commands.[25]

The history of Sutera serves as an excellent reminder that Sicily has long been a conquered land. For centuries, Sicilians watched one invader after another land on their shores. The Greeks, Romans, Byzantines, Normans, Spanish, English, Bourbons, and finally the Italians all claimed the right to rule, but few were able – or willing – to create a strong, centralized state. Each conquering army seemed content to claim superficial control over the basic infrastructure. In the void, local elites claimed control over a large portion of the islands' political and economic resources.[26]

This climate meant that the fate of residents in charter towns such as Sutera remained closely linked to the expanding latifundia. The Suteresi had been freed from living under a domineering baron but they still did not have access to the resources they needed to invest in land and claim independence. In Sutera, the church and the local elite divided the arable lands between themselves, and this prevented most residents from entering the ranks of property owners. Suteresi rented fields from local landowners in neighbouring towns in exchange for part of the crop, or they worked as day labourers on the surrounding latifundia. The agricultural contracts between workers and owners rarely enabled labourers to make a profit. The only tangible differences between the lives of Suteresi and their neighbours who owed feudal obligations to a baron were that the local government tended to give rural agricultural workers greater access to land for pasturage, and that the contract system created a relatively large sharecropper class.[27] When feudalism was finally outlawed in 1812, many ex-serfs became *braccianti*, landless wage workers. In Sutera, the *braccianti* class was comparatively small, as most residents had sharecropped the land for centuries and were considered *contadini* (small farmers) or *mezzadri* (sharecroppers).

By the nineteenth century, Sutera had developed characteristics typical of other agrotowns: a nucleated village that provided a stable labour pool to work the surrounding wheatfields. Landowners rarely lived on their country estates, choosing instead to reside in their urban palaces, where they enjoyed the amusements of city life on the income from their land. Proprietors rented their land to a *gabellotto*, a middleman, for three to six years in exchange for a fixed cash amount and a portion of the harvest, with the additional stipulation that he would have the land ploughed at the end of his contract. In the area around Sutera, the contract was usually for six years.[28] Landowners recruited their *gabellotti* from the few rural residents who had succeeded in making a profit by farming or by lending money at high interest rates to other residents. Otherwise, these middlemen tended to be people who had established personal authority in the area, usually through coercion or threats. Landholders often gave the position to a guard, a tax collector, or a rich foreigner in exchange for protection or financial rewards.[29] Once in possession of the estate, the *gabellotto* divided the land into smaller portions and sublet them on an annual or biennial basis to local rural residents.

Contracts between *gabellotti* and agricultural workers were broadly similar across the island, although they varied in their details. In Sutera, residents usually sharecropped the land under a two-year contract.[30] As in other agrotowns throughout the province, contracts were based on oral agreements and were rarely put in writing. The first year the land would lay fallow, or the renter could plant legumes; the second year he had to plant grain. On the owner's behalf, the *gabellotto* provided the seed. Over the course of the two years, the sharecropper received approximately 70 litres of grain for each hectare of land, with repayment due at the end of the harvest. After sharecroppers had repaid the borrowed grain and given the owner his share of the crop, they divided the remainder with the *gabellotto.* Besides the rent, the landowner received 25 per cent of the first year's harvest and 19 per cent of the second year's. The sharecropper then paid back the seed advance from what remained. Another 18 per cent of the annual yield went to pay the guards hired to watch the crop in the fields. In addition, the renter was required to pay a variety of taxes. In Sutera there were property taxes, employment taxes for people who did not qualify as landowners, and taxes on the importation or exportation of goods. Taxes alone could equal 50 per cent of a family's yearly income.[31] Those who could not afford to sharecrop were hired as wage workers on an estate for a specified time. In 1900 a man earned between one and 1.25 lire a day working in the wheatfields.[32]

The system was extremely corrupt, breeding a combination of resentment and fatalism among the residents. *Gabellotti* lent out at high interest rates the tools, cash, and extra seed the sharecropper needed to start working the land. Reports of agricultural conditions in Sutera at the end of the nineteenth century describe the vicious circle that trapped sharecroppers:

> Owners and overseers impose enormous burdens on the system, instead of

giving out grain of decent quality, they hand out grain that is rotten and of the worst quality that falls through the sieve; [sharecroppers] are not given enough grain for their land, and therefore, the poor peasant must buy the extra from [the overseer], and repay it at double the amount; the interest rates are exaggerated, the grain is measured out [to the sharecropper] with a normal measure, but when it is repaid [after the harvest] the [overseers] use another, larger measure; [the sharecropper] is made to pay the guard, the candles, and other charges; by the time he has harvested the half that is his, there is not enough to pay the owner, and the man who sweated blood on his hoe remains in debt, or there is just enough left and he returns with his pitchfork on his back. If a small amount still remains he must sell it to pay the debts accumulated by the family.[33]

Few people could make a decent living, let alone put any savings aside. Most rural Sicilians lived with constant debt.[34]

The system conspired to prevent workers from ever gaining access to land. Even so, rural Sicilians still dreamed of someday owning enough land to live comfortably off the rental income and join the ranks of the landowners. Land brought social status and security. In the nineteenth century several attempts were made to institute land reforms and create a larger class of landowners and a more productive economy. The first step toward the dismantling of feudalism came when the Bourbon government returned to Naples in the wake of Napoleon's defeat in 1815. Back from exile, the government accepted French administrative and legislative reforms, including the official dismantling of feudalism. A series of laws, beginning in 1806, erased the traditional privileges of church and aristocracy and demanded the privatization of all feudal lands.[35] Reformers believed that these laws would lead to the breaking up of the latifundia. In practice, however, they created more large estates. Also, the new legislation abrogated the common use rights previously guaranteed under feudalism, with the result that villagers lost access to the land. A new class of landowners was created, but these were not the small proprietors the reformers had hoped to create. In the previous century, many barons had mortgaged their estates, and after the reforms they quickly sold their property for needed cash.[36] In most regions, the *gabellotti* bought up the estates. The law thus facilitated the transfer of land from the aristocracy to the island's growing entrepreneurial and professional groups, the *civili*. The the intended beneficiaries – the sharecroppers and day labourers – remained landless.[37]

Many social critics and economists saw the transformation of land ownership as a positive step toward alleviating the worst abuses of Sicily's agricultural system. They believed that these new owners would adopt a more capitalistic approach to agriculture, introducing advanced farming techniques and improving transportation and communication.[38] Their expectations were never fulfilled. For the *civili*, land was a means to increase personal profit and obtain privileges previously reserved for the aristocracy. Once they had their land, they mimicked the old nobility, who admired and respected people who lived off rents and who sneered at any sort of work.[39] These new landowners lacked the authority that came with centuries of wealth and power, and many Sicilian farmers perceived them as gredier than the traditional landed aristocracy had been.[40] In the 1890s, as peasant rebellions spread across the countryside, it was often these new landholders who became the target of local protests.

With political unification came a new round of land reforms. The extension of northern anticlerical laws across Sicily dissolved many of the monastic orders. Huge tracts of church land were sold at public auctions. Through intimidation and corruption, Sicilian landowners made certain that these church lands would augment their own holdings, and not be used to create a potentially revolutionary class of smallholders. Only thirty years later, when municipal land was placed on the auction block, was it possible for all residents to participate in the sales.[41] By the 1880s it was clear that neither the collapse of feudalism nor the sale of ecclesiastical lands had radically changed the distribution of property. In his analysis of the effects of early land reforms on the island, Senator Jacini commented: 'When the latifundia are divided into small parcels, the result is that they are then sold to one person, who then declares at the auction that he is buying them for the same number of individuals as there are lots on sale, but the fact remains that he alone will be the owner of each parcel of land.'[42]

After all these reforms, over 50 per cent of the land was still held by large landowners. People owning medium-sized holdings bought up 40 per cent of the land at auction; small landowners were able to acquire only 7 per cent of ecclesiastical lands.[43] High debt among rural workers ensured that even those residents willing to confront the hired thugs had little hope of outbidding their wealthier neighbours.[44] Despite their good intentions, nineteenth-century land reforms precipitated a decline in the amount of available arable land on the island.

The first land cadastre (register) in Sutera, completed in 1855, clearly illustrates the uneven distribution of property that characterized the island's land tenure system. Less than 1 per cent of the landholders accounted for 60 per cent of total property values. Local land struggles involved the two largest proprietors, the church and city government. The Benedictine order owned over 200 hectares near Milocca, and their holdings accounted for more than one-third of the taxable income from all the land in the territory.[45] The struggles between the church and the village began fifty years before the decree of 1860 went into effect, when the monks attempted to restrict use rights enjoyed by residents for centuries.[46] After decades of court battles, the town lost the final decision in 1828. However, the 1841 decree, stipulating that all landlords must compensate villages for any use rights taken away, required the Benedictine monks to give one-fifth of the ex-fiefs of Capraria, Milocca, Aquilia, and Cimicia back to Sutera. The monks fought the government's order, producing documents stating that the land in question had never, under any conditions, been accessible to the villagers. In 1853 the village won the case. Twenty years later the parties agreed on the exact conditions of the settlement.[47]

By the end of the nineteenth century the focus of the struggle had shifted to the municipal holdings. In 1896 the *Commissariato Civile* created by Di Rudinì required all municipalities to sell any land not under cultivation. A few local administrators in Sutera were anxious to avoid this forced sale and to take over the estates of Aquilia and Milocca themselves, but they failed. In 1898 the property was divided into 157 sections of one salme and a half each (roughly 2.6 hectares), and the local government held a lottery to distribute 112 tracts of land. It sold the remaining lands in 1903.[48] Close to one thousand people entered the lottery. The land was supposed to be divided among the needy and landless. As one local official lamented, this unfortunately meant that much of the land fell into the hands of people who did not intend to work it including 'women of questionable morality, and even people who never had the honour of holding a hoe in their hand; people who then sold the land to the many speculators and the few peasants who had any sort of savings available.'[49]

In effect, those people not qualified to participate profited from the lottery. Even if the sale had been free of corruption, the amount of property did not even come close to meeting demand, and the vast majority of rural workers continued to sharecrop. These attempts at land reform served only as further evidence of the state's inability and unwillingness to bring about real change that could improve the lives of the majority of rural Sicilians.

In Sutera, sulphur mines provided an alternative to agricultural wage work. Engineers discovered sulphur around Sutera at the end of the nineteenth century. In 1902, miners uncovered a large vein at the base of San Paolino itself. These mineral discoveries placed Sutera on the government's official list of mining towns, along with the neighbouring towns of Serradifalco and Racalmuto, but they did not transform the economic base of Sutera, whose inhabitants chose to stay out of the tunnels and continue to work in the fields, as their parents and grandparents had done. Companies based in Racalmuto and Caltanissetta operated the mines, employing workers from surrounding mining towns.[50]

Even so, sulphur improved the local economy. Sutera benefited from the taxes on the mines, and from the migrants who had come to the village to work in them. The mines alleviated the worst effects of the 1890s depression. There are no records of Suteresi dying of starvation, though some people did in nearby towns.[51] The presence of the mines also delayed transoceanic migration. Although a few people migrated before 1901, Suteresi only began to leave in significant numbers after 1905, when several sulphur companies closed or cut back their operations.

Work in the mines was extremely difficult and dangerous. By 1902 only one company had installed steam engines. In the other mines, men carried the sulphur out in large wicker baskets balanced on their backs. Miners tunnelled deep into the ground in a haphazard fashion, with little supervision. As the mine shafts lengthened they grew increasingly dangerous. San Paolino-Lupo, the consortium that worked the sulphur vein in San Paolino in the centre of town, was among the worst offenders. In 1903 the *Giornale di Sicilia* published an article describing the imminent danger faced by Sutera as a consequence of unsafe excavations, but its public warning had little effect on the authorities, who were dazzled by the potential profits.[52] On 12 September 1905 a screeching sound followed by a series of loud bangs swept through the mountain. 'In the mines a state of indescribable confusion and panic broke out. The miners in the underground tunnels ran toward the entrances, leaving behind their tools, candles, and clothing.'[53] The next day the miners returned to retrieve their belongings but refused to go back to work. They told the mayor they would rather go without bread then return to the tunnels. In the days that followed, a group of fifty women and children, holding aloft a flag decorated with a postcard of the King and Queen of Italy, marched on the city hall shouting, 'Down with the mine! Close the mine!'[54] While the mine managers attributed the tremor to an earthquake in Calabria, municipal authorities expressed serious doubts about the mine's safety. The mayor of Sutera requested an immediate government inspection, but it came too late. Just a week later, on the night of 20 September, one side of Mount Paolino came sliding down, crushing the houses on the edge of town, killing one woman, Rosaria Pardi, injuring five others, and leaving 2,500 homeless.[55] After the landslide, mining operations in San Paolino ceased. The mines seemed to justify the townspeople's reluctance to work underground or to trust the government to protect their interests or lives.

Rural residents did not passively accept their economic or social position. In 1876, Sonnino wrote that peasants had two options to better their living conditions and raise their wages: organization and migration. The people of Sutera tried both.[56] Sicilian rural workers had been forming peasant associations since the late nineteenth century. Sonnino described how people in several villages would pool their resources and tools and form peasant cooperatives. Together they would rent land directly from the owner. He commented that 'among Sicilian peasants the spirit of association is alive, although lacking the instruction or education to bring forth from these associations all the fruit they are capable of bearing.'[57] By the 1880s, villagers across the island were organizing mutual aid societies. These organizations formed the basis for the more militant worker associations that emerged a decade later.

The Sicilian economy had been in crisis since the 1870s, and by the late 1880s, residents were beginning to demand reforms. Cheap wheat from the Americas, combined with the protectionist measures of 1887, sent the agricultural markets into crisis. Exports from Caltanissetta (cheese, grain, and citrus fruit) fell sharply at the end of the 1870s. While they showed some improvement between 1880 and 1882, the markets remained very unstable. After 1884 the economic situation worsened, with prices falling and rents continuing to rise.[58] By 1888, workers had established the first *Fasci Lavorativi* in the cities of Palermo and Catania. Over the next five years these organizations spread far into the countryside. These urban committees were organized along the lines of trade unions and were closely tied to the nascent socialist movement.[59] However, as Francesco Renda notes, the links between peasant movements and the Italian Socialist Party were not so clear. Rural protesters were not advocating communal ownership of the land, but rather the redistribution of private property, or at least fair contracts.[60] The target of the peasants' anger was not the aristocracy or the system itself so much as the state's failure to recognize their grievances and the rising wealth of the non-noble landowners.

In the countryside, resistance generally took the forms of direct occupation and strikes aimed at employers and the state. During a strike, villagers refused to work the land, to send their children to school, or to have any contact with the government.[61] Both men and women participated in these protests. Although women did not usually work in the fields, their families and communities depended on agriculture. In May 1893 the prefect of Palermo lamented how 'even the women, forgetting their traditional modesty and their mission, perverted by revolutionary ideas have begun to enroll in a few of the *Fasci*, taking part in their public and private meetings, giving speeches and inciting people to resistance and violence against the bourgeoisie and the government.'[62]

As the movement spread across the island, local governments joined forces with landowners to confront the demonstrators. In many towns, local government officials forbade marches and public protests and called in the police during municipal elections to stop members of the local sections from voting. Rural residents who joined these organizations or who participated in the demonstrations faced severe reprisals. Many lost their jobs; some lost their lives. The bloody clashes between workers and peasants, and owners usually ended in death. The degree of police violence was in direct proportion to the pressure placed on the local government by the landowners.[63]

The *Fasci* arrived in Sutera in the summer of 1893. In early August, agricultural workers organized a local section, and within a few weeks they held their first protest march. A month later, members of the local section in Milocca staged a demonstration protesting the unjust arrest of their leaders. The protestors attacked the jail, disarmed the police, and liberated the prisoners.[64] The local police lieutenant commented that both sections 'showed themselves to be audacious and resolute.'[65] However, before any real change could be accomplished, Prime Minister Francesco Crispi, urged on by the Sicilian deputies in Parliament, sent down government troops. The strikes and demonstrations were quickly and violently squashed.

Suteresi continued to organize even after the *Fasci* were crushed. In 1901 a group of agricultural workers and artisans formed the Vittorio Emanuele III Society (V.E.III), and 380 people quickly joined. Within a year, membership had shrunk to 246, a result of migration to America, death, and expulsion.[66] The society's stated goal was to better the economic and social conditions of the workers. Instead of occupying the land, members vowed to 'make agricultural contracts and taxes just and honest.'[67] The society instituted a strict moral code. Anyone who 'abandoned themselves to drunkenness, frequented brothels and houses of ill-repute, or gambled away money earned by many days of sweat, will be admonished by the president the first two times and then expelled.'[68] A few years later another section opened in Milocca. Over the next twenty years, rural workers in Sutera opened twelve cultural, social, and financial institutions.

In the first decade of the twentieth century, these clubs organized several demonstrations and marches. In the early fall of 1901, a group of men marched through town shouting, 'Long live the King! Long live the Queen! Down with the land tax!' A few years later, the Peasant League staged a rally again demanding lower taxes. In December 1908, it staged two more demonstrations. The first was attended by two hundred angry villagers. A week later, residents staged a second protest march, and this time over a thousand people participated, demanding new roads.[69]

Villagers kept trying to break up the large estates in the first decades of the twentieth century. Suteresi established local cooperative financial institutions that funded attempts by the agrarian societies to buy the land directly from the owners. However, these combined strategies of collective ownership and direct occupation did not bear fruit until the 1920s.[70] Attempts to claim land through force and protest before 1914 ultimately failed to transform the system. Before the First World War, the only way a villager could acquire land was to buy it, and to do so he had to somehow get out from under the heavy burdens placed on him by the agricultural contracts. Despite the blood and violence, attempts at peasant organizing did not bring change quickly enough. After 1900 many residents turned to migration as an alternate means for realizing their dreams of land ownership.

This brief history of struggles over property in Sutera illustrates the power of land in the island's past. Since land equalled wealth, its acquisition and use were enmeshed in the island's society and politics. People's experiences of political and economic change were filtered through family, blood, and honour. Kinship networks and notions of respect located each person in this world, creating social networks that crossed class boundaries. A local proprietor might be an oppressive landlord, the target for attack, yet also be the godfather of his workers' children. Family ties complicated class divisions, privileging geographical proximity over individual success and informing people's actions and choices. Gender played a central role in shaping these social connections. So to understand how migration transformed the lives of rural women in the midst of political and economic turmoil, we must explore the ways family and community fashioned individual and collective identities.

Men, Women, Family, and Honour

In rural Sicily a person's sex and blood influenced how he or she moved through this world and how he or she experienced economic, political, and social change. In 1880 Sutera's resident population over the age of fifteen was fairly evenly divided by sex: 2,022 men and 2,262 women. The vast majority of villagers were engaged in agriculture; according to a local survey, over 88 per cent of the male Suteresi worked on the land. Roughly half these men were *agricoltori* – that is, they owned a small plot of land and rented out sections of the large estates. More than 35 per cent of the men worked as *braccianti* – that is, day labourers paid a set wage.[71] Only 4 per cent worked as artisans – as cobblers, tailors, bakers, pasta makers and so on – although many of these craftsmen owned a small plot of land on the outskirts of town.[72] State employees, clergy, and the landed aristocracy made up the remaining 12 per cent of the men. Fewer than 1 per cent of the women claimed any sort of profession. There were three female schoolteachers, a midwife, a baker, and four women employed by the municipal government. The rest of the women were listed as 'without a profession.'[73] This rough statistical portrait of Suteresi suggests the presence of powerful links between the economy, family, and the individual. These numbers make visible the influence of the *latifondo* system in shaping this world, in which physical and social spaces were deeply gendered.

Family defined a person's place in the social hierarchy. Family ties crossed class boundaries, creating different social and economic circles, but family roles were determined by sex, just as they were determined by work. In Sicily a person belonged to a multiplicity of families that were in a constant state of flux, spreading outward in overlapping circles mixing blood, affection, and pragmatism.[74] Birth rooted individuals in a nuclear family, but the ritual families created through baptisms and marriages were equally important in situating a person in the community. Sometimes, strangers entered into a family out of genuine fondness, for example, when childhood sweethearts married; more often, new people joined a family as a consequence of mutual interest. Marriages were arranged to improve a child's economic or social condition, and hopefully that of the extended family as well. Similarly, parents appraised possible godparents according to wealth and power, hoping the entire family could eventually capitalize on the relationship. Every birth, marriage, and death reshaped each person's immediate and extended families and his or her social and economic relations within the town.

Tracing the development of the Sicilian family is a difficult task that raises a number of methodological problems. Historical studies of the family long focused on the household, since residential patterns are far easier to trace over time than families.[75] Families are constructed differently by every culture. They can include distant relations or be limited to parents and children. The biological and cultural bonds connecting people of part times are difficult to reconstruct. The household is a much more tangible construction. By limiting family reconstruction to co-resident groups, it is possible to recreate the size and shape of households past.[76] These studies have been useful in writing the histories of the physical families, by showing that the formation of small households is not a recent historical phenomenon, but they cannot uncover the different meanings and functions of family in different places. They also fail to recognize the unequal power relations that resulted in men and women constituting family differently. In nineteenth-century Sicily, focus on the household alone would be misleading, since each household was enmeshed in multiple, constantly changing kinship networks that informed who people married, where they lived, and what they did. These family circles articulated the gendered nature of power and belonging that permeated Sicilian society through a rigid code of honour that defined respect in relation to the control of female sexuality.

Studies of the Sicilian family are further complicated by its identification with southern backwardness. Since the publication of Edward Banfield's work *The Moral Basis of a Backward Society* in 1958, scholars and experts have considered the southern Italian family as one of the principle obstacles to modernization in the region. Pointing to the overwhelming desire of the family (defined strictly in terms of parents and unmarried children) to improve its material condition, they have argued that southern Italians are incapable of acting for the collective good. The family is the basis for clientalism and weakened relations between citizens and the state. Immediately after publication, Banfield's argument came under blistering attack and has been largely discredited; however, the echoes of his original idea have not fully disappeared. As Gabriella Gribaudi noted, recently, the notion that the family is an essentially conservative institution whose power lies in tradition has not been challenged. The resistance to certain aspects of Banfield's original thesis is linked to prevailing gender stereotypes. The idea of the southern Italian family as dominated by a powerful and protective mother supports Banfield's assertion that the principle cause of amoral familialism is the absence of an extended paternal family. Even if we categorically reject Banfield's work, we are left with the idea of the southern family as a profoundly conservative, regressive, and female institution.[77]

In rural Sicily the family appears as a much more flexible institution, grounded in the past but also looking toward the future. In many respects it does seem to be an insulated, inward-facing institution, yet a closer study suggests that the family is also constantly looking outward. The family is both a private institution and public one that facilitates relations with the state, employers, and the church. The nuclear family – husband, wife, and children – stood at the centre of the intricate social and economic networks that made up family throughout southern Italy.[78] In general, people who lived to adulthood expected to marry, have children, and set up their own households. Marriage was the only socially acceptable entrance into the adult world as fully sexual and productive beings.[79] A religious calling, poverty, or a loss of family honour could leave any man or woman celibate for life. Political upheaval could also affect a person's chances of marrying. Wars and revolutions could pull young men from the community, leaving many women dependent on their parents or siblings for the rest of their lives. But, in general, people chose to marry. In Sicily as a whole, over half the people born in 1880 eventually married; this would represent the majority of those who survived to adulthood. By age fifty, only 12 per cent of women were single. Marriage patterns in Sutera reflected these regional patterns; over 50 per cent of people born in 1880 eventually registered a marriage at city hall.[80]

Contrary to common belief, rural Sicilians did not marry young. In Sutera, between 1880 and 1900, the average age of first marriage for women was twenty-four. For men the average age of first marriage was twenty-nine. Marriage ages reflected class position. Children from wealthier families married younger than children of agricultural workers and artisans, since they did not have to wait to inherit land or learn a trade.[81] Regardless of class, people sought their partners within town limits. In over 95 per cent of marriages celebrated between 1850 and 1900, the bride and groom both came from Sutera.[82] Proverbs such as 'the mother raises the daughter, the neighbour, the wife,' and 'a stranger's love is like water on bread' reinforced the common wisdom that it was best to marry someone born nearby.[83]

The importance of family meant that choosing a partner and arranging a marriage was a family event, although the protagonists did have some say in the matter. Young men and women had the opportunity to meet in church, in the piazza during the daily *passeggiata*, and in the homes of mutual friends. When two people did fall in love, they turned to their parents for permission. If the mothers found the prospective spouses acceptable, they would enter into preliminary negotiations and, with luck, announce the young couple's engagement within a few weeks. If an agreement could not be reached, a young couple could elope to force the families to agree to their wedding. Marriages driven by personal passion were tainted with scandal for years. As Charlotte Gower Chapman wrote: 'The attitude is not so much that they have done wrong in any serious way, but that they have failed to follow the proper procedure. They have made an individual matter out of what is really a concern of the family and of society; they have exercised a freedom which was not theirs.'[84] Eventually, however, the community accepted these couples.

Sicilians, at least publicly, held that the parents were best equipped to choose a partner who possessed the necessary qualities for a long-term relationship and who would benefit both the family and the community. Love was pleasant and to be enjoyed, but it did not necessarily constitute the best foundation for such a partnership. The pragmatic character of rural marriages led many outsiders to conclude that they were uncaring relationships. Salvatore Salamone-Marino commented: 'There is nothing, then, of the more or less sentimental love for the peasant, nothing idyllic.'[85] Certainly, these relationships did not reflect nineteenth-century middle-class notions of love; however, though romantic interest was not the primary factor in choosing future mates, residents generally expected mutual attraction and tenderness to develop over time. A wedding was a passionate celebration of the continuation of the family rather than a public ceremony attesting to the undying love between bride and groom. For this reason it required the attendance of the entire extended family. Ideally, a marriage brought the families involved greater material and social opportunities by expanding kinship networks.

Once married, the extended kinship networks eagerly awaited the announcement of the arrival of a child within the year. The newly wedded couple attained social legitimacy with the birth of a child. In 1913 Giuseppe Pitrè observed: 'Without a child's love the conjugal life lacks the force that sustains, illuminates and enriches the family.'[86] Contrary to contemporary nineteenth-century descriptions that rural Sicilian residents were just as happy to bury a child before his or her first birthday as to see him or her survive, Pitrè and other ethnographers noted that parents were very protective of their children. Children solidified the couple's position within the community. Also, the birth of each child provided an opportunity for the family to enlarge its network by choosing appropriate godparents. A child's parents and godparents referred to each other as *cummari*, or *cumpari* (co-mother or co-father). The relationship was similar to a close friendship that cannot be torn apart by rivalry, jealousy, or greed. If possible, parents tried to choose godparents for their children who were wealthier and more powerful and able to provide for the child's spiritual and physical well-being. Godparents, like in-laws, were permanent members of the family. They extended the kinship network and thereby optimized the nuclear family's economic and social possibilities.[87]

Marriage and family meant different things for men and women. According to local folklore, marriage was the 'ardent desire of every woman' and the 'duty' for every man.[88] Only through marriage could women gain a measure of independence; for men it marked a loss of freedom. Married women and mothers enjoyed a degree of respectability and autonomy denied their spinster sisters. Although marriage did not grant a woman freedom from male authority, her status within the family and the community changed. Marriage and motherhood marked a woman's entrance into the world of adults, and enabled her to form her own female support networks. Women who remained single were incomplete. The community did not blame unmarried women for their condition. Rather, townsfolk pitied the unfortunate woman who was somehow physically deformed or who was born into a family that could not or would not provide an adequate dowry. Local residents did not even hold prostitutes, unwed mothers, or the mistresses of the local elite solely responsible for their situations. Their plight was a result of the failure of their families to protect them as young girls, and everyone bore some degree of guilt. The 'house nuns' were the only women condemned outright for their spinsterhood, since they had chosen their celibacy and had affected an 'unnatural virtue.'[89] Whatever the reasons these women remained single, their status left them dependent on their parents and siblings for their material well-being for the rest of their lives. As a member of her father's household, a daughter was expected to obey her father, her mother, and her brothers. Her freedom was restricted, and she had little say in family decisions. Marriage kept women subordinate, but it also offered them the space to carve out networks that increased their personal and social power.

As a wife and mother, a woman held together and even helped strengthen the family's complicated social networks. In his ethnographic study of Sicilian families, Pitrè concluded: 'The mother contracts marriages for her children, chooses the spouse and arranges the business, and there remains nothing left but for husband and son to agree.'[90] For their sons, mothers sought young, honourable brides with a decent dowry. For their daughters, they looked for men from respected families who worked hard and could support a wife and children. Once a possible bride was identified, a woman approached the potential fiancée's mother and began negotiations. Sometimes a third party – usually an older woman or a close friend – acted as an intermediary between two families. Women relied on their kinship networks to gather information about a prospective spouse and his or her family. Was the family wealthy? Was the potential groom vicious and mean? Were the in-laws under consideration decent and hard-working people? Did they suffer from strange maladies or from insanity? The information a woman gathered reflected the character of the in-laws, and was used to decide whether to continue negotiations.[91] Once initial discussions had established a mutually acceptable marriage contract, the families met formally and announced the engagement together. On a Sunday afternoon the future bridegroom arrived bearing gifts at his fiancée's house, surrounded by his immediate family and kin. At the *canuscenza*, or introduction, the families agreed on the final financial arrangements and announced the date of the wedding.[92]

For men, marriage represented a more ambiguous transformation. It granted the new groom adult status within the community as a worker and head of household, but it also signalled the end of a life marked by greater sexual freedom and mobility and little responsibility.[93] Unmarried men occupied a distinctive place within the family: they were dependents, yet they also carried within them the future authority they would realize through marriage. This position of temporary dependence gave them greater autonomy within the father's household than their sisters could ever possess. Marriage brought young men's freedom to an end. It identified them as fully adult, with all the responsibilities and privileges that accompanied the position of head of household. However, it also tied them to one woman and her children, who became the source of their social existence.[94] For better or worse, marriage shaped the private and public relations that linked men and women to each other, to family, and to the community. All of this is best illustrated in the organization and meaning of housing and work.

Although people lived in nuclear-family households, residency patterns strengthened the physical and social ties that linked kinfolk together. A survey of the *foglio di famiglia* (family registers) indicates that only 5 per cent of villagers lived with members of their extended families – usually a widowed parent.[95] Average household sizes in Sutera support the image of a community organized around nuclear families. According to the census of 1901, the average size of households in the village was only four.[96] High infant mortality rates and the presence of older couples whose children had moved out account for the relatively small family size. Elderly residents moved in with their adult children only if they were unable to care for themselves. In general, elderly parents resisted moving in with their children and the accompanying loss of personal autonomy and authority. For men in particular, the loss of independence was associated with fading prestige and respect within the village.[97] However, nuclear families did not exist in isolation. Housing patterns suggest that family ties extended beyond the household, linking neighbourhoods together through blood.

The physical location of each separate household testified to the new social relations created by every marriage. In Sutera and Milocca, neighbours were usually related through birth or ritual. Newlyweds moved into their own houses, but there were not far away from their parents or siblings. According to the manuscript census of Sutera for 1911, parents commonly lived next door to a child, and siblings generally lived in the same neighbourhood. In Milocca, on average, a person was directly related to three out of nine families in each *robba,* or neighbourhood.[98]

Kin networks strongly influenced housing patterns because residential property was generally acquired through family. A child generally received his or her portion of the family patrimony in the form of housing (and land in the case of sons) on marriage or the death of a parent. If a family was too poor to buy or build a separate house for the adult children, existing houses were divided among family members.[99] In 1888, Paolina C. inherited a two-storey house in the centre of town. Two years later she divided the property in half, creating two separate houses. When she died in 1903, her daughter and son inherited the two separate apartments.[100]

While housing in Paolina's family was relatively simple, oftentimes the division of property became quite complicated. It illustrates the way property could foster either independence or dependence, depending on the circumstances of family members. When Anna R. passed away in 1931, she divided her one-room house between her three children and two grandchildren. Obviously, physical division of the property among her heirs was impossible. To avoid dissension, use rights and ownership rights were carefully defined, and the terms of the agreements reflected the needs of individual family members. According to Anna R.'s will, her husband Vincenzo B. had the right to use the house until he died. Although he did not own any part of the property outright, her testament ensured that he would not become dependent on one of their children. Their daughter, Calogera B., a single mother, inherited 5/8 of the property, along with use rights when her father passed away. Anna's other two children, Pietro and Maria, both married and living in their own houses, each inherited property, rights to 1/8 of the building. Her grandchildren, Giovanni and Vincenzo together received 1/8 of the house. In practice this complicated division of property meant that while Calogera and her son could live in the house, she could not sell the property without the consent of the entire family. Calogera could never become the head of her own family, even though she had her own child and her own house. Her mother's inheritance ensured that she would remain under the tutelage of her siblings.[101] The complex links between housing and domestic power relations ensured that place of residence bound individuals to family groups.

In Sutera, residential patterns strengthened the social bonds that united a woman, her sisters and her new female in-laws. When a bride moved into her new home, her nearest neighbours were often her sisters and brothers, and these households formed the centre of the new family's social network. Even in Milocca, where matrimonial customs and inheritance patterns favoured settling near the husband's family, women maintained strong ties with their birth families. Regardless of where women settled after marriage, most maintained closer ties to their parents and blood siblings than to the husband's relatives.[102] That is not to say that a bride did not recognize or utilize her ties to her in-laws. Although a woman formed stronger bonds with her in-laws than her husband did with his, she remained closer to her birth family. A woman's mother and sisters were often the first ones she turned to for help in times of crisis or when someone needed an extra hand. Since women stood at the centre of a family's social relations, children tended to grow up closer to their maternal relatives than to their paternal ones.[103]

Rituals surrounding childbirth attest to the strong influence of female social networks in shaping a hierarchy of mutual dependence. When Paolina N. gave birth to her children, her husband Giuseppe D. appeared at city hall to register the newborns if he happened to be in town. If he was working in the fields when the child was born, Paolina turned to her sisters for assistance, and they formally presented the child to the municipal clerks. Her sisters Assunta and Maria assisted at two of the births, while her sister-in-law was present at only one. Paolina in turn assisted her sisters when their children were born, and appeared a number of times to present her newborn nieces and nephews at the civil registry. In Sutera and Milocca, a woman who was giving birth turned to her blood relatives – her mother, her sisters, her aunts (usually her mother's sisters), her brothers, or her father – for assistance 64 per cent of the time. A husband's relation was present nearly 32 per cent of the time; neighbours appeared in 4 per cent of the cases where someone other than the father presented the child at city hall.[104]

Practical needs strengthened the physical and social bonds that united *la famiglia*; they also underscored the deeply gendered nature of any one person's role. Few families were self-sufficient; most relied on their neighbours, in-laws, siblings, and cousins for help. Goods and services were shared between families. If a man needed a mule to plough his fields, he could borrow his brother's on the implicit understanding that he would somehow return the favour. While men often shared material goods, women were responsible for creating strong social networks that bound the household to the family.[105] Women's work encouraged cooperation: sisters, in-laws, and neighbours shared childrearing and household tasks, helping one another with the weekly baking and washing. Women also joined together to prepare a new loom or share a precious sewing machine. They also formed information networks. Thus, younger women would seek the advice of elderly women, who were considered the authorities on household problems. Older women also acted as the community memory, storing information about other families that could prove useful in arranging marriages or business deals.[106] Female neighbours and relatives lent their assistance in times of crisis, providing food in case of illness or death, or helping at the birth of a child.[107] The ability to call on relatives for physical assistance during childbirth, funeral preparations, and marriage celebrations was based on reciprocity. A woman had to participate in order to be able to depend on her relatives and neighbours when her family needed assistance.

By helping sisters, aunts, cousins, and neighbours, women developed crucial economic and social resources for their immediate and extended families. The discussions that took place in kitchens and doorways and on the streets were not strictly limited to judging the behaviour of other residents. These conversations often overlapped with 'men's issues.' Casual conversations about a neighbour's marriage prospects easily slid into talk about money matters, job prospects, property rights, the upcoming harvest, or local elections.[108] Networks among women were strong, but this is not to suggest that men's social organizations were weak or unimportant. Men, especially day labourers, shared information with one another in the fields. However, the nature of agricultural work meant that these contacts were transient and could rarely provide the long-term, concrete material and physical assistance provided by women's networks, which were enmeshed in family. In sum, the borders between 'male' and 'female' worlds were permeable.

Women's friendships were an invaluable resource for families, but they could also do harm. Within the village, female networks served as powerful means of social control. Gossip had the power to make or break a family's reputation.[109] Blood alone was not enough to guarantee admittance to the group. Kinship defined the perimeters of a particular social circle, but behaviour determined the woman's position – and her family's – within that circle and the wider community.

Gender also shaped work. When work was available, Sutera seemed to be a town of women, children, and the elderly: except for the local gentry, schoolteachers, and priests, and a handful of artisans, few able-bodied men walked the streets during the week. The distance of the fields from town kept men away from their homes for most of the week. Women worked in the home, caring for their children and looking after their families' interests. Work reinforced the identification of women with the household and their position as kin-keepers within the family, and the identification of men with the outside world of waged work and their position as head of household.[110]

In the harsh environment of interior Sicily, the rhythms of daily life meant that men and women inhabited virtually separate spheres, their worlds colliding only within the confines of the house and on special occasions. On this land where wheatfields bordered on malarial swamps and outlaws roamed the countryside, women and children remained in the relative safety of the village. The lives of Giovanni S. and Antonia A. illustrate the impact of environment and land tenure systems on daily life. They married in the summer of 1889 and established a new family, yet they spent relatively little time together.[111] Giovanni worked in the fields most of the week, usually returning to Sutera late on Saturday evening. Even if he was lucky enough to find work closer to the village, he left home well before dawn and returned long after sunset.[112] When there was no fieldwork, he left the house early in the morning, joining his friends and family members in the piazza or the social club. The house belonged to Antonia. In the course of a typical day, Antonia rose before dawn and joined the other women on their way to get water. As she waited her turn at the fountain, she passed the time chatting and gossiping with her neighbours.[113] Back home she dressed and fed the children, emptied the chamber pots, made the beds, and washed the floor. Once the house was straightened, she went downstairs to clean the chicken coop and gather the eggs. By the time she had finished these tasks it was usually time to begin preparing the midday meal.[114] She spent the afternoons doing laundry, weaving, or baking bread, depending on the season and the day of the week.

However, the division between male and female worlds did not correspond to public and private spheres as defined by the four walls of the house. Women spent a good portion of the day outside. Often they would bring chairs into the street. Surrounded by her neighbours and friends, a woman would sit and weave, feed her children, and do her mending or whatever chores needed to be done. The public space appropriated by Sicilian women became an extension of their homes and the domestic world.[115]

Although Antonia did not work for wages, her work was considered as important as Giovanni's. Proverbial wisdom held that 'a house without a woman becomes poor.' Without a wife, a man owned nothing, for 'a good wife is the primary wealth of the house.'[116] Women's roles within the family were recognized as vital to the prosperity of the entire household. In his tour of Caltanissetta, Giovanni Lorenzoni described his visits to two families. The first family rented seven *salme* of land and owned two others outright. Out of eight children, four were capable of working the land. The second family owned only one *salme* of land and was able to rent only two others. Only two of the couple's five children could work in the fields alongside their father. Despite the obvious economic inequality, Lorenzoni concluded that the second family was better off than the first: 'In the first family everything was going badly: the house was dirty and miserable, the debts grew each year, and there was dirt everywhere even on the faces of the people; it screamed of misery: in the second [we saw] the opposite phenomena: a well-ordered house, no debt, very clean and dignified. When I marveled at the extreme diversity of the two situations, my guide responded shortly: 'the two women deserve the merit and the fault.'[117]

A woman's capacity to fulfil her role as wife and mother reflected on the prestige and prosperity of the entire family. No one ever questioned the importance of a woman's work, even though women did not work for wages. The community measured a family's honour in large part based on its ability to keep its house and women in order. A good reputation enabled a Sicilian man to compete for scarce natural and social resources, including jobs, land, and loans. Yet townsfolk judged no man by his actions alone. Rather, they assessed each man's character by the condition of his family.[118]

Although the Sicilian family worked as a cooperative enterprise, the relative position of men and women was not equal.[119] The gendered meanings of marriage, housing, and work reflect the centrality of male authority, which was articulated through a rigid culture of honour, which located each person within the framework of family. In the Sicilian family, according to Pitrè, 'the father holds absolute and indisputable control ... The mother governs the house and the children, almost as an extension of her husband, who she obeys and loves even when he does not deserve it.'[120] Men dominated the family; however, their power rested on the actions of wives, sons, and daughters. The male and female worlds framing the meaning and function of family were interdependent, and this sometimes led to conflict within the family, as the various members sought to realize their own dreams. In a family with very limited resources, the decision to invest savings in a mule for the father, or land for a son, or a trousseau for a daughter, could lead to tension.

Relations between men and women within the family are clearly visible in the patterns of daily life, but they cannot be fully understood outside of the code of honour. A family's ability to ensure its social and economic prosperity and better its material circumstances depended on its reputation. A family's most important asset was its honour. While honour is often used to refer to an individual's reputation, among Mediterranean cultures the concept of honour was an attribute of the entire family.[121] By the turn of the century, honour had become a tangible quantity in Sicilian culture, something that could be measured and traded, a valuable commodity in a land where few claimed significant wealth.[122] In agrotowns like Sutera, where cash was not readily available, the only means of ensuring good marriages and strong social networks that translated into increased access to jobs and land rested on a family's reputation. Honour brought a family prestige, power, and wealth regardless of its actual economic circumstances. Neighbours, friends, and acquaintances judged a family's honour on the basis of its members' ability to conform to expected social roles. In a world where people had little control over the environment, death, disease, or even their work, they could control their reputation. So honour became the quality that most accurately reflected a family's character.

This code of honour informed family organization and shaped how men and women fashioned their sense of identity. To claim a good reputation a man had to feed, shelter, and protect his wife and children. A man measured his self-worth by his ability to provide a decent dowry for his daughters and see that his sons were employed. Women defined themselves in terms of their ability to care for their homes, raise children, feed and clothe their families, and observe traditions and rituals. Female sexuality played a crucial role in all of this.[123] A man's honour rested on his ability to keep his women chaste. A woman's reputation depended on her behaviour in public.

A young girl's father and brothers were responsible for protecting and preserving her chastity until she married. Mothers closely monitored the behaviour of unmarried girls and limited their contacts with neighbours. If a young girl lost her virginity and the family could not quickly arrange a suitable marriage, all members suffered. Fellow residents saw her father and brothers as weak and foolish men incapable of protecting their own interests, and this placed them at a disadvantage in competing for scarce resources. The disgraced girl's mother would have difficulty finding good husbands for her other daughters and arranging marriages with well-dowered wives for their sons.[124] An unmarried girl's sexual misconduct also raised fundamental questions about the family's unity. If the accusations were true, then the guilty woman had betrayed the interests of her family, revealing a fundamental weakness in familial allegiances that outsiders could exploit. Honour, based on sexual hierarchy, was the public articulation of a family's social position and its assets.

The southern Italian family structure fixed individuals in the economic and social landscape. Cultural ideals, geography, and economic necessity combined to sharpen gender divisions, which were clearly visible in Sicilian villages. Yet this structure, so rigid in many respects, was also quite flexible. Familial roles and duties met the demands of the *latifondo* system, which pulled men out of the village for most of the week. Male and female networks proved critical to the family's survival, and in different ways often fulfilled similar tasks. Through relatives, friends, and neighbours, rural Sicilians sought to better their own economic and social opportunities as well as those of their extended families. These vast, overlapping networks wove each person into a complex, gendered web of mutual obligations and shared resources. These relations were fraught with tension as households and families vied for access to scarce resources, yet they also created a system of mutual support and allegiance. No matter how competitive or contradictory this world appeared from the inside, families showed a united front to outsiders. When faced with the outside world, Suteresi transferred their familial allegiances to the community.

Myth, History, and Identity

If family located each person in the social and economic environment in a particular way, these complex social webs also facilitated the construction of a shared collective identity. Every family passed on the same legends and stories telling of the moral and physical superiority of Sutera and its people. Residents claimed that their village was older than its neighbours, that the air they breathed was purer, that their ancestors were braver and more honourable. Even though many Suteresi have settled in Campofranco over the years, there is still a powerful rivalry between the towns. Local residents explained to me that thieves, murderers, and runaway servants settled in Campofranco, which was first established as a free town outside the jurisdiction of local authorities. Today, Suteresi look down on Campofranchesi as rude, ill-educated buffoons with a markedly different accent. The divisions between families in Sutera disappeared when the villagers compared themselves to the people of neighbouring towns.

As in towns throughout the southern provinces, Suteresi attempt to connect their personal histories to great historical events. In the myths and stories that comprise Suteran folklore, the primacy of Sutera and the courage of its people are unsurpassed and unquestioned. Despite its isolation and its relatively insignificant size, Sutera and the Suteresi take centre stage in the island's history. Why Sutera was lucky enough to be central to every major historical event is never addressed. It was the fate of the village, an accident of geography. In their reconstruction of their past, Suteresi see themselves as rebels challenging any threat to their autonomy from outside authority, any attack on their way of life. The town is older than the nation and demands complete loyalty and allegiance.

Suteresi pride is founded on the antiquity of their village. Locals recount how the caves on the outskirts of the village attracted the first people who roamed the island. According to local historian Antonio Vaccaro, these caves became the 'habitations of the first men who came to Sicily.'[125] Vaccaro cited the pottery shards and bits of silver and bronze found by local inhabitants as evidence of these ancient settlements. The caves are spread out across the territory, and Vaccaro believed that these early settlers slowly 'abandoned their solitary caves, and joined with others on the high plain of our mountain to lay the foundation for our primitive village that rose to the northeast.'[126] Suteresi claim these dwellings as evidence that their land was special enough to attract the first human beings on the island.

Legends tell how the descendants of these cave dwellers were the first to convert to Christianity. In his local history, Vaccaro quoted from the life of Saint Onofrio written by Biagio Simi, and from a biography of the saint by Pietro Propono, as irrefutable evidence that 'Sutera was the first to embrace Christianity, and to have welcomed the evangelists Saint Onofrio and Saint Archileone to preach within its walls ... In the year 57 those who came before us, who walked the land that we walk today, who breathed in the pure air that we breathe today were baptized.'[127] Historians since Vaccaro agree that Christianity did not reach the island for at least another hundred years, but residents pay little heed to these scholars' arguments. They see their Christianity as rooted in the land itself.[128]

Suteresi claim that a connection between their land and Christ existed even before the evangelists reached the island. At the edge of town, above the cemetery, is a hill that seems to have been split in half, probably by a long-ago earthquake. Local legend holds that the mountain broke open when Christ died on the cross.[129] When an older woman in the village recounted the story to me, she claimed the mountain had cracked open because it could not contain its sorrow when Jesus died. In the early twentieth century, immigrants who had settled in America raised money to replace the rickety wooden cross on the mountain with a solid metal one firmly embedded in a concrete base, thus reaffirming their connection with the village and its past.

Local myths also attest to the power of land. Suteresi believe that the hills surrounding their town are magical and hold great wealth, and that given enough time the earth will eventually yield their treasures to the people. The legends vary. One emphasizes the local people's strong sense of fate; another focuses on the promise of future wealth for the entire community. All legends revolve around San Marco, a hill outside the town. At the top of the hill, massive rocks are piled one on top of the other, creating bizarre rock formations. One legend tells of a man who was returning from his fields long ago. It was late, around midnight, and as he approached San Marco he heard a huge crowd of people. Much to his surprise, when he rounded the corner he found a lively fair in progress. Merchants were busy selling horses, cows, grain, and fruit. The tired man stopped and bought a sack of oranges, tucked them into his saddlebags, and led his donkey home. The next day the oranges had turned to gold.[130] According to legend, this fair is held one night every hundred years, and if fate leads you to the market, whatever you buy will turn to gold by sunrise. Another story claims that the rocks themselves are filled with gold and that when they tumble down the entire village will be wealthy. Even if greedy landowners and corrupt politicians made land ownership impossible, the land remained – at least in myth – the people's source of past and future glory.

Suteresi take great pride in their village's connections with ancient Greece. Northern Italian communities summon their links with ancient Rome to emphasize their importance; Sicilians look even deeper into history.[131] In this regard, Suteresi focus on a ruined castle above the town on the path up Mount San Paolino. In the nineteenth century a few scholars argued that Dedalus built the castle when he took refuge from the wrath of the Cretan king Minos in the mythical city of Camico, allegedly located on a mountain somewhere north of Agrigento. When Minos came in search of Dedalus, the king of Camico attempted to distract him by offering food and wine. Minos took advantage of the king's hospitality, and one of his daughters. The king of Camico ordered his men to drown his guest in his bath. Uncertain whether their king's death was an accident or murder, Minos's henchmen left the village, vowing revenge. A few years later the Cretan king sent an expedition to Sicily to avenge the death of Minos, and Camico was destroyed. Few experts, even in the nineteenth century, believed that Sutera was built on the ruins of Camico; even so, local residents are loath to give up any connection with the famous town. Vaccaro, for instance, argued that refugees from Camico, fleeing from Cretan forces, first settled in the shadow of San Paolino.[132]

Suteresi have constructed a past that emphasizes their resistance to oppression and their struggle for independence from any sort of outside authority. The town has defined its struggle during the Arab conquest in terms of its own independence and as a defence of the Christian faith. Sutaresi took part in the great revolt led by the residents of Caltabellotta – a rebellion that took the Arabs eight years to quell. A few decades later they joined Agrigento in a second rebellion.[133] Under Norman, French, and Spanish rule, the villagers more or less accepted their place in the feudal system, but still they did not hesitate to rebel any time they felt that the baronial demands had grown too excessive. In 1282 they participated in the Sicilian Vespers, the uprising that ended Norman rule on the island. Fifty years later the Suteresi killed the tyrannical Baron

Scandolfo when he attempted to impose his will on the town.[134] Shortly after that the village was freed from baronial rule altogether. Whenever invading forces threatened their independence, the local elite fought back until they regained their freedom. Vaccaro recounts that in the nineteenth century, Suteresi courageously protected their town from brigands in the chaos of 1860. When 'the news of the advancing enemy spread through town, men and women left their houses and heroically defended their town.'[135] The bandits, facing a united front, turned around and rode toward Campofranco.

Antonio Vaccaro, who wrote the only local history of Sutera, was a prominent doctor. Throughout his work there is a tension between his desire to emphasize the independence of the villagers and his desire to create a historical connection between Sutera and Italy. At times he seems to imply that Suteresi had an emotional bond to the Italian nation long before Italy even existed. In describing Sutera's resistance to Arab rule and the arrival of the Normans, he wrote how the town 'awaited the arrival of the [Norman] army with great anxiety unable to support the tyrannical [Arabic] yoke and a religion in direct opposition to its own, and remembering, as the illustrious C. Cantu said, what it meant to be Christian and Italian, they could not resign themselves to living under the domination of those that offended their national pride and domestic integrity.'[136]

Vaccaro's account ends with the arrival of the Piedmontese and the fall of 'Bourbon tyranny.' The last few pages of Vaccaro's history briefly outline the wondrous changes wrought by the new government in Rome. However, despite his attempts to create a sense of historical national identity, the townspeople see themselves as a fiercely independent people whose loyalty is tied to kin and town and not to the Italian nation.

The village's physical isolation forced the Suteresi to depend on themselves, and these stories created a sense of common purpose. Feelings of *campanilismo* were reinforced by the stories and legends they used to create their history. In the nineteenth century the villagers used their reconstructed past to justify their actions in the present. Stories of the town's heroic resistance to Arabic and Spanish rule shaped their attitudes toward the Italian government: Rome was just another foreign invader. These myths created fierce local allegiances in men and women, which in turn shaped the notions of Italian nationalism and patterns of assimilation in immigrant communities in the Americas.

Blood and honour circumscribed the individual and collective identities of rural Sicilian men and women at the end of the nineteenth century. Families created by birth and ritual served as the principal means for locating each person in the social hierarchy. A family name defined a person's power in the adult world; it improved one's chances of making a good marriage, finding work, and settling into one's own house. Family linked each person to the wider community, which had been created through stories and myths. In this world, power was located within the family, and gender conferred authority and assigned each person a position in both the domestic sphere and the community. Family also acted as an agent of change. Decisions about family size, housing, work, marriages, and even politics reflected residents' responses to economic and political change. In the wake of failed land reforms, failed rural cooperatives, and strikes to change the land tenure system, residents were left with a difficult choice: immigrate, or accept the status quo. While many chose to leave, many more decided to stay. The same forces that held so many rural Sicilians to their homes – to this world that held so little hope of improvement – impelled others to seek their fortune overseas.

Chapter Two

'Gone to America': Migrating Men and Abandoned Women

In late September of 1908, Paolina B. bid farewell to her husband, Rosario M. He and his older brother, Onofrio, were bound for the coal mines of Birmingham, Alabama. Rosario was a seasoned migrant. He first left home in 1906 when he was twenty-four, returning in 1907 to marry Paolina. Now, less than a year after their wedding, he was once again setting out for Alabama, leaving Paolina, eight months pregnant, at home. Paolina's sister-in-law, Rosaria, was in a roughly similar situation. She and Onofrio had married eight years earlier, and his departure left her with their four children, the youngest only a month old. Paolina and Rosaria, like their husbands, believed that the family's separation was temporary. There was no need to postpone plans to immigrate because Paolina was pregnant or Rosaria had an infant to care for. The men would be home shortly. Onofrio returned in 1910, and Rosario followed a few years later.[1] The two families saw migration as a chance to better their lives, to improve their material conditions and their social status back home in Sicily. The money Rosario and Onofrio sent to them from the Americas would buy land and better housing and ensure that their children would not have to work as day labourers. Emigration was a necessary sacrifice to improve their lives in Sutera, not an opportunity to create new ones in faraway lands.[2] While the men were away, Paolina and Rosaria would raise their children and look after their families' interests. In 1909, Paolina built a new house in the middle of town with the money Rosario had sent her.[3] The stories of these two families are typical of the experiences of thousands of rural Sicilians at the beginning of the twentieth century.

All across the island, men left their families at home to seek work in the Americas. Contemporary observers, much like historians, novelists, and film makers today, focused their attention on the adventures of the migrants, largely ignoring the role that migrants' wives played in the process. As Sicilian men crowded onto ships bound for New York in ever larger numbers, critics concentrated their growing fears of social chaos and economic ruin on the women who remained behind. Politicians and landowners argued that if left unchecked, mass male migration would undermine the agricultural workforce and the integrity of the family. Supporters of migration viewed it as a potentially beneficial force, as it resulted in rising incomes and a shrinking workforce and might weaken existing forms of economic relations that had stymied development of the southern provinces; however, they agreed with its critics that mass male emigration had the potential of creating social chaos. Left on their own, the 'white widows' could be forced into begging, prostitution, or crime. Their inevitable decline into vice and depravity would cause the social fabric to unravel; as families disintegrated, the nation would experience rising rates of infanticide, abortion, and female insanity. Italy as a whole would lose its ability to compete in the world's marketplaces. The image of the abandoned wife left destitute, a widow before her time, became the symbol of the heavy price exacted by mass migration. By the First World War, time had proven these dire predictions false. Migration had transformed the lives of the women who stayed behind but it had not driven them insane or into crime.

The images of women that appeared in political discussions and popular fiction do not reflect the experiences of rural women; they do, however, illustrate the deeply gendered nature of transoceanic migration. In this chapter, in order to show how notions of gender and female sexuality informed public debate and popular attitudes toward migration, I examine how the women who remained behind were portrayed. These cultural notions contrasted sharply with the experiences of rural women. In the cultural imaginings, the migrant and the act of migration became identified with characteristic male traits (strength, virility, and action), whereas the people who chose to remain behind became imbued with female qualities (weakness, passivity, and dependence). The strength of these images suggests that migrants crossed both national and sexual boundaries when they chose to emigrate. Female migrants were masculinized; the men who remained behind or who returned were feminized. In Sicily, political debates merged with popular literature and scientific culture, both of which drew on notions of masculinity and femininity rooted in the island's code of honour, to strengthen the cultural gendering of migration. The way Italian culture gendered emigration, however, is profoundly different from the way men and women experienced transnational migration.

Far from being abandoned or forgotten in a world populated only by women and weak men, the women who stayed in Sicily actively participated in the migration process. As household managers and 'kinship keepers,' these women often helped arrange and finance their husbands' voyages. These women did not cross the Atlantic; instead they invested their own dreams in the decision to send a family member overseas. Mass male migration did not leave rural women behind; instead it provided the resources to carve out new economic, social, and political spaces in their rural world.

The Forsaken and Abandoned

In 1905 Angelo Mosso, a young professor from Turin, toured the hill towns of southern Italy and Sicily to see firsthand the effects of mass migration on the region. As his train pulled into the small railway station outside the village of Castelfillipo in the province of Caltanissetta, where hundreds of migrants were preparing for their departure, the women left standing on the platform captured his attention:

> A woman, pale as a corpse and supported by four people, passed in front of us with her head hanging lifelessly on her breast. Other women were crying; their faces once browned by the sun turned to grey, their large mouths and whitened teeth twisted in screams; they turned to[ward] the back of the train oblivious to us. [When the train began to move] there was a strident scream, a thunder of tears which burst from the crowd at the moment of their misfortune ...
>
> A woman broke from the crowd and ran screaming. We had already left the station and as she ran she kept shouting 'Give him my best, remind him that I am waiting, make him send me money for the voyage; tell him that I'm waiting for him, that if I do not leave I will die!' Her words were cut off by her tears and lack of breath. She stopped, supporting herself against a telegraph pole, then suddenly leaned forward and fell to the earth.[4]

A few kilometres outside the station the train rounded a curve and a woman with her children appeared on horseback. Mosso wrote: 'The figure of that mother weakened with pain, motionless between the two children she held in her arms, stirred me and I stretched my hand out to wave to her with my eyes full of tears.'[5]

Mosso's descriptions of women left on railway platforms and standing alone in fields tearfully pleading with their husbands not to forget them reflected some of the striking characteristics of Sicilian mass migration. Most migrants were male, and many were married, and their wives remained behind. The presence of these wailing women, however, does not support the conclusion that they were abandoned – a position that Italian politicians and social critics were so quick to embrace. Political and economic considerations and ideas about women's nature fuelled the logical leap that these women had not chosen to remain in Sicily. The assumptions behind Mosso's analysis informed early twentieth-century political discussions about migration. As the numbers of migrants from the southern provinces climbed into the hundreds of thousands, debates between the supporters and the opponents of unrestricted migration reached fever pitch. Closely linked to fears that the loss of manpower would weaken Italy's industrial development and its military strength was the image of the forsaken woman. Politicians offered these weeping women as proof that even 'temporary migration is fatal to morality.'[6]

In Sicily, as throughout the South, those who saw transoceanic migration as a degenerative force that would ruin the island's productivity and undermine social mores often pointed to these women as the harbingers of chaos. Conservative politicians and landowners vehemently opposed unrestricted emigration. Large landowners in Sicily and the South were especially hostile to any form of government support for emigration. The apparent exodus from the hill towns of Sicily and Calabria drastically depleted local labour pools. The diminishing number of available workers was forcing landowners to raise wages, and many landowners were demanding that the government pass legislation to prohibit emigration altogether. The landed elite readily admitted that most Sicilians lived harsh lives with few possibilities of improving their living conditions, but they did not see why the wealthy had to suffer. 'It is true, our peasants live in misery,' lamented the landowners, 'but it is not our fault. Now that they emigrate, it is difficult to find anyone who will work the land for reasonable wages. Now we are ruined.'[7] Unrestricted emigration set a dangerous precedent, encouraging even lowly day labourers to exercise their freedom to leave and sell their labour to a higher bidder. When the migrants returned, property owners complained, they were arrogant and refused to 'raise their hats' in deference to the local gentry.[8]

Those who believed that the growing exodus of Italians should be

Emigrants in the port of Palermo 1902. (Alinari/Art Resource, NY)

curtailed – or at least closely regulated by the state – inflated popular fears of sexual licentiousness, infidelity, and cuckoldry, and fused them with the image of the abandoned woman. Critics of emigration argued that a woman left to fend for herself would inevitably find protection in the arms of another man. To buttress their positions, they pointed to rising rates of adultery and prostitution.[9] In 1911, Professor Luigi Rossi stated that 'migration has, in part, contributed to the rise in instances of adultery, illegitimate births, abortions, infanticides and a host of other crimes connected to the weakening of family ties.'[10]

Liberal supporters of emigration believed that unrestricted mass migration would rid the island of the last vestiges of its feudal past and force the island into the industrial capitalist world. They were quick to show that the conservatives' arguments rarely held up under scrutiny. In his study on crime and delinquency, Francesco Coletti pointed out that though infanticide was a frequent crime in several southern provinces – in particular Abruzzi, Molise, and Sardinia – the northern regions of Tuscany and Umbria consistently reported higher rates. Calabria, on the other hand, reported one of the lowest rates of infanticide, even though it had a history of high male migration.[11]

Those who favoured unrestricted migration viewed it as an invigorating movement that would bring new ideas, new markets, and hard currency back to Italy.[12] Emigration was a sign 'of growth and of a sober industrious people.'[13] They argued that most Italian migrants intended to return home and would introduce much-needed cash into local economies. Supporters of migration contended there was no reason for the state to intervene as long as emigrants eventually repatriated.[14] Some even suggested that mass migration might alleviate the worst social and economic problems plaguing the new state.

The Italian state had long looked with alarm and a sense of hopelessness at its poverty-ridden southern provinces. The government commissioned several studies and senate inquiries to try to solve the worst of the region's economic and social problems before residents took up arms in a full-scale rebellion.[15] In the late 1890s the government passed legislation favouring development of the South, but the problems of underdevelopment, inefficient agriculture, high unemployment, and overpopulation never disappeared, nor did the threat of social unrest. After 1900, as emigration from the southern regions reached massive proportions, officials saw the movement as a safety valve – as allowing them to hold off making any serious economic or social reforms. By encouraging overseas migration, the government avoided having to address the region's problems. Mass emigration would cause the population to fall and offer the residents who stayed behind the opportunity to enjoy a 'growing sense of well-being.'[16] Emigration held the possibility of ending the cycle of poverty and starvation. In the conclusion of his study of social and economic conditions in Sicily, Professor Giovanni Lorenzoni wrote that emigration 'could be compared to a catapult destined to upset the economic and social foundations of the island: however it would not just destroy society, creating a wasteland, but reconstruct the island on a more prosperous and more modern basis.[17] Francesco Coletti agreed, pointing to improved health, rising literacy rates, and declining crime rates as solid evidence of the benefits of emigration.[18]

Many advocates of unrestricted migration were more cautious. Giuseppe Bruccoleri believed that emigration would eventually force needed reforms on the backward and corrupt Sicilian economy, but he also viewed it as a harsh and cruel engine of change. He questioned whether the economic gains were really worth the physical and emotional price the emigrants had to pay, noting how migrants commonly returned alcoholic or broken in health. Furthermore, he argued, mass migration was a symptom of the island's difficulties, and by lauding emigration as the solution the government was evading responsibility for the troubles that plagued Sicily's infrastructure. Emigration, a consequence of the lack of roads, antiquated farming methods, deforestation, drought, and a corrupt political system, was incapable of fixing these problems. Bruccoleri warned: 'If upon hearing the rising anthems to emigration, on occasion we rush to calm the flames, it is not because we wish to negate the benefits resulting from emigration; but because we fear that these continuous shouts of joy benefit us in ways similar to morphine: that is, we sink into a rosy dream, from which we could sadly awaken.'[19] Even Senator Pasquale Villari, who firmly believed that mass migration was beneficial, recognized the difficulties involved and questioned whether returnees would in fact serve as agents of modernization. In 1909 he noted that when emigrants returned with enough money to build sparkling white houses in the centre of town, they could not easily readapt to village life. 'They end up becoming Americans, or they remain [home] and become useless Italian citizens.'[20]

These more cautious supporters of mass migration, who believed that emigration would in the end improve living conditions in the rural South, tended to agree with their conservative opponents that transnational migration caused untold suffering among the women left behind. Their misery was the unfortunate price that had to be paid for the long-term benefits of emigration. A few suggested that the condition of these women was only temporary. Angelo Mosso, who so vividly described the pain and suffering of the wives and mothers left behind at the railway stations, argued that ultimately even these women would profit from their plight. Left to survive on their own, they would seek paid work. The loss of able-bodied men would translate into higher wages, better jobs, improved literacy, and a greater degree of autonomy for all rural women. 'This reawakening of woman ... ensures that the next generation will be better than the present.'[21] Other writers were more pessimistic. Bruccoleri, citing cases where men anxious to migrate married in order to raise the cash they needed to buy a ticket to America, sometimes abandoning their brides even before the marriage was consummated, saw migration as an unmitigated disaster for these women.[22] However, despite the sorrow caused by mass migration, he too concluded that even these women would benefit if migration improved general economic and social conditions on the island.

This image of 'abandoned' women circulated in political debates; it also appeared often in popular literature in more lurid and graphic forms. By the First World War, to portray the social impact of mass migration, Sicilian authors were turning regularly to the image of the crazed and dissipated woman abandoned by her migrant husband or son. In Maria Messina's short stories depicting the everyday trials of Sicilian women, the tales of women left behind by husbands and sons are by far the most poignant. Born in Palermo in 1887, Maria Messina, the daughter of a poor nobleman, spent her life writing stories portraying women as forsaken castaways in a world dominated by the desires and dreams of men. In her stories touching on migration, even the women who actively sought to keep their husbands at home inevitably failed, unable to compete with the promises of wealth and success in America. Once their husbands had left, these women went crazy or died. In 'La 'Mèrica,' when Catena's husband announces his intention to emigrate she forbids him to go unless he takes her with him. They fight for weeks, and eventually he gives in and books passage for her and their small son. They arrive at the port of Palermo, where she is diagnosed with trachoma and sent back to her village. At home the local pharmacist treats her condition with caustic poultices and she goes blind. Mariano never writes, and he gradually slips away, lured by the riches of America. Lost in the darkness, Catena goes crazy and waits for the next boat to carry her to Mariano.[23] *Gli Americani del Rabbato* (The Americans of Rabbato) by Luigi Capuana opens with a woman's screams echoing through the streets. When a neighbour rushes to the window she is told that *la scarsa* (the halfwit) has just received news that her husband had taken another wife in *la 'merica.*[24] Neighbourhood women readily accept this final proof of her abandonment as the explanation for her descent into madness.

In the popular literature, wives were not the only ones to suffer when the men left. In these novels and stories, mothers of migrants also fell victim to despair. When a woman's son left for America, so did her old age insurance. According to Sicilian custom, family obligations dictated that sons care for widowed mothers; however, it was also recognized that time and distance could undermine filial loyalty. Sicilians believed that if a woman's son left for America there was a good chance he would forget his responsibilities to his widowed mother. The bond between mother and son was the strongest tie between any two family members. A mother sacrificed everything she possessed for her son, including her life if necessary. Maternal love was total love, and long after his marriage a man's first loyalty was toward his mother.[25] The relationship between a mother-in-law and daughter-in-law was the most hostile among all familial relations, reflecting the mother's jealousy as her son's affections gradually shifted to his wife.[26]

Authors often incorporated the image of an elderly woman left behind to die alone without her children's love and support. In 'Nonna Lida,' another short story by Maria Messina, a young man left alone after the death of his wife decides to immigrate to North America. Before he leaves he asks his widowed mother to care for his only child. For a while her grandson keeps her so busy that she rarely has time to reflect on her son's absence. Then a year or so later he writes to tell her he has married a woman from a neighbouring town. She is unhappy: 'Now with the new family he would no longer have time to think of the old one. But patience, at least the little one, when he is grown would support her, he would stay with her.'[27] Within a few months a letter arrives instructing her to use the money enclosed to buy a ticket for her grandson and put him on the next boat to America. A day after the little boy sails, Nonna Lida is found frozen to death in a nearby field. Messina's story reflects the importance placed on the mother/son relationship, which was fundamental to a Sicilian woman's self-image. With her grandson, the last physical tie to her son, on a boat bound for America, Nonna Lida dies.

Political debates, novels, and short stories linked migration to men and modernity. When women tried to migrate, they usually failed. These women, literally and figuratively, symbolized the backward world that migrants left behind. In these stories the rural countryside of the South, emptied of able-bodied men, who have been lured to America by promises of wealth and power, is a barren, ineffectual, and passive land. In Luigi Pirandello's short story 'L'Altro Figlio' a poor woman pines for her two sons, both of whom left for the United States fourteen years earlier. She wanders through the town, filthy and sweaty: 'Her yellowed face was a tight-web of lines in which her eyelids bled, ruined, burned by continual tears.' She sleeps on steps and doorways, searching for news from America. Whenever she hears that someone is planning to travel overseas she begs them to carry a letter to her sons, convinced that if they know of her plight they will come to her rescue. Her fellow townsfolk humour her. A local woman, abandoned by her own husband but flourishing under the protection of a new lover, pretends to write letters for the illiterate Maragrazia. Departing migrants promise to deliver the letters, only to throw them away before they even arrive at the port. Her one son who remains in the vicinity, a product of rape, is invisible. This son is the essence of Sicily. Physically ugly, he is a hard-working and dutiful son, but he is inconsequential. He is a constant reminder of the corruption and violence so closely identified with island life. Although the two sons who left are morally bankrupt, they appear as the only source of life and salvation for this poor widow. The homeland appears in literature as a source of life and a place of death. These are the same qualities commonly ascribed to women in Sicilian culture.[28]

Whether unmarried, widowed, or temporarily separated from their husbands, single women were the most dangerous to the wider community. These women threatened the honour of their own kin and the reputations of all other families in the town. Widows were considered especially dangerous to rural life, especially if they were childless. Popular belief held that marriage awakened the powerful force of female sexuality, and once roused the only curb on a woman's lust was her husband. After a woman became a mother, the danger was mitigated in part, as her children exerted a controlling force over her nature.[29] If a woman's husband died and she had no children, there were no external controls on her sexual appetites, and she would certainly succumb to the offers of the first man who came along. If no eligible man happened along, she would seduce a neighbour's husband to satisfy her desires. Unless a widow remarried, she was a constant threat to the honour of her neighbours and her family.

A widowed woman had to live in complete seclusion for at least two years after her husband's death to claim a position of respect within the community. She kept her house tightly shuttered and only ventured outside to attend mass. In the most extreme cases, relatives even brought her meals so she could avoid shopping. Once two years had passed, she occasionally left her house, but continued to wear black for the rest of her life.[30] Only if a widow was carefully hidden behind closed shutters and her behaviour strictly regulated could her family's honour be protected.

The wives of emigrants were as dangerous to the community as widows were. Often these women were left alone soon after their sexual awakening. In their husband's absence these *vedove bianche* (white widows) would surely dishonour their families. The position of emigrants' wives was similar to that of women whose husbands had been carted off to jail. In Milocca, the wife of an imprisoned man lived her life as if she were in deep mourning. After her husband was led away, a respectable woman dared not leave her house except to attend early-morning mass. Whether the separation was voluntary or imposed by the judicial system, as long as their men were away these women had to behave as carefully as widows to avoid bringing dishonour and shame to their families.[31] They were neither widows nor wives according to conventional definitions, yet they had been freed from the direct supervision of men. They did not fit into any of the well-defined social roles, and this may have made them more dangerous than other single women and caused the neighbours to be even more suspicious. The fictional images of the old abandoned mother left to die, and the wife who sinks into insanity, mitigated the precarious social position of these women.

The scientific community lent further support to popular attitudes toward women. With the weight of scientific methodology behind them, the medical community provided physical evidence that the absence of a man could irrevocably harm a woman. Physicians in small villages actively encouraged the association of migration, insanity, and sexual depravity that Capuana and Messina described so vividly and that Sicilian culture embraced. In 1903, Dr Vaccaro from Sutera admitted Onofria I. into the mental hospital in Palermo. According to the medical report: 'A little jealousy on the part of her husband, a few beatings, perhaps a few blows to her head, and the absence of her husband who had immigrated to America, are the causes presumed to have influenced the development of her mental illness.'[32] Apparently the combination of a jealous husband and a history of physical abuse left her unable to face life without her husband. When a rural Sicilian woman seemed to be insane, and a son or husband had emigrated, local doctors in Sutera and Milocca never hesitated to conclude that emigration had caused the woman's condition. To support their diagnoses, doctors relied on accepted medical notions linking female sexuality with mental health.[33]

In 1912, Giovanni S. committed his forty-seven-year-old wife, Concetta V., to the insane asylum in Palermo. He recounted to local authorities how for the past two years, ever since their son left for America, Concetta had shown signs of mental illness. She spent her days wandering through the streets armed with a large stick, searching for her son. Her neighbours reported finding her screaming and crying outside her home, threatening anyone who passed by. After one especially violent outburst, when she attacked her daughter with a knife and nearly killed her husband, Giovanni appealed to local authorities for help.

Concetta's diagnosis fused ideas of sexuality, insanity, and migration, echoing the fictional characters in the works of Messina and Pirandello. The official medical report stated that though Concetta V. had lived with her husband for a number of years, recently 'she had conducted a libertine life; though she dedicated herself to Venus, rather than to wine.'[34] When asked to describe the probable causes of her condition, Dr Vaccaro wrote: 'The departure of her son for America influenced her current mental state. She had also been subject to spontaneous abortions, and suffered severe headaches.' He concluded by reiterating that 'her only fixation is that of her son.' Dr Vaccaro's diagnosis reflected common attitudes regarding the relationship between a mother and her son. In Concetta's case, it was emigration, not marriage, that marked the final physical separation. The medical community considered emigration a powerful enough event to cause insanity in some situations.

Dr Vaccaro was assuming that women were essentially weak-willed and susceptible to the temptations of the flesh. In detailing Concetta V.'s past history of amorous adventures and spontaneous abortions, the report was implicitly connecting a woman's personal reproductive history and sexuality to her mental state. Only the physical presence of a woman's husband (with the implication of normal sexual relations) or her son (the product of her womb) could control her ferocious sexuality. The mother/son relationship was as intimately connected to female sexuality as the husband/wife relationship, and may have been even stronger. Dr Vaccaro's diagnosis lent medical support to the social assumption that there was a direct connection between marriage, motherhood, and a woman's powerful sexual drive, controllable only through external forces and reason. Medical opinion held that a woman was wife or mother, and it was the presence of a man that provided her with security, sanity, and protection from her own inherent self-destructive tendencies. The medical explanation of Concetta's condition illustrates how physicians utilized science to support commonplace attitudes about the accepted social position of women.[35]

Politicians, doctors, social critics, and emigrants commonly agreed that women left behind, bereft of male guardianship, would surely sink into prostitution or commit adultery.[36] The prevailing belief that without the presence of a man, a woman would give in to her physical and emotional weakness and seek out another male companion informed assumptions regarding the inevitable fate of emigrants' wives.[37] Men and women both agreed that women were weak when it came to controlling their sexuality. Common proverbs described a woman as 'a worn old cane' – that is, something easily broken. Sicilians expected that a woman would succumb to a man's advances, given the opportunity. As everyone knew, 'a match held close to the fire will eventually light.'[38] The only way to ensure a wife's fidelity – or a daughter's virginity – was constant vigilance. Common beliefs about the female body informed the popular image of women as sexually insatiable, weak-willed creatures who, when left by their emigrant husbands, had to immediately find substitutes. Contemporary understandings of female physiology linked unfulfilled sexual needs with madness. Attitudes toward these women who were left behind reflected deeply rooted ideas of female sexuality and honour.

These medical theories and fictional stories echoed deeply held ideas about women in society; they also pointed to new ideas about masculinity and femininity in rural Italy. In these narratives, migration shatters traditional gender roles, and in the wake of this, men and women must reconcile their long-held notions with the demands of modern life. In this new world the ideal modern man is a provider, husband, and father who has been forced to leave his family and fields to fulfil his familial duties. He bravely crosses the ocean and suffers the difficulties of life in a barbarous land, far from his kin, to make the family's fortune. The new man must find a way to negotiate the industrial world while remaining a man of honour, able to protect his women from starvation, seduction, slander, and innuendo. The entire process is fraught with the possibility of failure. An emigrant often found it difficult to protect his honour so far from his family. The economic and emotional difficulties arising from physical distance left his wife and daughters vulnerable to both real and imagined attacks on their reputation and bodies. The new masculine ideal shifted to accommodate an absent man who could still keep a close rein over his family. This compromised the manliness of men who remained at home, or who returned.

It seemed that transnational migration could turn men into women and women into men. Southern Italians admired returnees for their good fortune, their money, their new clothes, and their sophisticated ways; yet they also looked on these men with suspicion. Rural residents saw the act of return as some sign of weakness (spiritual if not physical or financial). A good man was supposed to return, yet the act of returning was equated in literature with abandoning the future for the past, and undermined the returnee's manliness in a number of ways. The decision to return to Sicily identified a man with 'the old, the women and the children.' Furthermore, Sicilians believed that prolonged exposure to 'America' undermined traditional values and morals and weakened a man's capacity to act honourably. Common songs and sayings equated the emigrant with a cuckold. By dwelling on the pitiful sight of the emigrant's wife sinking into economic despair and sexual licentiousness as she faced life without a man, popular literature was suggesting that to survive, these women had to become men. Forced to care for their families, they took on men's burdens. They went out to work, hiring themselves out as day labourers, servants, or prostitutes. The images of the migrant man and the abandoned man associated with transoceanic migration reflect attitudes toward female sexuality and honour deeply rooted in nineteenth-century Sicilian society.

The Sicilian code of honour supported the complicated cultural imagery surrounding gender and transnational migration. The central position of honour as a measure of status and respect, and as a form of social control, directly related a man's social position to female sexuality. According to the Sicilian concept of honour, the most basic measure of a society's strength was its ability to keep its women in seclusion. Sicilians assumed that if husbands, brothers, and fathers kept leaving en masse, men would no longer be able to protect their women and ultimately society would disintegrate. The women who remained behind found themselves in an ambivalent position in Sicilian society. They were to be both pitied and feared. Their presence threatened accepted social mores and challenged the rigid code of honour that shaped village life. To mitigate the dangers these women posed, residents viewed them as victims of migration. Their position was so untenable that if their husbands abandoned them, insanity or death would surely follow. In effect, women who did *not* sink into despair brought dishonour to themselves and their kin.

The risks that migration posed to a man's honour were reflected in popular song and poetry. The faithless harlot was a common figure in song lyrics. Emigrants readily believed that most women left behind would find another man. A husband's ability to keep his wife loyal rested on his physical presence, and any prolonged absence inevitably ended in deception.[39] Thus, the promised wealth of the Americas could only be obtained by sacrificing one's honour. As one Calabrian saying claimed: 'America, brings money, food, and horns.'[40] A song popular in Milocca at the end of the 1920s expressed similar sentiments:

The wives of *Americani*
Eat and drink like dogs
They go to the church and pray to God:
'Send me money, my husband'
For if you do not send me money,
I will change your name
And christen you Pasquale[41]

In popular culture, *Americani* described those men who had returned home from the Americas, and *Pasquale* referred to a cuckolded man. Men easily believed that women were weak, and quick to succumb to temptation, but they also maintained that their own wives were exceptions. In this way they could hope to claim a position of respect when they returned.

The sexual voracity of the 'wives of the Americans' symbolized male weakness. If a woman became the target of gossip, her husband had three choices. He could kill her and her lover, and repair his personal honour by destroying his family. Or he could defend his wife's reputation and actions, even if this meant overlooking blatant infidelities. Or he could abandon his family. One man from Milocca returned from the United States to investigate rumours that his wife was involved with another man. Although the report appeared to be true, he still took her back to America with him. By choosing to forgive his wife's transgressions, this man saved his marriage but lost his reputation and the respect of the townsfolk. He had little hope of returning to Milocca and claiming a position of wealth or respect. Another man returned to find his family quite a bit larger than when he had left, and abandoned his wife and settled in another town.[42] The additional children could not be ignored, and there was little hope of saving his marriage. However, by choosing to leave rather than to avenge his honour through violence, he too lost the respect of his neighbours and had to leave town. Exposure to American culture weakened the cultural code that legitimized murder as a means for a man to salvage his personal and familial honour.

Traditionally, if a woman dishonoured her family or her husband there were two ways to restore familial honour. If the girl was single, relatives could force the man involved to marry her, or her brothers could kill them both.[43] If a married woman was involved, the responsibility for controlling her sexuality shifted to her husband. Any suspicion around her behaviour now reflected directly on her husband, and indirectly on her birth family. A married woman was not as much of a threat as long as she was not left alone, because in theory her sexuality was firmly under the control of her husband.[44] If she strayed from her husband, the townsfolk did not blame her alone for her actions – after all, she was only following her instincts. Her husband had failed in his duties as a man, and as a consequence respectable residents shunned the entire family. The only recourse the man had was to kill his wife and her lover. If the man was unwilling to take such a drastic action, his relatives often forced his hand.[45]

The family could cover up the incident only if the seducer was socially superior to the woman; since the family was already in an inferior position relative to him, no loss of honour had really occurred. With respect to the rich, the poor man was always a cuckold. Only when the two families involved possessed a relatively equal amount of honour was retaliation expected.[46] One way that an emigrant could honourably respond to accusations of infidelity was to claim that the *signori* was at fault, not the woman. During his tour of the island, Lorenzoni asked the provincial doctor from Caltanissetta if emigration posed a grave threat to society by weakening family bonds. The doctor replied:

> In regards to our family we have a clear conscious; if not for them, then for whom do we submit ourselves to the risks and rigors of emigration? And if it is true that during our absence our women are disloyal, it is strange that the *signori* are upset, for *they* are the most active accomplices in that infidelity, and even before emigration they never worried themselves about our honour, except perhaps when they profited from our poverty to violate it.[47]

In central Sicily a man could also protect his honour by playing to the widespread distrust and hatred of the clergy. A poor man had little recourse against the all-powerful church. Sicilian proverbs and sayings reflected similar attitudes about monks and priests as they did about

America. As one proverb stated, 'Where there are monks and priests, there are horns and clubs.' The church and America were necessary for the good life on this earth and in heaven, but both could bring dishonour. Because the local priest was an unmarried male, his actions were often viewed cynically and his chastity always suspect.[48] His regular visits with house nuns (women who took an informal vow of chastity) and rural housewives offered plenty of possibilities for illicit encounters.[49] Opportunities for local clergy to take advantage of unprotected women increased with the rise of mass migration. Across the South, clergy acted as mediators between husbands overseas and their wives in Italy. Since most rural women were illiterate, the priests read the letters they received and wrote the responses. Close, unsupervised contact between the clergy and these unprotected women fed rumours of more secular relationships.[50] If emigrants suspected their wives of being unfaithful, they often blamed the priest. By identifying the church as the source of their seduction, these men could claim that they themselves were victims of a powerful and hypocritical institution.

Some Sicilians who returned home from the Americas challenged the church and acted on their suspicions and the rumours they had heard abroad. In the province of Caltanissetta a few emigrants who claimed that local priests seduced their wives complained to the bishop. Rural residents filed accusations against the clergy in Vallelunga, Mussomeli, and Sutera. In 1905 the highest-ranking priest in Sutera, Don Nicastro, reported to the bishop that an emigrant who had recently returned from America was accusing one of the local priests of 'having relations with his wife during his absence, saying he [the emigrant] could prove his accusation with love letters.'[51] These accusations sometimes ended in tragedy. In one village in southern Italy, an emigrant returned so enraged that he shot and killed the local priest.[52] Whether they ignored the rumours or took action, the emigrants embraced the notion of the sexually voracious and unstable women left behind.

These sensational stories and medical cases are important for what they tell us about how popular imaginings of migration fused with ideas of family and honour, but they shed little light on how women actually experienced migration. The widespread belief that women who remained behind would take lovers or become prostitutes expressed the underlying fear that emigration would destroy Sicilian society. It did not reflect the experience of most people. (In Sutera and Milocca there were only three publicized cases of unfaithful women.) This belief *does*, however, reflect a culture that relied on a rigid code of honour centred on female chastity to regulate social and economic behaviour, and that saw emigration as a real threat to the traditional order. This fear combined with political debates and popular culture and folklore to create a description of mass male migration that reflected old and new ideas of manhood and womanhood.

The migrants' destinations were identified with manliness, and the homeland with femininity. Recognizing this helps us understand the cultural impact that transnational migration had on ideas of gender, and why the women who stayed behind have remained invisible. However, it does not help us understand how rural women experienced migration. How much of this image reflected the actual lives and experiences of the women who remained behind? Once their husbands and sons had set sail, were these women transformed into crazed sexual demons? If we go back to Sutera, the haunting heroines in the stories of Maria Messina and the comic images of the 'American wife' appear to be exceptional cases. The experiences of Rosaria M. and Paolino B. were far more common. Most women continued to live their lives, raising their children and caring for their houses until their husbands returned. Tracing the history of migration in Sutera – who left, who stayed behind, and who returned – provides another way of understanding the gendered nature of transnational migration. The stories of the women of Sutera clearly show that men and women experienced migration differently. However, their experiences did not mirror the cultural imagery. Far from being the passive victims of emigration, women actively participated in the process.

The Emigration Experience

The history of emigration from Sutera shows clearly that men and women experienced and participated in the process in different ways. It also indicates that migration was identified with a new masculinity, and at the same time offers a vastly different understanding of the homelands and the women who remained behind. Contrary to the imagery surrounding transnational migration in popular culture, the rural world does not appear as an abandoned wasteland, home to weak, enfeebled, feminized men and sexually voracious women forced into the man's world of paid labour. The women who remained behind, like the migrants themselves, invested their own dreams in their husbands' overseas voyages. A general history of migration from Sutera, combined with a close analysis of the age, sex, civil status, and class composition of the emigrants, provides an in-depth picture of emigration from one community that can serve as a case study for uncovering who left and who remained behind. It reveals that Sutera's men migrated later than most and returned in high numbers, which supports the argument that migrating men did not rush off, abandoning their wives and children. The history of this community also illustrates how women who did not emigrate participated in the decision-making processes underlying mass male migration.

Until 1901, Sicilians accounted for only a small percentage of the total number of Italian emigrants. Migration from the island did not reach massive proportions until after the turn of the century, in particular after 1905. The densely populated coastal provinces of Palermo, Messina, and Trapani experienced the highest rates of migration before 1900. Between 1900 and 1905, however, the source of the migrant stream shifted toward the interior, as more people from the mountainous regions decided they would do better in America. In a 1904 report the U.S. Consul in Naples neatly summarized the reasons so many southern Italians chose to leave home. 'Discontent has been greatly contributed to by the fact that the needs of the people have outstripped the means of satisfying them. With the extension of railroads in Italy and the diffusion of information there has not been a proportional increase in the advantages of life among workers of the soil.' He went on to note that specifically, 'high taxes, import duties on the products of neighboring places, a currency at times depreciated, high rates of exchange, and often the idea prevalent among the population that local administration is not always honest tend to augment discontent and promote the idea of emigration.'[53]

By 1906 the provinces of Agrigento and Caltanissetta respectively boasted the highest rates of emigration on the island.[54] Although the number of towns in Caltanissetta reporting high rates of migration (over 5 per cent of the population) had jumped from one to eight by 1906, Sutera was not among those eight. Sutera experienced a more typical pattern. Like most towns in the province, emigration rates hovered between 4 and 5 per cent of the population. In Sutera in 1906, forty-six out of every thousand residents emigrated – only slightly higher than the provincial average of forty-two. In some Sicilian towns such as Serradifalco, Villarmosa, and Santa Caterina, all the men seemed to be abroad; in contrast, emigration from Sutera rose significantly but not dramatically.[55]

At the end of the nineteenth century, transoceanic migration was

TABLE 2.1
Population movement of Sutera, 1861–1921

	1861	1871	1881	1901	1911	1921
Population						
Resident	4,021	4,198	4,569	5,892	6,748	7,294
Present	3,725	3,897	4,424	5,685	6,407	6,869
During the previous decade						
Births		1,137	1,826	4,657	2,455	1,980
Deaths		1,104	1,208	3,237	1,514	1,331
Net births/deaths		33	618	1,420	941	649
% births/deaths		0.1	2.0	3.0	2.0	1.0
Actual population change		172	527	1,261	722	462
Difference between population change and net births/deaths		139	–91	–159	–219	–187
Annual difference		14	–9	–16	–22	–19
Annual % difference		4	–2	–4	–4	–3

Source: Stefano Somogyi, *Storia demografici dei comuni siciliani dal 1862–1971* (Palermo: Tip. Lux., 1979), 167, 168, 241–2. The difference between the actual population change and the net births/deaths is the basis of conservative estimates of emigration. See Sam Baily, 'Chain Migration of Italians to Argentina: Case Studies of the Agnonesi and Sirolesi,' *Studi Emigrazione* 19 (1982): 77, for further analysis.

still a rare event in Sutera. Conservative estimates of emigration (see Table 2.1) show that few Suteresi left before the turn of the century, and only during the first decade of the 1900s did they begin to emigrate in significant numbers.[56] In the 1890s only six families requested permission to travel abroad. After 1900, emigration rates steadily increased. Between 1900 and 1910 the number of emigrant Suteresi rose from 2 per cent to 4 per cent. These net migration rates provide an extremely conservative estimate of migration.[57] Other sources indicate that the number of emigrants may have been much higher. According to data compiled by the local historian Mario Tona and the population records held in the provincial archive, nearly 700 out of 6748 residents left Sutera between 1900 and 1909; in 1909 the mayor of Sutera estimated that at least 900 people had emigrated.[58] According to these figures, more than 10 per cent of resident Suteresi had been to North America by 1910.

Biases within the sources account, in part, for the disparity between the two estimates. Local government officials compiled their emigration reports based on passport requests; however, not everybody who applied for a passport left, so the reported rates of migration are somewhat inflated.[59] Since passports were free after 1901, lack of money did not inhibit people contemplating emigration from requesting one.[60] Even those who used their passports often made two or three requests before finally setting sail. Back-and-forth migration partly mitigates the bias in the passport registers. Some residents requested a passport but never left; others made multiple trips using one passport. The frequency of multiple trips to the United States means that passport registers tend to overstate emigration rates. On the other hand, calculations of net migration generally underestimate the number of migrants.[61] Estimates of emigration based on net population loss often overlooked those who emigrated and returned within four or five years, assuming that once a person received his or her passport, that person was gone forever. High rates of return migration explain some of the discrepancies between population loss and passport registers. By any measure, however, Suteresi began to leave shortly after the turn of the century and continued to emigrate until the outbreak of the First World War.

Residents of Sutera seemed reluctant to join the rapidly rising stream of Sicilian emigrants for a variety of reasons. In particular, the discovery of sulphur and the nature of the agricultural system slowed emigration. Before the Lupo mine opened in Monte San Paolino in 1902, nearly two hundred people had requested permission to emigrate. In 1903, one year after the discovery, the number of requests dropped to sixty-six. Although few residents worked in the mines, the discovery of sulphur strengthened the local economy. Miners who came from Serradifalco and Racalmulto increased the size of the local market; more bakeries and dry goods stores opened in Sutera than in most towns its size. The sulphur mines bolstered local demand for agricultural goods; it also improved working conditions. In 1904, when the mines were operating at full capacity, fewer than a dozen people left Sutera.[62] The local administration also profited, through the taxes the mining companies paid for extraction rights. The economic benefits from sulphur combined with the large number of sharecroppers and renters (as opposed to wage workers and artisans) to slow transoceanic emigration.[63]

Local and global economic conditions also influenced patterns of migration from Sutera, as they did throughout southern Italy and the islands. Residents chose to stay home if alternative sources of income were available. Transoceanic migration was only one way to earn money, buy land, or build a larger house. People carefully weighed the pros and cons of migration against local opportunities, and chose to stay home as

The mine in San Paolino. (David Tager)

long as they could find gainful employment. In Sutera, mining provided one such alternative, even though Suteresi themselves did not work in the mines. In the nearby town of Marianopoli, a strong agricultural economy lowered migration rates in that community. Fewer people chose to emigrate in a given year if they could make enough money at home.[64] The number of Suteresi who left remained relatively low until 1906. A strong local economy combined with the news of economic and political insecurity overseas, generated by the 1904 presidential election in the United States, kept people close to home. Within a few years this trend had reversed, and the number of people who set sail for the Americas rose dramatically.

The 1905 landslide in Sutera convinced many residents of what they already suspected – sulphur mining was too risky and not worth the money. The closing of the mines coincided with an especially bad winter. Months of heavy rains flooded fields and left hundreds of men unemployed. In the winter of 1906 the *Giornale di Sicilia* reported that across the island people were suffering from hunger and were demanding government aid.[65] In addition, the sulphur economy was sinking into a depression. Technological innovations made it possible to mine the vast mineral reserves in Louisiana profitably. The ready supply of cheaper sulphur quickly affected world markets. The newly established Union Sulphur Company succeeded in breaking the Sicilian sulphur monopoly, and the effects were felt within a year.[66] The transformation in the global mineral market had a dramatic effect on small Sicilian mines. Between 1905 and 1906 the owners of the sulphur mines, as well as distributors and shipping agencies, had laid off more than five thousand Sicilian workers.[67] In Sutera, the San Paolino mine shut down for good a few years after the landslide.

By the spring of 1906, Suteresi were beginning to see emigration as the best alternative to working the fields around town. In 1905, seventy-eight people emigrated from Sutera. One year later, in 1906, more than two hundred people left. The following year, 263 people sailed overseas.[68] The sudden increase bolstered a growing sense that Sutera was on the verge of disappearing. At the end of July 1907 the mayor wrote to the provincial school director that 'the emigration current is so strong that in one neighborhood a person can count the able-bodied men on the fingers of one hand.'[69]

Changing economic conditions in the United States directly affected Sicilian transatlantic migration. Emigration from Sutera remained strong until 1910, when economic conditions in the United States discouraged newcomers. In January 1909, notices sent by the Italian government arrived in Sutera warning that the demand for manual labourers had declined in the United States. The panic of 1907 had led to the postponement of a number of railway projects, and the harsh winter of 1908–9 had further depressed work. In spring 1909 the Italian government was still actively discouraging emigration, warning prospective migrants that Italians who decided to travel to North America often found themselves unemployed and living in squalid conditions.[70] Migration rates began to rise again after 1911 as economic conditions in the United States improved, only to be sharply curtailed again by the outbreak of the First World War.

Technological and commercial innovations revolutionized global transportation and played an important role in Sicilian migration. New technology made the passage to North America faster and cheaper than ever before. By 1880, steamships were rapidly replacing sailing vessels in the Atlantic and the cost of a one-way ticket had dropped sharply. A ticket from Naples to New York cost only twenty-eight dollars by 1900, and the trip took only a few weeks.[71] It was also much easier to purchase tickets locally. In 1905 only two shipping lines had agents in Sutera. By 1906 three more had opened offices, and by 1907 licensed agents in the town were representing seven shipping companies.[72]

Steamships, falling ticket prices, rumours of work, and the presence of agents made transoceanic migration more attractive, but were not enough to seduce Suteresi from their homes. Rural Sicilians were well aware of the difficulties awaiting them overseas. In 1907 Professor Giovanni Lorenzoni reported to the Italian Parliament: 'The life of an emigrant is not rosy. From the moment he leaves his village accompanied by his wife, screaming and crying all the way to the train station or the docks where he holds her tightly to his chest one last time, to the voyage, to his arrival, to the long days toiling in different climates under brutal overseers, he sees the difficulties, the dangers, and travails growing in his life.'[73]

Few residents of Sutera and Milocca believed the myth of an America paved with gold. In Milocca, they recounted how when Columbus returned from his first visit to the Americas he reported that he had found 'flowers without fragrance, foods without flavor, and women without love.'[74] There was no Garden of Eden awaiting the migrants. The only reason to leave home was the chance of finding steady work that paid better than working the fields at home. Most Sicilians who chose to seek their fortune in the Americas knew their new lives would be hard – that work would be scarce at times and that there would be moments of intense homesickness.[75]

Table 2.2
Civil status of emigrants

Age	Married	Single	Per cent of male or female emig. pop. Married	Single
Men				
<15	0	10	—	3
15–22	4	59	1	16
23–40	149	117	41	32
>40	23	1	6	1
Women				
<15	0	7	—	15
15–22	5	4	11	9
23–40	23	3	50	6
>40	4		9	—

Source: Data are taken from the migrant file I created from birth records, passport records, and ship manifests. In this table I used only those people on whom information was available from all sources. The total sample comprises 363 men and 46 women – slightly more than half of all the migrants in the file.

In Sutera, as throughout Sicily, sex, civil status, and class influenced individual decisions to depart or stay home.[76] Thus migration from Sutera appears, on the surface, to closely resemble descriptions in popular literature – men left in droves, abandoning their women. In Sutera, 86 per cent of migrants were men and the average age of these men was twenty-nine (see Table 2.2).[77] Nearly half these men were married when they left. The proportion of married men was higher among older migrants. Only 7 per cent of the migrants between sixteen and twenty-two were married when they left, but nearly 60 per cent of men over twenty-three left a wife behind. Most of these married men were not newlyweds – on average they had been married six years and had at least one child.[78] Just as in popular fiction, men from Sutera left their wives and children behind when they set off for the Americas.

The existence of two distinct migrant groups, young single men and older married men, was partly an effect of conscription. The chance to avoid military service encouraged younger men to migrate before they married. Single males between eighteen and twenty-two were significantly more likely to migrate. In 1904, 10 per cent of the draft-age population was reportedly living in North America; the general rate of migration from Sutera was less than half that. Each year when the military called up a new class of recruits, the number of young men living in the United States increased substantially. At the height of the exodus in 1907, nearly one-quarter of the class of 1887 was living abroad. As the rates of emigration from the town fell after 1907, so did the number of draft-age men who chose to leave; between 1907 and 1913 the number of men eligible to serve in the armed forces who were living abroad hovered around 16 per cent. As the possibility of impending war drew closer, the chance to escape the draft proved irresistible once again. The number of men eligible for military service who chose to emigrate rather than serve rose sharply before the government could stop them from leaving; in 1914, 43 per cent of the draft-age male population resided in the United States.[79] Those men drafted into the military at eighteen generally returned home to marry and settle down after their service ended. If they decided to emigrate, they generally did so in their early thirties, likely motivated by the demands of their growing families.

Along with sex and age, class marked migration from Sutera. Most migrants were rural workers or artisans; neither the wealthy nor the poor chose to emigrate overseas in significant numbers. Wealthier residents had little need to improve their lives by working abroad. Occasionally a noble family sent a younger son, with little prospect of a substantial inheritance, to the Americas to seek his fortune. However, in Sutera, where the church and state owned the largest estates, few families were in such a position. Professionals and landowners who had recently acquired their property and access to political power and social status comprised the wealthy in Sutera. As long as their main sources of income remained intact, they had little reason to go to North America and dig ditches.[80] This lack of personal motivation merged with official policy. The U.S. government, supported by Rome, explicitly discouraged professionals from emigrating. The United States did not want doctors or lawyers: it wanted labourers. In 1909 the Italian government sent a memo to all rural towns asking local officials to encourage 'students, lawyers, property owners' to stay home. Officials argued that people from professional classes did not possess the 'necessary physical or moral strength to adapt to and resist the harsh demands imposed by the shovel.' Furthermore, 'these men discredit the Italian laborer and constitute a grave danger for our good name – driven by necessity they lie and pretend to be experts in work they do not know – they accept work to which they do not demonstrate any capacity.'[81] It is impossible to tell how many landowners or pharmacists in Sutera lied on their passport applications, transforming themselves into humble day labourers. In at least one case, a doctor's son emigrated without listing a profession.[82] However, it is doubtful that many people chose to leave their privileged positions at home to suffer the hardships faced by southern Italians in the Americas. The poorest residents in Sutera also rarely migrated, since they lacked the resources to provide for themselves and their families until they could begin to earn in the United States.

Agricultural workers and artisans comprised nearly 90 per cent of emigrants, reflecting their proportion of the village's total population. In Sicily, *contadini* and *braccianti* were not as mobile as local artisans and petty bourgeoisie. This holds true for Sutera. By 1915 around 17 per cent of all agricultural workers living in Sutera in 1881 had emigrated at some point in their lives, but nearly 63 per cent of the village's cobblers, shopkeepers, carpenters, and metal workers had been overseas.[83] Transatlantic migration drew heavily from the relatively small artisan class. Artisans accounted for nearly 10 per cent of the emigrants, yet only 4 per cent of the general population.

This pattern can be found across the island. Scholars have proposed a number of possible explanations for the high emigration rates among rural artisans. Historian Donna Gabaccia argues that artisans have always been more mobile than agricultural workers. According to Gabaccia, their craft and inheritance practices contributed to greater mobility. Their work brought them into contact with suppliers and clients from neighbouring towns and cities, so they were most likely the first to hear of better opportunities overseas. She also suggests that inheritance practices did much to shape the class differences underlying migration patterns. In her study of Sambuca, a Sicilian agrotown in the province of Agrigento, she notes that among artisans one son generally inherited the family property, while the other children were encouraged to learn a trade and migrate. It was customary among rural workers to distribute family lands among all the heirs, reducing the need for migration as long as there was enough land to go around.[84]

Class divisions affected migration patterns in Sutera, though not as obviously as in Sambuca. Sutera was much smaller than Sambuca and did not have a large, distinct artisan class. Occupational divisions overlapped. Local records show that most everyone, including cobblers and carpenters, owned some land or worked as day laborers. Antonio P., the father of Vincenzo and Baldessere, both of whom emigrated in 1906, was an iron worker and day labourer. The family also possessed a small amount of land, a portion of which had been part of his wife Maria's dowry.[85] Both of Antonio's sons declared themselves to be *braccianti* on their passport applications, instead of identifying themselves as skilled artisans.

Despite blurred lines that often left craftsmen indistinguishable from rural wage workers, there is one characteristic of migration from Sutera that supports the argument that inheritance patterns combined with class effected migration patterns. Over 55 per cent of emigrants who practised a trade or who were engaged in commerce were single, whereas 45 per cent of field workers were unmarried when they left. The fact that artisans emigrated before they married suggests that the lack of opportunities to set up a workshop and settle down at home encouraged them to choose emigration. In Sutera, as throughout Sicily and southern Italy, employment was a prerequisite for marriage.

Although a relatively high percentage of artisans left Sutera, most emigrants claimed to be sharecroppers or wage workers. The presence of so many *contadini* is somewhat surprising. Historians have often argued that 'middle peasants' (sharecroppers, renters, etc.) are more likely to rebel than to emigrate.[86] Until recently, migration scholars readily accepted the assertion that where peasant organization was strong, emigration was weak, and vice versa.[87] Recent scholarship has challenged this idea, arguing that militancy did not preclude migration at all. In Sambuca, where labour protests were common, rates of overseas migration were also high.[88] In Sutera, peasant protest was not especially strong, and emigration rates were not especially high; this implicitly suggests that rural workers approached the decision to emigrate pragmatically.

Faced with the choice between resistance and emigration, Suteresi chose whichever option was more advantageous. Suteresi saw political action and emigration as economic choices – alternative ways of bettering their lives through increased access to land. If political action could not succeed in redistributing the land, perhaps U.S. dollars could buy it. In Sutera, participation in the *fasci* uprisings of the 1890s came late; Suteresi were not particularly militant. Far from advocating revolution, the social clubs formed at the turn of the century bolstered traditional values and respect for the system. When militancy failed to reform traditional land tenure patterns, residents chose to emigrate. In Sutera, where class identification and blood relations were were closely linked, it is difficult to understand emigration as a predominately working-class or peasant movement. Migration was just one option available to families to improve their livelihood.

From the preceding discussion, a picture of the emigrants emerges. The typical emigrant was male, married, and nearly thirty. To him, the United States offered an opportunity to earn higher wages and perhaps realize his dreams of buying property back home; it was not a place to start a new life. He usually owned a small piece of land near the village, but rarely enough to support his family. In the course of the year he worked as a sharecropper. High rents, bad harvests, recession, or a failed land reform movement convinced him it was time to join his brother, or his wife's brother, in Alabama. This description also sketches a rough portrait of the people these migrants typically left behind. The women who remained in Sutera were young and recently married. Most of them had a child or were expecting their first. In many ways they closely resemble the popular image so vividly described in popular literature. The average age of the women who remained in Sutera was twenty-eight, nearly four years younger then their emigrant husbands.[89] Most of these women had lived with their husbands for a few years: over half had been married for less than five years, while another third had been married somewhere between six and ten years. Only 20 per cent of the emigrants' wives had been married for more than ten years. Most women who remained home were not alone. In Sutera, over 70 per cent of migrant wives had at least one child, and over half were expecting a child when their husband left. Despite these superficial similarities with the popular image of the emigrant's wife, these women were not the abandoned victims of migration. They saw migration as a necessary separation that would only last a few years. An analysis of emigrants' family records and repatriation rates indicates that they supported their families in their absence, and then usually came home.

According to the provincial statistics gathered by the Commissariato dell'Emigrazione, the composition of the emigrant groups shifted after 1900.[90] In the nineteenth century when emigrants left for Argentina and Brazil, officials labelled them permanent emigrants because they tended to travel in family groups. Over half the Sicilians who left the island in the nineteenth century emigrated with their immediate families. By the turn of the century, however, single men were beginning to outnumber families among emigrant groups. In 1900 only 30 per cent of Sicilian emigrants were accompanied by their immediate families.[91] Sutera does not appear to differ radically from provincial or regional trends. Passport registers show that individual migrants began to outnumber family groups in the late 1890s. In the summer of 1893, four Suteresi families requested passports to sail to Brazil. Their trip turned into a nightmare in Britain, when customs agents refused to allow them to continue on to the Americas. On the return voyage a woman and her infant son died. Their story discouraged other prospective migrant families from making the trip. This was the last expedition to South America from Sutera. The next passport requests recorded in the register came five years later. In 1898, Gregorio M. and his sister requested permission to emigrate to Horatio, Pennsylvania, and a year later Mariano. D. requested a *nulla osta* to emigrate to New Orleans.[92] Among the hundreds of applications for passports made after 1900, very few people requested documents for their wives or children. Overseas emigration accounted for less than 5 per cent of the families eliminated from the municipal records after the turn of the century.[93]

The number of female migrants visible in the records reflects the shift away from nuclear family emigrant groups. Throughout the nineteenth century, the proportion of women, children, and families in the total migrant population was on the rise. In 1880, women comprised one-quarter of all migrants; by 1899, they comprised 35 per cent of emigrants.[94] After 1900, as the number of Sicilians emigrating rose to unprecedented levels, fewer women and children appeared alongside the male migrants. By 1903 the percentage of women among all Sicilian migrants had dropped back to 25 per cent. Only after the First World War did the percentage of women once again reach 30 per cent.[95] As women stopped migrating, so did their children. Before 1900, one-quarter of the migrant population was under fifteen. After the turn of the century until the first World, only one-sixth of emigrants were children.[96]

At the height of emigration to the United States, very few women chose to leave Sutera. Between 1900 and the First World War, women comprised 15 per cent of the migrant population, far below both national and regional levels. If a woman did emigrate from Sutera, it was likely that she was young and recently married. The typical female emigrant was twenty-five and married. With only one exception, these women were all going to join their husbands, who had already settled overseas. Rarely do children appear on ship records or passport requests; only 3 per cent of the emigrants from Sutera were under fourteen. Almost all these children travelled with their mothers, who were joining their husbands in Alabama or Pennsylvania.[97] Parents brought girls and boys to North America in almost equal numbers; over 40 per cent of the children who left were girls.

Most of the women and children who left southern Italy intended to leave forever. All of the emigrants from Sutera who requested passports in 1901, and who stated that they were not planning to return, were women.[98] If a man took his wife and children with him, the plan was to settle permanently. The majority of Suteresi, however, chose not to bring their women and children to America. Most Suteresi, like other southern Italians, saw emigration initially as a temporary absence rather than a permanent condition. In a 1904 report the United States Consul in Rome noted: 'It is believed that most migrants who do not go to America to join friends and relatives already established there leave Italy with the idea of returning sooner or later. One does not hear much about settling on free lands in foreign countries. The idea is to work for someone else in the company of compatriots and to return to Italy later on.'[99]

Rates of return to Sutera, and to southern Italy as a whole, support the idea that emigrants saw the United States as a means to improve their lives back home, not as an opportunity to create new ones overseas. Emigrants did not suddenly decide to return after living in the Americas for a few years. Nearly 90 per cent of the emigrants who requested a passport in 1901 stated that their stay was only temporary.[100] Suteresi were no different from other Sicilians. In 1907, Lorenzoni noted that the majority of Sicilian emigrants 'did not intend to permanently establish themselves overseas, but they wanted to return home. They did everything possible in order to return after three or four years, as soon as they managed to save a respectable amount of money.'[101] Robert Foerster reported that 82 per cent of the emigrants who returned in 1908 had been in the United States for less than five years.[102] Even when economic conditions in the United States improved and conditions in Italy deteriorated, emigrants came home; in 1916, nearly 60 per cent of returning emigrants had lived abroad for less than five years.[103]

Repatriation rates for Sutera were very high. According to the local population records, nearly 70 per cent of Suteresi who left between 1901 and 1909 returned before 1910. Between 1907 and 1909, when the American economy began to weaken and unemployment rates rose, nearly four hundred Suteresi returned home to Sicily. Out-migration from the village took on new life after 1910, but the movement came to an abrupt halt with the First World War. The war actually encouraged some men to return home to be with their families; in the first nine months of 1915 more than fifty men returned and enlisted in the army.[104]

The proportion of Suteresi who returned was much higher than for Italy as a whole. Betty Boyd Caroli estimated that 45 per cent of all Italian emigrants returned. Italy's return rates, she noted, were higher than those of any other European nation. Even so, they were still far below those of Sutera.[105] One explanation for this relates to regional differences: southern Italian migrants were far more likely to return; over 86 per cent of those who repatriated came from the islands and the southern provinces.[106] Social and economic factors also accounted for the high rates of repatriation in Sutera. Obviously, the prevalence of married men in the migrant population encouraged many emigrants to come home. However, class structure also played an important role. Many of the migrants had been sharecroppers, and this made for strong links to agricultural rhythms. Most emigrants left between September and February, after they harvested their crops and paid off their yearly debt. This is when they had a lump sum of money to spend for passage to North America. Since a family's income generally appeared at one time, sharecroppers did not have to sell their own small landholdings to finance their passage. After they left, their lands remained fallow unless a close relative had agreed to work their fields.[107] The ties that bound these men to the land remained intact, so that they had every reason to return home.

Conditions in Alabama offer another reason for the high rates of return among Suteresi. According to the Dillingham report, over three-quarters of the southern Italians working in the Birmingham mines had been in the United States less than five years. In part this reflects the recent arrival of Italians in the American South and the lack of a well-established immigrant community. However, the declining numbers of southern Italian workers after five years also suggest high rates of repatriation.[108] As soon as they arrived in Pratt City or Thomas, Alabama, southern Italian men found work at wages that far exceeded what they could have earned at home. Italian men started in the mines earning on average more than seven dollars a week, and their wages rose over time. Even allowing for illness and frequent shutdowns, southern Italian men in the Birmingham mines took home, on average, 286 dollars (1,520 lire) a year.[109] In five years working abroad Rosario M. could easily have saved close to three thousand lire. Had he stayed home he would have made about 1,700 lire as a day labourer, if he was lucky enough to find work for two hundred days of the year – probably less if he sharecropped.[110]

While working abroad, men tended to save as much money as possible by living as cheaply as possible. Dillingham's report noted that Slavs and southern Italians often boarded with a family to save rent money. In the company houses near Birmingham the investigators found families who had taken in as many as fifteen boarders. If a migrant could not find a room with a family, he often moved in with other single men, sharing a room or a house depending on their numbers. By sharing their meals, their pots, and even their beds, these men could save a good portion of their weekly wages. Southern Italians also preferred to pay cash for their food at the Italian grocery stores in town. This way they avoided the punishing interest rates charged by the credit plans at company stores.[111] By scrimping and saving, living in poorly furnished rooms in bleak surroundings where few trees or flowers grew, these men could return home in a few years with the means to live in comfort and beauty.[112]

Household records support the notion that people saw transoceanic migration as temporary. The women of Sutera did not set up legally independent households while their husbands were away. Family records *(foglio di famiglia)* in Sutera listed a woman as the official head of household in nearly 20 per cent of the cases. These women were either widows or single women living with their siblings. Only two women appeared as *capa famiglia* because their husbands transferred their residence to America. Emigration did not transform wives into widows. Despite their husbands' absence, these women still saw themselves – and the town saw them – as part of a family.

Throughout Sicily there was no significant increase in female-headed households. Between 1901 and 1911 the percentage of households presided over by women was around 19 per cent across the island. By 1921 that figure had fallen to 13 per cent.[113] These rates are surely conservative estimates. Even if a woman was the head of her family for practical purposes, she may not have chosen to formally admit her status to the census taker. The cultural stigma attached to single women in Sicilian society probably encouraged a woman whose husband had migrated to America to continue to act as if he would soon return. Most women who remained behind did not claim to be their families' principal providers.

There is little evidence to support the popular image of the abandoned wife. Men did not dream of emigration as an escape from their families but rather as a means to better their lives at home. Migration patterns support the assertion that husbands and wives believed that the separation was only temporary; this undermines the assumption that women were the passive victims of male migration. Rural residents used the popular image grounded in real fears of separation to control the behaviour of women who remained behind, and the nation used it to buttress specific political positions. It was not representative of the experiences of the wives and mothers of the emigrants.

Far from being passive victims of their husbands' ambitions, Sicilian women participated actively in the decisions that sent their husbands and sons overseas. We see their agreement in the passport records, in which mothers and wives officially gave their permission. According to the new laws regulating emigration that went into effect after 1901, a prospective migrant had to prove he was not abandoning any dependents.[114] Local officials took this seriously and often requested written permission from the migrant's wife. In Sutera, Carmela S. declared on her husband's application that she was granting her husband permission to emigrate 'in the hope that he will find work and send his savings back to his family.'[115] In 1905 the law changed: a migrant no longer had to officially present a statement attesting to his wife's consent in the matter, although she retained the right to oppose his request.[116] How often a woman's approval resulted from coercion is unclear. Certainly some men physically or emotionally forced their wives to consent. However, some women took exceptional steps to stop their husbands from sailing overseas. In September 1920, Francesca G. went to the police department in Palermo with a written declaration opposing her husband's decision to emigrate.[117] Although it seems she was unsuccessful, she believed she had the right to prevent his departure. In another case from a neighbouring town, Concetta Amenta was able to prevent her husband from emigrating without her consent. Vincenzo Castiglione married Concetta in the church of Centuripe. 'A few days later, unknown to the young bride and with a false passport, he left for America; after his wife brought charges he was arrested in Napoli on board a departing boat.' He was sentenced to two years and required to marry Concetta in a civil ceremony.[118] If a woman vehemently opposed her husband's decision to leave, she could take action to stop him.

Official consent represents just one form of female participation. Sicilian men were motivated to emigrate mainly by the desire to improve the family's economic and social status. The same goal encouraged women, in their traditional capacity as wives and mothers, to play an active role in the decision-making processes underlying mass male migration. As kinship keepers and household managers, these women shaped migrant networks and helped finance voyages.

Sicilian migration was not driven by individual desire for personal gain or adventure: it was a sacrifice undertaken for the good of the family. It was part of a broader family survival strategy and was undertaken to accomplish specific goals.[119] With the money the migrant sent home or brought back, the family first paid off any outstanding debts incurred as a result of emigration. Returnees and their families then spent a portion of the money to improve their housing, building new additions and purchasing new furniture. They invested the rest of the money in property in the hope of rising in society – the goal that had fuelled the initial decision to emigrate. If the family was lucky and skilful, migration would enable them to live off rents and never work in the fields again. Property ownership brought honour and respect, turning *braccianti* and *contadini* into *signori*. The acquisition of land brought freedom and independence. As landowners, rural labourers would no longer be forced to work for low wages or under unfair sharecropping contracts.[120] Their children would be able to attend university and study to become professionals. The family could become part of the *benestanti*, the wealthy. But a family had to pay a price to reap the benefits of migration, and each family carefully weighed the costs against the possible benefits. Some families decided that steady work and high wages offset the short-term economic and psychological hardships involved in transatlantic migration; others concluded that the possibility of financial gain was not worth the suffering and decided to try to improve their fortunes at home.[121]

Whatever the local and global economic conditions at the time, the actual decision to emigrate remained a personal choice made within the confines of the family.[122] Migrants sought the advice and influence of the entire family. Women often encouraged their husbands or sons to leave, convinced that it was the only way for the family to improve its social position and resolve its immediate economic problems. Some women actively pressured their husbands to leave. In Milocca, Zia Maricchia was said to have 'driven her husband to emigrate to America by her unwifely behaviour. She had among other things refused to eat of the same dish with him, and insisted on having her own drinking glass at meals.'[123] Her refusal to accommodate her husband may have extended to other aspects of their marital relationship as well, with perhaps more effectiveness. Milocchesi accused Zia Maricchia of emulating the behaviour of the elites, acting above her social class, in order to convince her husband to emigrate. Only by going to North America could he hope to make enough money to buy his wife the material goods and property she required to buttress her claims of social superiority. The other villagers gave Zia Maricchia a great deal of credit for her husband's eventual decision to emigrate. Whether she actually had as much influence as people believed is unclear. The point is that the townsfolk accepted the notion that a wife had a great deal of leverage over her husband.

As wives and mothers, Sicilian women exerted good degree of control over the family's finances and resoures, including its children. Since the men spent most of the week far from home, it was the women who made the everyday decisions about a family's resources. Sicilian women were in charge of all the cash that came into the house – the weekly wages the men earned as well as the yearly profit from fields they rented. A housewife took care of the small expenditures herself, and made the decisions to buy larger items (furniture, mules, or land) jointly with her husband.[124] In the absence of their husbands, women were also responsible for creating and maintaining reciprocal support networks that the family could turn to in times of trouble or heavy work. Women also held sway over their children. As their children's chief educators, they taught their sons and daughters the rudiments of the Catholic religion and their expected duties as adult men and women.[125] Mothers commonly chose their children's prospective spouses, relying on their own female networks to make all the preliminary arrangements, and transforming the necessary paternal approval into a mere formality.[126] Through their financial and social roles, Sicilian women exercised a great deal of power within the family and influenced decisions affecting the entire household.

The idea that Sicilian women possessed any power within the family contradicts most descriptions of Sicilian peasant life contained in the nineteenth- and early-twentieth-century ethnographic and government publications. Many studies of rural Sicilians noted the strong patriarchal and authoritarian structure of the family.[127] Fathers dominated every aspect of family life, and a good wife obeyed her husband without question. As Pitrè wrote: 'She served the best food and wine to her husband, and she never looked him in the eye or challenged his decisions.'[128] A female-run household signalled a failed family. Charlotte Gower Chapman observed that the women of Milocca seemed to accept the implicit right of their husbands to command. Wife-beating, common in both folktales and proverbs, seemed to be accepted as a husband's prerogative, even if he only infrequently resorted to physical violence.[129] Gower Chapman summed up popular attitudes among men and women toward conjugal relationships in this way: 'A man should treat his wife with kindness if she is good, but always firmly. Like a good weapon, she should be cared for properly; like a hat she should be kept straight; like a mule she should be given plenty of work and an occasional beating.

Above all, she should be kept in her place as a subordinate, for there is no peace in the house where a woman leads her husband.'[130] When the family faced the public world, women were expected to appear deferent and obedient to the male head of household.

The absence of Sicilian women in public spaces reinforces the private image of female deference.[131] In Sutera, women never participated in local government or the legal system or joined mutual aid associations. Women rarely trespassed in male-dominated public spaces, the main streets and squares. When a woman left her house, she draped a black shawl around herself and clutched it tight across her face with both hands.[132] On the way to market women kept to the side streets and avoided the main square, where the men congregated. If a woman had to cross the square to attend mass, she walked quickly with her shawl covering her face and her eyes cast downward.[133] The image of a cloak-covered woman scuttling along the back streets, hiding her physical presence from all onlookers, is admittedly a powerful one, and speaks to the commanding patriarchal structure of Mediterranean culture. However, invisibility alone does not constitute definitive proof of total female subservience.

The lack of women in public spaces and public displays of obedience do not tell the whole story of relationships between men and women.[134] Anthropologists have openly challenged the idea that such things automatically support contentions of gender inequality.[135] These scholars suggest that a society organized around separate male and female spheres, such as characterize gender relations in Sicily, does not necessarily locate power exclusively in the male domain; nor are these relations inherently oppositional. Sicilian women had little access to formal institutions of power and authority, but they were not completely lacking resources. As Michelle Rosaldo wrote: 'It is necessary to remember that while authority legitimates the use of power, it does not exhaust it, and actual methods of giving rewards, controlling information, exerting pressure, and shaping events may be available to women as well as to men.'[136] Women in Sicily possessed power within the family, in a society where the family was the foundation of society. And as Ernestine Friedl noted, in communities where the family is the most important social and economic unit, 'the private, and not the public sector, is the sphere in which the relative attribution of power to males and females is of the greatest real importance.'[137]

In her study of a Greek village, Jill Dubisch suggests one method of measuring relative power within the domestic sphere. Dubisch outlines four criteria for gauging the influence of husbands and wives within rural families: how much respect one spouse shows the other, in public and private; whether or not one spouse interferes in the other's world; the ability to control and allocate family resources; and involvement in childrearing and in arranging marriages for children.[138]

Going by this model, the women of Sutera and Milocca possessed considerable power within the domestic sphere. Open displays of affection between married couples were rare in Sutera, as throughout Sicily, yet observers never failed to notice that men usually accorded their wives a great deal of respect.[139] As we noted earlier, men publicly acknowledged the importance of women within the family. The same economic and social conditions that divided Sicilian society according to gender made it difficult for men and women to interfere in each other's tasks. Men rarely interfered in how women raised their children or ran the household. As the family financial manager, a Sicilian woman had access to family resources. A woman's dowry, comprised of property and material goods, was often the only valuable possession a family owned.[140] From the birth of her children until they reached puberty, a mother was the primary caretaker and educator of both sons and daughters. Sicilian women played a crucial role in arranging marriages for their grown children, and these marriages furthered the economic and social interests of the family. Analysis along the lines suggested by Dubisch does not lead to the conclusion that women were equal to men, but it does encourage us to re-evaluate husband/wife relationships in rural societies.

Sicilian women had little formal authority, but they did have access to economic and social resources that enabled them to influence important family decisions. Rural Sicilian women employed these resources when the family was faced with decisions affecting its future. Sicilian women were not silent partners in the family. When migration emerged as a possible means of improving the family's social and economic position, women were involved in the decision-making process and the preparations, just as they always had been. A close analysis of Sutera and Milocca indicates that female participation in the migration process was especially visible in two areas: the creation of migrant networks, and money. These aspects of transoceanic migration drew heavily on traditional female roles in the family and in the community.

When migrants left their homes they did not leave one at a time, but in larger groups linked by kinship, association, or class.[141] In Sutera and Milocca, blood shaped the social webs underlying mass migration. Migrants usually set out for the Americas with an uncle, a brother, or a cousin. Familial networks, which defined individual identity and bound households and families together, formed emigrant groups. Women, always central to the creation and maintenance of kinship networks, were pivotal players in the construction of these transoceanic networks.

Once transnational migration became a viable economic opportunity for rural men, women turned to their traditional networks to gain information about emigration and to arrange migrant groups. How villagers obtained information about conditions overseas, wages, employment opportunities, and the cost of steamship tickets is complicated. Certainly, men had access to this information through contact with other men in the fields and their Sunday conversations in the piazza. The Italian government kept local authorities well informed about conditions abroad and new legislation pertaining to migration.[142] When a man appeared in City Hall to apply for a passport, or met a local clerk on a coffee break, he could hear the latest news from overseas. Information about employment and wages spread quickly through town as the men passed on what they had heard. It was far more difficult to get information directly from the emigrants themselves. Since nearly 70 per cent of adults were illiterate, letters from the Americas were infrequent, but news from relatives sometimes did filter back.[143] Prefects in many southern communities reported that whenever the rare letter arrived from abroad, someone always read it out loud in the main square. Another important source of information was the returnees themselves. Each year a steady number of emigrants returned, bringing news from overseas.[144]

While these information routes generally flowed through men or utilized male means of communication – the local government, for example – women developed their own information networks. Women spread the news contained in the few letters their families received. Often the letters announced family news – an illness, a marriage, the birth of a new child – and described life across the ocean. In Milocca, reports that a neighbour had just inherited money from America passed quickly among neighborhood women.[145] Women wove this information into the family histories that shaped social relations in the community. When a woman's husband returned from abroad, she passed along his stories to her sisters and neighbours. At the public laundry, at the water fountain, in the bakery, and in the streets, women stopped to report the latest news from overseas.

Besides providing information to potential migrants and their families, women helped organize emigrant groups. Although most Suteresi left their immediate families behind, they did not emigrate alone. Usually an emigrant and a close relative joined a larger group of *paesani* and sailed together. Even a brief survey of Italian ship manifests indicates that people rarely emigrated alone. Although seldom accompanied by immediate family, they generally travelled with at least one relative. Usually, rural Sicilians emigrated in groups of ten or more, representing three or four different families from the same town.[146] The personal migration history of Rosario M. illustrates this pattern. When Rosario first sailed to the United States, he accompanied his nineteen-year-old nephew, Baldessere P. They landed at Ellis Island and immediately caught a train bound for Birmingham, Alabama, where fellow emigrants lived. When Rosario returned to Sutera to marry Paulina B., he convinced his older brother, Onofrio, and Baldessere's younger brother, Vincenzo, to go back with him to Alabama. All of these men migrated with relatives, yet on their documents they were listed as travelling alone. Another common method of encouraging migration involved men already in the United States sending prepaid tickets to their sons, brothers, or nephews at home. Literate migrants preceded a ticket with long letters home extolling the virtues of the new land and encouraging others to join them. In 1909 the U.S. Immigration Commission reported that over 60 per cent of new immigrants from southern and eastern Europe were travelling on tickets bought by a relative or friend in the United States.[147]

Generally, migrants preferred to travel with their own brothers. If a migrant did not accompany a blood sibling, he usually travelled with one of his wife's relations. When passenger ship lists are compared with family reconstructions, it is found that seemingly unrelated migrants from the same town are linked by marriage. It is common to see a man sailing with his wife's uncle, brother, or cousin. When twenty-six-year-old Giuseppe G. landed at Ellis Island with fifteen dollars in his pocket and told the customs official he was on his way to Birmingham, Alabama, to meet his wife's brother, it was already a familiar story. In Sutera, over half the male migrants were travelling with or meeting a wife's relative or the husband of an older sister. Young single men often accompanied a maternal relative overseas, reflecting the strength of a mother's influence in her son's life. Emigrants who left unaccompanied by maternal kinfolk or close relatives of their wives were usually accompanied by a brother. Only a few migrants announced their intention to meet a paternal uncle.[148] The construction of migration networks was a complex process that involved the resources of all family members. Emigrants did not choose their partners or their destinations alone. The women who remained behind, the wives and mothers of migrants, affected Sicilian patterns of transoceanic migration, influencing the composition of migrant groups and settlement patterns.[149]

Female participation in the migration process is also visible in how migration was financed. Sicilian women controlled the household budget. Each Saturday evening when the men returned from the fields they would hand their earnings to their wives. Sharecroppers turned their yearly profit over to their wives after the harvest. Women also controlled the earnings of their unmarried sons. Men received a small allowance from their wives for cigarettes, shopping, and daily expenditures.[150] In general, families made economic decisions cooperatively. Any large purchase – a dress, furniture, or even a mule – required the approval of both husband and wife.[151] Certainly, the purchase of a steamship ticket was considered significant.

The local economy in Sutera and Milocca made it difficult to raise money for emigration. Even the most thrifty housewife had difficulty scrimping and saving the 150 or 200 lire (half the family's annual cash income) necessary to purchase a ticket. In 1903 the cheapest fare from Palermo to New York was 150 lire ($30).[152] Even if a friend or relative sent a prepaid ticket from the Americas, as was often the case, a prospective emigrant still had to scrape together at least 50 to 100 lire for the trip. According to U.S. Customs regulations, immigrants had to have at least ten dollars (approximately 50 lire) in hand when they arrived. The exact amount depended on sex, age, and physical fitness.[153] Women, children, and older men had to have nearly twice that amount in order to prove they could support themselves and that they would not resort to crime to survive.

A family needed to raise nearly 200 lire just to send one member to North America, not including the cost of living abroad, where rents were much higher. At the turn of the century a day labourer in Sutera made only 250 to 300 lire annually depending on how many days he could work out of the year. From his salary he had to feed and clothe his family.[154] Sharecroppers fared little better. Abele Damiani estimated that the cost to work one *salme* of land in Caltanissetta was at least 450 lire, including rent, seed, fertilizer, and labour.[155] After the middlemen and owners took their share and debts from the past year were paid, a *mezzadro* in Sutera was left with slightly over 100 lire worth of grain and legumes, if he was lucky. Commonly there was not enough money left at the end of the year to settle old debts and the accumulated interest. Families were trapped in an endless cycle of revolving debt.[156] Even those fortunate few who managed to break even, or bring a small amount of cash home, rarely had enough money to feed their families during the winter or to provide seed for the next crop. Often those who rented land also had to work as day labourers to make ends meet. It was difficult if not impossible to finance a trip to Alabama on the annual income from field work. Families needed to find alternative sources of money.

Often migrants financed their trips through loans or by selling family possessions. These financial decisions required the cooperation of women, if not their participation. Many emigrants turned first to banks and moneylenders before they sold their houses, mules, and family heirlooms. Interest rates were often usurous – typically 20 to 30 per cent and sometimes as high as 100 or 200 per cent. People used the first money that arrived from overseas to pay off these loans.[157] Returnees often used the money they made in the United States to subsidize other migrants with low-interest or no-interest loans in order to demonstrate that they were no longer part of the poor peasantry, who needed to profit from their money.[158] To what extent women were directly involved in arranging loans is unclear. Given the restrictions on women's lives, it is doubtful that they secured loans from banks or public moneylenders. However, since Sicilian women played a decisive role in other family economic decisions, it is highly likely that they participated in decisions to take out loans to finance trips overseas.

There is evidence that rural women acted as informal moneylenders. Although excluded from obtaining bank loans, they had access to other cash sources. In Ficarazzi, a coastal village near Palermo, an emigrant complained to the mayor that for the past fifteen years he had been sending money and clothing home to his mother, fulfilling 'his duty as an Italian son.' Recently, however, he had received word from his brother that their mother was selling the clothing he had given her and was lending the money at high interest rates.[159] It is not clear to what extent her behaviour was typical. Historian Patrizia Audenino found evidence of female moneylenders in northern Italy, which suggests that Italian women arranged financial deals.[160] It is conceivable that given the strong informal networks the women of Sutera created and their access to family finances, they also loaned money to fellow townsfolk.

Property sales were another potential source of cash for families trying to finance a trip overseas, and here women also played a central role. Women were directly involved in most familial property transactions, and certainly in all those where they had sole or joint ownership rights. When a woman from Sutera or Milocca married, she retained full possession of her dowry. A husband could manage his wife's property but could not dispose of it without her consent.[161] At the end of the nineteenth century a bride's dowry consisted of embroidered linens, small parcels of land, money, and perhaps a house. The most valuable items were the handmade linens.[162]

A woman's dowry often represented the family's sole valuable possession. Cash-strapped families resorted to selling or pawning their household linens. Although in some instances, coercion surely played a role in a woman's decision to sell her trousseau, most husbands did not violate a woman's right to dispose of her own dowry.[163] Folklore and proverbs offered sharp warnings to women not to sell their dowries. However, not everyone heeded these warnings. According to oral histories recorded by anthropologist Jane Schneider,

> Sometimes women pawned whitewear at local grocery or yardgood stores to purchase food or sheeting for their daughters' trousseau. Itinerant merchants secretly negotiated with women who were eager for a 'family allowance' but ashamed that anyone would know they would trade *corredo* to get it. Church sponsored pawnshops, the *Monte di Pietà,* dating back to the seventeenth century, made loans against whitewear, too.[164]

Even before transoceanic migration began, there was an established market for embroidered linens and bed covers accessible to women. Sometimes a couple married for the purpose of selling the bride's dowry to raise the money needed for the bridegroom's passage:

> Some peasants, who possessed nothing but two strong arms and the will to work, were married shortly before they emigrated, and with the consent of their wives they sold or pawned the dowry and they left home. Often the marriage was not consummated, or they celebrated only the civil ceremony, which is held as insufficient to be considered married, according to the religious sentiments of the peasants, reserving the religious ceremony and the consummation for their return, if they returned.[165]

The cooperation of Sicilian women was essential to raise the capital needed to emigrate, and tradition dictated that it was within their province as household financial managers to find the money. Women's economic power sometimes proved dangerous. In one town a young man murdered his aunt and benefactress when she refused to finance his passage to North America.[166]

In the early twentieth century, critics of Sicilian migration pointed out that aspiring emigrants were selling everything they owned to raise the money to leave. Rural residents were auctioning off their houses, mules, and parcels of land to purchase a steamship ticket. In communities where a woman's dowry included land, critics assumed that women would sell their property to finance the trip. This does not seem to be the case in Sutera and Milocca, where a woman's dowry often included land. Rarely did a newly married woman sell her property. There is no indication that couples married in order to sell the land the woman inherited. In addition, a survey of land records from Sutera shows that women rarely sold their land before their husbands emigrated. A few couples even bought a small piece of land – usually on the outskirts of town – the same year the men migrated. In a number of cases, couples registered land jointly in the name of the wife and her husband, or in the wife's name alone, shortly before or immediately after a request for a passport.[167] Within a year before Paolino L. left for America, he and his wife Giuseppa R. jointly bought a small piece of land. Possibly, the purchase of property was part of a family's preparations for sending a member overseas. Especially if the primary wage earner was departing, the family had to arrange to live in some fashion until he was able to send money back. This reluctance to sell land to raise money for a voyage reminds us how important property was to families. The main reason for emigrating was to raise money to buy land back home. Surely it was not in the family's best interests to sell off land it already owned.

A close study of female participation suggests that the different ways men and women experienced transoceanic migration translated into familial tensions as the ambitions of emigrant men clashed with the dreams of the women who remained behind. In helping their husbands prepare to leave, women invested their own dreams in the voyage. Usually the goals of the women reflected the original dreams of the migrants themselves. When an emigrant left his town, he set out determined to make as much money as possible, as quickly as possible, to better his family's position at home. Emigration was a sacrifice, but a temporary one. On their return, migrants recounted stories of the deprivation they suffered while living abroad, the years spent in rented rooms shared with two or three *paesani*, eating little and saving as much of their meager earnings as possible to send home to their loved ones. Overseas, Sicilians tended to live on the margins of the host societies, working and saving for the day they could return.[168] However, the experience of emigration changed the lives of these men. The original goal of buying land sometimes faded after they saw how much money they could make in the Americas. Many emigrants returned home after a few years fully intending to settle down, but soon grew restless. The memories of their home villages that had sustained them through the difficult years abroad turned sour after they returned. Returnees constantly compared their rural towns with the cities and towns in the Americas. They extolled the New World for the grandeur of its cities and the opportunities it offered, and recounted their own successes there. Returnees found themselves envied for their wealth and despised for their arrogance. After a few years people often re-emigrated, as the cities they left behind in the Americas took on the mythical splendour that their towns had enjoyed while they were living abroad.[169]

Economic considerations also played a crucial role in back-and-forth migration. Sicilians who returned found that their hard-earned American savings were insufficient to buy enough land to be able to live off the rents. The desire for a certain piece of land – one they had sharecropped or one that was especially prestigious in the village – often led returnees to pay far more than market value for the property. Often a returnee used almost his entire savings to purchase land, which left little for the improvements it needed to return a profit.[170] Whether through bad luck, mismanagement, or price gouging, many new property owners soon found themselves working in the fields as they had done before. The wage differential became all too obvious. In North America, immigrants earned 2 to 3 dollars a day (between 10 and 15 lire) in skilled professions, compared to the 1.50 lire that day labourers earned in Sicily. One returnee lamented:

> I was in North America where I worked on the machines at a large agricultural firm earning between 9 and 14 lire a day. Now I have returned; but not one day goes by where I am content. We have nowhere to go during the evenings and we suffer a lot. The *signori* enjoy themselves and travel around Europe; we work too much and don't earn anything.[171]

The U.S. Consulate in Naples noted that returnees commonly complained about conditions at home. Those who chose to return to the Americas often announced that they were 'going to stay this time.'[172]

Dissatisfaction among the returnees led to family tensions. The women who stayed behind did not experience the changes that accompanied the migration experience; for them, emigration remained a temporary condition. They found it difficult to accept that the United States could fundamentally change their loved ones. Emigrant's wives maintained the original goal of bettering the family's position within the context of rural Sicilian society. As tensions increased, the differences between women's and men's experiences of transoceanic migration became clear.

For those women who encouraged their husbands to emigrate and helped finance the voyage, emigration was supposed to improve their status at home. For them, the original purpose of migration never changed. They too had sacrificed for their husbands, and many women believed they had a right to the money that was sent back. As a result, they accepted few excuses for late payments. Carmelo M. first migrated to Alabama when he was twenty-one, in 1902. He worked in Birmingham for five years before he returned to Sutera to marry. In 1907 he married Giuseppa T. Two years later he left his wife pregnant with his first child to return to Birmingham. For the first few years, Carmelo sent twenty-five or thirty lire home whenever he could. In 1913, however, the money stopped. For two long years Giuseppa heard nothing from her husband. Finally, in October 1915, Giuseppa went to the mayor for help.[173] The mayor wrote to the consulate in Alabama, who called Carmelo into his office. Carmelo explained that for the past three months he had been unable to send back money because he had been ill and then unemployed. However, he did promise the government agent that he would resume payments by the end of the month. Carmelo also insisted that the clerk explain to the authorities how, 'for the last three years or so he had sent his wife a prepaid ticket from Palermo to this city for her and her seven year old child; but she had returned the said ticket assuring him that she would never ever cross the ocean to join him, and that if he wanted to see his family to come to Sutera.'[174] Furthermore, he stated in a postscript to the letter, he was still willing to send tickets to his wife and child, but that he would not return. Giuseppa never left Sutera, and Carmelo never returned. Giuseppa insisted that her home was in Sicily, as was her husband's, and that it was his responsibility as a father and husband to send her money.

For the next five years Carmelo sporadically sent money home. In 1921 these payments stopped. Giuseppa waited four years before she went back to the Mayor and asked him to write to the Italian Consulate once again.[175] This time, it seemed as though Carmelo M. had disappeared. In February 1926 the consular office in New Orleans informed Giuseppa that her husband had been committed to an insane asylum in Ohio a few years earlier and had since escaped. Since then he had been in and out of jail a number of times on vagrancy charges. He eventually returned to Alabama, where other emigrants from Sutera tried to convince him to return to Italy, but there was no one to accompany him to New York, so he remained penniless in Alabama.[176]

Giuseppa was not the only one who refused to emigrate when her husband decided to settle in the Americas. Other women in the village asked the mayor to write to the consul for information about their husbands, and continued to make their requests for money, yet very few chose to emigrate. Giuseppa D. and Pasqua Z. went to City Hall many times to ask the mayor to write to the consulate for information about their husbands. After years of silence, Maria M. finally requested that the government declare her husband dead.[177]

The women of Sutera were no different from women across the island. One migrant from the nearby city of Riesi returned home after nine months in the United States specifically to bring his family to the Americas. His wife and children refused to leave, so he planned to re-emigrate alone.[178] From the perspective of women married to migrants, permanent emigration was not a viable option – if these men wanted to see their wives and children, they had to return home. Women saw emigration as a means of achieving prestige and social status as defined by tradition and custom. With the American money the family could buy a small house and a plot of land and secure good marriages for their children. For male emigrants, the migration experience itself often changed this original dream: migration became a means of creating a new home in North America. For women, emigration meant new possibilities and opportunities for themselves and their children as defined by Sicilian society. They rarely perceived the decision to emigrate as a permanent one.

The sharp contrast between the image of the migrant wife in popular culture and political debates and the actual experience of rural women testifies to Sicily's radically changing place in the world economic system. Migration to the Americas was in many ways an extension of the traditional patterns of work. For generations rural men had left home for weeks or months at a time to work in the fields, returning with their weekly pay if they worked as wage labourers, with their annual earnings if they sharecropped. Overseas migration stretched months into years and transformed Sicilian wheatfields into Alabama coal mines.[179] By the same token, it was also something quite new: transnational migration represented the reordering of social and economic relations. The deep anxiety that accompanied this new form of work was expressed through public concern about the dangerous position that transoceanic migration placed women in and the long-term effects it would have on Italian men. The gendered descriptions of transoceanic migration that equated migration with masculinity and modernity, and identified those who remained at home with femininity and rural backwardness, while often conflicting with lived experience, have profoundly shaped our understanding of mass migration at the beginning of the twentieth century.

Men and women did experience transoceanic migration in different ways; that being said, their stories do not reflect the cultural imaginings. The stories of the women from Sutera show that far from being abandoned, the wives and mothers of migrants actively participated in the migration process. From helping organize migrant groups to financing voyages, women played key roles in the creation of the back-and-forth migrant networks that linked the New World to home villages. As the following chapters show, the process of migration transformed women's lives. Just as migration redefined notions of work and nationality for male migrants, transoceanic emigration inevitably redefined women's roles as mothers, workers, and Italians.

Chapter Three

Motherhood, Marriage, and Migration

In *La Donna Italiana,* published in 1899, Lodovico Frati described the philosophical and psychological makeup of women according to the most recent scientific studies. Negating women's ability to reason, while lauding their capacity for affection, he argued that sentiment was women's greatest virtue. He went on to write that: 'women's love passes through two distinct but coexistent phases: conjugal love and maternal love. In their love for their children women achieve self-sacrifice, and are capable of great acts of heroism. Only in the family, where nature erected woman's throne, can women as mothers and wives best satisfy their moral dignity, and give full expression to the faculties of their sex: such as the spirit of order, domestic economy and conservation.'[1] Although Frati supported his argument with modern psychiatry and anthropology, citing the works of Kraft-Ebbing and Cesare Lombroso, his thoughts echoed descriptions of women's nature previously set out by church teachings and tradition. At the turn of the century, his belief that women were fully realized only through marriage and motherhood was widely accepted throughout Italy.

From the northern cities to Sicilian hill towns, folk customs and religion testified to the importance of marriage and motherhood in a woman's life. Proverbs spoke strongly to the social significance of marriage, especially for women: 'A house without a man, is a house without a name'; 'A man without a wife has nothing good; a woman without a husband has no friends'; 'Heaven, for woman, is marriage.' A woman still unmarried after her thirtieth birthday was worthless ('Women in their thirties, throw them in the sea').[2] Faith and religion supported Frati's 'scientific' conclusions regarding female nature. Throughout Italy, especially in the South, the Madonna was the preferred recipient of fervent prayers. As the mother of God, Mary exercised enormous power. Sicilians said 'God refuses nothing to His mother,' making Mary a far more effective intermediary than any saint. Marian cults were popular throughout the South. In her honour, Sicilians generally refrained from marrying during the month of May (the Madonna's month), and celebrated her feast days (the Immaculate Conception, her birth, the Purification, the Annunciation, and the Assumption). Even the daily rosary included prayers directed to the Virgin.[3] Science, religion, and tradition agreed that female potential was fully realized through husbands and children.

At the beginning of the twentieth century, two of the most important events in the lives of southern Italian women were marriage and childbirth. A woman's wedding marked her entrance into the adult community. Status, respect, and autonomy were inextricably linked to her maternal and conjugal standing. In the cities, a few women found the courage to forgo family and become writers, artists, or revolutionaries; in the South, childlessness and spinsterhood were viewed as tragedies, not choices. Although, in rural Sicily the acts of matrimony and childbearing were central to the lives of generations of women in the nineteenth and early twentieth centuries, the consequences of these acts changed over time. Invasions, revolutions, and economic booms and busts all influenced the material and symbolic formation of families. Between 1880 and 1920, transoceanic migration altered family composition and changed the meanings of motherhood and marriage. It became possible for families to improve their social position; rural women and men could now make choices about family size that reflected prevalent social ideals. At first this meant having as many children as possible; later it meant having only one or two children. These changing notions of family redefined the roles of mother and wife. The experience of transoceanic migration also transformed the timing of marriages and births. At the beginning of the twentieth century, these rituals long connected to the agrarian economy began to adjust to the demands of the industrializing world.

Maternity and Migration

As emigration from Italy swelled, critics voiced concern about its long-term impact on the state. Central to the heated discussions was the fear that prolonged mass male migration would weaken the country's population. Politicians calling for tighter restrictions on emigration argued that if the current migration rates continued, there would be no men left to work in the fields or to enlist in the army. In 1907, Pasquale Villari observed that in a northern province that had a history of sustained male migration, the men who remained were already noticeably smaller and weaker.[4] When Antonio Mangano travelled through the rural towns of southern Italy, it seemed to him that the worst fears of the Italian politicians were coming true. 'In town after town,' he wrote, 'I scarcely saw an able-bodied man. Only the old men, women and children are left.'[5] These men prophesied that the loss of healthy young men would cause birth and marriage rates to fall so quickly that within a few years now bustling towns would completely disappear. Critics predicted that moral decay would surely accompany the physical degeneration of Italian men. Mass migration would undermine the sanctity of marriage and family. Without male supervision, the women who remained behind would sink into prostitution and adultery.[6] Legitimate births would decline, and Italy would become a nation of immoral women and bastard children.

Supporters of migration acknowledged that sustained emigration would undoubtedly affect demographic patterns, but they disagreed that the impact would inevitably be harmful. They pointed out that the provinces reporting the highest rates of male migration were the most overpopulated, and that emigration would relieve pressure on scarce resources. The endemic problems of too little land and too few jobs could finally be resolved without recourse to government intervention. The economic benefits would outweigh any harm to the population.[7] Whether they believed that the population decline was good or bad, Italian politicians all agreed that it was an inevitable consequence of transoceanic male migration.

Debates over migration's impact were especially intense in Sicily. Despite the island's history of overpopulation and underemployment, Sicilian politicians and social critics tended to view the rapidly rising rates of male migration with alarm. Many islanders agreed with Biagio Puntero's prediction in 1910 that 'if emigration rates continue at the current pace ... our Sicily will be a vast desert, a depopulated region that sooner or later will be left silent, alone, abandoned and uncultivated.'[8] In the same speech, given at a conference on emigration held in Caltanissetta in 1910, Puntero lamented: 'Emigration bears away our most economically productive and active youth, those most vigorous and best suited for legal unions. It has caused the marriage and birth rates to fall, and increased the death rate.'[9] No amount of money could compensate for the loss of a generation of young men. Puntero described how emigration left only the crippled and infirm, those who were incapable of raising either crops or children. He predicted that the number of illegitimate children and single mothers would inevitably increase as the women who remained behind struggled to survive. Without immediate government intervention, the Sicilian family – the backbone of society – would disintegrate.

There was the general agreement that long-term migration would inevitably lead to fewer marriages and lower birth rates; yet the experiences of Suteresi and Milocchesi tell a very different story. Mass male migration did not cause marriage rates to decline, fertility to fall, or illegitimacy rates to rise. Contrary to popular expectations, the reproductive lives of the women who remained behind were not radically disrupted by the absence of their husbands. In fact, mass male migration initially encouraged women to marry younger and to have more children than their mothers and grandmothers. The discrepancy between critics' expectations and the actual effects emigration on rural life is a product of the social and cultural ideals that shaped Sicilian society and family life. Large families and property were signs of wealth and power. Throughout the nineteenth century only the nobility and the wealthier members of the bourgeoisie could support large broods of children. Large families were admired among the wealthy but were derided among the poor. In general, rural Sicilians found that too many sons and daughters overburdened scarce resources. For the poor, many children meant hunger. In hard times, couples postponed the birth of their next child; in periods of prosperity, they had as many children as they could.[10] Decisions about reproduction were linked to a family's economic condition. American money provided emigrants with the means to support large families and realize their dreams of upward mobility. Emigrants chose to work overseas to improve their families' economic and social position at home, and houses and large families were the easiest ways to advertise their success. Only when cultural ideals equating success with numerous offspring began to change in the 1920s did migrants begin to have fewer children.

Rural Sicilians believed that fertility was affected by outside forces. Married couples welcomed as many children as God wished them to have, but this did not mean they considered themselves helpless in the face of God's will. Nearly everyone understood that individual actions could delay or hasten conception. Residents had recourse to a variety of methods to affect a pregnancy, some more effective than others.[11] Nineteenth-century ethnographers found that across the island, Sicilians enlisted a number of herbs, medicines, and spells to either promote or hinder the birth of another child. Coastal residents maintained that a small dose of grated cuttlefish bone taken on an empty stomach for three consecutive mornings would make a woman sterile. Rural residents across the island were well aware of possible abortifacients. If the potions failed, a woman turned to the local midwife to end an unwanted pregnancy.[12]

In 1890, Dr Vaccaro noted that abortions were common among Suteresi women, and residents believed that a woman could induce a miscarriage. Mothers thought they could control the fate of their fetus by choosing their activities and their foods. Most abortions occurred within the first few months of pregnancy and were attributed to 'exaggerated physical exertion or to unsatisfied desires.'[13] By the 1920s, drugs designed to induce abortions were available in local pharmacies. Charlotte Gower Chapman described how young men often claimed a pharmacist as a close friend in their efforts to seduce a woman. After the First World War, condoms were available in rural towns like Sutera and Milocca, although withdrawal remained the most popular method among both married and unmarried couples.[14] The use of contraception did not contradict faith in divine will. God determined the efficacy of human action, but it was up to the individual or couple to take the necessary steps to avoid or encourage pregnancy.

After a woman had given birth, nursing allowed her some control over the timing of pregnancy. Demographic studies indicate that lactational amenorrhoea is an effective means of contraception for eighteen months after delivery. Research has concluded that women who exclusively breastfeed, or who use little supplemental food, are 98 per cent protected from another pregnancy for at least a year-and-a-half after giving birth.[15] Sicilian women were expected to nurse their children for at least one year, and most breast-fed their children for two years. If a woman from Milocca or Sutera had difficulty nursing or developed a breast infection, she prayed to Saint Zaccharia or Saint Agata; both were considered adept at curing breast-related illnesses.[16] A new mother was given certain foods to ensure enough milk for the newborn. Semolina bread sprinkled with sesame and soaked in wine, then toasted in the oven, was believed to stimulate breast milk. Pasta with onion and fresh ricotta was also said to induce lactation.[17] Studies have shown that the effectiveness of lactational amenorrhoea is linked to diet. A low-fat diet seems to prolong postpartum amenorrhoea; however, once menstruation has resumed, a diet higher in fat will continue to delay conception as long as the woman continues nursing. Until the mid-twentieth century, rural Sicilians ate relatively little fat. Most of their protein came from vegetable sources. Meals commonly consisted of a touch of olive oil on boiled greens with bread, or a piece of bread and an onion. At least once a week the family ate pasta. Only the relatively wealthy ate meat and dairy on a regular basis. This low-fat diet, combined with the popular wisdom encouraging new mothers to eat more dairy foods, increased the efficacy of nursing as a means of controlling fertility.[18] Sicilian women took active steps to breast-feed their children as long as possible. It is not clear whether they chose to nurse for two years because it was an economical way to feed their children in a world where milk was not plentiful, or in order to delay the arrival of the next child. Whatever their motivations, the tradition of breast-feeding among Sicilian women, and their customary beliefs about pregnancy, suggest that women not only believed they had limited control over reproduction, but in fact did.

Sicilian attitudes toward family size were linked to class. Among the local gentry, large families were traditionally symbolic of success and power.[19] As long as a man could provide for all his heirs, children were signs of wealth. Children could actually increase a rich family's wealth, if the parents were able to arrange marriages between their sons and well-dowered women. Daughters' marriages, admittedly more costly, could establish profitable political or business alliances. The vast majority of Sicilians, however, were not members of the gentry. Among the rural poor, large families were usually considered a curse. Proverbs reminded residents that 'two or three [children] are a pleasure, seven or eight a torment,' or more succinctly, 'family, famine.'[20] Poor women who had many children in rapid succession were considered weak, foolish, or born under the wrong moon. Certainly they were not to be envied or emulated.

Cultural attitudes toward family size, combined with the belief that fertility could be affected by human action, tied birth rates closely to economic conditions. Throughout the nineteenth century, prosperous times brought a significant rise in birth rates. Demographic patterns in Sutera and Milocca illustrate the close connection between reproduction and economic opportunity. In Sutera, the 1870s and 1880s witnessed especially high population growth and strong economic expansion. In the 1880s the town's total population grew by 18 per cent, compared with 14 per cent in the 1870s and only 5 per cent in the 1860s.[21] Through-

TABLE 3.1
Average bride age at first marriage and births per marriage ratio (BMR), 1860–89

	Bride age	BMR
1860–9	25	7
1870–9	24	5
1880–9	24	6

Source: Average bride age is based on the bride age in the *Atti di matrimonio 1860–1889* in the Archivio Comunale di Sutera. It represents the average nuptial age of women in 909 marriages where both the bride and the groom had never been married before. The birth per marriage ratio (BMR) is based on Somogyi's data. See Stefano Somogyi, *Storia demografici dei comuni siciliani dal 1862–1971* (Palermo: Tip. Lux., 1979), 93, 167.

out these decades, births far exceeded deaths, spurred by a simultaneous rise in the birth rate and a sharp drop in mortality. From the 1860s to the 1880s the birth rate rose sharply, from 38 live births per 1,000 residents to 47 in the 1870s, to 51 during the 1880s. The increase in births coincided with a rise in marriage rates. At the same time, mortality rates fell from 37 to 31 deaths per 1,000.[22]

During the 1870s and 1880s, Suteresi watched their families grow. A rough estimate of marital fertility based on the average number of children born to each marriage (births per marriage ratio)[23] shows an increase in family size. Couples who married in the 1880s tended to have, on average, one child more than those who married a decade earlier (see Table 3.1). The growing number of children is partially accounted for by a decline in the age of first marriage for local women. Between the 1860s and the 1870s the average bride age in Sutera fell from 25 to 24, and it remained low throughout the next decade. The falling age of women at first marriage was a consequence of fewer brides over thirty, rather than of women marrying at an ever younger age. The proportion of women marrying between twenty and twenty-four rose from 35 per cent to 47 per cent between 1860 and 1879, and remained relatively high at 38 per cent through to the end of the nineteenth century. Meanwhile, the number of women who postponed marriage until their late twenties or early thirties fell. These rising rates of marital fertility and changing marriage patterns occurred during periods of economic prosperity.[24]

Between 1860 and 1885, industrial growth in the region coincided with a series of good harvests that ushered in a period of relative prosperity, encouraging women to marry young.[25] After Italian unification, Sicilian industry profited from foreign investment and government intervention in the local economy. The French and English invested heavily in the nascent wine industry and in mining and shipbuilding companies. Hoping to encourage industrial growth, the state reorganized regional financial institutions, allowing local banks to extend credit to these industries. The government also expanded the island's railway system, in particular improving connections between the sulphur mines and the ports. By 1881, mining towns – including Sutera – were beginning to reap the benefits of the lower costs of production and of increased investment in sulphur.[26]

Suteresi also profited from the growing market for Sicilian wheat. Despite the newly imposed grist tax and other onerous duties on agriculture, production increased significantly during the first twenty years after Italian unification. As the French and English demanded more grain, and the price of wheat rose on the global market, landowners ploughed under land previously used for pasture. By the end of the 1880s the annual yield on the island was nearly 8 million hectolitres a year – an increase of over 2 million from 1870.[27] The rise in grain production was the result of increased commercial activity and a series of good harvests. During these years Sicily was spared severe droughts and destructive storms. The absence of serious food shortages contributed to the decline in mortality rates and rising birth rates.[28]

By enabling local governments to fund sanitation reforms, economic progress had immediate benefits for the island's population. In 1874 the city council of Sutera purchased new pipes to bring clean drinking water from the spring 9 kilometres away to thirteen fountains scattered throughout the town. Four years later a cemetery was built on the outskirts of town. Previously the dead had been buried underneath the churches or in ravines on the outskirts of town. Both measures improved public health; in particular, they reduced infant mortality rates. In the 1870s, after the new pipes were in place, death rates dropped to 31 per thousand, and they continued to fall throughout the first part of the 1880s.[29] However, Sutera's population growth cannot be attributed solely to structural improvements in transportation and sanitation. A close analy-

TABLE 3.2
Average family size, 1880–99

Year of marriage	Rural workers	Artisans	Gentry
1880–4	6	7	6
1885–9	5	5	4
1890–4	5	7	4
1895–9	5	5	6

Source: Data are based on a total of 485 family reconstructions from *Atti di nascita 1880–1899* and *Atti di matrimonio 1880–1899* in the Archivio Comunale di Sutera.

sis of birth and marriage patterns in the village suggests that residents made reproductive choices according to personal financial circumstances. And although the economic boom improved most people's daily lives, it did not benefit everyone equally.[30]

In Sutera, the 1870s and 1880s were especially good for the local gentry and artisans. The sale of ecclesiastical lands enabled local landowners to increase their wealth. Their affluence is visible in the many civic improvements undertaken between 1870 and 1885. In the 1870s the wealthy residents raised enough money to move the town hall into the ex-Benedictine monastery, a far more spacious and elegant building.[31] A few years later the gentry pooled their money to buy instruments and uniforms for a town band. They even hired a music teacher for the town, who was paid 1,000 lire a year – more than the local schoolmaster earned. The town cut the funding for the position a few years later; however, Dr Vaccaro insisted that the combined ineptitude of the bandleader and the administrative committee was to blame, not a lack of funding. In 1883 the gentry raised enough money for streetlights.[32] These projects attest to both a growing civic pride among the elite and to their financial strength.

These years of prosperity encouraged the local gentry to marry as soon as possible and begin their own families. There were no financial reasons to delay marriage or children. Between the 1860s and 1870s the average age of first-time brides who married into prominent families fell from twenty-five to twenty-two.[33] Well-to-do women who married during the height of the economic boom, between 1880 and 1884, had an average of six children each (see Table 3.2). Although they did not have significantly larger families than other Suteresi, the lower incidence of

TABLE 3.3
Average number of months between children's birth, by year of marriage, 1880–99

		Year of marriage			
Children	Class	1880–4	1885–9	1890–4	1895–9
1 and 2	Rural workers	28	28	31	31
	Artisans	35	25	23	31
	Gentry	26	22	37	—
2 and 3	Rural workers	34	32	36	32
	Artisans	36	26	30	29
	Gentry	24	32	26	—
3 and 4	Rural workers	38	36	32	33
	Artisans	46	27	32	29
	Gentry	35	36	24	—
4 and 5	Rural workers	31	40	32	32
	Artisans	34	32	32	30
	Gentry	30	32	28	—

Source: Data are based on 374 family reconstructions where at least two children were born. It is culled from the *Atti di nascita 1880–1899* and *Atti di matrimonio 1880–1899* in the Archivio Comunale di Sutera.

infant mortality ensured that most of their children survived to adulthood.[34] Elite women also tended to have their children in quick succession. On average, women who married during the early 1880s usually had their first three children within six years of their wedding (see Table 3.3). As long as the economy was flourishing, the local gentry continued to have one child after another.

Local artisans benefited from the good fortune enjoyed by the elite, and their prosperity also translated into larger families. The various public works projects and the growing private demand for larger houses provided steady employment for local builders, bricklayers, and artisans. The cemetery, built in 1878, employed a large number of stonemasons. Relocation and renovation of the new city hall provided many people with jobs during the 1870s. More orders were placed with local craftsmen as landowners sought to display their wealth and status through material possessions. Tradesmen and shopkeepers found a demand for ready-made fabrics among residents. Wealthy women walked through town wearing high-heeled shoes made by the local cobblers and dresses sewn by local dressmakers. According to a government survey conducted in 1885, two tailors were 'officially' working in Sutera.[35] Marriage records

TABLE 3.4
Births per marriage ratio, 1880–1909

	1880–9	1890–9	1900–9
Rural workers	4	4	6
Artisans	4	5	6
Gentry	6	5	3

Source: Data are based on *Atti di nascita 1880–1909* and *Atti di matrimonio 1880–1909* in the Archivio Comunale di Sutera. Rates are calculated from a total of 4,420 births and 1,032 marriages.

show that at least two women also found work as seamstresses.[36] With jobs plentiful, artisans had no reason to prolong courtship or postpone marriage, and women were marrying at an ever-younger age. During the 1870s the average age of brides fell by two years.[37] Newlyweds began their families immediately after the ceremony, seeing no reason to delay having children.

The first decades after unification were not as good for agricultural workers as they were for cobblers, metalworkers, professionals, and landowners. Sharecroppers and day labourers saw their economic opportunities diminish between 1860 and 1880. Expectations of a better life, awakened with the arrival of Garibaldi, faded along with the promises of real land reform. Good harvests only marginally offset the lower wages and higher rents. Also, the grist tax had been reinstated. Despite increased production, few agricultural wage workers found themselves better off in 1875 than they had been in 1865. Government efforts to encourage local industry through protectionist legislation exacerbated the position of the sharecroppers.[38] In the 1880s there were only four births registered for every marriage among rural workers (see Table 3.4), and family size did not rise as rapidly as among artisans (see Table 3.2). Although rural women married two or more years earlier than artisans or gentry, they usually delayed the birth of their children for a longer period (see Table 3.3).[39]

By the 1890s the good times had ended. Over the next thirty years, wealthy families began having fewer children as they adjusted to the changing economy. In the wake of the agricultural depression and the phylloxera epidemic, Sicilian investors and their foreign partners pulled out of the island's industry, and the economy fell into severe crisis.[40] As members of the elite felt growing pressure on their shrinking resources, they began to postpone marriage if they were single, and married couples began delaying their children.

By the end of the nineteenth century, fertility rates among the gentry had shrunk to three births per marriage. They continued to decline in the following decades (see Table 3.4). In Sutera, family sizes began to fall almost as soon as the agricultural depression came to the island. During the difficult years of the early 1890s, when Sicily's local elites were facing worker uprisings and strikes combined with shrinking profits, average family size fell from six to four children. Some sort of birth control was needed to preserve the family patrimony.[41] By the early 1890s, wealthy couples were choosing to delay the birth of their first child by six months and the arrival of their second by fifteen (see Table 3.3). Also, daughters of the local gentry began to defer marriage for a few years. The average age of brides at their first wedding rose three years, to thirty.[42] When the economy improved after 1895, marriage ages fell and family sizes rose slightly, only to fall again after the turn of the century as emigration and land reform undermined traditional sources of wealth. By 1910 the average size of wealthy families had shrunk to one child, and marital fertility rates had fallen to three births per marriage.

Gradually the idea spread that fewer children symbolized success and wealth. By the 1920s this idea had taken hold among the non-elite.[43] Once the economy began to shrink, artisans began to delay marriage and postpone the arrival of their children. Couples who married during the most prosperous years, between 1880 and 1885, had seven children on average; those who married between 1885 and 1889 had only five (see Table 3.2).

Rural workers in Sutera reacted differently to the economic crisis of the 1890s than the local gentry. Although agricultural labourers faced rising unemployment, the rural rebellions and land reforms initially offered some improvement in sharecropping contracts and daily wages. Daily life changed little for these people throughout the 'good years' of the 1880s and the depression of the 1890s. Agricultural workers saw little reason to delay their marriages or alter their reproductive choices. The average woman still married at twenty-four, and after the birth of their first child, couples often chose to wait before having their second. Between the 1880s and 1890s the time between the births of first and second children rose from twenty-eight to thirty-one months (see Table 3.3). In the last decades of the nineteenth century, marital fertility and the average family size among rural workers changed far less than among the gentry and artisans.[44]

Changing attitudes toward family size influenced the reproductive decisions made by migrants. The falling price of a steamship ticket and plentiful work made the coal mines of Alabama and Pennsylvania valid alternatives to working the wheatfields at home. Overseas, a hard-working man could make enough money to support a large family. In Sutera, where migration patterns were characterized by high rates of repatriation and many trips back and forth across the Atlantic, couples did not have to put off having children. The promise of America held little incentive to limit family size. When Salvatore C. set sail for America in the fall of 1905 he left his wife, Onofria R., one month pregnant with their fourth child.[45] Onofria R. had just turned thirty, and with Salvatore C. overseas, it appeared as though this would be her last pregnancy. In fact, Onofria R. went on to have three more children with Salvatore, giving birth to her youngest child in 1913 at thirty-eight. Despite her husband's multiple trips to the Americas, Onofria R. had more legitimate children in less time than her sister, whose husband never left Sutera.[46]

In his study on Italian fertility, Massimo Livi-Bacci suggested that migration acted as a conservative force, slowing fertility declines in the South. Evidence from Sutera bears out his initial findings but not his explanations. He argued that 'emigration attracted those more inclined to change and innovation, those more receptive to new ways of life, those less adaptable to a static, and of course, undeveloped society.'[47] Based on this assumption, a community with heavy emigration loses its most imaginative and innovative members, those most likely to change traditional family patterns. According to Livi-Bacci, migration relieved the worst of the economic and social pressures – unemployment and overpopulation – that would force people to change their reproductive behaviour. Emigration acted as a conservative force by removing the strongest forces for change. This may be true in certain cases, but it does not explain the experience of the women of Sutera. It seems that in rural Sicilian hill towns, migrants and their families were the most resistant to demographic change.

A comparison of reproductive patterns between couples who opted for emigration and those who did not supports the conclusion that at least initially, migration acted as a conservative force in communities, but not because the most innovative people left. Emigrants from Sutera who left before 1905 had a stake in maintaining traditional reproductive patterns. The individual migrants and their families back home had gambled heavily that migration would provide the resources necessary for realizing their dreams of upward mobility, which were tied so closely to family size. Indeed, the psychological and economic investment that went into the decision to emigrate placed a greater emphasis on children as a visible symbol of the family's success. Sicilians who chose not to emigrate may have been quicker to abandon traditional assumptions equating large families with success, as they faced the economic and social changes affecting the island.

When Paolino S. married Giuseppa I. in March 1899, he wanted what his father and grandfather had sought in their lifetimes: a wife, a house in town, and enough land of his own to support his hopefully numerous progeny. Like most residents, he dreamed of being a respected member of the community, a *signore.* He believed that emigration could help him realize his dreams. Before their first wedding anniversary, Giuseppa I. gave birth to a son. Shortly afterwards, Paolino S. requested a *nulla osta* to sail to New Orleans.[48] Two years later, in 1903, he left Sutera. Paolino S. was gone for nearly five years this first time – his longest stay in the United States. When he returned to Sutera in 1907 he stayed home for less than a year, leaving Giuseppa I. expecting their third child. After the birth of their third child, Giuseppa I. joined her husband in the United States, but within two years she had returned to Sutera with her four children. Within months after her homecoming, she gave birth to their fifth child. A year later Paolino S. rejoined his wife in Italy. By the time Paolino S. had permanently resettled in Sutera, he had fulfilled a good portion of his dream. He was the proud father of six children, at least five of whom survived to adulthood and together with his wife he owned three houses in town. The reproductive choices made by Paolino S. and Giuseppa I. reflect those of the nineteenth-century gentry, rather than rural workers in the twentieth century.

The tendency for migrants and their families to cling to traditional family patterns is visible in a comparison of crude marital fertility rates between women married to migrants and those whose husbands never left home. Despite the prolonged absence of their husbands, wives of migrants had more children. In Sutera, marital fertility increased from four to five births per marriage in the first decades of the twentieth century. Among non-migrant residents, the BMR (births per marriage ratio) did not change, whereas among families where the father had gone abroad, net marital fertility rose by five between 1905 and 1914 (see Table 3.5).

The increase in births per marriage after 1907 corresponded to the return of hundreds of emigrants. In 1907, 234 migrants returned to Sutera. The following year 74 came home, and in 1909 another 70 came back. Most of these returnees left for the Americas between 1905 and

TABLE 3.5
Births per marriage ratio between migrants and non-migrants, 1890–1914

Year of Marriage	Migrants	Non-migrants
1890–4	3	5
1895–9	3	5
1900–4	2	5
1905–9	4	5
1910–4	9	5

Source: Ratios are taken from the *Atti di nascita 1890–1914* and the *Atti di matrimonio 1890–1914* in the Archivio Comunale di Sutera. The total number of births among the migrant population was 699, and the total number of marriages was 183. Among those residents who did not emigrate, there were 3,003 births and 629 marriages.

1907 and stayed abroad three or four years, and according to government reports, most came home better off than when they left. Those who had emigrated as single men married shortly after their return and immediately started families. Married emigrants who returned felt little economic or social pressure to limit the size of their families, and had as many children as possible.

The families of migrants were able to grow so rapidly by extending women's childbearing years and adjusting the spacing between births. In the 1890s, wives of migrant men married nearly four years earlier than women whose husbands never left Sutera, and they had their last child at an older age (see Table 3.6). This is especially evident among women who married in the 1890s or earlier. Male migration affected the childbearing experiences of the women who remained behind, first postponing and then hastening the arrival of their children. Women who married in the 1880s, and whose husbands migrated, spaced their first three or four children over a longer period of time and had their last three children in quicker succession (see Table 3.7). Women who married between 1895 and 1899 often gave birth to their second child an average of three years after their first. Most likely their husbands left for the Americas after the first child was born, and their absence delayed the second pregnancy.

The effects of transoceanic male migration on the population of the

TABLE 3.6
Average bride age at first marriage, and average age of mother at birth of last child, 1890–1909

	Average bride age		Average age at birth of last child	
	Migrants	Non-migrants	Migrants	Non-migrants
1890–4	22	25	32	26
1895–9	22	26	36	35
1900–4	23	25	25	23
1905–9	25	21	31	30

Source: The average age of brides at their first marriage where the groom had never been married before is calculated based on 603 marriages in the *Atti di matrimonio 1890–1909* in the Archivio Comunale di Sutera. The average age of the mother at the birth of her last child is based on family reconstructions of 427 families

TABLE 3.7
Number of months between children, for migrants and non-migrants, 1880–1909

	1880–9		1890–9		1900–9	
Children	Migrant	Non-migrant	Migrant	Non-migrant	Migrant	Non-migrant
1 and 2	27	28	33	31	37	31
2 and 3	34	32	32	33	34	32
3 and 4	49	35	36	32	35	28
4 and 5	30	35	35	31	29	29
5 and 6	36	32	36	29	41	26
6 and 7	27	32	28	29	36	18

Source: Calculated from reconstructions of 612 families, based on *Atti di matrimonio 1880–1909* and *Atti di nascita 1880–1909* in the Archivio Comunale di Sutera, and the migrant file created by the author.

community varied with each generation. In Sutera, couples who married in the 1880s or 1890s and then decided to send a family member abroad had more children over a longer period than their non-migrant counterparts. In contrast, women who married migrants in the 1900s and 1910s had the same number of children or fewer than the wives of non-migrants. These younger women also tended to stop having children at an earlier age. The shift in reproductive strategies that occurred among these families of emigrants reflects a fundamental change in attitude toward family size and notions of success that occurred at the beginning of the century.

TABLE 3.8
Average family size, for migrants and non-migrants, 1880–1909

Year married	Number of children	
	Migrants	Non-migrants
1880–9	6.3	5.0
1890–9	6.4	4.9
1900–9	3.7	3.6

Source: Data are based on the reproductive histories of 765 couples who married between 1880 and 1909.

After 1905, culture codes associating fecundity with wealth and status weakened. In the 1890s, local elites and wealthy bourgeois couples began choosing to have fewer children. By the First World War, there was a significant drop in family size among all residents. The shift to smaller families seems to have been more readily adopted by younger generations of emigrants than by older migrants. Among women who married after 1905 and whose husbands migrated for even a few years, there was a marked drop in family size (see Table 3.8). Despite the absence of their husbands, these women did not choose to extend their childbearing years. On average, women who married between 1900 and 1905, and whose husbands migrated, had their last child at thirty-three. Women married to men who did not migrate continued to have children until thirty-four. Over the next ten years, wives of migrants stopped having children at a significantly younger age. By 1910, wives of migrants were choosing to stop having children five years earlier than those whose husbands stayed home. By the First World War, there was little difference in the general reproductive patterns of families of migrants and non-migrants through the first five children. Women married to migrants, like those married to men who did not emigrate, shortened their childbearing years and had fewer children. By the interwar years, all rural Sicilians, regardless of class, were consciously limiting family size.[49]

The experiences of women in Sutera suggest that mass male migration did not radically disrupt the lives of rural women who remained behind, nor did it act alone as a conservative force on fertility patterns. Based on the reconstructions of families in Sutera, the wives of emigrants and their husbands continued to make reproductive choices based on assumptions equating children with wealth, and these women were not left barren or childless. Emigration reinforced Sicilian attitudes about family. Only when rural views regarding family size changed did women who were married to migrants limit the number of children they had. The social goals underlying emigration that encouraged women to continue to have more children – or fewer, if they were married after 1905 – explain why predictions that the wives of migrants would abandon their husbands, leaving a trail of bastard children in their wake, were not borne out.

Contrary to most expectations, migration seems to have had little impact on changing illegitimacy rates. The ratio of illegitimate births to live births fell sharply after 1900 in Sutera and throughout the province. From 1890 to 1895, 7 per cent of the births in Sutera were registered at city hall as illegitimate. In 1900, babies born out of wedlock accounted for 3 per cent of all the births residents reported to the civil authorities. As migration intensified, the number of reported illegitimate births continued to fall. By 1914 they comprised only 1.3 per cent of all registered births.[50]

At the turn of the century, illegitimacy rates in the southern provinces were much higher than in the northern regions; however, this was not the consequence of mass male migration.[51] The number of children born to unwed mothers rose most rapidly prior to emigration, in the last decades of the nineteenth century. After 1900, when southerners began to emigrate, illegitimacy rates dropped sharply.[52] In 1901, Sicily reported that 5.8 children out of one hundred were born out of wedlock. By 1913 only 3.2 children out of every one hundred appeared as illegitimate.[53] The relative high rates of illegitimacy at the beginning of the twentieth century are actually an indication of southerners' attitudes toward the state; they were not an effect of mass male migration.

National marriage laws inflated the number of children defined as illegitimate. In 1866 the Italian government passed a law mandating civil marriages throughout the kingdom. In the eyes of the state, marriages celebrated by the church alone were invalid, which meant that in official terms, children born to couples married only by a priest were illegitimate. Despite the government's efforts, rural residents continued to recognize the authority of the church in matters of the heart.[54] Between 1860 and 1920, children considered perfectly legitimate by their parents, their parents' families, and the community were labelled illegitimate by municipal clerks. In Sutera, couples often delayed the civil marriage or ignored it altogether. In May 1886, Mariano S. and Anna L. were married at the local church, surrounded by their friends and family. They quickly settled into their new life together as a married couple. A year later Mariano S. appeared at the office to register the birth of their first child, a daughter named Luigia. On her birth certificate the clerk wrote that the mother was 'a woman who wished to remain anonymous.' Although the community recognized their marriage, Anna L. appeared as an unwed mother in the eyes of the state and its clerks. This couple was not deeply troubled by the legal status of their children. Eventually they were married in a civil ceremony at city hall, but only after five children and fifteen years of marriage.[55] Throughout Italy, clerks defined thousands of children as illegitimate who were eventually recognized by one or both parents.

As municipal weddings were gradually incorporated into local marriage rituals, the number of these technically illegitimate children dropped dramatically. In Sutera, parents of over 70 per cent of the children registered as 'natural' recognized those children as their offspring.[56] Of these, 57 per cent were considered legitimate by townsfolk who had witnessed the parents' marriage in church prior to the birth of the child, or who had attended the religious ceremony shortly after the child arrived. Single fathers recognized 8 per cent of the children, and unwed mothers recognized 6 per cent. Fewer than one-third of these illegitimate children were never acknowledged by either parent. Many of the children of parents who chose not to marry were the products of long-standing relationships rather than accidents of passion. It was common for the same person to appear two or three times over the course of a decade to report the birth of an illegitimate child. Well over half the forty-two illegitimate children born between 1880 and 1889, whom their parents eventually officially recognized, were presented to city hall by the same eleven people.[57]

Esposti, or unrecognized foundlings, are a much better indication of actual rates of illegitimacy in Sutera. Each year, residents found two or three infants on their doorsteps. One cold winter's morning in 1880, Carmela V. found a baby girl on the front steps of her house in Rabato. Carmela took the newborn inside and that afternoon went to the city clerk's office to announce the birth of Paolina F. The mayor decided she should keep the child until a nurse could be found.[58] Every town had a special fund set aside to pay women to care for foundlings. The provincial government provided slightly more than half the money, and the town raised the rest through local taxes. The province determined the size of the annual budget based on population size. Only 14 per cent of these foundlings were ever recognized by their parents.

Despite rising rates of emigration, local governments were not burdened with a glut of illegitimate children. In 1904, Sutera had a total of

1,719.43 lire to care for foundlings; by the end of the fiscal year the city had disbursed less than half this money. By 1913 the provincial authorities had reduced the budget to 1,124.74 lire as the population declined.[59] During the peak years of emigration from the town, the city council was not forced to raise taxes to care for unwanted children. Fears that migration would destroy the moral fibre of society, causing the women who were left behind to take up with any man available and abandon the fruits of these illicit relations on a neighbour's doorstep, were unfounded.

Evidence from Sutera suggesting that emigration did not cause illegitimacy rates to rise is not surprising, considering the nature of rural life and the emotional and financial stakes these women invested in the migration process. In a town the size of Sutera, it was not easy to keep an unwanted pregnancy secret. Women who remained behind who engaged in extramarital affairs would have been hard pressed to keep their actions private. When a swollen belly accompanied rumours of infidelity, women had to face the wrath of their husbands overseas and their family members at home, and they suffered the same social stigma usually attached to unwed mothers. Within the community an illegitimate child was associated with immorality. At least three of the women who recognized their children had been accused previously of being prostitutes.[60] Clearly, it was difficult for a woman who gave birth to a child out of wedlock to claim the same position of honour among her neighbours and family members as her neighbour whose children were all publicly recognized as the legitimate offspring of her lawful husband. The community condemned married women who engaged in extramarital affairs more harshly than young unwed girls who found themselves pregnant and alone. Everyone knew that women were inherently weak and that an inexperienced girl could not resist the wiles of older men. Fathers, uncles, and brothers along with mothers, aunts, and sisters were expected to restrain and protect her, and if she brought dishonour to the family, everyone was partly to blame. A wedded woman had to be more cautious. She was no longer an impetuous girl but a wife and mother responsible for her emotions and actions.[61] Any hint of impropriety by a married woman weakened her position in the community. If a child were born from her indiscretions, her ability to climb the social ladder would be severely limited. She would probably find it difficult to arrange prestigious marriages for her children or improve her family's condition. For women whose husbands had emigrated, sexual promiscuity would compromise the success of the venture. These women had urged their husbands to emigrate to acquire the capital necessary to improve their lives and their status. Rumours of an illegitimate child would undermine their ability to realize their dream of bettering their families' lives.

The experiences of the women of Sutera suggest that mass male migration did not depress fertility or increase illegitimate births. In many ways migration was a conservative force, encouraging rural residents to have more children when their neighbours were actively curtailing family size in response to the new economic and social conditions of an industrializing world. Only when residents began to associate smaller families with wealth and success in the 1920s did emigrants also seek to limit family size. Although mass male migration did not have the social impact that so many critics and politicians predicted, it did affect women's roles within the family. By accelerating the trend toward smaller families at the beginning of the twentieth century, transoceanic migration helped change the experience of motherhood. Women married after 1890 no longer spent the same amount of time pregnant and caring for small children. The changing marriage and birth patterns that accompanied mass male migration redefined the meaning of motherhood.

In nineteenth-century Sicily, mothering meant raising sons capable of following their fathers into the workshops and fields, and daughters skilled in running a household. Mothers groomed their sons to be hardworking young men, to be responsible and dutiful labourers; they trained their daughters in domestic arts such as weaving, cooking, and childcare. Mothering also entailed moral instruction. Women were responsible for children's early religious education.[62] A mother guided and protected her children. She was the sympathetic parent, more likely to express her affection physically and emotionally. In exchange for her love, a mother expected complete loyalty. Proverbs from the late nineteenth century expressed the strong belief that parents deserved blind obedience from their children, and emphasized that individual happiness sprang from filial fidelity. 'Those who obey their fathers and mothers live a rich, happy, and contented life.'[63] According to Salamone-Marino, 'when parents have taught a son or daughter the how and why of behaving, to be useful at home, an endless respect and blind obedience to themselves, the authors of their lives, they have satisfied every obligation that natural and civil law imposes.'[64]

Mothering meant more than guiding children to adulthood, arranging marriages, and ensuring the continuation of the family; it also involved certain economic obligations. In Sicilian households each member contributed his or her wages to cover family expenses. Mothers managed the household and the financial relations that held the family together. It was the mother who ensured that the family could provide for everyone's needs, and she often decided what those needs were. A good mother made her children contribute to the family as soon as they were able, either by working around the house or by earning money. By age ten, sons were sent to work. Usually they helped their fathers or were apprenticed to a local craftsman; the most unfortunate were sent to work in the sulphur mines.[65] Daughters contributed by helping their mothers with household chores and by raising chickens and pigs for a few extra lire. As the mayor of Caltanissetta noted, mothers recognized the value of education as the 'first step up on the social scale,' but few could afford to keep their children in school year round. The family needed children's labour, and even if children could not earn money, a frugal housewife could save the family the expense of new clothes and books required for school attendance by keeping their children home.[66] By the 1890s, married women had little opportunity to contribute financially to the family; even so, their roles as mothers and managers ensured the family's survival.

As in the northern cities, the identification of smaller families with wealth and success marked a transformation in family roles and relations. The physical and emotional experience of mothering changed. Smaller families meant a woman spent less time pregnant and nursing. However, as couples chose to have fewer children, childcare assumed a more important place in a woman's life, and a greater portion of her time.[67] As transoceanic migration brought more cash into the region, raising the general standard of living across the island, Sicilians began encouraging their children to learn new skills and careers. Parents kept their children in school instead of sending them out to work at the first opportunity. As a consequence, women spent more time watching over their children. Migrants' wives were among the most vehement in demanding their children attend school and in encouraging them – especially sons – to seek professional careers instead of toiling in the fields like their fathers and grandfathers. They also encouraged their daughters to learn skills that would be useful in the new economy. Daughters needed to learn to read and write and were sent to school. Mothers were now raising their children to surpass their parents. This meant they had to play a much more active role in their children's lives, making sure they attended school and found partners suitable for their new position.

The importance of children in realizing the migrant dream gave new significance to a mother's responsibilities.

The transition to smaller families did not immediately weaken the ideal of motherhood in the family; however, changing family relations did produce tensions between generations. Mothers continued to exercise all power over the youngest children. Sicilian culture continued to idealize the mother/child relationship, identifying maternal love as the greatest love and 'stipulating that mother's requests never be denied.'[68] Cultural codes still held children financially liable to the family. In 1928 a father in Milocca wrote to his son's fiancée in America that while they had no personal objections against her, they could not agree to the marriage because their son had 'made no contribution to the upkeep of his own family.'[69] In some ways mass migration even fostered a renewed maternal reverence. In emigrant communities, nostalgia for the homeland often translated into sentimental remembrances of a mother's love.[70] A close analysis of popular culture and expectations, however, reveals growing tensions between children and their mothers as children sought to claim more autonomy.

When Charlotte Gower Chapman did her research in Milocca in the late 1920s, she observed that contrary to the cultural ideal, children often disobeyed their parents. Beyond the traditional rights of children to elope, she noted that mothers and children often quarrelled, with the latter talking back, telling their mothers to 'be still' and belittling their knowledge and experience.[71] A mother's wisdom was antiquated and held little authority over modern youth, well schooled in the ways of the world. Migration seems to have fuelled youthful rebellion, encouraging children to challenge their mothers. Emigrant sons used distance as an excuse to shrug off their filial responsibilities, and claimed their autonomy by choosing their own partners and marrying overseas, sending little of their earnings back home, and permanently settling in the Americas. These children also broke with tradition by deserting the family trade. Daughters who remained home were also influenced by the new ideas filtering home. In a popular poem by Rosario Baglio of the neighbouring town of Serradifalco, a daughter tells her mother of her plans to marry:

> The mother then began to howl
> 'Bitch, stinking of innocence
> Is it fever that makes you rave?

To speak thus at your age makes no sense
For you are hardly arrived at sixteen'
'Mamma, I am losing patience,
You tell me to listen to you –
It is useless to make such an answer
I cannot stay like this always
The American says: Take a Chance
If you won't marry me I will marry myself any way'
The Mother responded: I will kill you!
May you have a bad fall.[72]

While mothers and daughters surely quarrelled in the nineteenth century, the nature of the rebellion reflected in this poem, with its underlying themes of independence and personal autonomy, was unique to the twentieth century. The mother's apparent overreaction in Baglio's epic is directed not at her daughter's desire to marry, but at her desire to decide on her own when and whom she will marry. As Rudolph Bell wrote: 'The forces of passion and romantic love appeared in Sicilian lore in their traditional form, as threats to the happiness and perpetuation of *la famiglia*, not as a basis for marriage.'[73]

These themes of conflict and change were played out in the short stories published in the *Giornale di Sicilia* between 1900 and 1920. In 'Il Bisogna d'Amore' (The Need to Love) by Amalia Guglieminetti, the young widow Santelli adopts a small boy to fulfil her maternal needs. She raises the child, who adores his mother as if she was his birth mother. Under her guidance he transcends his lowly origins to become a doctor. Her love for her son is the principal reason for her existence. She cannot not bear the idea that her son will marry: 'The only impurity in this pure love was a confused, latent jealousy.' Her son also feels uneasy about replacing his mother, and so seeks a woman who will be a good companion but who will not challenge his mother's love. He goes home and announces his engagement to his mother. 'Who is this woman?' she responds. 'Do you love her?' He tells her she is his fiancée, the daughter of his professor, who will open many professional doors for him: 'But I don't love her: I only love you.' After the marriage the young couple moves in with the widow, who watches the interloper capture her son's heart. The young bride is a cold creature who does not return Enrico's love and soon begins to cheat on him. The mother tells her son about his wife's infidelity, and the son, distraught, returns to his mother. 'Holding her tightly between his arms, he shudders, "I have no one but you."'[74] Stories like this illustrated the increased emotional investment required of mothers, yet at the same time they reiterated the traditional theme that a child's independence was dangerous. Other writers celebrated youthful autonomy in their stories. In 'Vaghe Stelle dell'Orsa' by Clarice Tartufari, a young girl sets her sights on a young student staying with the family. Through her persistence and simplicity, she conquers his heart. Her parents have no say in her choice of a husband.[75] In the wake of transoceanic migration, these stories describing modern mothers and daughters echoed throughout the Sicilian countryside.

Changing Seasons

Mass male emigration disrupted the close links between late-nineteenth-century parenting ideals and the rhythms of agricultural life, where weddings and the birth of children revolved around planting, sowing, and harvesting. Male emigration changed the agricultural calendar to incorporate the rhythms of the industrial world.

Before 1900 Suteresi, like most Sicilians, lived in a world where time was measured in seasons.[76] They did not measure time by years, days, or hours. Rather, they marked it according to the cyclical rhythms of ploughing, planting, and harvesting. Rites of passage and rituals came and went in accordance with the seasons. In this world, little seemed to change from year to year, and few people harboured expectations that their lives would be different from those of their parents. People planned their lives on the premise that what had occurred the year before would happen the year after. The past predicted the future. Every year, townspeople planted their crops in fall, hoed their fields in spring, and harvested their wheat in summer, just as their parents had done, and just as their children would do when they were grown. Children replicated the lives of their parents, and life experiences were passed on from one generation to the next, yet with each individual life, new opportunities and choices appeared.[77]

In traditional agrarian societies, cyclical time coexists with linear time. Although each crop is the same, specific years stand out in the collective memory marked by disease, hailstorms, flooding, or political change. Linear time refers to a temporal structure where each event in a person's life is unique and impossible to replicate. In a society dominated by linear time, the primary life course is that of the individual, not the family or kin group. People move through their separate lives with few reference points in the past.[78] They recognize that people are different, but individual lives are placed in a communal and historical context. This combination of cyclical and linear time enables people to recognize and acknowledge gradual change, while providing precedents for their actions in a common past.

How a community constructs time shapes patterns of daily life. When people marry, when they have children, and even when they die are inextricably linked to the environment, to their work, and to their conception of time.[79] In Sutera at the turn of the century, the seasons affected the biological processes and cultural rituals that defined everyday life. In this society, work patterns were defined by gender, and cyclical constructions of time reinforced the separate worlds of men and women. Each season brought different tasks for men and for women. In conjunction with work, marriages, pregnancies, births, and deaths followed seasonal fluctuations, further dividing the ways men and women experienced their lives and the passage of time.

According to custom, the year in Sutera began each fall when the harvest was finished and debts were paid.[80] This was especially true for men. As soon as the wheat was harvested, communal festivities marked the end of the agricultural year. Residents celebrated the feast of Saint Onofrio, the patron saint of Sutera, on the second Sunday in August, and rural workers made a special effort to return home from the fields for it. Early fall was a time for negotiations, for renewing land contracts and planning for the next year. September was the most popular month for requesting passports; over half the applications were made in that month.[81] By October the men had returned to their fields to begin ploughing and planting so that the next season's crop would be in the ground by mid-December.[82] It is not coincidental that so many people married in the fall, the time of completion and renewal. In Sutera between 1880 and 1900, one-third of all marriages took place between September and early November (see Figure 3.1). People planned their weddings around the summer harvest. By late summer the men were back home and the townsfolk had the money and time to celebrate. The First of November, the Day of the Dead, marked the end of fall celebrations, after which the men retreated indoors to their homes or social clubs to wait out the rain.

For women, except for new brides, the fall was a continuation of the past year rather than the start of a new one. Women spent the autumn preserving and storing the year's harvest for the winter. While their husbands were in the fields planting the next crop, they passed the cool, sunny afternoons cracking almonds, readying flax for winter weaving, and harvesting grapes and olives. Their work was fixed in the present; in

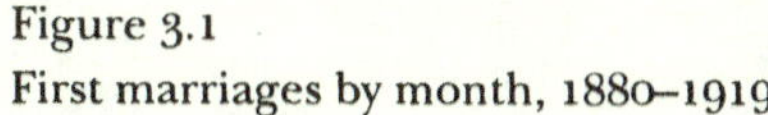

Figure 3.1
First marriages by month, 1880–1919

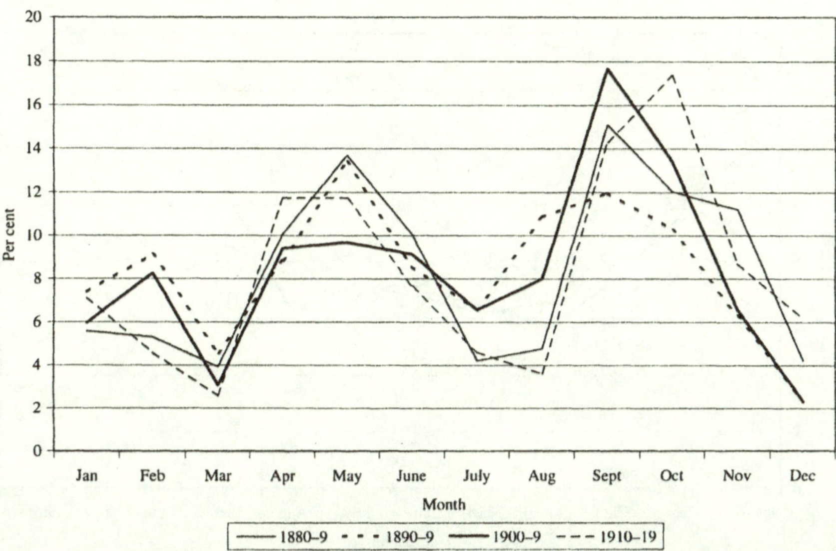

contrast, the men were planting next year's seed and dreaming about the future. Biology also tied women to the previous year: many women did this work in the last trimester of pregnancy. Nearly 20 per cent of the children born in Sutera each year arrived in September and October (see Figure 3.2).

The winter months marked the halfway point between sowing and harvesting. It was a time of waiting, when men watched the skies and hoped for a good harvest. There was little fieldwork to be done. On the few warm, sunny days, men would work in the family gardens planting fava beans and lentils. Only a few couples married in December. Religious law, bad weather, and fieldwork made it difficult to find a free day during the month to wed. The church did not perform marriages on holy days and prohibited weddings between the first Sunday of Advent and the Epiphany.[83] Couples could marry at city hall, but the marriage was not officially celebrated until after the holidays. By February the men from Sutera had returned to the countryside to cultivate the fields before the wheat grew too high.[84] Men passed these months alternating between working intensively in the fields and waiting for the wheat to grow or the rains to stop. Trapped in town, they gathered in the main plaza to discuss politics, exchange information, and plan the future.

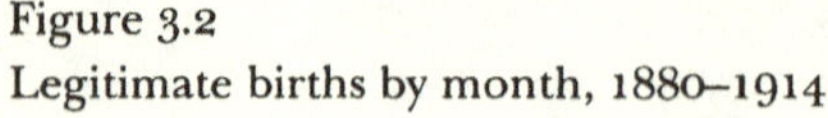

Figure 3.2
Legitimate births by month, 1880–1914

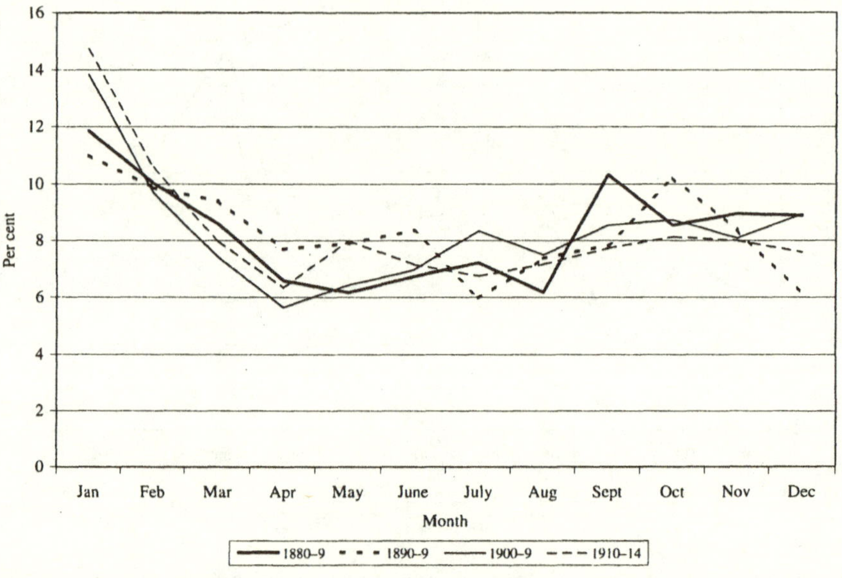

March was the second most popular month for men to apply for passports to emigrate.[85]

By late November, everything harvested in the fall had been dried, bottled, or preserved. When the rains came, women moved indoors, where they began spinning the flax gathered during the fall and waiting for children to be born.[86] Most of the children conceived the previous spring and summer were now due, and women were often called from their work to assist a neighbour, sister, or friend during labour. Birth rates began to climb in early December; they peaked in January, when over 11 per cent of all births for the year occurred see Figure 3.2). The cries of newborn babies brought a joyful end to the anxiety and fears that had haunted these women over the past nine months as they worked in the fields or bent over their looms. Each birth was greeted with great rejoicing and congratulations, and each new child changed a woman's position in the social hierarchy. Her first child enabled her to join the ranks of adult women and gain the respect and honour accompanying motherhood. Subsequent children symbolized the growth and success of her family. Men were equally proud parents. For them, however, these births may have further reinforced the sense of renewal that accompanied the late fall and early winter months, since they were virtually excluded from the processes of pregnancy and birth.

Winter was a time of death. The icy January rains seeped into the stone houses, making it difficult to keep warm. Infants and the elderly succumbed to pneumonia and other forms of respiratory failure.[87] Death was inextricably linked to birth cycles. Infant mortality rates were extremely high throughout the nineteenth century; in 1850, children under a year old comprised 30 per cent of deaths. There was an excellent chance that a baptism would be closely followed by a funeral. January reported the highest birth rates and the highest death rates, followed by March and August. In 1850, 15 per cent of the people who died were buried in January, and one-third of the funerals were for children under six months old.[88] And a child who survived to the first birthday had only a slim chance of seeing adulthood. Nearly half the people who died in 1850 were under ten.[89] This pattern of death changed little over the century. In 1899, well over half the people who died were under ten. The seasonal regularity of death continued into the twentieth century. In 1909 over 24 per cent of the deaths in Sutera occurred in January.[90]

Spring began when the March rains ended. Warmer weather ushered in a period of intense activity for rural men, who spent most of the month away from home, working in the wheatfields. By April, the wheat was nearly grown. There was little to do, and the men came home to hope, pray, and watch the sky. Like August and September, the next two months were popular times to marry. The family had survived another winter, and the future was promising. April was a busy time for the parish priests as couples posted their banns. Between 1850 and 1899, nearly 30 per cent of marriages were celebrated during late April, May, and early June (see Figure 3.1). By mid-June, the threshing had begun and there was little time for celebrations. This was the season for elopements rather than family festivities, as a family could ill afford to lose a son's labour during the harvest and usually accepted the marriage.[91] Spring celebrations symbolized people's faith in the future rather than expressions of thanks.

For women, spring marked the beginning of the year. By April women were starting to shift their attention – and their work – from the past year toward the next year. The past harvest was stored; the children conceived over the previous twelve months were born, and some were buried. The winter funerals tapered off. Women set up their looms in spring, and by May most had finished weaving. The old year was finally over. The spring weddings, combined with rising conception rates, marked a new cycle. For men, these weddings came right before the harvest and the end of their year.

The summer harvest closed the agricultural year, leaving the land washed out under the white-hot sun. By Saint Onofrio's feast day, the men were back home, their work finished once the wheat was sold at market. Women's work had just begun. Women had only just finished weaving the flax harvested the previous fall. In August, while their husbands gossiped in the main plaza, the women busied themselves bottling tomatoes and preparing for the next winter.[92] Like winter, midsummer was a time of death. Mortality rates rose. July and August were especially dangerous months for newborns and infants. The hot sun and the water shortages that plagued the town in August often led to severe diarrhea. Gastroenteritis was listed as the principal cause of death among infants during the summer.[93]

In Sutera, marriages, births, and deaths characterized each season as strongly as weather and work. The biological and economic influences on the annual calendar reinforced the sense that women and men lived their lives in separate but interdependent worlds. By the First World War, however, the traditional balance between cyclical and linear time had shifted. Changes in the global wheat market left many Sicilians scrambling to find supplemental work as wage labourers; they could no longer afford to rent enough land to make a living by sharecropping. In Sutera this meant that the agricultural year no longer began when leases were negotiated in the fall or clearly ended when the wheat was harvested in the summer. Weekly wages altered the patterns of work and redistributed the influx of cash in the local economy. Women's lives also changed as machine-made cloth, sewing machines, and canned foods made their way up the mountain. Many household chores and seasonal tasks disappeared, altering the traditional rhythms of housework and childcare that defined the worlds of wives and mothers. Migration did not cause this transformation, but it encouraged the transition to a consumer wage-labour economy and redefined women's roles in the family. By altering the timing of births and marriages, transoceanic migration weakened the influence of the agrarian calendar over rural women's lives and strengthened the importance of the industrial world in shaping the rhythms of daily life.

A cultural and temporal shift occurred when rural workers left their fields and farms to work in factories at home or abroad.[94] Factory work entailed a transformation of work skills, attitudes, and ultimately a community's perceptions of time. Most of the men of Sutera who arrived in

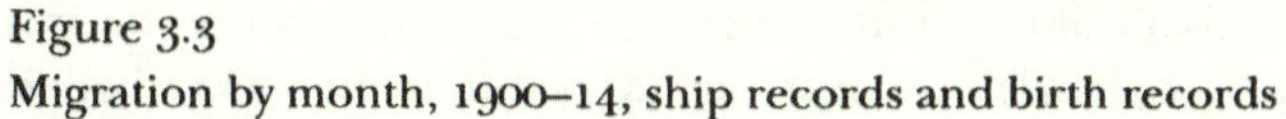

Figure 3.3
Migration by month, 1900–14, ship records and birth records

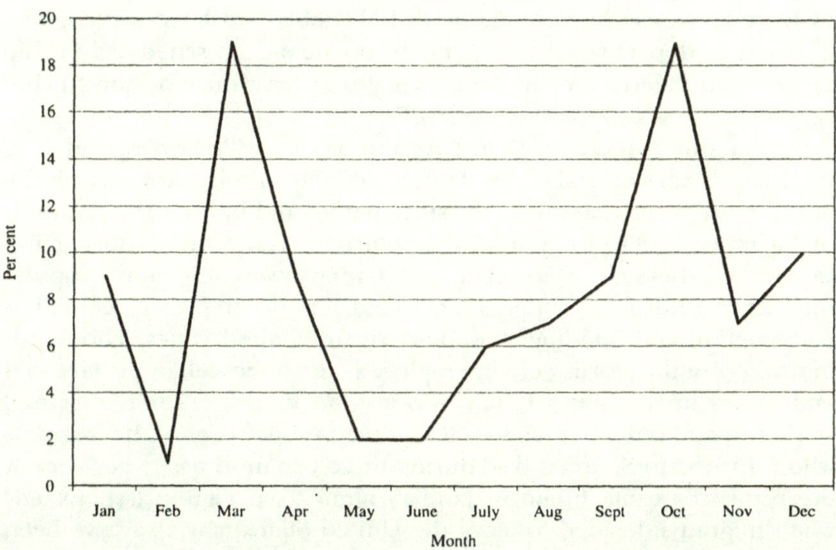

Pratt City or Thomasville had never worked under the watchful eye of a boss. As sharecroppers or part-time wage labourers at home, they rarely worked under close supervision.[95] In Alabama they had to be at work at a specific time and quit when the whistle blew. In the Birmingham district, most workers were employed year round, and the mines usually paid their wages at the end of the month or every two weeks. Pay was based on the quality and quantity of coal mined in an eight-hour day.[96] Each day mirrored the ones that came before. The work itself never varied with the seasons; the men performed the same tasks day after day. Weeks merged together, broken only by paydays.

The emigrants had to adjust their lives according to the requirements of 'industrial time'; even so, the demands of the steel mills and coal mines did not end the influence the agricultural calendar had on their lives, and patterns of migration reflect this. Emigrants from Sutera usually left in the early spring or in the fall after the harvest was sold at market. Rarely did anyone emigrate during the summer harvest, November, or February, when fieldwork was most intense (see Figure 3.3). March and September were the two most popular months to leave. A man who left in early spring could arrange for his fields to be harvested, and rest assured his family would survive the following winter in his absence. The spring crop also provided collateral for any loans needed to finance the trip to the United States. September was an excellent time to leave since the harvest was in and all debts had been settled. The decision to depart was not dependent on steamship schedules (a ship sailed from Palermo to the United States at least once a month), but rather on the seasons and the crops.[97]

The labour markets in Pratt City and Thomasville corresponded to the island's agricultural cycles. Patterns of return migration were influenced both by fluctuations in the steel market and by the rural economy of Sicily. Over 80 per cent of the returnees came home during five months of the year. December and January were the most popular months to return. In winter the demand for soft coal and steel fell as construction and building slowed across the United States. Thousands of workers in the North were unemployed, and wages fell in the factories and mines in the South.[98] This was a good time for a miner or mill worker to go home. Between 1908 and 1910, 47 per cent of the migrants who returned to Sutera did so during these two months; 37 per cent of the returnees came home in January alone (see Figure 3.4). Exactly when migrants decided to leave the United States may also have been influenced by the rural world they had left behind. Migrants who intended to remain in Sicily and farm probably tried hard to be home by mid-December at the latest, in time to buy land and plant their fields for the following year. People who were homesick could spend the Christmas holidays with their families. March, May, and June were also popular months to come home. Decisions to return home in spring were probably influenced more by the agricultural calendar than by fluctuations in the steel and coal industries. These were among the three busiest months in the fields for Suteresi, and emigrants who returned were guaranteed steady work. Back-and-forth migration forged links between the two worlds, gradually transforming the seasonal rhythms for people who lived on both sides of the Atlantic.

The wives of emigrants, like the emigrants themselves, adjusted their lives to the demands of the new economic order. Throughout the nineteenth century, marriages, pregnancies, and births had been linked to the agricultural calendar; now, seasonal patterns of emigration were influencing when women married and when their children were born. Although no one yet has studied the relationship between migration and patterns of marriage and childbirth, it is clear that transoceanic migration changed the traditional relationships between biology, work, and the environment that had shaped women's lives for generations.

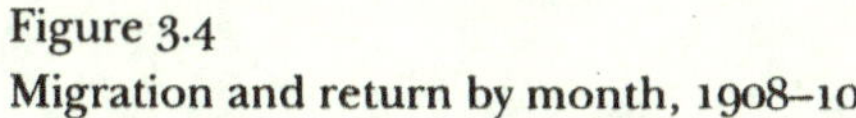

Figure 3.4
Migration and return by month, 1908–10

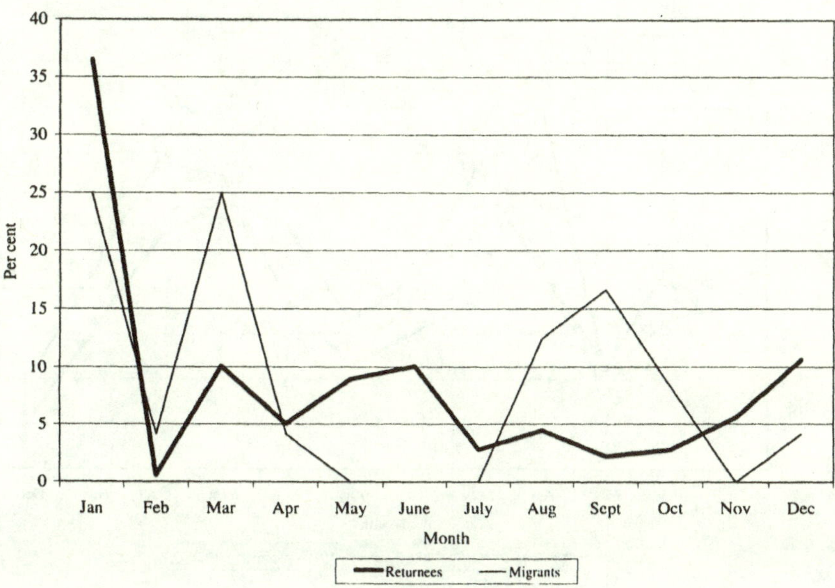

Marriage patterns in Sutera began to change shortly after the turn of the century. Between the 1890s and 1920s, more Suteresi chose to marry in the fall (see Figure 3.5). Marriages began to cluster around the months of April, September, and October. In the 1890s less than one-quarter of marriages took place in September and October. Between 1900 and 1919 nearly one-third of marriages were celebrated in those two months alone. Spring ceremonies were also growing in popularity. In contrast to the nineteenth century more people were choosing to marry in April and May rather than May and June. These changes were partly a consequence of the new economic opportunities opening overseas.

Migration seems to have affected the seasonal concentration of marriages. As Figure 3.6 illustrates, women married to migrant men were more likely to marry in early spring or fall and less likely to marry in winter. Among these couples there was a sharp decline in the number of people who decided to marry after May, compared to a steady increase of marriages through June among couples where the husband stayed home.

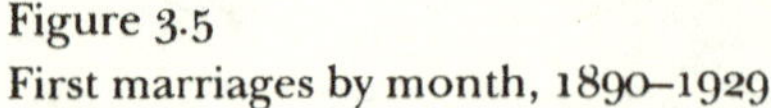

Figure 3.5
First marriages by month, 1890–1929

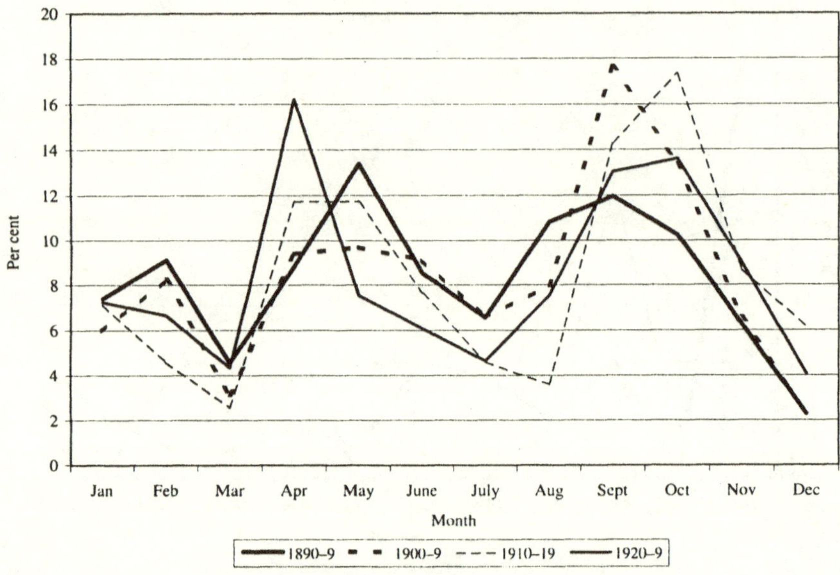

The intention to emigrate was an important factor in marriage plans. Women who bid farewell to their husbands shortly after the wedding usually married in April or July, shortly before or after the harvest (see Figure 3.7). Over 20 per cent of marriages where the groom went abroad were celebrated during these months, compared to 12 per cent where the groom had no plans to emigrate. Return migration had a different effect on the seasonal concentration of marriages, causing weddings to cluster around two months, April and September. Nearly half the men who returned to Sutera married during these two months. Returning migrants rarely married during the harvest months or between October and December – traditionally popular times to marry.

Transoceanic migration also affected reproduction, weakening the effects of agriculture on patterns of conception and births. Women married to migrants no longer conceived their children according to the rhythms of the agricultural calendar alone. Pregnancies and births were linked to migration patterns. Since the decision to migrate was tied to the rural economy, there was no decisive change in fertility, but rather a gradual shift in seasonal concentrations.

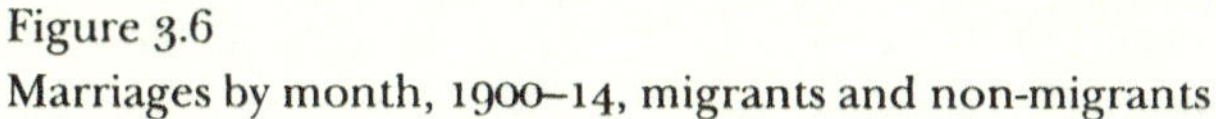

Figure 3.6
Marriages by month, 1900–14, migrants and non-migrants

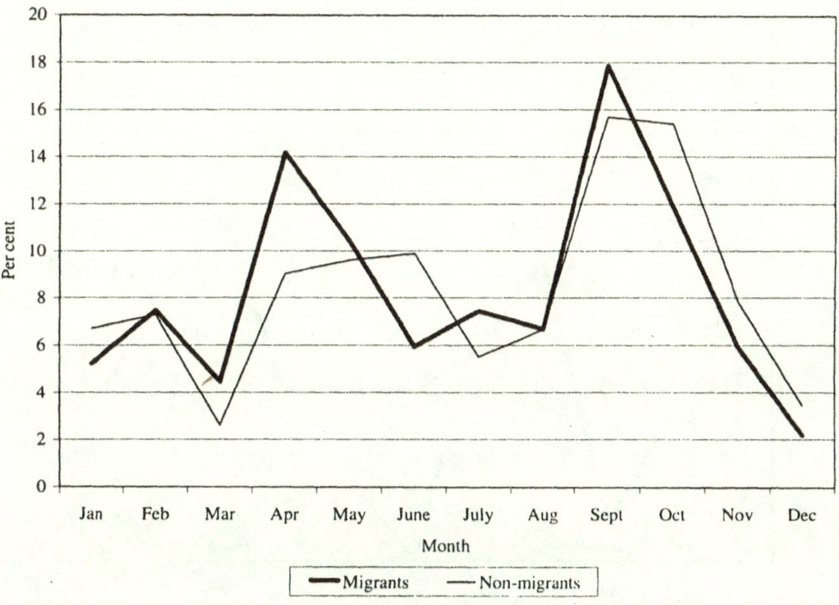

Women married to emigrants were far more likely than other women to get pregnant in October, December, February, and March, and less likely to conceive a child in April. These months coincided with patterns of migration. Nearly 40 per cent of the emigrants who returned came home in January, and over one-quarter of the emigrants left town in March and April. Both these factors influenced the higher number of conceptions in February (see Figure 3.8). Men who were working in Sutera usually spent most of February in the fields far from home, so traditionally it was a time when fewer children were conceived. Spring emigration offset the effects that migrants who returned in the spring to marry had on the number of children conceived. Women married to migrants conceived more children in May than other women. Emigration seems to have delayed the traditional decline in spring conceptions and shortened the time before rates began to rise again. The intention to emigrate in September and October affected the number of women who got pregnant in the fall. Conception rates for women married to migrants fluctuated greatly in the fall months, relative to women whose

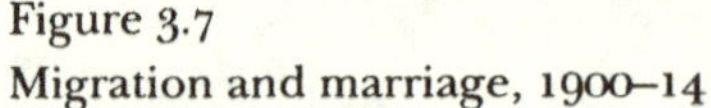

Figure 3.7
Migration and marriage, 1900–14

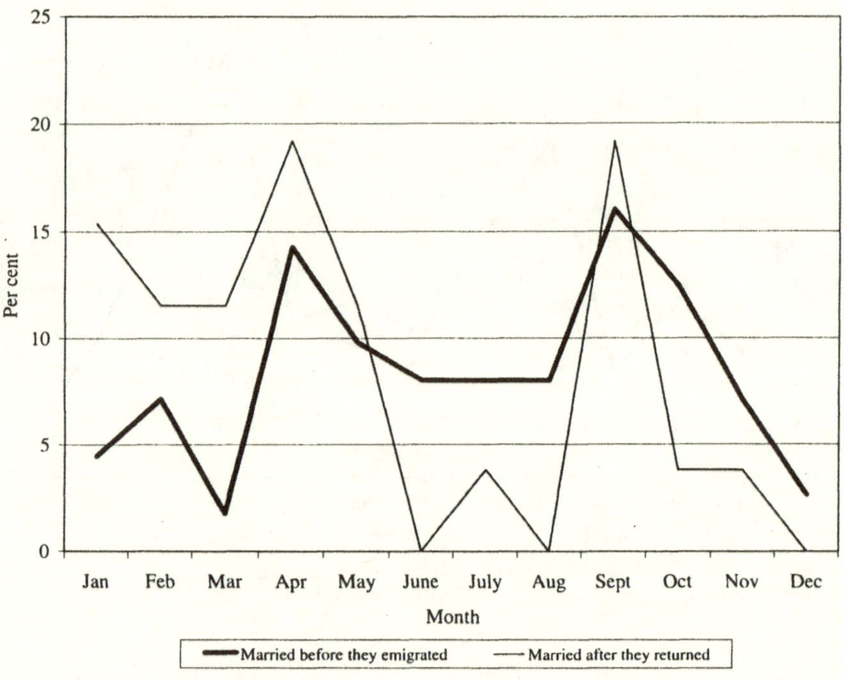

husbands did not emigrate. The reproductive cycles of women married to migrants no longer conformed to the fertility patterns that characterized couples who had no intention of emigrating. Like their sisters, women married to emigrants usually conceived their children in the spring and fall; however, the cycle was no longer tied only to the agrarian calendar.

Even these slight changes in patterns of conception affected the timing of births and the rhythms of a woman's year. Women married to migrants had more children in the fall and fewer children in the winter than women whose husbands stayed home (see Figure 3.9). This meant that more women than usual were tending newborns in September and November – usually the busiest time of year for women. The high number of conceptions in October increased the number of births in July, when infant mortality rates were also high. Migration changed the

Figure 3.8
Migration and conception, 1900–14

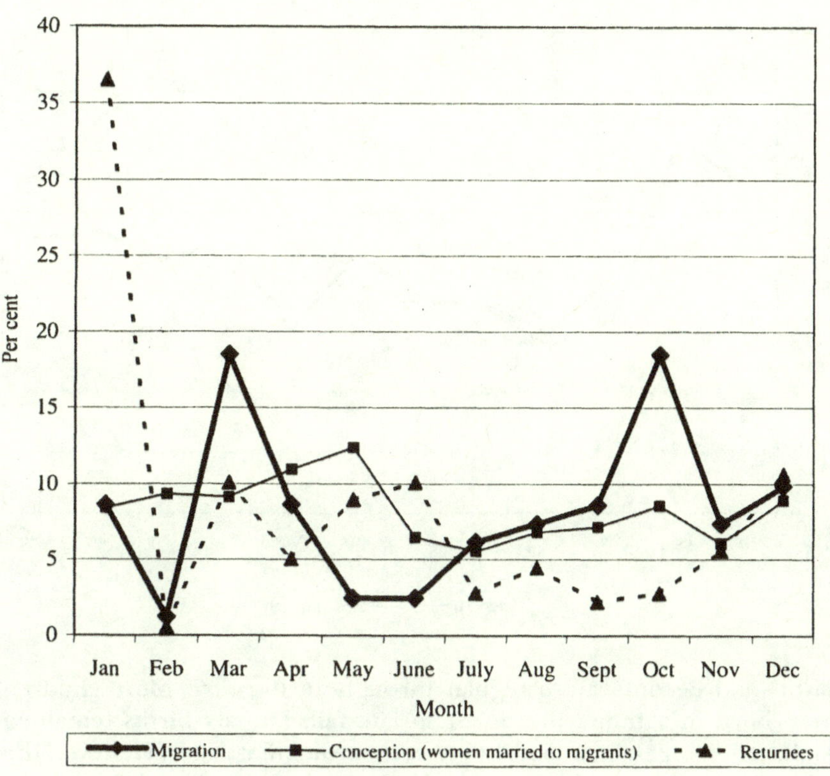

seasonal cycles that shaped women's lives, just as it redefined the relationship between men and the seasons.

Emigration softened the impact of the agricultural calendar on decisions to marry and have children, but did not eliminate it.[99] In rural communities like Sutera, industrialization did not destroy traditional rhythms of daily life; rather, it changed the foundation of the cycles, merging factory time with agrarian seasons. Transoceanic migration was not the only factor influencing decisions regarding marriage and family. Changes in the rural economy also had an impact. The shift to wage work began to eliminate the sharp seasonal concentrations that characterize the traditional calendar. By the First World War, the timing of

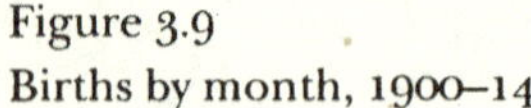

Figure 3.9
Births by month, 1900–14

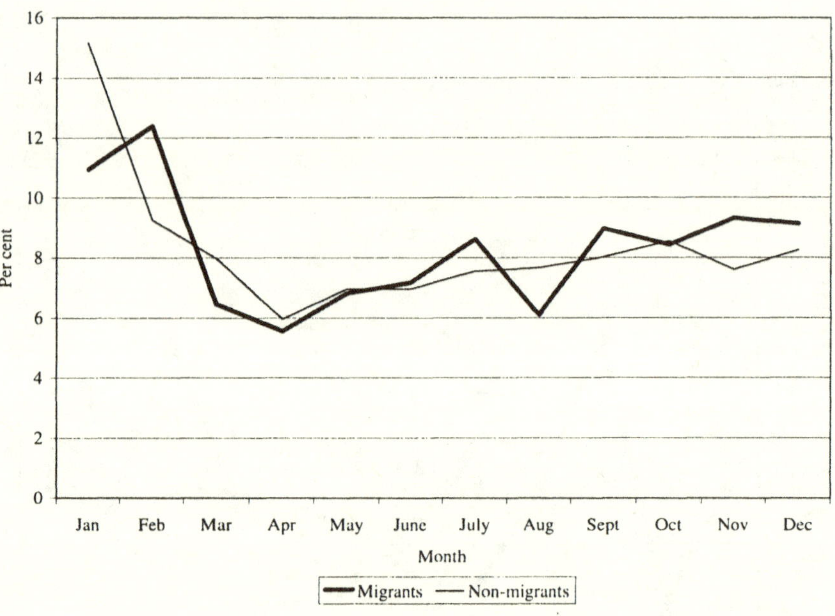

births had become more regular throughout the year. More children were born in summer and fewer in late fall. January births remained high, reflecting the general shift to early spring marriages. However, the integration of Sutera into the global economy through male migration and wage labour changed how women experienced marriage and childbirth.

Today in Sutera the effects of migration on the rhythms of rural life are still visible. Every August the sons, daughters, brothers, and sisters of the townspeople all come home to celebrate the feast of Saint Onofrio. Most European factories, governments, and retail establishments close by 15 August, and Suteresi rush home to honour their patron saint and bask on the nearby beaches. For a few weeks each year, Sutera is transformed into a cosmopolitan town as the streets fill with the sounds of English, German, Sicilian, and Italian. People still plan their weddings around the return of the migrants, just as they once set the date according to the harvest. As one resident told me, August is a good time to marry as the emigrants return bearing generous gifts. Just as in the nineteenth century, the middle of August is a time of celebration – only now the holiday is based on factory hours and not on the harvest.

Debates surrounding transoceanic migration focused on the demographic effects on Italy's population. Most people feared that long-term separations would inevitably result in higher illegitimacy rates and a general decline in fertility. Yet in Sutera, male emigration enabled women to have more legitimate children than otherwise would have been possible. Economic and social conditions informed reproductive decisions; as one result, women married to emigrants sought to recreate the families of the wealthy. These men and women saw in transatlantic migration the possibility of achieving success in traditional terms. However, the long-standing cultural codes connecting fecundity with wealth began to change. This was first visible among the local elite, then among artisans. The first residents to migrate were most resistant to these changes; their long-term strategies were firmly linked to traditional conceptions of success. Migration encouraged couples to initially have larger families, and only later to limit their families; it also redefined women's domestic roles. Mass male migration altered the image of the ideal mother and the actual experience of motherhood. Smaller families and a new emphasis on education and social mobility meant that mothers experienced different physical and emotional responsibilities. Mass male emigration did not immediately lower birth rates or undermine the institution of marriage, as so many critics predicted; however, it did have a profound effect on notions of marriage and family. By linking marriages and births to rhythms of the industrial world, transoceanic migration tied these rural women to a radically new economy and society. Even through these women never migrated, worked in factories, or moved to large cities, they participated in one of the most significant events associated with industrialization – the decline of fertility and the shift to smaller families.

Chapter Four

Fulfilling the Dream: Houses, Land, and Work

By 1910, American money had begun to transfigure the face of rural Italy. Each year, emigrants sent home millions of lire from the Americas. Back home their families used this money to pay off family debts, build new houses, open small businesses, and buy land. By using the money to change where they lived and worked, rural men and women sought to realize the migrant dream.[1] Houses built by these 'Americans' were considered the visible symbols of a family's and a community's material success and moral improvement. Responding to a survey sent out by the Royal Italian Agricultural Commission, the mayor of San Giovanni in Fiore wrote: 'Most of the houses are very dirty; only in the high quarter of the town are there many new and clean houses, without pigs, mules or chickens in the interior. These were built by peasants who returned from America, so that one must admit that if a little civilization has penetrated into this district, it is certainly exclusively owing to emigration.'[2] Land also conferred status and respect on individuals and communities. If, after the migrant returned, family members continued to work as day labourers or sharecroppers on another man's land, the emigration enterprise had failed. Though land ownership was the surest way of joining the elite, it was also the most difficult. Lack of arable land combined with inflated prices made acquisition costly. Often migrants and their families opened a small dry-goods store and purchased a small piece of land instead of waiting until they could afford enough land to live comfortably off the rents. These new homes and new businesses were physical monuments to the changes brought to rural Italy as a consequence of mass migration.

Rural women played a critical role in this transformation. In southern agrotowns, mass male migration enabled women to participate in the real estate market as consumers at a time when the number of female property owners seemed to be declining. Though Sicilian women had long appeared in the land and housing cadastre, they usually inherited their property from their families. In the late nineteenth century, the number of women in the property registers seemed to be declining, a consequence of changing inheritance patterns. Increasingly, those women who continued to register new properties tended to appear in the housing cadastre as purchasers rather than heirs. Remittances helped slow the disappearance of women in real estate markets by providing the means to buy new properties. Most women invested their family's first savings in housing – a reflection of cultural ideals, individual interests, and economic realities. Arable land was expensive and difficult to find, especially for women; it was easier to buy or build houses. The quick appearance of these 'new and clean' homes testifies to the role women played in investing money earned in the Americas.

Women also used remittances to carve out new work opportunities. While Italian students of mass migration predicted that rural women, abandoned by their husbands, would be forced to leave their homes to earn a living in the wheatfields, creating a new class of female wage workers, it was clear by the First World War that this was not happening.[3] As a consequence of mass male migration, rural women were able to participate in the changing rural economy as entrepreneurs and professionals rather than as wage workers. These women from the small towns of southern Italy chose not to sail overseas, and not to join the growing number of female factory workers in northern cities. Instead they participated actively in the expanding world economy.

Buying and selling houses and land altered women's position within local and national economies. Larger homes required furnishings; dressers, mirrors, rugs, and lamps were ordered from local craftsmen and big-city department stores. With their access to ready cash and their new businesses, these rural female consumers and entrepreneurs drove the creation of a consumer culture that altered social and economic relations between regional, national, and global markets at the beginning of the twentieth century. Remittances transformed the economic position of women but did not radically alter class or sex-specific notions regarding the nature of work. In certain respects, transoceanic migration was a conservative force, buttressing deep-rooted attitudes associating property ownership with the wealthy and field work with the poor or immoral. 'Women's work' remained centred in the home. The cultural and social meanings of work continued to reflect the unequal hierarchy that characterized relations between men and women.[4]

Women and Property

Sicilian women had long been property owners. Unlike in other rural Italian regions, many Sicilian women owned a house or a small piece of land at some point in their lives. Throughout the nineteenth century, houses and land were often included in women's dowries or as part of their inheritance. Women also purchased property. According to the 1881 census, Sicilian women comprised 38 per cent of property owners, and 13 per cent of all women living on the island held property in their own name.[5] Although women held all kinds of property, the vast majority owned houses. In Sutera women were registered as sole or partial owners of 27 per cent of the property acquired in 1881. These women comprised more than 14 per cent of the resident female population.[6] Cultural and social strictures defining women's lives in terms of family and household combined with land tenure patterns to reinforce sex-specific patterns of real estate.

Every Sicilian family sought to own a home. Ownership provided a sense of security; it also marked a family's social status. Even a miserable one-room hovel, sheltering family members and animals under the same roof, eased fears of eviction. In the 1890s the poorest Suteresi lived in dark and smoky one-room, one-storey houses where the mule's manger stood next the kitchen table and chickens huddled under the bed. Most residents lived in two-storey, two-room houses, where the first floor served as a stable and tool shed and the upstairs room as the living quarters. The houses of those who were somewhat better off had at least three rooms upstairs – a bedroom, a kitchen, and a pantry – while the wealthy lived in two or three storey houses with many rooms.[7] In 1894 Lorenzo C., a landowner and politician worth more than 30,000 lire, lived in a two-storey, seven-room house that his wife had inherited.[8] Home ownership and house size were measures of a family's honour and a visual symbol of its economic and social position.

In central Sicily, houses were the centrepieces of marriage contracts, bequests, and commercial transactions. In some rural hilltowns a bride's dowry included a house. If the bride's family was unable or unwilling to provide a house for the newlyweds, the groom's family furnished one. In the 1880s, roughly one-quarter of all women held a house in their own

A view of the Sicilian hills from Sutera. (David Tager)

name. At the end of the nineteenth century, 35 per cent of the women who registered buildings in Sutera acquired their property as part of an inheritance, a dowry, or a gift.[9] Once married, women worked to save enough money to buy or build a bigger house and provide housing for their own children. In rural Sicily a woman's ability to provide a house for her daughter was an important factor in securing a good son-in-law. In the nineteenth century more than 40 per cent of Suteran women registering property reported purchasing or building a new home. Nearly 60 per cent of the houses purchased in the 1880s were passed on to children.[10] The presence of women in the real estate market reflected the deep-rooted belief that fieldwork was men's work and that a family's land – its economic support – should be held by its menfolk. Women's lives, centred on childcare, domestic tasks, and weaving, revolved around the physical structure of the house; thus, female home ownership was a seemingly natural arrangement.

A few Sicilian women owned land. In Sutera, women appeared in 17 per cent of the land transactions recorded in the cadastre between 1870 and 1900. These women represented nearly one-quarter of Sutera's female population in 1881.[11] Most women who owned property received their lands as part of their marriage settlement or an inheritance. Rarely did women purchase land on their own. Lands held by women tended to be quite small. The average size was two acres, and the plot was usually located on the outskirts of town and used to grow the family's fruits and vegetables. The value of the property rarely exceeded more than a few lire. Only a handful of women from wealthy families received large tracts of valuable land suitable for growing wheat and other cash crops when they married. When Giovanna S. married into the Bongiorno family, one of the most powerful families in the valley, her father gave her more than 33 acres of land. Her holdings alone comprised nearly one-third of all the land registered to women in the 1880s. Giovanna S. retained control of her property until the 1920s, when she sold portions to her neighbours. Giovanna, however, was an exceptional case. Women seldom inherited the family's large wheatfields, and even when they did, they often turned ownership over to their sons, reserving use rights for themselves. Carolina G., Giovanna S.'s mother-in-law, inherited her husband's property after he died in 1893. The widow immediately named her two sons as joint proprietors, and retained use rights for herself until her death in 1907. Women's roles as mothers and wives framed land ownership. Female landowners usually held small plots, which they used for kitchen gardens. Only among the wealthiest landowning families did women possess profitable wheatfields, and even then these women commonly turned their possessions over to their sons.

One consequence of Sicily's new place in the global marketplace was that property was removed from women's dowries and women gradually disappeared from property markets.[12] Between 1880 and 1920, patterns of female property ownership in Sutera and Milocca began to change. Fewer women inherited property from their families when they married or after their parents died. The 1890s were pivotal years in this transition. During the 1870s, 15 per cent of women in Sutera registered the acquisition of a building. By the 1880s, only 7 per cent of women appeared in the cadastre. In the 1890s only 5 per cent of the women were active in real estate, and by 1911 the presence of women in the housing market had fallen to less than 3 per cent.[13] This sharp decline was partly a consequence of fewer women inheriting property. Between 1890 and 1910 the percentage of women in the housing records who received a house as part of their inheritance or their dowry or as a gift fell from 37 per cent to 28 per cent.[14] The 1890s saw the sharpest decline in the number of houses dowered to village women. In the 1880s nearly 10 per cent of the houses registered to women were marriage gifts; a decade later only 5 per cent of the houses transferred to women were part of a dowry. By 1910, few women could count on inheriting a house. Between 1880 and 1900, nearly one-quarter of all women who registered a house received the property as a bequest from a parent or relative. In the first two decades of the twentieth century, only around 11 per cent of the buildings registered to women had been inherited from family.

By the turn of the century, those women still appearing in the cadastres were more likely buying or building a new house. The percentage of women in the housing market rose from 36 per cent to 64 per cent by 1910. Increased demand stimulated sales and new constructions. Hundreds of residents of Sutera were left homeless after a rockslide destroyed the neighbourhood of Rabato in 1905. In addition, the families of the first Suteresi who emigrated at the turn of the century had saved enough money to build additions or buy larger houses.

Changing inheritance patterns had a similar effect on women's ownership of land. As the nineteenth century came to an end, land cadastres reported a noticeable decline in the number of women receiving land as part of their patrimony, and a slight increase in the proportion of women purchasing land. In the 1890s, dowered properties accounted for 17 per cent of land registered to women. By the first decade of the 1900s, they comprised only 8 per cent of the lands held by women. As the proportion of women who inherited land fell, there was an increase in the number of women who purchased land on their own or jointly with their husbands. In Sutera between 1890 and 1900, the percentage of women who bought land increased from 21 per cent to 53 per cent of all female landowners. As in the housing market, the shift from inheritance to commercial transactions seemed to curtail women's real estate activity.

While women in general withdrew from all real estate markets, property records show that mass male migration played an important role in keeping rural women in the housing market. The story of Rosario M. and his wife Paolina B. illustrates the ways women utilized money from abroad to fulfil their dreams at home. Rosario M. left Sicily in December 1908 aboard the *San Giorgio* bound for New York, on his way to Birmingham, Alabama.[15] During his years overseas he worked hard and sent most of his wages home. Within a year Paolina B. had saved enough money to start construction on a two-storey, two-room house in the centre of town. Workers began building in the summer of 1909 and completed the house in November, just in time for her to move in before winter.[16] During these months Rosario M. continued to work overseas and send his savings home. When he returned, the couple began searching for a plot of land. This proved to be far more difficult. There were few small plots available, since most of the arable land was owned by large landowners. The few pieces that were available were being sold at highly inflated prices fuelled by the demands of returning emigrants.

Throughout the first decade of the twentieth century, men like Rosario sent home the fruits of their labour and self-deprivation. Savings accounts swelled. In 1907, migrants from the district of Caltanissetta sent their families nearly two million lire by registered mail, insured letters, and international money orders; the average migrant was saving five hundred lire a year.[17] By 1902, district officials from all corners of Sicily were reporting a huge influx of cash into local banks and post office savings accounts.[18] Critics and supporters of migration pointed to the estimated five hundred million lire flooding into the Italian economy from abroad as the main benefit of temporary transoceanic migration. In 1907, emigrants sent more than fifty-five million lire to Sicily through international money orders from the Banco di Napoli.[19]

Rural Sicilians deposited their money in postal savings banks or *casse rurali* (rural banking cooperatives) until they were ready to invest in property. Savings deposits rose from approximately four million to more than six million lire between 1902 and 1906.[20] Families used a small portion of their remittances to cover their pressing needs and to pay off any debts incurred financing the voyages of family members. After this, they used some of the remaining money to improve their housing, then saved the rest to invest in land.[21] In Sutera, deposits in the Cassa Rurale di San Paolino and the Banca Popolare rose dramatically between 1905 and 1920. These savings institutions provided low-interest loans to their members. The Cassa Rurale di San Paolino was the oldest and largest cooperative in Sutera, founded on 14 May 1903 by Giuseppe Nicastro. The original membership list had only twelve names. By 1907 more then 230 men had joined, and each member paid two lire in annual dues. Deposits in the bank earned interest of 5 to 6 per cent. In 1907 the bank reported more than 60,000 lire in deposits; by 1920 it was holding deposits amounting to 939,206 lire. It offered loans at an interest rate of 7 per cent. In Milocca, the Cassa Rurale 'San Giuseppe 'was established in 1907 with fourteen active members. Within two years its membership had risen to nearly two hundred and it had two full-time employees and nearly 20,000 lire on deposit, not including the money lent to members or already invested in land.[22]

The influx of cash created new opportunities for Sicilian women. As household managers, they saved or invested the money as they saw fit, often before their husbands returned from overseas. Most women used the money to purchase or build a new home as soon as possible. Just over 60 per cent of migrants' wives bought a house between 1900 and 1920 (See Table 4.1). Another 16 per cent built a new house or added a second floor to one they already owned. Only 10 per cent of the women reported receiving a house as a gift or as part of an inheritance. In contrast, fewer than half the women whose husbands remained in Sutera purchased property, and only 10 per cent built new houses or renovated their old ones. Women whose husbands stayed in Sutera were more likely to acquire a house as part of their patrimony than to buy it themselves. American dollars allowed rural Sicilian women to improve their families' lives significantly; and breathed new life into women's real estate opportunities.

The visibility of the wives of migrants in the housing records shows that women had some independent control over remittances. Like Paolina B., many of these women did not wait for their husbands to return before buying a new house or renovating their old one. Nearly one-quarter of the women on the housing cadastre whose husbands were working overseas registered new or renovated houses while their husbands were gone. One-fifth of all sales transactions were undertaken by

TABLE 4.1
Property ownership (buildings) by women and migration

Type of acquisition	Year of acquisition 1880–9	1890–9	1900–9	1910–9	1920–9
Women married to migrants					
Inheritance, gift, dowry, division	0.00%	0.00%	16.67%	5.26%	11.76%
Sale	0.00	100.00	72.22	52.63	64.71
New construction	0.00	0.00	11.11	21.05	0.00
Other	0.00	0.00	0.00	21.05	23.53
Women not married to migrants					
Inheritance, gift, dowry, division	36.49%	39.29%	30.25%	25.81%	0.65%
Sale	27.70	32.14	52.10	45.16	44.57
New construction	21.62	0.00	9.24	11.83	1.09
Other	14.86	28.57	8.40	17.20	33.70

Source: Catasto dei Fabbricati – Sutura, 1870–1930, in Archivio di Stato Caltanissetta; information on migrant's families from migrant file.

these women while their husbands were absent. Even when women waited for their husbands to return before purchasing a house, the property was usually registered in both names. More than two-thirds of the women married to migrants who bought a house between 1900 and 1920 were registered as joint owners with their husbands.[23]

The wives of migrants used remittances to increase their purchasing power in the housing market; they were unable to accomplish the same in the land market. Male migration did little to reverse the gradual disappearance of women from the land registers. Rarely did migrants' wives invest their family savings in the large tracts of arable land – land that was at the centre of families' dreams of social advancement. When these women bought land, they tended to buy the same small garden plots that women used to inherit in the previous century. The average size of the plots purchased by the wives of migrants, alone or jointly with their husbands, was less than one acre. Sometimes women invested a small amount of money in land before their husbands returned. In 1910, one year after her husband sailed to the Americas, Paolina I. purchased two very small pieces of land on the edge of town; combined, they amounted to less than one-tenth of an acre.[24] In 1909, Assunta C., whose husband had left seven years earlier, bought four plots of land that combined were even smaller than Paolina I.'s. The land these women purchased provided food for the family – vegetables, olive oil, and fruits – but it did not help them achieve their dream of becoming landowners, able to live comfortably off rents.[25]

Women whose husbands remained home actually acquired larger tracts of land: on average, they registered three-acre parcels of land. Class accounts for this disparity. While the wives of migrants were the daughters of agricultural workers, masons, or tailors; many of these other women recorded in the land cadastre were the daughters of some of the wealthiest men in Sutera. In 1907, Carmela G, the widow of a prominent industrialist, bought more than thirty-five acres of land. The widow of Ignazio N., a notary public who had been a member of the city council, bought twenty-four acres in her own name, most of which she passed on to her sons within a few years.[26] These women from wealthy families, who were married to prominent men, inflated the holdings of women whose husbands did not migrate. Most of the wives, widows, and daughters of sharecroppers and day labourers were unable to purchase more than an acre or two whether their husbands migrated or stayed home. Male emigration made only a slight difference to a woman's ability to purchase land. Whether they had access to cash or not, cultural codes and the scarcity of available land limited a woman's access to the most profitable lands.

The sharp gender divisions that characterized rural society influenced how women invested their family savings. Land represented the world of men. A man's relationship to the fields, as owner, overseer, renter, or worker, marked his place in the community. Women's social worth was measured by their children and houses and were excluded from fieldwork and from direct access to information about the quality and quantity of available lands. In their travels between the fields and their homes, men exchanged rumours of impending sales, rentals, or wage work. Sharecroppers exchanged information about land transactions when they met on the threshing floor to negotiate their annual contracts, or in the main square as they strolled on Sunday afternoons. Day labourers surely kept one another apprised of the latest transactions when they gathered in the predawn light in the main square, hoes in hand, waiting for the estate representatives to arrive with weekly or daily job offers.[27] Rural women were cut off from this male information and employment network. They had to rely on their own contacts in town to get information about property: nearly 40 per cent of the women who bought land between 1900 and 1919 purchased their property from other women.[28] The land that circulated through these women's networks tended to be garden plots inherited during the nineteenth century. Typically, these lands were on rocky hillsides near town, suitable for olive groves, orchards, prickly pears, and flax. These lands grew household crops for family use – literally, 'domestic' crops.

Even if women had the desire and the means, the scarcity of available farmland severely limited their ability purchase any. The latifundia system kept the most fertile lands in the hands of a few. In the province of Caltanissetta, one estate owner held over 60 per cent of the land.[29] Information and money were not enough to break up the latifundia, and the influx of ready cash at first only exacerbated the problem by inflating the price of properties that were available. By 1910, emigrants' savings and demand made it nearly impossible to find affordable land for sale in Sutera.[30] Almost unanimously, district officials told Lorenzoni that 'the principal causes for the increased price of land were: more requests for land following the return of emigrants; and the improved conditions of the families that had remained in the village.'[31] The lack of available land is evident in the number of transactions recorded in the land cadastre of Sutera. Between 1900 and 1909, residents registered 1,321 land transactions. Over the next decade, Suteresi reported 1,071 new registrations despite the increased demand and available cash.

In the short term, mass migration, like the rural uprisings of the 1890s and the land reforms of the nineteenth century, had little impact on land tenure patterns, apart from raising prices. Many reformers held out great hope that mass migration would force the local gentry to break up their vast holdings and allow a larger class of small landowners to develop. But instead of selling off land, the gentry responded to the loss of labour by taking land out of production.[32] It was not until the savings accumulated by migrants in cooperative lending institutions combined with postwar protests to restructure agrarian contracts that land tenure patterns began to change. In the countryside around Sutera, conditions began to improve after 1920, when rural men and women joined together demanding land reform and occupying the surrounding estates.[33]

Not everyone agreed that women's ability to buy land was limited by culture, access to information, and lack of lands. Some critics suggested that rural women were stubbornly refusing to invest their family savings in profitable land far from town and were actively discouraging their husbands from acquiring wheatfields. In 1933, Enrico Taddei wrote:

> The reasons that peasant families do not want to move into the countryside are not only found in the usual problems of security, poor hygiene, etc. ...

> but principally in the fact that women, used to living in town do not want to adapt to the solitary life of the country. They prefer to remain far from their husbands – who live uncomfortably from Monday to Saturday in their wood huts, where they are forced to cook for themselves – rather than give up town life, where most of their time is spent in *gossiping* with the other women.[34]

Women, they argued, would rather undermine their family's economic condition than lose their support networks by moving to the countryside. In their analysis, migrants' wives were responsible for the failure of transnational migration to redistribute land.

For whatever reason, migration did little to change assumptions that landed property reflected a man's honour and that houses marked a woman's status. If anything, women married to migrants were even more reluctant than their sisters whose husbands never left to invest in wheatfields or cash crops. As long as her husband was abroad, no woman could risk any action that might tarnish her reputation or cast a shadow on her honour. Activities associated with land that fell outside traditional patterns of female ownership could easily undermine a woman's status in the community. And if women *had* invested any savings in wheatfields, their families would have been hard pressed to make ends meet. Rarely were remittances or incomes from land enough to pay the rising wages of hired hands. Returnees found it difficult to make a profit out of the land they bought even when they worked it themselves. Often they ended up selling the land they had worked so hard to buy, and emigrated again, disillusioned and disappointed.[35] Whether a consequence of cultural codes or availability of land, Sicilians chose to invest their money in houses rather than land. By 1907 nearly twice as many Sicilians owned houses as owned land – the opposite of property patterns for the rest of Italy.[36]

Women's ability to use remittances to buy properties redefined their economic roles in the community. As consumers, they increased their social and economic clout. When a woman bought a new house, it was more than just a home: it represented the opportunity to purchase the physical appearances of the bourgeois world. Emigrants' wives did not settle for just any house. They searched for roomy two-storey houses, preferably with a small kitchen off one room. The average house registered by the wives of migrants had two stories and two rooms. The average size of the buildings owned by women whose husbands did not migrate was one floor.[37] Often it was difficult to find an acceptable house to purchase, so the wives of migrants, like other women in town, settled for smaller, one-storey houses. Some women, like Maria P., were unwilling to compromise. In 1909 she and her husband, who had just returned from America, built a three-storey, three-room house with a small separate kitchen. For many women in Sutera the money sent home by their husbands meant they could realize their dreams of living like the *signore*, in large houses with separate bedrooms, kitchens, and living areas. The houses registered in the land cadastres between 1900 and 1909 emigrants' wives had an average net worth twice that of the houses owned by women whose husbands did not migrate.[38]

A new house was merely the first step toward social advancement. As soon as families moved into their new homes, they replaced their old furnishings with iron bedsteads, dining-room tables, and ornate dressers. Mirrors were hung on the walls, and floors were covered in carpets. Charlotte Gower Chapman noted that by 1928 a few women in Milocca even owned sewing machines.[39] When Maria P. moved into her new home with a separate kitchen, she probably built a tile stove with a chimney, the best kitchen stove available in the region, according to Gower Chapman.[40] Good furniture, and a lot of it, was yet another mark of prosperity and status. Kitchens in particular carried a great deal of significance. Even today some women have two kitchens in their homes: one is outfitted with the most modern appliances and is mostly for show; the other is smaller and has a small range and sink for daily use. The money sent home from overseas enabled rural women to purchase more things for the home, along with enough space to display them. By the First World War, American money was bringing modern consumer goods into the most remote hill towns of Sicily.

Male migration provided rural women with a new entrance into the rapidly changing rural economy. They could no longer rely on patrimonial gifts of property, but they could use cash to purchase houses and land on their own. This encouraged rural women to see themselves as consumers rather than producers or wage earners, and as household overseers and managers. This in turn altered their familial roles as wives, mothers, and workers.

Sicilian Women and Work

When Sidney Sonnino, a parliamentary deputy, toured Sicily in the spring of 1876, he was struck by the absence of women in the fields and quickly concluded that 'peasant women contribute little to the family's income.' He observed: 'Women usually remain at home, spinning flax, taking care of the pigs and children, and cleaning as little as possible.'[41] Later studies modified Sonnino's opinion but did not change his assertion that Sicilian women had a negligible impact on the family's cash earnings. Abele Damiani and Giovanni Lorenzoni agreed that Sicilian women rarely worked on the wheat estates. Only poverty-stricken widows or disgraced single mothers forced into the fields by the threat of starvation and death could be seen bending over hoes. Respectable women raised the family's vegetables but worked for wages only during the harvest, alongside their husbands, sons, or fathers. Sonnino, Lorenzoni, and Damiani readily acknowledged that woman contributed to the family's financial prosperity through their household activities – spinning, weaving, selling produce at the market, raising chickens and pigs, and the like. Lorenzoni in particular emphasized the importance of women's financial and managerial skills in the family economy.[42] Even so, these scholars and politicians held that women's absence from wage work excluded them from being counted as productive workers.[43]

In the debates surrounding transoceanic migration, everyone agreed that the exodus of young, able-bodied men would end this female seclusion. Lured out of their homes by higher wages, women would take work in the wheatfields. Scholars and politicians, however, disagreed on the consequences of this change. Some feared that the next generation would suffer as a result of women being forced to pick up a man's tools, to do men's work for hours under the hot sun, their sleeping babies in baskets on their heads. 'The evil is already apparent,' noted Antonio Mangano. 'Government reports show that the physical standard of young men examined for military service is much lower than twenty years ago.' Even though the young men Mangano pointed to as evidence of physical degeneration were born before mass migration forced women into the fields, his argument that the nation's decline was linked to the economic plight of these abandoned women sparked fears surrounding transoceanic migration. Other critics agreed that fieldwork was difficult and dangerous, but contended that as long as Sicilian men could not earn a living wage, their women had to go out to work. This was the only way rural residents could hope to improve their lives. Angelo Mosso even argued that it was a sign of social progress. The presence of women in the workforce brought southern culture one step closer to the ideal world of separate spheres that, for some, represented the pinnacle of civilization. After providing a harrowing description of women working in the fields, Mosso went on to suggest that a society's evolutionary progress can be measured by the position of women in the workforce. 'In the lowest civilized state (as in the case of the southern provinces) women do not work: in the next stage women work and share the maintenance of the family with their men: in the highest condition of social evolution, women, completely conquered and rejected in the fight with the workers, return to close themselves up in their houses.'[44] In Mosso's vision of an orderly society, women did not work because they did not need to, and could devote themselves to children and home. Whatever their opinions concerning the relative merits or problems with women in the workforce, all the critics agreed that in Sicily, migration would at least initially transform women into wage workers.

The conclusions of these politicians and scholars rested on the belief that the absence of women in the agricultural workforce was evidence of Sicilian backwardness and a holdover from Arab rule. What they were actually witnessing was the impact of global capitalism on the island's economy, filtered through traditional notions of women's work and appropriate female behaviour. Contrary to the opinions of these northern men, Sicilian women were not lazy or content to live as prisoners in their homes. Cultural codes stipulating that respectable women should not work in the fields, or as subordinates in another person's house, shaped developing patterns of female work. A woman seen working in the fields brought dishonour to herself and her family. As a consequence, women who sought to improve their family's social condition – the wives of migrants in particular – did their best to avoid field work. Work and status were associated in such a way that mass male migration would never encourage women to seek work in the wheatfields. Despite rising wages on the surrounding estates, rural women chose to make money in other ways. Careers that required a good education or that were extensions of women's family duties, such as commerce, were perfectly honourable occupations for women, and the remittances from overseas provided them the means to open their own businesses. The effects of mass male migration on rural women's work attest to the fundamental changes occurring in the region's economy and the changing meanings of work itself. Sicily's integration into an expanding world capitalist system created an economy based on the exportation of male workers and the transformation of rural women into entrepreneurs and consumers.

The exclusion of Sicilian women from paid work began in the second half of the nineteenth century, before men began to migrate.[45] According to census figures, between 1881 and 1921 there was a dramatic decline in the number of female wage workers in Sicily. Within forty years, the proportion of Sicilian women appearing in the census as engaged in productive work fell from 38 per cent to 8 per cent.[46] The apparent departure of women from the workforce was an effect of northern industrialization. In the first half of the nineteenth century nearly half the Sicilian women who worked were employed in the cottage textile industry.[47] Over the course of the century, as mechanization moved looms from houses to factories, fewer women were able to earn cash from spinning or weaving at home. By the late nineteenth century, manufactured goods were available throughout the island. The market for domestic cloth – the most lucrative women's work in the South – had nearly disappeared. Women were unable to compete with cheaper and better-made machine-woven textiles.[48] In northern Italy, as throughout France and England, the textile industry offered factory jobs to women, creating a female wage-labour force. For rural Sicilian women the northern cloth factories eliminated a traditional occupation.[49] Between 1881 and 1901 the number of Sicilian women employed in textiles fell by 78 per cent, from 189,270 to 41,216.[50] In Sutera one-third of the women who married during the 1880s described themselves as spinners or weavers; in the 1890s only two women were listed as *filande* in the marriage records.[51] The decline in the number of female wage workers was accompanied by a sharp increase in the number of women listed as *casalinghe* (housewives) or *senza professione* (without a profession). In 1881, 40 per cent of Sicilian women were described as *senza professione*; by 1901, the number had risen to 65 per cent.[52]

The transition from a household mode of production to a cash economy entailed new definitions of female labour, which contributed to the disappearance of women from industry. In 1901 the government began excluding home production from the official definition of textile work in the census. They argued that including cloth woven at home obscured the industrial progress in the North. This new method severely underestimated the number of southern women still making cloth.[53] In Sutera, women continued to spin and weave, only now they were categorized as housewives or agricultural workers because they no longer sold their work at market. Despite statistical evidence of a decline in female textile workers, the number of looms in Sutera increased from 50 to 200 between 1876 and 1895.[54] Women continued to spend the long winter months at their looms weaving rough cloth for everyday use. But now their work was no longer defined as economically productive. By the 1900s the long tradition of women's industry in the village seemed to have been completely forgotten. In 1904 the Caltanissetta chapter of the cooperative Le Industrie Femminili Italiane asked the mayor of Sutera to describe the artisanal or craft occupations dominated by women. Carruba replied: 'In this town there is no sort of female industry other than women's work limited solely to housekeeping.'[55]

New definitions of female labour also account for the apparent rise in the number of Sicilian women engaged in agriculture. Jole Calapso noted that between 1870 and 1880 the number of women engaged in agriculture rose from 78,774 to 157,799.[56] Evidence from Sutera suggests that this increase is as misleading as the decline in the number of women spinners and weavers. Marriage records from Sutera indicate that between the 1860s and the 1870s the number of women who listed themselves as *contadine* (female agricultural workers) rose dramatically from 6 to 232. However, when these women went to register the birth of their children, they either left the occupation line blank or defined themselves as spinners or as housewives. In the 1880s more than one-third of brides identified themselves as spinners or weavers. Most women who married in the 1890s were categorized as either agricultural workers or housewives.[57] Yet according to local records the women of Sutera were not working in the fields any more than they had in the 1880s. In 1895, Dr Vaccaro proudly asserted that in Sutera, 'women are responsible for the housework, while their husbands tend the fields.'

Female occupations seemed to vary according to who was filling out the official documents. When Onofria C. married in 1875, she was listed as a rural worker just like her husband. Five years later, when her husband went to city hall to report the birth of their son, she was described as a spinner. In 1904, when another child was born, she was recorded as a housewife. Women who appeared in the records as housewives one year could be classified as agricultural workers the next, and spinners the next.[58] Women worked at a variety of activities. Depending on the season, Onofria spent her days cooking, cleaning, sewing, spinning, working in the family's gardens, or storing vegetables for winter. It is unlikely that women's daily lives had changed dramatically with the new titles. The occupational categories of women reflected government regulations, changing definitions of work, and the family's economic condition more than they reflected women's daily activities. The flexibility of these descriptions of female employment must have had a significant impact on the national census, probably inflating the number of female agricultural workers.

Women themselves contributed to this confusion. Gender ideals influenced how they described their lives to the outside world. Agricultural wage work had long been associated with poverty and immorality, so few women proudly declared they were actively employed in fieldwork. Lorenzoni, echoing Sonnino's contention that only the most miserable women work in the fields, wrote: '[The] ruling prejudice in many towns within the island asserts that a respectable woman must not work for wages in the countryside. Only the poorest women, those abandoned by their husband, widows or dishonoured girls request such work. Respectable young women refuse to work in the fields, or for wages, only agreeing to help their families.'[59]

Even during the First World War, when customary taboos were loosened, women who chose to work in the fields were condemned by other women. Charlotte Gower Chapman recounts how when 'Pippina the cow,' a strong, hard-working young woman from Milocca, decided to organize a group of friends to hire out for the harvest, her actions were considered 'so extraordinary as to be beyond approval or disapproval.'[60]

Women who were driven by economic necessity to leave their homes to work were morally suspect. In her travels across the island, the reformer and writer Caterina Binetti-Ventura argued:

> There is no industry for a woman, and if a woman is constrained to leave her house and earn her bread, watchful eyes follow her with suspicion and contempt as she walks down the street to the stores and workshops accompanied by her mother or a relative, or more often a companion, a marginal figure somewhere between a hag and a procuress. In exchange for her services, her scrupulous supervision, she receives a small compensation ... she could be compared to a eunuch that watches the honour of beautiful oriental women.[61]

According to Binetti-Ventura, women forced into wage work by desperate circumstances were quick to stop after they married. 'Once they had found a husband, they were shut away in their houses far from prying eyes. Jealousy and hunger were the price they had to pay for the trappings of respectability and the title "*signora.*"'[62] A woman who had to continue working once she was married brought shame and dishonour to herself and her husband. A woman who trudged to the fields with her hoe in one hand and her newborn infant at her breast was announcing to the world that her husband was unable to support his family. He was a failure.

Sicilian women did not view all work with the same mixture of disdain, suspicion, and horror that they directed toward agricultural wage work and domestic service. Women who were not forced to work out of poverty could choose to work outside the home without suffering public humiliation. Girls from *borghesi* or wealthy artisan families were sent to Palermo to study for a teaching certificate or a midwifery licence. When they returned home, they were expected to marry well – the son of an artisan if not a *signore*.[63] Their education was their dowry. The women born in Sutera who went on to teach at the elementary school all came from well-to-do families. Carmela C.'s father ran a small store. When she returned from the city with her diploma, she taught the female elementary class in Rabato. After a few years she married Pietro M., a lawyer. Calogera V., another teacher, came from an artisan family and earned her diploma in Palermo. She returned to Sutera, and after working in the classroom for a couple of years married Bartolomeo B., a fellow teacher.[64]

Midwives were also respectable. Grazia C. received her diploma in midwifery from the University of Palermo in 1872. Two years later she married Carmelo N., an elementary school teacher in Sutera. She continued to practise even after her marriage. In the 1890s she was hired by Sutera's city council as the town midwife. The city paid her more than 600 lire a year to care for indigent women.[65] By 1900, two other authorized midwives were practising in Sutera and Milocca for a slightly lower salary. Carolina D. received her diploma from the University of Palermo in 1900. She worked for the city of Sutera and then went into private practice for a few years. In 1909 she married Ignazio M., a wealthy tailor, and afterwards continued to practise her trade. When examinations were announced for two additional positions the year Carolina D. married, she did not hesitate to apply. Carolina D. and Marianna I., the daughter of a wealthy landowner who had received her diploma in 1905 and had only recently returned home to practise, won the competition. They were the only two midwives who regularly appeared in the birth records after 1909. The appointment carried a stipend of 400 lire – less than half what the village doctor was paid but still a sizable sum.[66] These women were protected from slander and innuendo by their background, marriage, and education, despite the ambiguous nature of their profession, which required them to rush to the poorest families in the middle of the night. Unlike the domestic servants and the laundresses pitied by Caterina Binetti-Ventura, these professional women entered homes from a position of social superiority. Their honour and status were never questioned despite the hours they kept and the wages they earned.

Commerce was also considered an acceptable activity for women, since it did not require them to leave the house or work for wages. Most businesses in Sutera operated out of the ground floor of a family home, so women did not need to leave home and subject themselves to the public humiliation that involved. A shopkeeper's wife stood behind the counter and waited on customers while her husband travelled around the valley buying merchandise for the store. These women were well respected in the village and were generally addressed as *Donna*, a title reserved for the well-to-do.[67] Women who spent their days in these small, dark shops were not technically wage workers. They worked alongside their husbands to earn income for the family. Tending a store was an extension of women's economic duties as family managers.

A woman's occupation reflected her family's honour and status. The negative associations surrounding agricultural wage work kept migrants' wives out of the fields even though their earnings could have brought their husbands home sooner. Instead they opened stores, movie theatres, and coffee bars, and sent their daughters to learn a profession – all socially acceptable endeavours for women. Mass male migration contributed to this transformation and to the redefinition of women's work in a capitalist economy.

The significance of the cultural meanings of work in rural women's lives is plain in women's refusal to toil in the fields during the peak years of migration. As soon as emigration emerged as a real alternative to working in the fields for low wages, or for contracts that left a man deeper in debt after the harvest than before he started planting, the traditional relationship between employers and employees ended. As labourers left, wages began to rise and the terms of agricultural contracts improved. By 1906, rural workers were earning 30 to 50 per cent more than they had in the 1890s.[68] Wages did not rise equally across the island. Landowners in the provinces of Agrigento and Palermo, which reported the highest rates of migration, found salary increases of 50 per cent. Several districts in the province of Siracusa that boasted low rates of emigration reported that wages actually fell between 1883 and 1906. Even moderate migration rates seem to have had a significant impact on salaries. Districts in Caltanissetta that reported a modest 5 per cent rate of emigration reported that men's wages rose 17 per cent, from 1.70 lire to 2 lire a day.[69]

In Sutera, wages for male agricultural workers rose significantly in the first years of the twentieth century. By 1906, men could command daily wages of up to 2 lire depending on the season and the type of work;

TABLE 4.2
Women in agriculture, 1881–1921

	Sicily	Province of Caltanissetta	District of Caltanissetta
Percentage of women working in agriculture			
1881	10.81	5.57	—
1901	4.86	2.58	3.83
1911	3.70	1.72	2.13
1921	4.41	1.50	—
Percentage of agricultural workforce that is female			
1881	22.15	10.52	—
1901	11.05	5.48	8.75
1911	10.09	4.36	5.97
1921	9.22	2.79	—

Source: MAIC, DGS, *Censimento 1881*, vol. 3, pp. 584–5; *Censimento 1901*, vol. 3, pp. 272–300; *Censimento 1911*, vol. 3, pp. 331–2; *Censimento 1921*, vol. 13, pp. 508–25.

fifteen years earlier a man would have considered himself fortunate to be earning 1.5 lire a day.[70] Wage workers were not the only ones to benefit from the labour shortage: so did sharecroppers.[71] In 1910 the mayor of Sutera declared: 'The consequences of emigration have been economically beneficial to the residents of the village, [especially] to the rural workers who remained behind who have obtained better agricultural contracts and daily wages.'[72] Men were not the only ones who found employers willing to pay more for their labour. Landowners also raised wages for female agricultural workers. By 1906 the women of Sutera could earn as much as men during the harvest.[73] Yet despite rising wages, Sicilian women did not rush out to work in the fields. The number of women engaged in agricultural activities in the district fell, as did the percentage of women in the agricultural workforce (see Table 4.2).

It is not surprising that mass male migration encouraged women to withdraw from the agricultural workforce, regardless of the higher wages. Suteresi were not driven to emigrate by economic necessity. While their husbands were abroad, the women who remained behind set out to move their families up the social ladder. The money sent home provided the means to buy the physical and material trappings of higher social status. However, possessions did not in themselves guarantee social mobility. A family's behaviour was as important as its possessions.

From the moment their husbands boarded the train to Palermo on their way to New York, the women who remained at home had to live exemplary lives. To claim a position of respect and status in the community, emigrants' wives – already placed in a morally precarious position by their husband's absence – had to emulate the lives of upper-class women as closely as possible. Fieldwork irreparably damaged a woman's reputation and status in the village. No matter how much money her husband sent back from Birmingham, she would be counted among the abandoned women, the 'poor, the widows, the beggars, the women whose husbands had left for America.' Commonly held notions about women's appropriate economic roles and men's activities shaped family decisions about work. Despite higher wages, the wives of emigrants shunned paid work in the surrounding wheatfields. The migration experience encouraged women to take up the trades and occupations generally associated with elite women in order to solidify their new position in society.

Between 1901 and 1911 there was an increase in the number of working women engaged in commercial activities in the district. This includes women licensed to run dry goods stores or to sell wine or bread. In Sutera, women who were married to migrant men and who found it difficult to make ends meet chose to open stores, selling dried chickpeas and other local produce, rather than work in the fields. While women made these economic decisions based on ideas about appropriate female roles, this shift also marked their entrance into a cash economy. The women of Sutera were part of a larger regional trend that began at the end of the nineteenth century, when Sicilian women began to find work in commercial activities. In the province of Caltanissetta, the number of women in the workforce engaged in commerce rose sharply between 1881 and 1901, from 0.6 to 8 per cent (see Table 4.3). By 1911, over 10 per cent of the female labour force were in commerce.

Male emigration provided some women with the means to open small businesses. In 1902, Calogero F., a twenty-five-year-old bachelor, migrated to Buffalo, New York, with his father. For five years he worked on the railway and in the Pennsylvania coal mines, saving his money to return home. In 1908 he returned to Sutera and married Maria M. Together they invested the 6,000 lire he had brought back from America in a small dry-goods store, a small piece of land, and a house in town. Maria worked in the shop while her husband travelled to the neighbouring towns to buy supplies. Years later, her son fondly remembered his mother as an 'excellent businesswoman,' the one who kept the shop profitable.[75] According to stories told in Sutera today, the wives of emigrants were among the first to open new modern establishments. The

TABLE 4.3
Women in commerce, 1881–1921

	Sicily	Province of Caltanissetta
Percentage of female wage workers engaged in commerce		
1881	0.63	0.58
1901	10.01	8.42
1911	14.94	10.26
1921	4.64	24.67
Percentage of Sicilian women working in commerce		
1881	0.24	0.23
1901	1.38	0.93
1911	1.30	0.47
1921	0.51	1.50
Percentage commercial workforce that is female		
1881	13.91	15.78
1901	16.22	19.46
1911	24.45	15.07
1921	11.23	45.94

Source: MAIC, DGS, *Censimento 1881*, vol. 3; *Censimento 1901*, vol. 3; *Censimento 1911*, vol. 3; *Censimento 1921*, vol. 13, pp. 508–25.

first bars and cinemas were opened by women whose husbands never returned from overseas.[76]

Mass male migration did not have the same effect on women's labour patterns as war. In wartime the state intervened to encourage women to sub for men in the fields.[77] During the First World War, some women from well-to-do families engaged in agricultural activities, but as property owners, not as workers. In 1917, twenty-nine women in Sutera and Milocca applied for the twenty lire prize the government offered to those women who worked their lands while their husbands, sons, or brothers were serving in the army. They eventually received the money four years after the war ended.[78] The women nominated for the prize were not poor women who had worked in the fields in the past. Most of them came from small land-owning families. The women who applied for the government prizes were relatively well educated. Twenty-two of them could sign their names when they accepted the prize. When the army called their menfolk away, these women planted and sowed, or at least hired someone to do the work; either way, they took stewardship of the family's fields. The absence of men enabled women to compete with men for scarce jobs, while the patriotic demands of a wartime economy allowed them circumvent traditional taboos and work the land without fear of social disparagement.

There were no similar incentives to encourage the wives of emigrants to work the lands their husbands left behind. Usually, families arranged for a close relative to work the land while the owner was overseas. When Calogero M. decided to emigrate to the United States in 1910, leaving his wife, Francesca Z., and their one child in Sutera, he arranged for his brother and brother-in-law to work the land until he returned in 1915.[79] Without the protection of patriotism, families arranged their affairs so that women like Francesca Z. would not have to work their own lands or hire themselves out as day labourers.

Women could not replace men in the fields. Emigration was intended to bolster a family's social position. All the money in America could not buy a higher social standing if the migrant's wife disgraced and dishonoured herself by working in the fields for wages while her husband was overseas. The principal role of the women who remained behind was to preserve the family's reputation, and this meant they had to avoid wage work. The quest for status and respectability meant that though mass male migration did not transform patterns of female agricultural wage labour, it did change the nature of women's work. Women could now become entrepreneurs or shopkeepers, and this repositioned them in the local and global economy.

This survey of the impact of mass male migration on patterns of female work and property ownership in rural Sicily highlights the changing meanings of work that accompanied the region's entrance into a new economic system. These new meanings altered ideas of what constituted male and female. The growing exodus of Sicilian men at the beginning of the twentieth century signalled the end of the island's agrarian economy. When labourers replaced wheat as Sicily's principal export, it marked a shift not only in what men did during the day, but also in the significance of their work. The island never fully recovered its traditional economic and social values after the agricultural recession of the late nineteenth century. The barons and princes, whose power was based on their landholdings, were challenged by commercial wealth and pressured to modernize their holdings. In di Lampedusa's *The Leopard*, when Don Fabrizio saw Don Calogero as 'the Revolution itself in white tie and tails,' he was speaking to the ascent to power of the nouveaux riches who had made their money from trade and were using it to buy their lands and titles.

The failure of late-nineteenth-century government reforms and rural protest movements to revitalize the land tenure system and create a dynamic class of small property holders heralded the creation of a wage labour economy. Increasingly, Sicilian men sought work as day labourers, working for wages rather than as sharecroppers. Although initially a strategy on the part of the estate owners to create a more flexible labour force to keep profits high, for men it shifted the idea of labour from producing goods to earning weekly pay. In northern Europe this transformation occurred during the Agrarian Revolution of the eighteenth century and contributed to creation of the free, mobile labour force that underpinned the Industrial Revolution. The factory model prevalent in England represented only one of the many avenues toward proletarianization. In Sicily, where there was little manufacturing, the shift to wage labour facilitated transoceanic migration. A man could just as easily sell his labour to the local landlord as to a mining company in Thomas, Alabama, or a construction boss in New York City. However, whereas in northern Europe both men and women became wage workers (although they experienced the shift in profoundly different ways), in Sicily at the beginning of the twentieth century, wages defined men's work and paid labour came to define work itself.[80] Among rural workers a man's sense of worth was increasingly linked to his ability to earn.

Over this same period, women's work was separated from wages. As Sicilian women witnessed the disappearance of the market for their finely woven cloth, they too seemed to vanish from the workforce. Once productive work was claimed as a central pillar of masculinity, rural women were set on a different pathway into the new global economy, one that circumvented the selling of labour for wages. The particular circumstances of economic change in the late nineteenth century left room for rural women to enter real estate and commerce. Though the devaluation of land as a source of capital and income did not immediately diminish its social and cultural value to residents, it did mean that certain kinds of property ownership remained open to women. Strengthened by cultural codes that associated shelter, food, children, and clothes with women, and by the infusion of cash from overseas, many women were able to contribute to the family economy by purchasing houses, engaging in intensive agriculture, opening grocery stores, or as working as seamstresses, teachers, or midwives. The economic transformations of the twentieth century that turned Sicilian men into a free, mobile labour force did not leave rural women behind, but rather offered them opportunities to carve out a space for themselves without leaving their homes.

In rural Sicily the masculinization of production accompanied the femininization of consumption. The new economic opportunities that accompanied mass male migration firmly linked women to the growing consumer culture, as sellers and buyers of the wealth of new goods and services. Their new houses needed furnishings, and their new social status required appropriate clothes. To meet the growing demand, women turned to their neighbours and friends, asking them to order new furniture or to sew new dresses based on the latest Paris fashions. Consumer demand spurred the growth of new businesses operated (if not owned) by women. Access to cash did not undermine the political or cultural power of men in these small rural towns, but it did offer rural women new ways to participate in the local economy. As the next chapters illustrate, their admittance into a growing global consumer economy also relocated them in the Italian state.

PART II

Shifting Borders, Shifting Identities

Chapter Five

Sicilian Women and the Italian State

In early January of 1908, Angelo A. stepped off the train at the Sutera station. He had been gone four years, working in the coal mines outside Birmingham, Alabama. In his store-bought suit, starched white collar, and leather shoes, he made a striking picture trudging up the steep, muddy road that led from the station in the valley to the main square. He had left his family as a sharecropper with only a few lire to his name. After four years in drab company towns, scrimping and saving his weekly pay, he was coming home with money in his pockets to open a store, buy a house in town, and invest in some land of his own. He had discarded his homespun clothing long ago. His appearance testified to his success as a migrant in the Americas: he had left a peasant and returned a respectable businessman. Angelo's sojourn in Birmingham did more than transform his wardrobe and his social standing in Sicily: it also redefined his sense of civic identity.[1]

For most of his life, Angelo's connections to the outside world had been defined by the social and physical boundaries of Sutera. His civil birth certificate testified to his family circle and social networks, while his baptismal certificate attested to his position in the wider Christian community.[2] His identity was firmly rooted in bloodlines and in the church, so that secular political institutions and national borders had little significance in his everyday affairs or in defining his sense of self. His kinship networks served as his primary means of communication and social advancement, and offered help when he needed it. Overseas, Angelo's world changed. He was no longer defined by where he was born, but by his own experiences and behaviour. From the moment he set sail from Palermo, he was no longer just a Suteresi. The passport he held out to the customs agent at Ellis Island defined him as an Italian.

To non-Italians his look, language and gestures made it clear he was Italian. To other Italians his dialect defined him as a Sicilian, but to other Sicilians he remained a Suterese. Daily life in the Americas strengthened an individual's identification with Italy. In the United States, Italian businesses and government agencies took on new importance. The central institutions linking immigrants to their homelands were the Italian consulate officials, the Banco di Napoli, and the Italian-American newspapers. Migrants also turned to formal and informal networks to find jobs, send money home, seek protection, and keep in touch with friends and family.[3] Once home, the migrant was seen as an *'Americano.'* These conflicting identities produced by transnational migration did not replace the migrants' identification with Sutera; rather, they testify to the complicated political, social, and cultural connections that linked individual migrants to their home towns, nations, and new communities abroad.[4]

Although Rosa A. never left Sutera, transnational migration redefined her place in the nation as well. Until her husband emigrated, Rosa's life had been shaped by the physical and social boundaries of Sutera. Since childhood, blood and baptism had defined her position in the community and the world. While Angelo worked abroad, Rosa did her part to fulfil the couple's dreams by ensuring that the family would be able to claim the cultural and material trappings of success. Her new familial responsibilities led her to seek the assistance of government officials, creating a new, more independent relationship with the state. Since Rosa could neither read nor write when Angelo left, any communication with her absent husband required the assistance of the mayor, the priest, or a friend. Rosa took over many of Angelo's routine tasks, from enrolling their children in school to depositing Angelo's remittances to registering property and paying taxes.[5] The migration process also encouraged Rosa to attend night school. These new duties and opportunities profoundly altered her relationship with the Italian state.

With their husbands absent, rural women began carrying out an autonomous relationship with the state. These new ties challenged assumptions about female civic inclusion incorporated into the founding of modern Italy. Rural Sicilians, both men and women, generally viewed the Italian state with the same suspicion and superficial acquiescence they had directed to the Bourbon, English, and Spanish governments. Unlike these previous governments, however, the newly formed Italian nation also set out to create a society in which citizens had specific rights and duties. The social model for the state reflected the family, and men by virtue of their household status were identified as the public representatives, while women as wives and mothers were private members. Men, then, defined female public space. The state's initial efforts to forge a body of citizens focused on men, reflecting nineteenth-century assumptions about the gendered nature of the liberal state.

Although the state was not greatly concerned about integrating women into the citizenry, paths for creating an autonomous relationship emerged as it took measures to mold a male citizen body. Military conscription, party politics, and compulsory education laws were directed at transforming the civic identity of men, but they also altered the relations between rural women and the state. National service offered men new experiences and mobility, the chance to travel to large cities and to meet other Italians. It accentuated women's secondary status, yet it also brought the totems of the Italian state into their homes and their lives. When their fathers, sons, and husbands returned, they brought home souvenirs, postcards from Rome, coins stamped with the King's face, and lace fans from Napoli. Meanwhile, in small Sicilian towns, the emergence of organized parties transferred the centre of public power from the city hall to local political clubs. This shift in the location of political power offered women the opportunity to appear at city hall. In a similar fashion, the expansion of public schools facilitated an unmediated link between the government and rural women. In rural Sicily, the state's efforts to forge a new kind of nation altered relations between men and women, and between both and the nation, by shifting the boundaries between public and private.

Male migration furthered women's integration into the nation. When the men began to migrate, family roles began to shift, altering the physical and ideological ties that bound men and women to public life. Women used their contacts in local government to keep the family together, even if an ocean separated them from their husbands, sons, or brothers. Migrants' wives came to see state institutions as tools to improve the family's social and economic position. The mayor's office provided access to the Ministry of Foreign Affairs and the consular networks that enabled women to keep in touch with their husbands or sons overseas. The same networks enabled women to enlist the help of government agencies to protect their family interests, to demand pensions and benefits, or even to take legal action against shipping agents. Transoceanic migration also encouraged women to enrol in school. As the ostensible representatives of the family, women needed to be able to read the letters and documents arriving from overseas. They had little choice but to learn to read and write, and once they were in the classroom, the textbook lessons in Italian, civics, and national history taught them their place in the state. All of this – the resort to government institutions, and experiences in the classroom – strengthened the association between reproduction and the 'nationalization' of women underlying twentieth-century state policies.[6]

Rural Attitudes toward Italy

The relationship of Sicilians to the state is a complicated one, built on a combination of distrust, resentment, and dependency. In the United States, political debates about citizenship have privileged rights over responsibilities. Most American citizens accept their civic duties, paying taxes, serving on juries, and going to war, knowing full well that these obligations are the sources of their individual rights. Under the constitutional monarchy that was established after 1860, few Sicilians saw their relationship to the state in terms of rights. Citizenship was understood almost exclusively in terms of obligations, those duties 'that invited state punishment if not performed.'[7] The state exacted taxes, military service, and even votes in a capricious and often ruthless manner. Rarely did Sicilians view Italy as their protector or as a source of justice. Usually, it was best to avoid the state whenever possible. However, many people recognized that if used astutely, state institutions could benefit a family. The judicial system resolved local legal disputes (even if the verdicts tended to favour the wealthy and powerful). The King and Queen could intercede on behalf of the poorest peasant, and their names were often invoked in popular protest movements. In nineteenth-century Sicily the state was viewed as a source of both repression and redress.

The relationship of Sicilian men and women to the new Italian state was in part a consequence of their attitudes toward all outsiders. In the eyes of rural Sicilians, strangers were always suspect. The occasional travellers, salesmen, clergy, and government officials were all looked on with suspicion tinged with curiosity. Strangers had no blood ties to the villagers, no shared past, and so they had no place in the social hierarchy. They were unknown and therefore not to be fully trusted.[8]

Distrust of the outside world was reinforced by the isolation of the interior hill towns. In 1880 most residents of Sutera had little connection with the outside world. Townsfolk rarely travelled beyond the neighbouring towns of Mussomeli and Campofranco.[9] Inadequate roads, bridges, and railways combined with crime in the countryside to make travel difficult and dangerous. Contacts with people from other parts of the island were limited to the few migrant labourers who passed through looking for work during the harvest, or who came to work in the local mines. When times were good, a few of these itinerant labourers settled down with local women. During the prosperous 1880s the number of people in Sutera and Milocca who married outsiders rose sharply, from slightly less than 5 per cent to nearly 15 per cent. When the economy faltered, however, fewer strangers appeared, and there were fewer marriages with non-Suteresi. Limited mobility reinforced a strong sense of *campanilismo* and suspicion of outsiders.[10]

Strangers who found themselves in Sutera were not shunned or ill-treated. Sicilian hospitality, courtesy and curiosity ensured that no one was directly insulted or went away hungry. Sicilians had a genuine concern for other people, and besides, there lurked the possibility that a foreigner could benefit the family in some way. Sicilians prided themselves on their shrewdness and cunning, their *furberia.* The knack for exploiting a situation for one's own gain was respected and admired, especially if a poor, humble peasant made a fool out of a wealthy, powerful man. Sicilians believed that people were motivated by self-interest and that they would pursue those interests at any expense.[11] Sicilian attitudes toward foreigners – suspicion mixed with an eye to possible profit – extended to the new state. When government representatives and schoolteachers arrived in Sutera from other towns, the craftier Suteresi looked for ways to exploit them. When Charlotte Gower Chapman appeared in Milocca in the late 1920s, the villagers assumed she was on some sort of government mission. One rumour held that she had been sent to negotiate the transfer of the island to the United States in payment of Italy's war debts. Another insisted that she had been sent to investigate the spate of recent arrests that had been made under Cesare Mori's anti-Mafia campaign. As long as townsfolk were convinced that Chapman could help them liberate their imprisoned husbands and sons, 'everyone sought to please the stranger.'[12] It was up to each individual, especially the women, to benefit from this opportunity to strengthen the social status or economic condition of the family. All institutions, people, and networks were possible tools for familial gain, or instruments of harm.

Unification also contributed to the uneasy relations between Sicilians and the government. When Vittorio Emanuele claimed the title of King of Italy, he inherited a sharply divided kingdom. Linguistic and cultural differences were exacerbating economic and political inequities. As

Massimo D'Azeglio recognized early on, territorial unification alone did not create a nation.[13] In unifying the Italian provinces, the founding fathers succeeded only in cobbling a physical state together; now they faced the far more daunting task of 'making Italians.' Immediately after Italian unification, Vittorio Emanuele and his ministers extended the political, legislative, and cultural institutions of Piedmont across the newly formed nation, regardless of their suitability for the southern provinces and islands.[14] The state imposed taxes, and it carried the menfolk off to prison or the army. After unification the only regular officials of the state present in Sutera were the *carabinieri* – the military police responsible for arresting local criminals – and the draft board that appeared each year.[15]

Italian rule, like French and Spanish rule before it, brought little more than trouble into people's lives. From this experience it was easy for residents to blame the state for the bad things that occurred in their lives, even for the sporadic outbreaks of cholera in the region. Dr Vaccaro lamented: 'With few exceptions, even the most educated people are convinced that cholera ... is a government plot to poison the people.'[16] State policies instituted in the late 1800s seemed to strengthen popular sentiment that the Italian government was an arrogant, dangerous enemy to be watched constantly.[17] As Leopoldo Franchetti wrote in 1876, 'from the day that Garibaldi entered Palermo, there began a huge misunderstanding between Sicilians and the Italian government that continues until the present day.'[18]

Piedmont's economic and political policies deepened the divisions between the central government and the provinces. Italian economic policy privileged manufacturing and commerce over the needs of the rural South, and in the process solidified the power of the local elites. The Italian government was committed to making northern manufactured goods competitive in European markets. In the South it encouraged a shift toward export agricultural production – citrus crops, wine, and olive oil – and it also bolstered the sulphur mines. At the same time it sacrificed the local textile and cigar industries.[19] The Italian government did little to address Sicily's lack of industry, chronic underemployment, and long-standing inequities of land distribution. If anything, its policies exacerbated political abuses and heightened the sense of wariness that coloured attitudes toward the state.

The emergence of a regional economy based on exporting raw materials and importing manufactured goods empowered local elites to act as economic intermediaries between Sicilians and the state.[20] Local entrepreneurs, professionals, and aristocrats entered into an uneasy alliance with one another and with the new state. In exchange for a virtual monopoly over public works, they ensured that the state received some kind of compensation, although they continued to resist what they considered inappropriate demands. The evolution of a new political economy in the South that granted a certain degree of autonomy to the *comuni* governed by new local elites deepened the divide between rural residents and the state, and undermined the effectiveness of institutions.

Any benefits that came from Italy were the consequence of the astuteness and intelligence of the new governing class, who were well positioned to exploit the new laws and regulations. After 1860, Italian government representatives sometimes appeared in Sutera, carrying plans for new roads and new schools and promises of industry and jobs. Rarely, however, did the government directly finance these projects. The new tax structure imposed by the national legislature shifted the burden of improving transportation, sanitation, and education onto the shoulders of each *comune*.[21] Any improvements came as a result of local initiative. In Sutera it was the elite, not the government, that subsidized gas lines, water pipes, telegraph service, and the local band.[22] In the early 1880s a governmental commission led by Senator Stefano Jacini sent questionnaires to the mayors of small towns across Sicily asking them whether the government had done anything to improve agricultural conditions or daily life. The mayors responded with an emphatic *no*.[23] Centuries of foreign rule had taught the islanders that only kin and the local elite could bring real improvements to daily life. The government could not.

After 1860 the Italian government took a series of more proactive measures to bridge cultural and social divisions. Its mission to 'make Italians' focused on men. Politicians believed that if a man's identification with his village and family could be weakened through military service, political reform, and public schooling, he would transfer his allegiance to the state and in turn bring his wife and children into the national body. This approach didn't work. It failed to erode local loyalties. It did, however, recast the relationship between rural men, women, and the nation.

The Gendering of a Nation

The government's efforts to forge a nation deepened and widened Italy's civic gender gap. The state intruded on the lives of adult men as household heads in a different manner than on women and on children. In rural Sicily, men increasingly experienced the state as an oppressive, coercive force that took their money in taxes and their bodies in military service. The plebiscites held during unification offered proof enough that the democratic promises of the new monarchy were empty. The local political system effectively silenced any man who voted against the wishes of the local elite. The reimposition of the grist tax that Garibaldi had eliminated, and the presence of the military police and the annual arrival of the draft board, did little to change public opinion.

The military draft was one of the most intrusive measures taken by the new state, and played a pivotal role in differentiating male and female civic identity. For the men who were drafted, military service often marked their first time away from home. They were often stationed in large cities on the mainland, where they forged friendships with other men of their generation who grew up in vastly different linguistic and cultural worlds. In classrooms, Venetians sat next to Sicilians, studying Italian and learning that they were all citizens of this country, whose history stretched back to the greatness of Imperial Rome. District officials in Caltanissetta lamented that while military service had improved the education of rural residents, it had also made them dissatisfied with their lives back home. In a 1904 report on the causes of Italian emigration, the U.S. Consul in Naples, A.H. Byington, echoed these sentiments: 'Military service, too, seems to have a disturbing effect, not because of the unwillingness to serve, but because the soldier, after enjoying better food, clothing and quarters in garrison, returns to the discomforts of life in his native place and finds that the effort to correct matters and introduce reforms is ineffective.[24] Young men wanted more than their towns had to offer, and now they knew it existed. Furthermore, military service had taught these young men that they were an active part of the government.

When the local draft board came to town to enlist all twenty-year-olds for their mandatory two-year service, residents rarely rushed to enlist. Few men refused to serve outright. Most tried to avoid being on the list in the first place, or engaged in passive resistance. In Sutera only half the class of 1862 – forty-two men – were even listed as eligible for the draft.[25] The villagers used kinship ties to try to get abstentions. The more farsighted and well-connected parents went so far as to register their sons as daughters at birth to complicate their draft status. They only corrected the 'clerical error' at the time of the son's wedding. As record keeping improved, more men were called up. However, the number of men who actually served remained roughly the same. Absentee rates and discharge rates increased at about the same rate as the number of eligible men. In the class of 1883 more than half the men obligated to serve were listed as AWOL, or discharged as unfit or unable to serve. Only forty-five of the 104 men called up in July 1903 showed up to enlist. Two of those men failed to appear for the physical, and six were found to be too short. Only one-third of the class of 1883 served in 1903.[26] Few families saw military service as an obligation to King and country. It was an onerous duty, best avoided if possible.

Draft avoidance techniques became more creative as the risks associated with military service became more pronounced. During the First World War the young men of Britain and France rushed to enlist and looked on anyone who lagged behind with derision and suspicion. In contrast, Sicilian men sought ways to avoid serving on the front lines. Two men in Milocca permanently blinded themselves in order to avoid being sent to the front, and suffered no loss of respect within the community. Residents considered self-mutilation justifiable, and even admirable in the circumstances. Other men boasted about tricking the draft board and failing their physical exams. Some ate cigars; others went to a friendly physician for a pill or an injection. Each of these men was proud to have evaded the state's demands, and justified his actions in terms of his duty to his family. As Charlotte Gower Chapman noted with some surprise, any one of them 'would have resented being called a coward: that was not the question. His life was very useful to himself, and he saw no reason why he should risk it. To resort to artifice to avoid military service was simply the exercise of proper Sicilian astuteness.'[27] Fifty-five years after unification, Sicilians still did not see the state as worth a man's life. Risking your life for your country brought no real benefit to family or community and was rarely considered a praiseworthy act. The townspeople celebrated those men who were cunning enough to trick the government and stay at home.

Conscription failed to replace local allegiances with patriotism; it did, however, differentiate between the relationships that tied men to the state and those that tied women to the state. Women were never conscripted, and this reinforced their lack of mobility relative to men and further excluded them from direct participation in the new nation-state; at the same time, conscription offered men the opportunity to see cities and meet people from other regions, to learn Italian, and to see themselves as active participants in national life.[28] For rural women, male military service imposed a new, physical separation from the rituals that marked the entrance of boys into adulthood. It also reinforced the physical isolation experienced by young girls in comparison with their brothers and husbands.

Until the state imposed conscription, girls and boys became women and men according to traditional rites of passage that clearly differentiated their roles within the community and the family, but that took place in the same world and involved the same people. Before the 1870s the basic boundaries that marked people's lives from birth to death were similar for men and women. Within that space they moved in separate but interconnected spheres. True, men worked in the fields while women stayed in town, but each could easily envision the world of the other. Military service physically expanded men's lives beyond the borders of the agrarian society. This expansion accentuated the limited horizons that delineated women's lives. The state seemed to be granting mobility to men and discouraging women from travelling – a situation only heightened by migration. When Charlotte Gower Chapman arrived in Milocca in 1929 she was struck by the limited physical boundaries of women's worlds: 'Most women have never been on a train or even seen one except when their excursions into the country have taken them to the heights at the edge of the river valley from where one can see far off the thread of tracks and, with luck, white smoke and a tiny train.'[29]

Male military service highlighted women's dependence in relation to the state. The draft made it clear that a woman's connection to the state came through a man. The stories that rural women heard about faraway cities and other people's lives were filtered through their husbands and sons. When the soldiers returned to their villages, they brought with them tales of the decadent cities on the continent and the immoral women who walked the streets of Rome and Naples.[30] Rural women learned that urban areas were dangerous and that foreign women were prostitutes. National service reinforced a woman's identification with her family and identified her position as a mother and wife as the basis of her relationship to the state.

Under the constitution of 1860, women were secondary citizens whose legal status was determined by their relationship to men.[31] As in the United States, the civic status of a woman was defined by the position of her father or husband, depending on her marital status. According to article 9 in the Italian civil code, a woman's national identity was subject to her husband or to the male head of household. A non-Italian woman who married an Italian immediately became a legal citizen, whereas an Italian woman who married a foreigner lost her birthright. Article 11 stipulated that the wife of a man stripped of his citizenship also lost her own.[32] The inclusion of the legal principle of coverture in the Piemonte constitution ensured that women owed their primary civic allegiance to the male head of household. The legal code guaranteed that female patriotism would be measured by familial loyalty, and it firmly placed women's public life in the domestic sphere.

A woman's position of legal dependence echoed her position in formal politics as a passive citizen. Electoral politics strengthened the social hierarchies and gender relations that characterized late-nineteenth-century Sicily. By 1900 electoral rights had been extended to Italian men over twenty-five who could read and write and who paid at least forty lire in direct taxes or between two hundred and four hundred lire in rent each year.[33] In Sutera, 165 men were listed in the electoral rolls for the 1899 elections, but only 108 made it to the polls. Overall, fewer than 10 per cent of Sutera's men were eligible to vote.[34] The extension of suffrage did not change the customary basis of political power. Wealth and land continued to shape the political landscape, and from the first parliamentary elections, held in 1861, large landowners controlled the votes.[35] The few men who were allowed to vote usually cast their ballots for those candidates supported by the landowners.[36] Local elites continued to believe that political power was a birthright conferred by blood and land. The expansion of the vote did not radically change the island's political system, based as it was on 'a certain reciprocity of favours' (to borrow Pezzino's words); however, it did sharpen distinctions between male and female citizens. Eventually, the party politics that accompanied a larger electorate would provide women with sufficient leverage to form their own autonomous relationship to state agencies.

Beginning in the 1890s, national political organizations began to change local politics. When the men of Sutera organized a chapter of the *Fasci*, it was a radical departure from past interactions with local and national governments.[37] For the first time, rural residents were organizing themselves across class lines in order to express their opposition to the protectionist policies of the central government. The *Fasci* marked the first conscious mass organization of Sicilian workers under the auspices of the socialist party.[38] By the turn of the century, Suteresi were joining a number of other political associations. The local branch of the Vittorio Emanuele III society became more and more influential in local politics. At least five of its members ran for city council in the 1905 elections under the newly created Partito Popolare.[39] Party affiliations did not eliminate the factionalism and clan rivalries that coloured local politics. However, grafting national organizational structures onto local factions shifted the locus of political power from city hall to political clubs.

After 1896, local conflicts were inextricably linked to national parties. Still, political affiliations reflected complex family networks rather than any ideological positions that bound people together. When national political parties formed in rural Sicily, residents utilized them as one more source of ammunition in long-standing family feuds.[40] In Milocca, the Angelilla family and its supporters took up the socialist banner when they found out their archrival, the Cipolla clan and its followers, had decided to follow the conservative party. Rarely did people express an ideological allegiance to a particular party. Followers of each family switched their loyalties with marriages or new family alliances. When Mussolini came to power, both families decided it was in their best interests to join the fascist party. One party, however, did not mean unity. When the Cipolla family was in power, the Angelilla family would not cooperate; its members refused to participate in local events and disrupted party meetings.[41]

These new parties bound Italian women to the political system through their husbands or fathers. The same feuds that divided men politically informed the activities of women. If the Angelilla family was in control of the local administration and the Cipolla family was excluded from power, the Cipolla women did not march with the *Fasci Femminili*.[42]

Although women's public activities continued to be defined by their domestic relations, the arrival of party politics offered a means for creating a new relationship with the state. Wth the growth of the Partito Popolare, in tandem with agricultural societies offering loans, burial services, and agricultural advice, the mayor and the city councilmen could no longer claim to be the sole access to local power. The physical structure of the town hall lost its political significance and was no longer defined as a men-only space. Toward the end of the 1880s, as rural Sicilians joined independent political organizations and mutual aid societies in ever-growing numbers, the *municipio* opened its doors to women. Though women continued to skirt the edges of the *piazza* with their black shawls clutched tightly around their faces, they were accepted in the town hall as clients – as official representatives of the family.

During most of the nineteenth century, contact between women and government officials was limited to the customary responsibilities ascribed to women within the family. When women appeared in the clerk's office it was usually connected to births, deaths, or marriages.

Birth records show the clearest shift in the relationship between women and local government, because women and their families could choose who would present the child to the clerk. Birthing and baptismal rituals were female-dominated activities. With few exceptions, only women were present at childbirth. Husbands, fathers, and sons remained outside while women attended to the birth of the child.[43] When labour began, most women called in one of the three practising midwives in Sutera. Wealthy women sometimes requested the presence of a male physician.[44] Once the child was born, however, it was the father in his capacity as household head who presented the child to the municipal clerk within three days of his or her birth, in accordance with the law. If for some reason the father was physically incapacitated or absent at the time the child was born, someone who had assisted at the birth could take his place. On these rare occasions the midwife, a close female relative, or a neighbour would present the newborn to the city clerk to officially register the infant's birth. In the 1880s, women comprised only 5 per cent of the declarants in the town's birth records, and not one woman appeared in the records to serve as a witness.[45] Apparently families waited a few days or weeks until the father had returned from the fields or had recovered his health and could register the child himself.

The invisibility of women in the city hall can be attributed in part to the exclusion of women from public spaces, to the acceptance of the male as the head of household, and to passive resistance to the state's demands. The city hall, located in the main square, was clearly outside women's traditional space. Unchaperoned women were rarely seen crossing the square. In addition, since the husband was the formal head of the household, it was his duty to publicly accept a new member into the family and to recognize the legitimacy of each of his children. As long as the city clerk's office was an extension of the local political culture, the responsibility for announcing the birth of a child had to remain the sole prerogative of the man. Most people did not believe that civil registration of births and marriages was as important as baptism, so it could easily be postponed. Reporting the birth of male children several months after the fact was an accepted way of delaying military service for a year.[46] Yet in the late 1880s, as political parties reshaped village politics, women's names begin to appear more often in the record books. Between 1890 and 1895, 174 women and 15 men appeared to register the birth of a newborn because the father was ill or absent. These women accounted for nearly one-quarter (22.5 per cent) of all the legitimate children born and registered in Sutera. The number of women who appeared in front

Figure 5.1

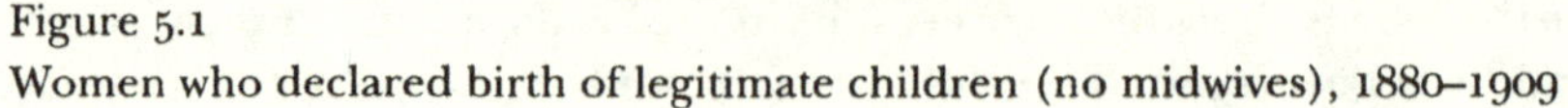

Women who declared birth of legitimate children (no midwives), 1880–1909

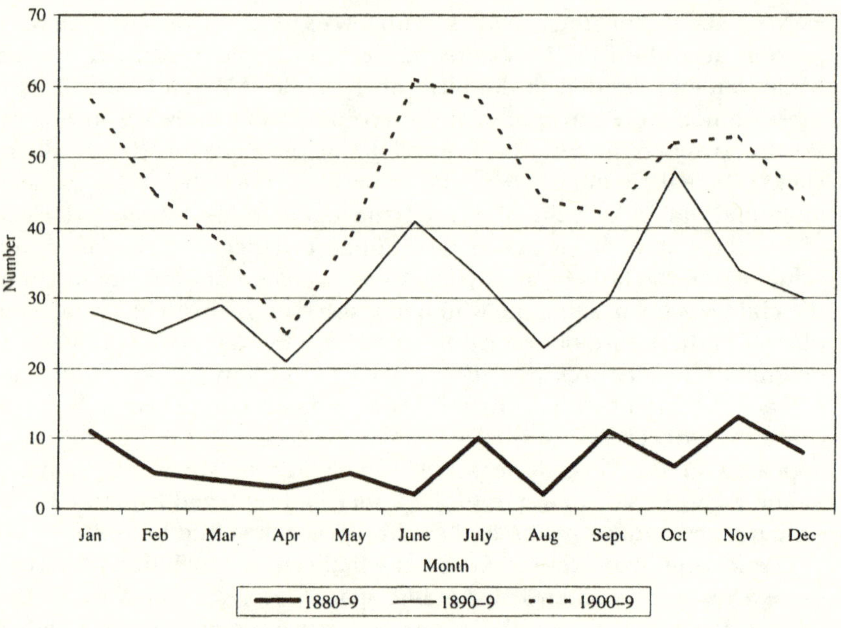

Source: Archivio Comunale di Sutera, *Atti de Nascita 1880–1910*

of the clerk with a babe in arms continued to rise through the decade. During the last five years, women were listed as the *dichiarante* in 27 per cent of birth records. Significantly, women were also appearing as witnesses to births. In the 1890s nearly 40 per cent of birth records were witnessed by at least one woman.[47]

Changing work patterns certainly contributed to this growing presence of women in the town hall. In the 1890s the agricultural crisis worsened. More men from the town had to seek work as day labourers, no longer able to survive by sharecropping alone. Often these men had to travel farther to find enough work and were gone for weeks or months at a time. More and more often rural men relinquished their role in presenting their children at the city hall, unable to return in time.[48] The rising frequency of women registering the birth of a child corresponds to the rhythms of the agrarian calendar (see Figure 5.1). Women were more likely to register a child's birth during the spring and summer, while sowing and harvesting were keeping the men in the fields. It seems that by 1900 the men were gone for most of June and July harvesting their own crops, and then working for wages the rest of the season. Men were absent from town for most of October and November, when it was easy to find extra work ploughing the fields for the next year's crop. Changing definitions of politics combined with new family roles for women to create the possibility of establishing a direct physical connection between rural women and the state, while at the same time highlighting the equation of female citizenship with domestic roles.

Along with military service and political reform, education was seen as a critical weapon in Italy's struggle to forge a national identity. Telegraphs, railways, and the military, municipal police, and tax inspectors forced even the wildest villages to begin to acknowledge – if not respect – state authority, but it was the schoolteacher who brought the language, the values, and the ideals of the new nation into people's homes. In rural regions the elementary school teacher was one of the most influential state missionaries. In the modern world, nation-states were increasingly being defined by a common ethnicity and language. The leaders of the new Italy knew that if they were to succeed in creating Italians, they would have to replace local dialects with Italian, local legends with a national history, and regionalism with patriotism.[49]

Between 1861 and 1900 the Italian government passed a series of education reforms making elementary school obligatory and providing for adult education classes. Yet forty years after unification, state laws had had only limited success in the rural southern provinces. According to the census of 1901, 71 per cent of Sicilian males and 77 per cent of Sicilian females over six were still illiterate.[50] A 1907 government study showed that most islanders only half-heartedly complied with the education laws, when they bothered following them at all. Across the island, rural schoolhouses were in deplorable condition and local governments were claiming they did not have the money to build new schools or to hire sufficient numbers of teachers.

Political ambivalence toward popular education undermined nineteenth-century education reforms. Conservative politicians feared that mass education would threaten the social order by expanding the electoral base to include all sorts of people easily swayed by socialist rhetoric. National education had to create Italians but at the same time preserve the privileges of the ruling classes.[51]

The first national educational reforms were founded on the assumption that though most rural Italians were too childish to participate freely in public life, rudimentary elementary and adult education was necessary to create a unified body of citizens. The Casati law, passed in

1859, required incorporated towns to provide free primary education to all boys and girls from six to eight. This was enough schooling that future citizens would accept their civic obligations, but not so much that they would question them. The approach to financing the new school system points to the new state's lack of enthusiasm for comprehensive educational reform. Local governments were responsible for funding elementary schools and adult education classes; the state supported the secondary schools and the universities that would shape the next generation of politicians, professionals, and industrialists.[52]

The tension between the recognized need for minimal education and the fear of too much education that shaped the Casati law also plagued efforts to combat adult illiteracy. Though the new state vowed publicly to raise literacy among adults, it committed few resources. An 1860 decree stipulated that elementary school teachers would be responsible for conducting evening adult classes, but it did not raise their salaries.[53] Teachers had no financial incentive to recruit students, and if classes were cancelled for lack of attendance, it meant less work for already overworked and underpaid teachers. Early legislation for elementary and adult educational reform served to create a system for reproducing the existing class-based social and political order.[54]

After the liberals came to power in 1876 there was renewed discussion about the importance of vocational and popular education. Although these liberal politicians argued for a more comprehensive elementary school system and for adult education programs, few believed that education was a tool for creating politically responsible citizens. Administrators and local officials throughout Sicily embraced the idea that popular education was supposed to produce a patriotic, passive, and contented work force. One Sicilian inspector wrote in his annual report to the Ministry of Public Education:

> The teachers' duty is to make the child understand the world in which he lives ... and teach him to love it with all of its privileges and defects, with its satisfactions and disillusions, and so to create an individual full of fire, of energy and activity, understanding of his duties and rights, productive for himself and for others, ready and willing to fulfil his role on earth.[55]

This attitude was echoed by the local elite. In Sutera, Dr Vaccaro wrote in his geography of Sutera: 'the economists clearly demonstrated the strong confluence between wealth, instruction and the education of the people, because the more instructed and educated the people are, the more hardworking and productive they are.'[56] These politicians believed that by creating a class of loyal labourers, they could control the influence of socialism in the countryside and reinforce the existing order.[57] The Coppino law, passed in 1877, raised the age of compulsory attendance to nine, mandated adult education classes be held in every town, and provided minimal funding to hire teachers and build schoolhouses. Despite its good intentions, the law had little impact in the poorer regions of southern Italy and Sicily. Twenty years later, a survey found that less than 1 per cent of the towns affected by the Coppino law had complied.[58]

The national government should not take the sole blame for the pitiful results of nineteenth-century education legislation. Class interests, combined with the cultural and material conditions of everyday life, also curtailed the growth of popular schooling.[59] Throughout the South, and especially in Sicily, hostility toward popular education among local elites made it extraordinarily difficult to carry out educational reforms. On the island, education had long been an accepted mark of wealth and social distinction. Only the wealthy had the time to learn to read and write and to spend their days reading newspapers. The gentry looked on state efforts to educate the masses as an attack on the social order. As one mayor bluntly wrote: 'Money for schooling is often harmful: obligatory education is useless and dangerous, serving only to create socialists and anarchists who are the ruin of Italy.'[60]

Local elites used their political influence to veto new taxes and to refuse to allocate funds for public schools or night classes as required by law. When the Italian Parliament passed the Orlando law in 1904, allocating additional funds to pay teachers extra for holding night classes, and making literacy a requirement for military service and for a variety of licences and permits, the provincial school boards often failed to enforce it. Professor Ingrao wrote to the district superintendent that Sutera was unable to comply with the Orlando law, because 'there had been no aid from either the [provincial] Patronato Scolastico, which had not even met during the year, or from the municipality which has little interest in the schools.'[61] State laws had little chance of success if the ruling elites responsible for their implementation refused to enact them.

Agricultural workers and artisans recognized education as a means of social mobility. Despite resistance from landowners and politicians, residents sought education for themselves and their children whenever possible. School attendance rose rapidly when political conditions seemed to offer hope for real change. In the 1890s, in the midst of the *Fasci* movements for land reform, Suteresi organized social cooperatives and hired teachers themselves. Mutual aid associations, organized by agricultural workers in the 1890s, offered adult education classes along with low-interest loans and burial insurance to all their members. Bylaws often stipulated that all members had to 'be sure that their children and dependents be given a Christian education, both in church and in school.'[62] By 1900, however, in the wake of hard economic times, rural residents could ill afford to send their children to school from November until May. Attendance in rural schools fluctuated with the agricultural calendar as Sicilians struggled to make enough money to provide for their families' needs. The everyday demands of craft and crops required the labour of all family members, and left little time for dreams of social advancement. Boys and girls continued to enrol in school each fall, but less than half these children attended throughout the year.[63] By spring, even the few who had regularly attended over the winter had left to work in the fields. Schoolteachers constantly lamented that as soon as 'the tiring work of the harvest arrives, students of both sexes are almost all absent from school, caring for the animals, gleaning or lending their small services to their parents.'[64]

The prevailing belief in the powers of education to improve a family's social position meant that residents supported education for both their sons and their daughters. According to the Jacini inquiry, girls comprised 46 per cent of students enrolled in elementary schools in Sicily.[65] In 1897 a group of concerned parents in Sutera petitioned the district superintendent to reopen the only girls' classroom in town after the city council closed it to save money.[66] Educated daughters were a clear sign of social status. Throughout the nineteenth century, women's education had been the privilege of the elite, and by the turn of the century there were practical incentives for relatively well-off agricultural workers to send their daughters to school. Educational reforms had increased the number of teaching positions, and teaching was a means of providing a dowry and a livelihood. Whenever possible, parents encouraged their daughters to study and to earn their teaching certificates, and these children of *braccianti* and *mezzadri* filled the island's normal schools.[67] Sicilians recognized the importance of education for boys and girls in principle; even so, most were not in a position to support the formal education of their children or to take advantage of the prestige that accompanied book learning. A sharecropper from the neighbouring town of Serradifalco told government inspectors in 1907: 'Sometimes we make the sacrifice and send our children to school; but many times we cannot because we lack the means to hire other workers.'[68]

The class antipathy and the demands of daily life that shaped nineteenth-century elementary education in rural Sicily also informed the development of adult education classes. Evening classes, *scuole serale,* were offered for artisans and day labourers who managed to return home each evening; Sunday schools, *scuole festive,* served the needs of rural workers who spent the work week in the fields. There was little support for adult education on the part of the local elite. Rarely did the town council offer more than one or two classes during the year, and these met only sporadically. Men who wished to learn to read and write rarely had time to attend weekend classes. Sunday was a day of rest and relaxation for sharecroppers, and wage workers often spent the day searching for work for the following week.[69]

Classes for women were held with even less regularity. Until the end of the first decade of the twentieth century, most adult women had little practical use for formal education. Until the early part of the twentieth century, there was no real economic or social incentive for women to enter classrooms. The only evening class for women held in Sutera between 1895 and 1899 lasted a mere thirty-six days.[70] By the beginning of the twentieth century, adult classes for women were being scheduled on Sundays. Reports sent to the Ministry of Public Education from rural Sicily noted that in the evening hours women were busy with household chores and family responsibilities. Even if women had the time, they would not traipse through the streets alone after dark. However, Sunday classes were ideal for women. If they were scheduled after mass, when the men gathered in the clubs to discuss their affairs or in the main square to arrange work for the following week, women could easily attend. Yet even after changing the time of women's classes, adult education classes were poorly attended the first few years.[71]

Legislative reforms brought schools and teachers into rural towns but could not change the economic and social conditions that placed the benefits of education beyond the reach of most residents. After half a century, educational reforms had not created a body of literate citizens, nor had they generated much interest in national education among rural Italians. By 1901, literacy rates had increased an average only 0.6 per cent a year across the island. The class interests and material conditions of daily life that limited the effectiveness of educational reforms had a greater impact on women than on men. The failure of popular education had increased the gap between male and female literacy rates.

In 1872, 14 per cent more men than women over twenty-one could read and write; thirty years later, 16 per cent more adult men were literate than adult women.[72]

The failure of secular school reform undermined all legislative efforts to unify the nation. In 1900, Sicilian dialects were still spoken in the island's homes and in the streets. According to the 1901 census, in the province of Caltanissetta fewer than one-quarter of the people over fifteen could read or write Italian.[73] Most literate Suteresi belonged to the local gentry or were professionals.[74] Only doctors, lawyers, notaries, and clerks and a few shop owners could read and write Italian. And even though they spoke Italian, these people conducted their daily affairs in dialect. For Sicilians the spoken language was more than a means of communication: it was a principal means of identification and separated strangers from *paisani*. Even today, Suteresi can tell a stranger's hometown by his or her accent. Slight differences in pronunciation permit residents of Sutera to immediately identify people from the neighbouring towns of Campofranco, Mussomeli, and Acquaviva. Italian was the language of the most recent conquerors and was only spoken by mainlanders and foreigners. Even educated politicians often refused to speak Italian as a matter of principle.[75] Business negotiations did not demand either written or spoken Italian. Labour contracts were generally verbal agreements. Since local officials usually came from the town, governmental transactions usually took place in Sicilian and were later translated into Italian by the clerks.

Despite national conscription, party politics, and educational reforms, rural Sicilians, continued to view the state as an interloper. However, the state's increased presence in rural life established new connections to the outside world for both men and women. By 1900, rural men were more mobile and political, and women were appearing more frequently in the corridors of city hall. Public education was gradually making its presence felt, and by the century's end literacy rates were slowly rising. Though Sicilians never came to see the state as a compassionate champion or a protector, they did begin to use it as an economic and social resource. Transoceanic migration built on these new relations. Migration strengthened the growing utilitarian relationship between rural residents and the state, creating a new sense of national belonging. Inclusion into the nation-state, however, did not replace blood and birth in fixing identity. Rather, national identity joined with the local and familial boundaries used to identify a person's place in the world. This process reveals the interwoven histories of local, national, and global networks and their roles in constructing the meanings of male and female.

Redrawing Boundaries

In the nineteenth century, transnational migration reinforced gender differences in the evolving relations between rural Sicilians and the state. Migration promoted the image of the modern Italian man as mobile and independent, and fostered the idea of the Italian woman as a fixed dependent within her family. Yet within these parameters, mass male migration also encouraged women, as mothers and wives, to use the bureaucracy and make claims on the state in their own right. Rural women began seeing the state as a means to keep their families together and even to fulfil their own private dreams of social advancement. Government agencies provided women with the means to seek redress from banks, shipping companies, and even their husbands. The demands of long-distance communication and money management, combined with the strong desire to improve the family's social status, encouraged women to take adult education classes and to send their children to school more consistently.

Mass male migration fostered a sense of national belonging among rural Sicilian women by altering their familial roles. With their men five thousand miles away, women shouldered new responsibilities at home. They registered the births or deaths of their children and enrolled them in school, and looked after the family's interests – tasks previously assigned to the male head of household. In discharging their added duties, rural Sicilian women entered into public spaces defined by the presence of the state, and this experience repositioned them in the national body.

The new position of rural women in public life is visible in town hall records. Between 1900 and 1909 the proportion of women who officially declared the birth of a legitimate child and who were not midwives rose dramatically, reaching 34 per cent by 1905 and 40 per cent by 1910.[76] This sharp increase coincided with rising rates of male migration. The wives of emigrants contributed to the high numbers: nearly one-third of the women who declared the birth of a child stated that the father was unable to attend because he had emigrated to America some months earlier.

Male migration did more than intensify the already growing presence of women in clerks' offices. It also changed the way women approached local government. Wives and mothers of migrants began to use the state as a means for communicating with family members overseas and for demanding support from their sometimes recalcitrant husbands and sons. When Giuseppa T. needed information regarding the whereabouts of her husband Carmelo M., she went to the mayor and asked him to write to the consulate. Although she surely made inquiries among recently returned migrants and sent messages to her husband with men who were just setting out for Alabama, she also believed that the state was a legitimate venue for pleading her case and for compelling her husband to send her the money she deserved.[77]

After their husbands had established themselves overseas and begun to send money home, financial matters grew more complicated. More rural women began turning to the government for assistance. The state became more than a means for keeping family members together. It also became a conduit into the intricacies of transoceanic business, providing access to national agencies that could look into difficulties with banks and businesses on both sides of the Atlantic. In 1907, Onofrio D. sent 1,100 lire to his wife Onofria V., 'the fruit of extraordinary privation and the work of three years far from his family in a strange land.'[78] The Credito Italiano was supposed to deposit the money directly into the family's account in the post office bank in Sutera. After several months of waiting and many inquiries, the money still had not appeared. Worried and frustrated, Onofria V. went to city hall with all of the receipts and paperwork and asked the mayor to write to the police headquarters in Naples to open an investigation. Onofria continued to press the matter until the problem was resolved.[79]

Greater contact with state officials did not translate into blind faith in the system. The correspondence between women from Sutera and various government officials suggests that these women had some understanding of their rights as wives under the laws of Italy and the United States and that they did not fully trust in the Italian government to look after their interests. When her husband died in a job-related accident in Boyles, Alabama, Onofria R. was aware that she was entitled to monetary compensation and went directly to the mayor. She soon realized that government assistance was going to be minimal. She requested a passport and went overseas to file the claim herself.[80] Leaving her two sons at home with relatives, she set out for Alabama, accompanied by her daughter. Although she spoke no English and had probably never been farther from home than Campofranco, she fought for the money that the mining company owed her, and returned home to Sutera once she received it.

When finances or business affairs were involved, women usually chose the state as their intermediary. When questions of honour, morality, and trust arose, women turned to the church. Few women from Sutera went to the local priest seeking advice regarding legal or financial questions, or even information about a missing husband or son. Reluctance to use the church as a mediator was fostered by deep-rooted suspicion of the clergy. Also, rumours followed women who sought out priests in private when their husbands were away.[81] Clerical avenues of communication were preferred when moral concerns were at stake. In the neighbouring town of Campofranco, Giuseppe R. wrote to the local priest when he heard rumours that his wife had betrayed him. He urged the priest to reprimand her for her behaviour and to pardon her if she showed remorse. When his wife refused to sell their belongings and join him in America to restore her lost honour, Giuseppe again wrote to the priest asking him to read her his letter offering her full forgiveness if she left Campofranco. Women turned to the church when they needed to discuss matters of the heart with their husbands overseas. People mistrusted priests, yet they still lent a certain moral authority to assurances of fidelity and devotion.[82]

The women of Sutera were not unique. Across the island, women were using local and national governments to protect family interests. The Ministry of Foreign Affairs archive holds many petitions from women asking the government to force steamship companies to reimburse them for the cost of their voyages, or for their children's passage. Generally these women had made their way to the United States only to be denied entrance at Ellis Island. Other women appeared as family representatives, seeking justice for sons who had been sent home by immigration officials.[83] Sicilian women had discovered that state agencies enabled them to negotiate family business and settle affairs with the outside world without violating the codes of behaviour that defined the lives of rural women.

The experiences of these rural Sicilian women help explain the apparent contradictions characterizing the lives of Italian women in the United States. Information from Italian-American communities in the northeast suggests that women turned to the state for assistance when they could no longer cope with abusive husbands, unemployment, or illness. Miriam Cohen wrote how Italian women went to government agencies 'in defiance of what all Italians had learned and believed about government.'[84] Yet evidence from rural Italy suggests that these Italian-American women were acting in accordance with Old World ideas about the appropriate relationship between women and the state. When these women crossed the ocean, social workers replaced mayors as representatives of the government, but women still viewed the state as a tool to protect themselves and their families.

The new relationship emerging between women and the state in the corridors of city hall was strengthened by the appearance of women in schoolhouses. The exigencies of male emigration, combined with their own dreams of improving the family's condition, encouraged rural women to send their children to school and to learn to read and write. While women could easily speak with local officials in Sicilian, if they wanted to read money orders, telegrams, or letters from abroad, they needed to learn Italian. Women began attending night schools, and kept their children in school despite the economic hardships involved. Personal experience, which gave practical meaning to reading and writing, succeeded where state reforms had failed.[85]

Between 1901 and the First World War, attendance rose in elementary schools and adult education programs across the island. Social commentators generally supported Giovanni Lorenzoni's assertion that 'all the oral and written testimony agree – emigration is the principal cause of the increase in school attendance.'[86] The migrant experience convinced rural residents that education was not a luxury but a necessity. Migrants living abroad and those who returned told rural Sicilians that workers who could read and write earned higher wages and were offered better jobs. Literacy also offered some protection against scams and con artists.[87] Migrants who couldn't read or write were easy prey for swindlers. Rumours that the United States would soon impose literacy requirements on all immigrants encouraged rural Sicilians to pursue their studies with greater diligence. Also, school lessons taught prospective migrants that literacy was their familial duty. In 1908, Francesco Paolo Minnetti wrote in the national teachers' journal:

> And so for the emigrant, as for the soldier, as for everyone who lives for a time far from their dear relatives and intimate friends, knowing how to read and write is a necessity, and at the same time a comfort. Only in this way can they write to their mothers, wives, and sisters without confiding their secrets to strangers; they can write from their hearts; they can write without worry, in full liberty, the words that they would say at their hearth, in domestic peace, when they are sure of not being overheard by anyone, and not exposed to people's indiscrete curiosity.[88]

In Milocca the number of men enrolled in adult evening classes jumped from 40 in 1900 to 104 six years later.[89] In the province of Caltanissetta, male enrolment in adult education programs more than doubled between 1904 and 1907.[90]

Historians have long been at odds over how much effect migration had on education. Scholars who have studied Italian immigrant communities in the United States have often concluded that Italian Americans had little use for schooling. They point to the higher rates of absenteeism and school leaving among Italians relative to other ethnic communities to support their argument that as soon as children could work and earn money they were pulled out of school.[91] More recently, research focusing on the sending communities has shown that transoceanic migration actually *increased* interest in schooling. Emigrants returning home packed their trunks with books and pamphlets; they even set up circulating libraries. Mark Wyman suggests that the new interest in reading came from returning migrants who were ashamed of their illiterate children.[92]

Evidence from rural Italy offers yet another way of understanding the renewed interest in education in the homelands. In central Sicily, migration inspired emigrants' families to learn to read and write in order to improve the family's condition. If a migrant, his wife, or any of his children were unable to read or write, the family had to rely on the help of a third party. When a woman in Sutera received a letter from her husband in Birmingham, she usually had to seek the advice of the local priest, the mayor, or a literate relative. As Antonio Mangano pointed out, this had a number of negative consequences. It was costly. Translation services had to be paid for either in kind or cash, and once someone outside the family read the letter, its contents were known throughout the village.[93] Women rarely admitted publicly that their husbands had failed overseas and were unable to send money home, and fewer still wanted even their closest relatives to know how much money their husbands sent home. The only hope of safeguarding a family's secrets lay in keeping all letters private. This meant that the wife, if her children were still too young, had to learn to read and write.

In addition, rural women's new familial responsibilities required some degree of literacy. Knowing how to read and write eased school registration, permit applications, and banking. Under the Orlando law, men and women born after 1890 had to provide proof of literacy before they could obtain permits to sell alcohol or tobacco.[94] Although male relatives or city bureaucrats probably helped these women with the paperwork, the ability to avoid the intervention of a third party again made it easier to protect the family's interests. Beyond these immediate and pragmatic incentives, education was critical if a family hoped to use migration as a means of acquiring wealth and social standing. The money earned overseas could purchase the physical trappings of success, but along with houses and land, the family had to attain the cultural and social symbols that defined wealth and status. Literacy and diplomas were as important as money when it came to claiming membership in the local elite. With transoceanic migration offering the real possibility of material improvement in the lives of rural women, schoolroom lessons took on new importance, providing a vehicle for upward mobility. In rural towns across Sicily and southern Italy, migrants wrote home urging their wives to learn to read and to 'keep their children in school at any cost.'[95]

The women of Sutera and Milocca acted on the advice of their husbands. Contrary to Robert Foerster's lament that 'children are torn from the schools to emigrate ... Or, as in Calabria, sent into the fields, especially for the olive gathering and the harvest, because their fathers are abroad,'[96] most families did not pull their children out of school when the head of household emigrated. In fact, elementary school attendance *rose* along with transoceanic migration, as mothers willingly enrolled their children each fall. The mayor of Caltanissetta noted in 1904 that 'enrolments are higher. People willingly rush to register their children, especially the mothers who are in the greatest hurry, poor things, feeling that this is the first step up the social ladder, and they look at their children and dream. Who knows, maybe they will see them rise.'[97] Not all families could actually realize their autumn dreams of seeing their children graduate to the next class. As the months passed, shoes wore out, uniforms frayed, and children stayed home. Still, enrolment in boys' classrooms doubled between 1900 and 1910. Because the state targeted young boys as future active citizens and as soldiers, educational reforms specifically encouraged their attendance, so it is difficult to attribute the steady increase in enrolment in male elementary schools in the course of the first decade of the twentieth century to transoceanic migration alone. However, it is important to note that sharp increases in registration and attendance among boys coincided with the peak years of migration. Not one child in Sutera was noted as having left school because his or her father was overseas.[98]

Transoceanic migration had a much more direct effect on enrolment in girls' elementary classes. For girls, class sizes rose most dramatically after 1905, when the mines were closed and the subsequent economic depression sent emigration rates soaring. Female enrolment in grade one classes in Sutera jumped from fifty-three in 1904 to seventy-six two

TABLE 5.1
Female enrolment in adult classes, 1904–9

	Town	Class	Enrolment	Attend	Pass
1904–5	Sutera	1	30	25	16
1906–7	Milocca	1	24		8
		2	8	6	
		3	5	4	
	Sutera	1	42	30	16
1907–8	Milocca	1	38	30	20
		2	33		4
		3	28		2
	Sutera	1	22	20	15
1908–9	Sutera	1	52	40	16

Source: Archivio Comunale di Sutera, Scuola Serale e festive, 1904–9, cat. ix, cl. 1, fasc. 9.

years later.[99] Between 1906 and 1909, girls' enrolments averaged seventy, and in 1909 the town had to reclassify one mixed grade one class to a girls' class to meet the growing demand.[100] Girls were also staying in school longer. In 1901, thirty girls registered for Ignazia Parravecchio's combined second and third grade class; by 1906 there were nearly eighty girls enrolled in the second and third grades.[101] At the time there were fewer legislative initiatives encouraging female education, so the increased enrolment and attendance of girls in elementary schools must have been motivated by private interests. The growing number of female students suggests that transoceanic migration offered residents real hope of improving their families' economic and social position, and that they were willing to make the necessary sacrifices to ensure their children stayed in school for as long as possible. Whether earned by sons or daughters, diplomas were a visible sign of a family's successful transition from *contadino* to *civile*, and therefore of the family's realization of the migrant dream.

Rural women not only sent their children to school, but also enrolled in adult education classes themselves. Female enrolment in weekend classes rose sharply between 1904 and 1910 along with migration from Sutera (see Table 5.1). Until 1906, few women attended the intermittent classes offered by the local government. On average, between twenty-five and thirty-five women annually enrolled in the one adult course offered. It was only after 1905, as families made the decision to emigrate, that more women enrolled in school. By 1907 the number of women in night courses in Sutera had risen by 40 per cent; a year later, more than fifty women registered for classes in Sutera alone. On average, at least forty women actually attended classes each week. In Milocca, attendance in the *scuole festive* tripled between 1906 and 1907.[102]

Although attendance in Sutera was steadily rising, the number of schools open for women in the province as a whole had fallen. The number of women officially registered for adult classes in the province of Caltanissetta fell by one-third between 1904 and 1907.[103] There does not seem to have been a decline in demand, since the actual number of women who attended classes rose. It is more likely that as city councils faced a rising demand for adult male classes, they cut costs by closing schools for women. Certainly, the records in Sutera and Milocca do not suggest that demand was any less fervent in 1907 than it was in 1904. The impact of enrolment and attendance on female literacy rates is visible throughout the province of Caltanissetta, where illiteracy rates among adult women fell from 84 per cent to 74 per cent between 1901 and 1911.[104] Since far fewer women were affected by the literacy requirements accompanying military service and licensing reforms, increased interest in learning to read and write among women seems to have been explicitly linked to transoceanic migration.

For women and their families, literacy brought a number of rewards. It provided a certain degree of social status and had clear practical implications. Calogero F.'s story is a case in point. Calogero spent five years working in the United States as a bachelor before he returned to Sutera and married.[105] He and his wife opened a small store and bought some land and a house in town. Calogero F. was not going to work in the fields as his father had done. Both husband and wife could read and write. He and his wife had eight children. Three of their children earned a high school diploma, and according to the family, one son was the first Suteresi to graduate from university. The younger children all stayed in school until the war broke out.

The motivational power of migration in bringing rural Sicilians into the classroom did not go unnoticed by educators. Curriculum guidelines for adult classes emphasized that schools should reflect daily life and the needs of rural communities, and many themes touched on the difficulties associated with transoceanic migration. Teachers were encouraged to use examples from rural life in classroom assignments. Arithmetic problems should focus on land use, rents, or buying seed. Yet at the same time, assignments should also promote the interests of the state. As the public debates surrounding migration grew more intense, rural schoolteachers were encouraged to include the topic of migration in their assignments. Initially, reading and writing assignments argued against emigration. Francesco Gazzetti's opening essay in his *Manuale di agricoltura ad uso della scuola popolare e complementare e d'ogni famiglia d'agricoltori*, published in 1885, is titled '*Non emigrare senza forte motivi*,' or 'Do not emigrate without good reason.' He writes: 'often a man is fooling himself who leaves his homeland and abandons his dear country in search of better fortune ... Sad experience teaches us that the majority of those who emigrate, instead of living better, as they hope, [find] their actual condition worsens.' He chastises emigrants for travelling overseas unprepared and without guarantees of work. He admits that a few men return home with savings, but then continues on describing the economic and social costs of emigration. Besides decimating the agricultural workforce, emigration dries up a person's 'love for their country and their family.'[106] In 1880, Bencivenni wrote in a book for boys and girls in elementary school: 'What is your country, you already know – try to leave it! – What palpitations – What undefined frenzy – What emptiness inside.'[107]

By 1905 the tenor of assignments discussing migration had shifted. In *I Diritti della Scuola*, suggestions for possible conversation and composition topics for night and weekend classes reflected new political positions and concerns. Migration was now recognized as a necessary but temporary evil. One writing assignment began, 'Lena writes to her husband in America and describes the miserable harvest from their land, the consequence of poor cultivation and lack of attention. She begs him to return as soon as possible.'[108] They never suggested that women write to their husbands asking for prepaid passage to the Americas. The lesson reinforced the idea that the women left behind anchored their husbands to Italy. By 1908, suggested conversation topics included discussions of emigration that described how

> poor workers leave their homelands, the houses they were born in, their dear relatives to go far faraway to search for work. They go overseas to America or elsewhere because they do not have the means to survive at home, or they cannot find work, they take with them memories and thoughts of their family and country. Judicious emigrants, even from far away know how to do their duties as excellent sons, husbands and father ... Emigrants work and dream of the fortunate day they can return home, content, happy to be able to pay off their debts, to buy a small house or garden, and marry off their daughters.

In the same issue of *I Diritti della Scuola*, dictation exercises appear asking adult students to copy down passages arguing that emigration is harmful to Italian agriculture and could be stopped if workers earned enough to support their families. Composition exercises ask students to write on such topics as 'Tonio must emigrate. Why? ... Where does he go?' or more simply, 'The return of the uncle from America.' Even the arithmetic lessons incorporate experiences of migration: 'Renzo sent his family 1,000 lire from America. With this sum his wife must pay a debt of 489 lire. How much remains for the family's needs?'[109] These lessons described male migration as means to relieve chronic underemployment and reminded emigrants of their duty to their families who remained behind. None of these lessons hinted that emigration could be permanent.

These classroom lessons reflected the personal experiences of girls and women. Students could easily relate to Lena's plight and to her need to send for her husband. In the same way, lessons in arithmetic and writing helped these women fulfil their dreams of upward mobility. The skills they learned would help them run businesses and look after their family interests. The schoolhouse experience also altered women's relationship to the state. As the women of Sutera learned to read and write, they also learned that as wives and mothers they were important to the strength and survival of the nation. In this new space where the state and rural communities met, rural women were able to create ties to Italy.

Although the women of Sutera and Milocca did not emigrate, migration fundamentally changed their relationship with the outside world. The new demands that the migration process placed on women's lives reinforced their independent ties with the state, and incorporated rural women into the emerging identification of Italian women as mothers and wives. Spurred on by their dreams for their families, rural women took advantage of the changing presence of the state in local life. This new relationship with public institutions – government agencies and schoolhouses – ultimately repositioned women in the state. The experience of transoceanic migration altered rural women's political ties to Italy, as surely as it transformed the political identity of migrating men. Although women appealed to the state as mothers and wives, mass male migration undermined women's dependent status as it was originally framed in law.

The consequences of schooling went beyond the ability to claim membership in the local elite. The classroom facilitated physical and symbolic integration into the nation-state. Schoolhouse lessons not only taught women to read and write, but also instructed them about their civic obligations, introducing them to the nation and to their duties as Italian women. Public instruction tried to teach people to appreciate the power and goodness of government.[110] The act of reading further strengthened women's sense of belonging in a national community. Literacy redrew the boundaries of rural women's lives, integrating them into new national and global communities as readers and consumers.

Exploring the emergence of an autonomous relationship between these rural women and the Italian state helps us understand the deeply gendered nature of citizenship. While these women also saw the state as a repressive force through the experiences of their menfolk, their own evolving independent relationship with the state stressed the notion that government institutions could aid families in their quest for upward mobility. Familial and personal interests aided in the formation of a particular kind of female connection to government institutions. In many ways, the relationship women had with government was conservative, grounded as it was in their roles as wives and mothers. Yet claims to pensions and for redress from steamship companies suggest the emergence of a new kind of rights-based politics. Increasing attendance in schools by adult women and young girls strengthened the sense of a belonging to a larger group of Italian woman, with different duties and obligations to the state then men. Perhaps the most important conclusion we can draw from the stories of these women is that notions of citizenship and national belonging are influenced by the personal dreams of women and men and by the world market. States do not define their nations alone.

Chapter Six

Beyond Sutera: Sicilian Women Join the Nation

By 1910 the women of Sutera were going to school and learning to read in greater numbers than ever before. Schooling and literacy did more than redefine the relationship between women and the state: learning to read redrew the boundaries of the world of rural women by integrating them into a distinctly Italian women's community. Classroom lessons taught girls and women to see their familial duties in terms of national responsibilities. In school texts, marriage and mothering became a woman's patriotic duty. The authors believed that properly run rural schools should produce girls who were 'adept in all domestic duties, punctual, orderly, well versed in cleaning.' Girls who were able through their daily tasks to teach children 'their many and sacred duties toward family, society and Nation.'[1] News stories and popular fiction published in regional newspapers underscored this notion of female community and citizenship. Serialized stories recounting the trials and triumphs of being a woman provided rural women with fictional models of the modern wife and mother. News items from mainland Italy, Europe, and overseas contrasted Italy and Italians with eccentric, exotic, and vaguely dangerous peoples in faraway lands. Advertisements extolling the virtues of modern appliances, furniture, clothing, and beauty products encouraged the women of southern Italy to identify their new social roles in terms of modern consumerism, fostering a sense of belonging to a nation. Mass-produced dining room sets, stoves, and sewing machines testified to a family's status. Modern commercial goods replicated the fine embroidery, silks, rugs, and handmade furniture that had distinguished wealthy Sicilians from the rest. Consumer products promising the latest scientific remedies to all sorts of common diseases appealed to a mother's duty to raise healthy and happy children. Although these advertisements rarely reflected a specifically Italian perspective, when read alongside textbook lessons and news stories they helped create a model 'Italian woman.' In this way the urban women of the North were linked to the rural women of the South.

Together, these texts provided a national and international context for Sicilian women to frame their personal experiences of migration. New economic opportunities and the shift to smaller families altered women's roles in the family community. Classroom texts and newspapers provided Sutera's women with opportunities to expand their roles as mothers, wives, and consumers; they also gave new meanings to women's duties. According to popular fiction, being a mother now involved more than bearing and caring for children. Having children brought with it a commitment to ensuring that they surpassed their parents socially and economically. Women as mothers and wives were expected to display their family's higher status and position through their own appearance. Advertisements promising happiness and beauty if only a woman bought their products shaped how these women articulated their family's new social status; they also linked these women to a national and international community of female consumers. The commercial iconography presented rural women with visual descriptions of the new cosmopolitan woman, separated from moral judgments and claiming little direct national allegiance.

When these advertisements are read alongside news stories and serialized novels, changing notions of femininity and motherhood take on greater political significance. The commercial images, popular literature, and accounts of personal tragedy and scandal that filled the pages of the *Giornale di Sicilia* attested to the emergence of a new national female figure, one linked to the nation through her position as a wife and mother in her family and community. These texts contributed to the nationalization of rural women and strengthened regional loyalties among these women. What emerges from this examination of what Sicilian women were reading and buying is that the experience of mass male migration contributed to a new understanding of what it meant to be an Italian woman.

The image of a national community echoed the multiple identities – local, regional, national, and international – created by transnational migration, and accentuated gender differences. Textbook lessons grounded the relationship between individuals and the nation in village and family. Each person's birthplace was the heart of the Italian nation. Lessons tried to draw the conclusion that residents of even the smallest villages could bask in national glory, celebrating the King's birthday and the heroic acts of Mazzini and Garibaldi; however, this approach emphasized regional differences by framing national belonging in terms of each individual's affiliation to hometown and family. In modelling the nation on the family, classroom readings emphasized the gendered nature of citizenship. In these texts the patriotic duties of adult men and women reflected their familial roles as husbands and wives, fathers and mothers. Mass media, advertising, and consumerism reinforced these classroom lessons and thereby strengthened Italian women's identification with their reproductive and familial roles. An examination of the changing nature of community and nation in rural Sicily highlights the complicated relationship between region, gender, and national unity that shaped modern Italy.

Many Italies: North/South, Male/Female

In 'Imagined Italies,' John Dickie writes: 'Nations ... are best thought of as *social fictions* rather than real entities.'[2] This notion, with its suggestion of multiple narratives, social relations, and even nations existing within one state, is especially useful in understanding the complicated nature of national identity among rural Sicilians. Dickie maintains that the idea of the nation refers to the people who claim to be a part of a recognized modern society, circumscribed by the state. A society's institutions, it is understood, make up the state. The nation's physical existence, embodied in the state, is subordinate to the idea of the nation.

As Benedict Anderson noted, nations are created in the minds of their members. Nations cannot claim a physical space; they can only exist in the ideas people have about them. All the individual members of a nation cannot know one another; it follows that people who claim a common national identity meet in the imagined spaces of literature, newspapers, and school textbooks.[3] The nation is described through the tales recounting its birth and through its moments of valour and disgrace – tales that are taught in elementary classrooms, moments that are memorialized in national holidays. The nation fuses disparate communities into one by creating patriotic myths and symbols (flags, coins, anthems) and by imbuing geographical formations with historical and spiritual significance. By offering the idea of the nation as a fixed, seemingly eternal entity, these stories, places, and talismans create common definitions of who is included in – and who is excluded from – from the national body. Among those who do belong, these landmarks and tokens create a sense of belonging to a place, a past, and a future that erases regional and class distinctions.[4] Yet within the nation itself, this sense of communion is grounded in difference. National belonging is rooted in each individual's immediate community, a distinct and special place that is also linked to the nation through a common history, culture, and administrative system. Each citizen identifies with the larger community though his or her self-identification as a man or woman in a local community.

Regionalism played a central if confusing role in the creation of modern Italy. Unlike France or England, Italy did not have a strong geographic centre or strong regional movements. The country's industrial, cultural, and political life was and still is fragmented between the northern cities of Turin, Milan, Florence, and Rome. Yet the absence of a centre did not give rise to strong regional states with cohesive economic and political systems.[5] Few regions could even claim a common language, let alone a shared past or land tenure system. To speak of regionalism in Italy is actually to describe a sense of allegiance rooted in cities, towns, and hamlets. These are linked together through commercial ties, kinship, and various kinds of personal contact. These regions defy cartographers' and politicians' attempts to describe them in terms of clear administrative or political boundaries.[6]

For Suteresi the 'region' included the neighbouring towns of Racalmuto, Grotte, Buompensiere, and Campofranco; it did not include the provincial capital of Caltanissetta. With transoceanic migration, the district of Sutera expanded to include Thomas, Alabama, and Pittston, Pennsylvania, but not Rome or Milan. As Charlotte Gower Chapman noted, rivalry rather than solidarity characterized regional relations: 'A Milocchese is never more Milocchese than when he is visiting one of the towns within his district.' The same can be said of a Suteresi.[7] A sense of being Sicilian was created in a similar fashion. A Suteresi identified with other Sicilians when faced with continental Italians or foreigners. For rural Sicilians, especially women, who were excluded from military service, a conscious separate identification with Sicily took on real meaning with the creation and expansion of the Italian nation-state, a process accelerated by mass migration. Personal and collective identity was constantly changing, depending on a person's situation and circumstances.

The deeply contentious and tangled relationship between the Italian nation and its regions began with Unification. From 1860 onward, the idea of national belonging was inextricably linked to the village. The state's efforts to transform local allegiances into national loyalties through holidays, memorials, and education only reinforced the importance of community and of regional differences. For example, when Italian was made the official language, this highlighted the diversity of dialects in the new nation and excluded many people from claiming full citizenship.[8] It was no easy task to piece together a legal state out of the various kingdoms, territories, and city-states under the Piedmont monarchy.[9]

Regional conflicts were especially evident in discussions about where to locate Italy's capital. The news that the government was contemplating a move from Piedmont to Florence was met with riots in the streets of Turino. The possibility of making Naples the capital brought fierce resistance from Sicilians. The depth of local identification contributed to the decision to make Rome the new capital. The Eternal City, long held captive by the Pope, had no history of administering a secular territory. It had been the capital of Christendom, not of a state. Arguably, Rome's lack of identification with a modern secular region, and its centrality to the twin founding myths of Italian unification – the Roman Empire and the Renaissance – made the city the logical place for the symbolic heart of the new state.[10] Only Rome, with its unique history as the centre of a world religion, could create the appearance of being above the long-standing regional feuds and friendships.

The decision to identify Italy with the glories of Imperial Rome and the southern Renaissance smoothed over many social, political, and cultural differences separating the northern provinces; but by the same token, it emphasized the differences that divided the North from the South. At first, in 1860, the Piedmontese viewed the southern provinces and the islands as a wealthy but mismanaged land. Too long separated from the civilizing power of northern Europe, the people and the culture of the South had sunk into depravity.[11] According to Italy's new rulers, the South was a wealthy but ungovernable land fixed in a feudal past. Government envoys sent to study the island operated under the assumption that the island's problems were a consequence of poor government rather than environmental or economic conditions. By the 1880s, Franchetti, Sonnino, Nitti, and Fortunato had dismantled the myth of a land of natural wealth, but not that of southern distinctiveness. In the decades after unification the southern regions and islands came to play a critical if unsavory role in the national mythology. The people of the South embodied the worst characteristics of the new nation. They were the outlaws, the backward children, the immoral and sinful. Politically and culturally excluded from the founding national myths, southern men and women could claim only a tenuous link to the national body.

Locating the spirit of Italy in an imperial past and cultural rebirth excluded the South from the national myths of Unification. Despite its wealth of Greek and Roman ruins, the South was linked to the atrocities and barbarism of Spanish and Bourbon rule. These regions had no connection to the great art, men, and ideas that flowed from the medieval city-states. As Benedetto Croce wrote: 'The South is almost extraneous to the second wave of civilization (the first being that of ancient Rome) which radiated from the Italian peninsula between the beginning of the communes and the height of the Renaissance.'[12] According to these authors, the 'civilizing force' of the Renaissance never reached Naples, Catanazaro, or Palermo, or any of the smaller villages between.[13] To erase the differences separating Tuscany, Lombardy, and Piedmont, national leaders created an Italy that could not include the South. In Sicily the sense of being excluded from the nation took concrete and violent form shortly after Unification. In the wake of rising crime rates, mass desertions, and rumours of insurrection, the leaders of the newly formed nation felt it was time to take drastic action. In 1863, government troops invaded the island, ostensibly to round up draft dodgers and criminals. During this campaign they placed military cordons around towns and cut off water supplies to villages in the heat of midsummer. Amidst swirling allegations of torture and abuse, Sicilian hostility and resentment toward the new government grew, heightening the sense of not being part of the new nation.[14] The narratives of Unification and the actions of the government depict the peoples of the South as cultural and social outsiders.

In Italy's national histories, founding myths, and lived experiences, a South emerged marked by corruption, violence, poverty, and barbarism. The southern regions defined what the rest of Italy was not and would never be. Sicily and the South could never truly be a part of modern Italy with its promises of progress and reform. History took a different path in the South. Consalvo Uzeda, Prince of Francalanza, the protagonist of *Viceré*, a novel by Frederico de Roberto, published in 1894, had this to say about Sicily:

> History monotonously repeats itself; the men have been, are and always will be the same. The superficial conditions have changed: certainly, a chasm seems to separate the pre-1860 Sicily, still almost feudal, and that of today; but the difference is completely cosmetic. The first official elected by universal suffrage is not a commoner, nor a bourgeois, nor a democratic; it is me, because my name is the prince of Francalanza.[15]

Frederico de Roberto was voicing the growing belief that after thirty years, the project of national unification had failed. Sicily remained invulnerable to the powers of liberty and democracy. By the end of the nineteenth century the regional tensions that marked the birth of Italy had been incorporated into the very idea of the nation itself. This, however, was not the fault of the founding fathers; rather, it was a sad testimony to the corruption and degeneration of the southern people.

By the end of the nineteenth century the idea of the South as a distinct historical, economic, and cultural world had been fixed in national narratives. Francesco Nitti eloquently described the situation in *Napoli e la questione meridionale* (1903):

> Between Northern Italy and Southern Italy the economic and social differences are greater than in 1860. There are now two Italies: one rapidly advancing, already entering the zone of the industrialized civilizations; the other is mired in its growing misery ... a close examination of the question leaves one with one inescapable conclusion. Political unification has been unequally beneficial; the same economic, financial and social laws that benefit the North often poison the South.[16]

Forty odd years after Unification, regional tensions still defined the Italian nation.

The idea of the South as other appeared with particular clarity in discussions about national education. Italian pedagogical principles reflected the belief of the founding fathers that elementary and adult education was essential to the creation of a national culture and the erosion of local allegiances. Language and civic education were identified as the two most important weapons in the struggle to create an Italian citizenry. Politicians believed that linguistic unity was a prerequisite to the creation of a liberal state, and that civics and national history taught patriotism, 'promoting and strengthening national sentiment.'[17] Yet by focusing on language and civics, these lessons reinforced the new nation's diversity.

In discussions about rural schools, teachers and professors inevitably pointed to the importance of language. By the First World War they recognized that fluency in Italian was crucial for both patriotic and practical reasons. Knowledge of Italian linked all residents to the soul of the nation and was essential for building a strong military and labour force. Grade one teachers were urged to 'always use the mother tongue when teaching, and through frequent conversations ensure your students do the same.'[18] Dialects, like foreign languages, cast suspicion on a person's patriotism and morality.[19] In rural hill towns like Sutera, Italian lessons created a bilingual citizenry. Those fluent in Italian and local dialect became the mediators between the state and villagers who could not speak Italian. The movement to make Italian the national language transformed local dialect into a symbol of Sicilian distinctiveness. Sicilians believed that continental Italians and foreigners could neither understand nor learn their language.[20] The presence of the two languages reinforced the special position of rural Sicilians within the national body.

Along with lessons in Italian, the first textbooks generally included a section on 'the rights and duties of man and citizens.' These readings identified the principal duties of citizens as 'respect for the laws and authority, payment of taxes, defense of the state, education and work.'[21] By the 1880s, curriculum guidelines published by the Ministry of Public Education had expanded the definition of an Italian citizen to include specific moral characteristics. Teachers were expected to instil in their students a strong sense of honour, obedience toward God and parents, respect for authority, and a belief in hard work, thrift, and honesty. By the turn of the century these themes were the foundation of the elementary school curriculum for boys and girls. In 1905 the Ministry of Public Education reiterated these original goals of education in their explanation of the new primary school curriculum. The first years of school should create 'honest citizens, industrious, respectful of laws and ready to serve the state.'[22] Similar injunctions shaped adult education programs. In the government publication *La Scuola in Azione*, educational experts recognized that hostility toward Rome accounted in part for poor attendance in schools: 'These people, are still used to seeing the state as an enemy, a tyrant that sucks the blood from the poor through taxes, and that steals children, at the age of twenty, from their families.'[23] Teachers were urged to teach basic reading and writing skills but to never forget that it was also their duty to teach the ignorant peasants their obligations as members of the Italian nation, and hopefully instil a sense of patriotism. In the curriculum guidelines published in 1905, the Ministry of Public Education wrote that teachers must 'clearly explain the duties and rights in a civil society to ignorant adults ... These people who have lived until now in a state of dependency, can in school and through school, acquire the necessary means to become conscious citizens and effectively participate in public life.'[24]

While the goal of creating a patriotic, obedient, and loyal citizenry was clear, the readings used to teach children and adults their common allegiance to Italy served to highlight regional differences. Textbooks built national loyalty through local allegiances, teaching students to conceive of the nation as an extension of their own village. In the lesson on *La Patria*, Rezzo opened with the teacher describing Italy from the point of view of the village: 'Today, on the map of Italy, the teacher had us look at a small, small point. – "Here" – She said – "our town, the place where we are right now!"' After teaching students that they lived in a particular geographic location, Rezzo went on to fuse the love of one's hometown with love of the larger state. Students read aloud, 'Oh, the town where I was born, it is more dear to me than any other.' They read how their hometown was defined by the presence of their house, their church, their school, and their parents and relatives: 'These are the reasons I so love my little town! It is a little part of my Nation!'[25] The lesson was clear: the nation should be conceived of towns like Sutera writ large.

Yet these same readings called attention to the disjuncture between official histories and lived experience by focusing history lessons on the 'virtues and glories of the Romans' and the Risorgimento.[26] In the biographical descriptions of the brave and wise Vittorio Emanuele II, 'who united all Italians into one people, made Italy one kingdom, and for this was called the father of the state,' students learned to see the King of Piemonte as their father and liberator. Garibaldi was usually portrayed as 'the hero of the people,' a man who sacrificed his life to free the South from an 'evil king.'[27] But to the people of Sutera the Piedmont army had not been the great liberator. And the heroes of the Risorgimento had not 'rescue[d] them from Tyranny,' but rather had arrived in force to draft their sons and quell their uprisings. By describing Italy as a vast web of villages and cities, these lessons taught rural Sicilians to see themselves as members of a community who formed part of the nation. But the same lessons also highlighted Sicilians' sense of separateness.

Migration reinforced the complicated relations between village and nation. As family members left their towns to seek work overseas, they physically redefined the borders of their hometowns. The experience of transnational migration expanded an individual's definition of *paese* to include scattered communities around the world, tied together through the bodies of absent fathers, sons, daughters, brothers, sisters, and cousins. The boundaries of the smallest southern villages stretched across the ocean to incorporate neighbourhoods in New York, San Francisco,

Buenos Aires, and Sao Paolo.[28] The map of the Italian peninsula hanging in every schoolhouse could not incorporate these new communities into the nation, yet they carried greater significance in the daily lives of rural Sicilians than Rome, Naples, or Turin. As the families of migrants flocked to the schoolhouses, classroom lessons underscored yet again the ways that their own communities did not conform to textbook descriptions of the relationship between nation, state, and village.

The symbols of the new nation – war memorials, statues of Garibaldi and Mazzini, tombs of unknown soldiers, coins, and national holidays – not only emphasized regional differences, but were also gendered. National myths and symbols reflected distinct ideas of masculinity and femininity. The image of the brave soldier defending the nurturing, fecund female land offered a compelling description of the new Italian man and woman. If men were the hardworking and honest protectors of Italy, women were the nation. The image of heroic, self-sacrificing, kind, and generous mothers/daughters became the model for the patriotic Italian woman. These notions of male and female citizenship gained new significance in rural Italy through the experience of transnational migration.

The most explicit descriptions of female patriotism appear in the schoolbooks used in elementary classes. Although the Ministry of Public Education did not officially distinguish between the civic duties and the moral virtues of boys and girls in the first two years of school, a gendered construction of citizenship emerged in these textbooks. The state was modelled on the family. As early as 1860 the conclusion of a popular text warned its young readers:

> Kingdoms do not rise and fall as fortune wills, but according to the good or bad works of their citizens. Just as families where the father is wise, prudent and just, the mother is loving and looks after the home, the children are docile, industrious, diligent, agreeable and affectionate with each other, prosper; so prosper cities, provinces and kingdoms where virtue flowers, and cities where vice prevails fall into ruins.[29]

The equation of state and family became the standard metaphor in textbook civic lessons published for boys, girls, and adults throughout the nineteenth century. Ildebrando Bencivenni reminded his students: 'Is the state, perhaps, the place where we were born? The mountains, the valleys, the endless plains? – No. The state is a vast family that lives together in a neighborhood.'[30] Within this family model, the ideal male citizen was idealized in the figure of the father/husband and the perfect female citizen in that of the mother/wife. Young boys were taught that their obligations to the state were the same as those to their parents and to their future wives and children. Young men must be obedient, work hard, and be willing to sacrifice their lives in defence of their immediate family and their extended national family. In the girls' textbooks, docile, obedient, and hardworking maids contrasted with these descriptions of active, strong, healthy, and impassioned young soldiers.

The familial model of female citizenship gave women a certain degree of authority as mothers, but at the same time emphasized their dependent status as daughters. 'There are, my daughter, two great things you must love with all of your strength,' concluded Guido Fabiani, 'your house, which is the sweet domain of your mother; and the mother of us all: *La Patria!*' To drive home this lesson, Fabiani concluded his textbook by exhorting his students to 'remember, good, prudent, hardworking women make a happy home; and happy homes make a happy state.'[31] In the conclusion of her reader for young girls, Ermelinda Fornari wrote: 'I hope to see you surrounded by those dearest to your heart, and always happy; I hope that in each of you has been permanently impressed the idea of duty. This should be your inseparable companion throughout your tender life. I do not want you to forget for even an instant that you are the daughters of this beautiful, noble, dear and glorious Italy, whose grandeur rests in the breasts, arms, minds and hearts of its children.'[32] Underlying the instructions of Fabiani and Fornari was the premise that these daughters would remain children of the state, even as they grew up to be mothers in their own right.

Textbooks written for girls' classes emphasized specific female forms of patriotic love and work that would produce virtuous and wise mothers. Young girls should learn to love and obey their parents and to strive to emulate their own mothers. Curriculum guides for girls' schools suggested that civic lessons 'should follow the general outline so that women know the duties and rights of men, [but] must, in the end, differentiate themselves, paying particular attention to the office of women in family life, as children and as adults.'[33] In the classroom, girls learned that their rights and duties consisted of housework and child care. The duty of Italian women to the state was to raise strong and courageous sons and daughters for the nation. They were expected to instil a sense of moral responsibility and obedience in their children. In *Casa Mia, Patria Mia*, a popular textbook for girls in grade three, Guido Fabiani included a lesson titled '*Madri di eroi*' (Mothers of Heroes) that clearly illustrated the patriotic duties of Italian women. One morning a classroom received a postcard of a monument in Rome. The statue of a woman holding a flag surrounded by her five sons was called *La Famiglia Cairoli* (the Cairoli Family). As the teacher passed the postcard around the class, she told her students of the sacrifice of Adelaide Cairoli:

> Many years ago, as I have told you many times, the nation lived through sad times; Italy was enslaved and divided. Patriots sought to free her. Adelaide Cairoli had nothing but her five sons who had grown strong and good around her; but when the people began to rise up, when the war against the oppressors was declared, Adelaide did not hesitate for one moment and said to her sons: 'I am a woman and I cannot fight; you are men and can: go: the country needs you.'

Her sons left to fight. Two died in battle. Luigi, who fought alongside Garibaldi during his ill-fated assault on Rome, died in Naples, exhausted from the campaign. Giovanni died in his mother's arms from wounds sustained in battle. Only Benedetto survived. After the war he became a deputy and minister, and in 1878 he saved Umberto I from an assassination attempt. Adelaide Cairoli deserved to be recognized among the nation's heroes because she had 'lived a simple and good life, ardently loved two equally great things: her country and her house.'

Luigi Natoli concluded his textbook with a similar message. After a long lesson on the how to serve the state, focusing on a soldier's duty, Bice, a young girl, asks the teacher: 'If everybody must defend the State to ensure its greatness and prosperity, what can women do? Can they go and fight?' The teacher responds: 'Women are not obliged to go and fight; but armies alone do not defend the state; nor does war alone make a state great and rich. Women must be virtuous and raise men from childhood to also be virtuous: they must teach them to do their duties, to obey the laws. When they are mothers they must teach their sons to be strong and courageous, and so learn to be good soldiers.'[34]

The fundamental purpose of female education was to prepare young girls for domestic life. It was not supposed to develop their intellect. Geltrude Malagoli preached this lesson to her young female readers in 1913:

> Your country, my daughters, has greater need of good housewives and wise mothers, than smart women capable of seizing the daily bread from male civil servants, or languid young ladies who study life through novels or

elegant charity ladies who abandon their children in the arms of nursemaids. These frivolous creatures are worth very little as daughters, wives and mothers![35]

The duties of young girls were embedded in the moral tales that comprised the readings for elementary schools. Usually set in a small provincial town, the stories depicted the lives of fictional girls who found happiness and praise in obeying their parents and helping with housework. Ill fortune inevitably plagued those classmates who were greedy, vane, and dishonest. Mixed in with these moral messages were practical lessons on personal hygiene, what clothes to wear in winter and summer, and how to shop, do laundry, and to care for household utensils. The implicit message in all these stories was that a young girl's future happiness rested in her domestic abilities. The warning was that if she failed to learn her lessons she could grow to be the ruin of the family and the state. Ermelinda Fornari, echoing Lorenzoni's tale of the two housewives and the condition of their families, cautioned young girls that a woman 'can be an angel or a demon, the smile and the joy of a family, or its greatest danger, the source of all its bad fortune.'[36] In warning young girls and adult women of their power to destroy the nation, these texts described the duties of a modern wife and mother. Girls were reminded of the influence they would have as adults over their husbands and children. A well-ordered, modest, and peaceful home would keep men out of the bars, cafes, and nightclubs and far from the evil temptations of drink, gambling, and immoral women.[37]

How women whose husbands lived and worked overseas personally received these lessons can only be imagined. Certainly, the warning that women could destroy the family, and therefore the nation, echoed notions of femininity embedded in the Sicilian code of honour. Rural women, especially the wives of migrants, could readily transfer their personal understanding of the dire consequences of their failure to live respectably (to appear chaste, avoid fieldwork, etc.) to the nation. These readings also provided a national context for understanding their new maternal roles. The notion of motherhood that emerges in these texts resonated with the personal experiences of rural women who came of age in the first decade of the twentieth century, and who associated status and success with smaller families. As Rezzo wrote in her text, mothers did everything for their children: 'She thinks of everything: food, clothes; she takes care of us when we are sick, advises us to be good, and to study, to grow strong and honest.'[38]

Practical courses such as home economics and gymnastics, integrated into the female elementary school curriculum after 1900, reinforced the links between motherhood, domesticity, and civic duties. Sewing, personal hygiene, laundry, ironing, cooking, and housekeeping comprised a woman's duty to her family and nation. Textbooks for girls and women included specific instructions on how to wash clothes (soak the clothes; add soap and scrub well; pour boiling water over a layer of ashes spread above the clothes, repeat; rinse well, soap, scrub, rinse; wring them out and lay them in the sun to dry), how to properly preserve foodstuffs, and how to wash lettuce. The lessons ended with hygienic explanations of woman's work: 'The earth and fertilizer contain dangerous germs ... Which is why intelligent and educated housewives never conserve water when they clean salad greens.'[39] Curriculum guidelines for adult women's classes insisted that lessons on domestic economy and housework be incorporated into all facets of teaching, including lessons in arithmetic, conversation, and dictation. Traditional forms of female labour acquired a modern, scientific aura and a patriotic significance in classroom texts. By the First World War, exhortations to let air and sun into the house, wash your clothes and your body regularly, and eat nutritious foods were being specifically directed toward girls and women. Knowledge of the principles of domestic hygiene would save the nation. Gherardo Ferreri made this perfectly clear when he argued that only by teaching all women the principles of basic hygiene could the state protect its future generations from alcoholism, tuberculosis, syphilis, pellagra, and malaria.[40]

Similar assumptions framed discussions of women's physical education. In an 1896 article on the benefits of physical education, Angelo Mosso wrote:

> Free movement, walking, jumping, running and games are more useful for women than for men. For the latter, gymnastic exercises that develop the arms and the back muscles can be useful. For a woman, these exercises are not as useful; maternity, a woman's reason for being, does not rest in her arms, but in the lower part of her torso where the largest muscles used to walk, to run and to play are located.[41]

Discussions about the curriculum for female education reflected the belief that women's duties were to ensure the health and well-being of future generations of dutiful, obedient producers and reproducers.

By the time the women of Sutera began to enter the classroom, texts and curriculum guidelines were offering a well-defined construction of the ideal Italian woman. How literally rural women accepted this model is impossible to judge. Certainly not all girls and women enthusiastically embraced the lessons extolling the joys of housework and motherhood and equating them with civic duty.[42] However, the idea of the Italian woman created through schoolhouse lessons resonated with the values and customs of the rural world. On many levels these stories and poems reflected the religious and traditional values that had long shaped female roles in the community. The general moral lessons embedded in the readers were similar to those preached in church every Sunday: obey God and your parents, do not steal or lie. Messages regarding the value of work and modesty echoed local proverbs: 'Good land and a good wife bring a man happiness,' 'Good habits, not beauty, bring love.'[43]

Literacy also integrated the women of Sutera into national life through daily newspapers. Serialized novels and stories of life on the mainland and overseas reinforced the growing sense of local and national identity shaped by textbook readings. By the late nineteenth century, Sicilians in even the most remote hill towns had access to regional newspapers. These newspapers reflected the complicated nature of the evolving relationship between town and nation. The pages of the *Giornale di Sicilia*, in particular, offer an opportunity to explore how access to newspapers at the turn of the century helped nationalize rural women and at the same time shape their sense of belonging to far-flung communities in the Americas.

In Italy, unlike in Great Britain or France, no one newspaper could claim a national readership: there was no *Le Monde* or *Times*. The strong regional character of the Italian press stemmed in part from the absence of a vigorous metropolitan centre, such as Paris, London, or Berlin. Most of the island's papers were published in Palermo or Catania; only a few came from the northern cities.[44] At the end of the nineteenth century some these newspapers became true regional papers by extending their readership beyond the city limits into the countryside. The *Giornale di Sicilia* enjoyed the widest circulation of all the island's papers. Founded in 1859 by the poet and patriot Girolamo Ardizzone, it sought to report on events across the island. At the beginning of the twentieth century the *Giornale* was being distributed throughout the island and even in Reggio Calabria. By the First World War, residents of Milocca had access to eight newspapers that came into town.[45]

As female literacy rates rose in the wake of mass male migration, popular fiction, news stories, and print advertising campaigns published in the local papers enjoyed a wider circulation among rural women. While devotional texts and the biographies of saints remained the most popular books among rural readers, women enjoyed secular stories of adventure and love, which were serialized in local papers. In 1930, Charlotte Gower Chapman noted that roughly 'a dozen people in town read for pleasure, mostly women, some of whom read religious pamphlets and others the few old novels which they might have or the serial story in the newspaper.'[46] The fiction and news stories that appeared in the paper reinforced schoolhouse lessons and became vehicles for creating a national popular culture that embraced rural women and reinforced gendered notions of citizenship. By romanticizing ideas of maternal love, sacrifice, and patriotism, these stories provided models of Italian womanhood. The heroines of popular novels echoed the descriptions of the ideal woman found in classrooms.

In the first decades of the twentieth century, serialized novels were directed explicitly at women and affected how women saw themselves and the world. The publishers of major newspapers carefully chose novels that would appeal to women. As Antonio Gramsci wrote: 'The man of the people buys only one newspaper, when he buys one. The choice is not even personal, but is often that of the family as a group. The women have a large say in the choice and insist on the "nice interesting novel."'[47] Although few publishers targeted rural women as their principal audience, they recognized the importance of female readers and sought out certain kinds of novels to boost sales and profits. Every major newspaper carried at least one serialized story to boost circulation. Many of the stories published in *Giornale di Sicilia* were purchased from national agencies. In 1899 an advertisement appeared in the *Bollettino della stampa italiana* announcing the opening of an agency that sold serialized novels to newspapers. They offered works from the greatest European authors, including Victor Hugo, Jules Michelet, and Leo Tolstoy. They asked editors to specify whether they were interested in 'novels that were bloody, historical, travelogues, educational, literary [or] patriotic.'[48] However, the *Giornale* also published works by local authors and popular female writers.

By romanticizing ideas of maternal love, sacrifice, and patriotism, these stories helped create models of Italian womanhood. Fictional heroines could serve as ideal role models, echoing descriptions of the ideal woman found in classrooms. In the historical fiction published in the *Giornale*, a specifically Sicilian version of the Italian woman appeared. Rural women could see themselves in the descriptions of the heroic exploits of Sicilian women of the past. The images of these historical heroines merged with the protagonists of romantic fiction. In these stories of love, female authors from the mainland described the model Italian woman in terms that reflected the portraits of women drawn in the historical narratives.

These stories created models for heroic women and men that took on a distinctly nationalist flavour. Between May 1909 and January 1910, the *Giornale* serialized Luigi Natoli's *I Beati Paoli* in 239 episodes. The novel is set at the beginning of the eighteenth century against the backdrop of the ascension of Philip V to the Spanish throne, the subsequent European wars of succession, the transfer of Sicily to the house of Savoy, and the struggles between church, state, and nobility on the island. It tells the story of a secret vigilante group that protected the powerless in the face of a corrupt nobility. In this story of adventure, orphan stepbrothers, Blasco and Emanuele, sons of a knight who died in the service of the House of Savoy, fight to regain their position from their evil uncle Raimondo. The female characters are divided sharply into good and evil. The mothers of the stepbrothers, Cristina, a peasant, and Alosia, a noblewoman, typify the good woman: they are humble, self-sacrificing mothers and wives who recognize their duties to their families, their children, and their lords. Both die protecting their young sons. In contrast, the noblewoman Gabriella, the wife of Don Raimondo, is a manipulative, conniving, selfish woman who betrays her husband and seduces young Blasco for her own pleasure. The depictions of Cristina and Alosia reinforced the teachers' lessons that the state did not need frivolous, selfish, or egotistical mothers and wives. While these historical adventures echoed the classroom lessons about the heroism of the leaders of the Risorgimento, they also focused on the particular characteristics of Sicilians. The exploits of Blasco and Emanuele bore witness to the innate cunningness, native intelligence, loyalty, and honour of Sicilians.[49]

These historical adventures alternated with stories of love, romance, and tragedy. Newspapers regularly published short, romantic stories alongside popular romance novels directed at women readers. In the early spring of 1913, the *Giornale* published Carola Prosperi's *Una Lezione d'Umilità* and Clarice Tartufari's *Vaghe Stelle dell'Orsa.*[50] In 'A Lesson in Humility,' Prosperi describes a playboy's self-destruction. Peppino Mari, she writes, was a man 'whom success destroyed.' The short story recounts his seduction of Marinetta, 'a delicious young woman who graciously wore her beautiful name, nothing other than a modest provincial bourgeois, recently moved to the city.' After a great deal of resistance, she succumbs to his advances. Basking in his success, he makes fun of her husband, boasting that no woman has ever betrayed him. Marinetta quietly nods, 'smiles ironically,' and responds, 'You are very sure of yourself.' Shortly afterwards, Marinetta disappears. A few weeks later she sends him a postcard from a coastal town. He rushes to her side, to find her living in domestic bliss with her husband. The young lover has been cuckolded by the husband. Prosperi's story is one of modern love. Marinetta's behaviour would not have been tolerated in rural Sicily. Yet rural women would have been receptive to the underlying message of the meaning of marriage. The themes of these stories focused on jealousy, betrayal, the beauty of marriage, and the power of maternal love. These newspaper heroines inevitably found fulfilment in marriage and family. Combined, they integrated the women of Sutera into a national popular culture, strengthening their civic and personal identification with marriage and motherhood.

Local and international news stories buttressed the fictional descriptions of good and bad Italian women. Even the most cursory survey of the news stories in the *Giornale* at the turn of the century leaves the reader with a clear sense of the characteristics of good women and bad women. In a September 1910 article, 'Patriotic Memorial for a Heroine,' the *Giornale* celebrated the exploits of Colomba Antonietti. Born in Perugia in 1829, she married Luigi Porzio in 1846. Two years later, disguised as an officer, she joined her husband's unit and fought in Veneto. The year after that she died fighting alongside her husband in defence of the Roman Republic. Sixty years later, Colomba's patriotism was framed in the context of her marriage. Her loyalty to Luigi and Italy were merged together; like a good wife, she had willingly sacrificed her own life for husband and country. Public homage to Colomba reinforced the idea that marriage and family defined the relationship between women and the nation.[51]

Except in popular fiction, positive images of women rarely appeared in the papers. Women usually appeared in news stories as victims of natural disasters or of conniving men, or to illustrate the horrors of a particular event, or as devious, adulterous, and evil. In 1909 the women of Sutera could read in detail how Giorgio Calvi shot the archpriest Domenico Oliva five times as he left church after celebrating mass in a small town in Calabria. 'The cause was the usual one. Giorgio Calvi returned from America after three years overseas, to find his wife pregnant. It did not take long for him to discover that his substitute during his absence was the archpriest.'[52] In another story a year later, Domenico Piasente made a surprise visit back home and discovered his wife in the arms of an officer in the Guardia Finanza. Armed with a large stick, he killed the young lover. His wife escaped into the nearby woods. In stories like these, the woman was construed as the victim, as too weak-willed to resist the man's advances. In other stories, blame was placed squarely on the woman. In 1913 a man sent for his wife. She was pregnant by another man and refused to leave Palermo, stating that 'American air was not for her.' His relatives quickly apprised him of the situation. Beniamino Schirò charged his brother with prosecuting the lovers, and both were jailed.[53] Suteresi could readily identify with these stories. At least one returned migrant lodged a formal complaint with the diocese in Caltanissetta, accusing the archpriest in Sutera of seducing his wife while he was working overseas. Whether women were to blame or not, these stories emphasized the idea that women were the moral centre of the family and the nation.

If regional differences were diminished by this printed evidence that indeed 'tutto il mondo è paese' (all the world is a village), so were class and national distinctions. The murder of the Countess Tregona, originally from Palermo, who was brutally pummelled to death by a male companion, clearly illustrated that money and titles were not enough to protect a woman's life or honour in the face of what many considered to be public licentiousness. Rural Sicilian women could follow the upcoming wedding of the Prince of Piedmont. Alongside the news of world events – trouble in the Balkans and Turkey, and Italy's manoeuvring in global affairs – were these stories that resonated with the traditional cultural mores of honour that defined village life. Rural women found their own experiences reflected in these pedagogical and fictional narratives.

The experience of migration contributed the shaping of Italian women and men by depicting an America that turned women into men and men into women. In February 1906, on page one of the weekend edition of the *Giornale*, ran the headline 'The Marriage of Two Women.' 'John Allaine Whitman and Miss Mariette Jolly were joined in matrimony, last Friday, by Judge Buchanan of Independence. Last night, the police, who had received a complaint regarding the identity of the groom, were able to ascertain that John A. Whitman was a ... woman!'[54] While there was little direct commentary on the story, it would appear that America blurred sexual identities. In the wilds of America the poor Italian could not even be sure that men were men or women were women. Whereas in

Italy, women dressed as men only in defence of their country as they followed their husbands into battle.

A few days later the *Giornale*'s readers were offered further proof of the perversion of American culture. In the column '*Italian-American Chronicles*' was the story of the unfortunate Nicola Murdaca, who was executed in the Jersey City jail on 11 February 1906, for killing his wife, Narua Varacalli. On 4 May 1905, Nicola could no longer take his wife's growing 'popularity,' as her conduct was described in the American newspapers, and ferociously attacked his wife with a hatchet. 'Peace in death,' continued the article:

> But we who, underneath, the gossip and the prostrate body of the woman, would give her a name that is anything but popular, to be precise and to remind our readers of the true nature of the crime we would say that the woman had become an adulteress, and the husband, in a moment of justifiable rebellion, after he had uselessly begged her to stop her deplorable conduct, went mad and killed her.
>
> In America, 'popularity' is not bad and Nicola Murdaca was condemned without one person coming to his defense ... There was the death, the killer, the testimony – consequence: the conviction; and we are left to note in our black book that Nicola Murdaca is the first Italian killed in Hudson county. We have said: killed, while to be more respectful of the law we should have said: executed. But having been said, it is not worth the effort of taking it back.

The point of this story was clear: in America, men were being murdered for acting like men. Poor Nicola, driven to extremes by his unfaithful wife, had done what any honourable man would have done – he had killed her in a jealous rage. But in the upside-down world of America, his understandable response to his wife's behaviour had led to his being convicted of murder and being hanged, while her behaviour was described in far more sympathetic terms, leaving her the innocent victim. To some extent, these stories justified the decisions of those Sicilians who chose to stay home, and of those women who chose not to join their husbands in the Americas. While life on the other side of the Atlantic promised higher wages and plentiful work, it was also morally suspect. The article about Nicola and Narua stands in sharp contrast to the ones about Italian vendettas, in which the actions of avenging returnees were generally described sympathetically.

News stories about the suffrage movement in England reinforced the negative image of Anglo-American women and highlighted the dangers of 'mannish' women. In March 1913 the *Giornale* published a photograph of Emmeline Pankhurst with the following commentary:

> Mrs. Pankhurst truly has *la physique de son rôle* writes Bergeret in the *Stampa* – her features are lined with such ingenious evil that a sudden encounter with this woman would even make the honourable Podrecca make the sign of the cross. She has the appearance of a ridiculous anti-Christ from her eyeglasses and her indescribable hair ... Looking at the photo, perhaps perversely retouched by the magazine, that I have under my eyes, the Leader of the suffragettes, clearly illustrates the crisis out of which suffrage was born: and through it runs one act of the vast female tragedy of our century. The crisis of the family, triumphant individualism, the new goals proposed by a life based on the satisfaction of greed and pride ... Our century is facing the catastrophe of the eternal tragedy of those who have mistaken their sex, as is so eloquently expressed in this portrait of Mrs. Pankhurst.[55]

The author here is warning readers of the dangers of women who claim the privileges of men and reject their sacred duties to family, house, and nation.

In Sicilian towns these stories bolstered a sense of moral and spiritual superiority in confrontation with the United States and Europe. Newspapers contributed to the nationalization of rural men and women without erasing regional or gender differences. In serialized novels and newspaper articles, the women of Sutera read about the exploits of fictional mothers and wives and about the sufferings of real women in faraway worlds. These narratives combined to describe notions of the new mother and wife. The fictional stories and historical notes described the qualities that comprised a good mother and wife in private and national life. National news items describing the fate of adulterous wives and negligent mothers enabled rural women to link their personal experiences to the nation. International stories offered a glimpse of the exotic and strange. Stories of women who dressed as men who married other women, of men sentenced to die only because they tried to protect their male honour when faced with an unfaithful wife, and of the horrors of female suffrage all reinforced the positive descriptions of the 'Italian woman.' These descriptions of early-twentieth-century femininity reinforced classroom lessons defining female citizenship in terms of domesticity to create the modern Italian woman. Educational readings, popular fiction, and news stories enabled rural Sicilian women to place their own personal experiences of transoceanic migration, mothering, marriage, and work in a national context.

A Nation of Consumers

Access to newspapers integrated Sicilian women into the national economy through their advertisements. Remittances and literacy enabled rural women to carve out a new economic position for themselves as consumers in a rapidly expanding world capitalist system. After paying off their debts and investing their savings in houses and land, rural Sicilians – especially women – turned their attention to buying new furnishings that could attest to the family's new position in the local hierarchy. Advertisements played an important role in integrating rural women into new national and cosmopolitan communities. Armed with the money their husbands sent home, rural women set out to realize their dreams of climbing the social ladder by purchasing the latest fashions and furniture. Advertisements, along with the growing recognition that rural Italy, particularly the South, was a profitable market, pulled women into a radically new economic and national space.

Mass male emigration improved the general standard of living in rural Sicily and changed islanders' lifestyles. In the fall of 1905 the American consul in Palermo, William Henry Bishop, wrote in glowing terms how 'from her children in all parts of the world a steady golden stream is pouring into her banks and industrial institutions.' He said much the same thing a few years later, reporting that remittances were going a long way toward improving the 'comfort of working families.'[56] The American consul at Messina noted in 1906 that a labourer or artisan could now 'afford himself and families more luxuries than was the case a few years ago.' Rural residents were beginning to demand access to new consumer goods, from food to furniture.

Between 1897 and the First World War, Italian commerce grew significantly. Italian exports (mostly raw materials and foodstuffs) rose by 24 per cent between 1896–1900 and 1901–5. Imports grew much more rapidly, increasing by 31 per cent in the same five-year period. In 1906, exports were 37 per cent higher than they had been five years earlier. Italians were producing and consuming more than ever before. In 1905, Germany and Great Britain were Italy's two largest trading partners, with the United States third. However, transoceanic migration accompanied a sharp rise in trade with the United States, especially in household and luxury goods. Between 1897 and 1901, imports from the United States rose by 46 per cent; between 1901 and 1908, the peak years of emigration from the southern provinces, imports from the United States rose by 56 per cent. By 1907 the United States had surpassed France, Austria, and the United Kingdom in trade with Italy.[57]

Both Italy and the United States recognized the importance of transoceanic migration to Italy's commercial growth. As early as 1902, Italy's commerce department was reporting that increased industry and emigration to the United States had increased the nation's exports. While they also warned analysts to be cautious about giving emigration more credit than it deserved in explaining Italy's commercial growth, there is little question that modernized portworks and the arrival of more steamships to handle migration traffic had done much to stimulate investment in Italy's infrastructure.[58] A year later, in 1903, Consul General Guenther of Frankfurt, Germany, credited transoceanic migration with improving the domestic economy and spurring consumer demand. Guenther wrote about 'the accumulation of money and property by the Italian emigrants in the United States. Brazil, Argentina, and other countries,' saying how 'every year a large part of their earnings is sent home to relatives and for investment in home securities.' Though disagreeing with Guenther's analysis of the impact of repatriation, U.S. Consul James Dunning agreed that migration had had a positive effect on disposable incomes, and that the new markets 'must be taken keen note of by American Exporters.'[59] Industrialization and transoceanic migration opened new markets and created economic demand.

In Sicily, commercial development lagged behind the continent. Italian commerce increased by 30 per cent per inhabitant between 1902 and 1907; in Sicily it grew by only 8 per cent. However, between 1905 and the First World War, commercial growth on the island rose significantly. In part this speaks to the timing of migration from the island, which did not really begin until the end of the nineteenth century. By 1907 the remittances sent home by migrants were spurring demand for consumer goods in local markets. While consumption in southern Italy never reached the levels found in northern urban areas, rural residents did begin buying more goods.[60] Rising consumer demand can be seen in the general rise in prices that plagued Sicily and southern Italy in the first decades of the twentieth century. In Sutera, a two-storey, two-room house sold for 600 lire in 1915, according to the property register at the Ufficio Conservatorio dei Beni Immobliliare. In 1920 the new owners of a similar house registered the sale price at 2,500 lire. In Palermo between 1907 and 1911, the price of potatoes rose by one-third; oil, rice, and flour for pasta nearly doubled in price.[61]

It was through consumption that migrants and their families could prove that emigration had succeeded for them. The acquisition of real estate marked only the beginning of the process. Consumption meant more than just the purchase of land or houses; it marked a new way of life and defined a family's new, higher social standing. The culture of consumption first made itself visible in its most literal form: food. In a 1904 report, U.S. Consul Byington noted that the Italian emigrant is 'accustomed in most cases to eat the simplest food, chiefly fruit and greens; he is sober but almost always drinks in moderation.' In 1908 he noted that the rising wage scale and cost of living in Italy were 'accompanied by a noteworthy intensification of the popular appetite and a considerable broadening of the national food table.' More often, pasta and meat were becoming part of a weekly if not daily diet.

The shift in eating patterns also highlights the gendered nature of consumption. Feeding the family was a mother's most important task. Which foods a woman served her family, and how she presented them, spoke to her family's respectability and wealth. A woman's ability to cook and serve meat and pasta on a regular basis marked her family's move up the social ladder. When there was nothing to eat, the family closed its doors and pretended to eat. In his memoir *The Heart Is the Teacher*, Leonard Covello recalled that in his boyhood home in Avigliano, a small village in Basilicata, 'there were times when there was no food in the house. Then we bolted the door and rattled kitchen utensils and dishes to give the impression to our close neighbours that the noonday meal was going on as usual.'[62] The smell of meat issuing from the kitchen was a sure sign of a family's well-being.

The potential profits associated with rising living standards did not go unnoticed by foreign industries. The problem in rural Italy, and in the South in particular, was one of marketing. Modern mail-order marketing techniques did not work well in the southern communities. The American consulates continually lamented how few American goods were being directly marketed in Italy. In 1891, General Consul Bourn in Rome explicitly stated that American industry must 'establish a physical presence in Italy.' American companies needed to send samples and salesmen. In 1905, Francis B. Keene, the American consul in Florence, noted that the English and Germans 'take the lead in the import business principally because they are represented by traveling agents familiar with the French and Italian languages, in which the Americas as a rule are completely lacking. Samples are of infinitely more value in securing orders then illustrations and catalogues.' Consul Heingarter in Catania fully agreed with his colleague, pointing out that in Sicily, large firms were generally represented by local agents and travelling salesmen.[63] Despite this sage advice, William H. Bishop in Palermo lamented three years later that 'except for raw materials, few American goods are brought in here direct. Some others are seen, as shoes, hardware and fancy novelties, but these owe their success to the visit of energetic traveling agents from large agencies in England, Germany and northern Italy, whence they are introduced.'[64] In 1909, James Dunning suggested that American firms study German methods. German salesmen, he noted, often spoke local dialects, in addition to Italian.[65]

The failure of catalogue sales to transform rural residents into modern consumers was a consequence of American arrogance and southern Italian culture and credit arrangements.[66] Many American firms sent catalogues to consulates printed only in English with prices in dollars and with no information on the cost or details of shipping. While catalogues were useful in creating interest in products, direct mail order was rare in rural Sicily. Most residents preferred face-to-face transactions, preferably with local storeowners who would acquire products for them, or with travelling salesmen. Furthermore, commerce in rural Italy was dependent on credit. Credit terms varied considerably. Generally, terms consisted of six months, minus 3 per cent for cash. American firms were often less generous, and this also limited their share of the market.[67]

What the consulate reports gloss over is the gendered nature of the growth in consumption. Food, fashion, and furniture all came under the purview of women as mothers, wives, and citizens. New products and new forms of marketing and payment strengthened the growing links between rural women's lives and national ideas of motherhood and marriage. Regional newspapers were full of advertisements for the latest furnishings and fashions that rural residents needed to decorate their new, larger homes and to dress themselves in keeping with their new status. Throughout the 1870s and 1880s, Peppino Ardizzone assiduously built up the advertising revenues of *Il Giornale di Sicilia.* Each day he paged through the continental dailies. If he found an advertisement that his newspaper did not carry, he immediately wrote to the company to solicit its business. By the First World War the newspaper was dedicating at least one full page, and usually two, to advertisements.[68]

By 1910 a reader of the *Giornale* only needed to glance at page five or six of the slim daily newspaper to find advertisements offering fine suits for men, Parisian shawls, and Spanish lace for women. Accompanying descriptions of the finest fashions were promises of beauty in a bottle and cures for illnesses. Products to get rid of grey hair, to restore hair, and to eliminate unsightly wrinkles nestled next to advertisements heralding the magical powers of a vast array of tonics, able to provide relief from liver disease, impotence, or 'female troubles.' These chemical miracles appeared alongside other products of the modern age: Singer sewing machines, gramophones, and farm machinery. Advertisers often aimed their messages, directly or indirectly, at women. They urged Sicilian women from the cities and the countryside to buy fancy machines to knit socks, new sewing machines to copy the latest fashions, and tables, rugs, dressers, and mirrors.[69] The wealth of goods and services advertised in regional papers offered the promise that even rural women could acquire the health and style of the modern urban woman. Advertisements encouraged these women living far from the cosmopolitan centres of commerce to enjoy the array of new consumer goods.

Many of the most prominent advertisements in the *Giornale* were for household goods. Their images and texts were designed to appeal to women. Iron bedsteads, walnut bedroom sets, armoires, and washstands appeared daily, often accompanied by small sketches. Tile stoves, irons, and porcelain and crystal ware were also visible. Between 1905 and 1913, advertisements also appeared for sewing machines, Philips light bulbs, bicycles, and phonographs. Local dry goods firms advertised linens for trousseaux and newborns; these ads were targeted exclusively at women, who no longer made their own linens and whitewear at home. All of these products could in some way ease a woman's life.

Ads for light bulbs would have had little impact in rural hill towns like Sutera, since most lacked electricity, but many of these advertised goods did make their way into Sicily's interior. The American consul in Palermo noted that there was an especially strong market for phonographs on the island. A ninety-four-year-old woman in Sutera remembered the arrival of the first phonograph in her neighbourhood (and perhaps in Sutera) in 1916, directly from the United States. She remembered how 'the phonograph arrived at her neighbors' house, and everybody danced.'[70] The phonographs, pianos, carpets, bedsteads, and sofas that appeared in rural towns, labouriously carried by mule cart up the rocky, muddy road, became families' prized possessions and marks of distinction.[71] These were luxury items that had once been reserved for wealthy residents. In a Cavallo, a town in Basilicata, the wife of a wealthy landowner, Michelina Ferri, brought the first piano to town in 1879. Herman Tak wrote in his study of Cavallo: 'It was an important status symbol for Michelina, an expression of the cultural capital of her family, and three years later she bought another one.'[72] Expression of social status through consumer goods remained strong throughout the early twentieth century. Perhaps the clearest example of the growing consumerism was the growth of sales of Singer sewing machines. In 1905 most of the machines in Italy were imported from Great Britain. Only a fraction of sales, amounting to only $28,100, came from the United States. In 1908, American sewing machine sales in Italy reached over $2,150,319.[73] The growth in trade was a consequence of better marketing and the appeal of the Singer brand. By 1913 the Singer Company had established agencies throughout rural Sicily. Near Sutera, agents were listed in Caltanisetta, Serradifalco, and Terrãnova. The proximity of these agents meant that Suteresi and residents from neighbouring towns could easily place orders with their local merchants, or wait for a salesman to arrive.

Sicilians demanded a certain aesthetic quality in their new possessions. While salesmen in Palermo readily acknowledged the quality of American pianos, they complained that they lacked the 'artistic finish, the case being too plain to satisfy the taste of the Sicilian who is fond of furniture of ornate finish. Another fault found is that it had no candle holders or metal handles.' A piano's cost (the average price was about 130 dollars) made it a luxury item and an especially clear mark of the owner family's new social position.[74] The same with stoves. The two most popular brands of stoves, 'l'American' and 'Stufa American Ressmer,' labelled 'American Stoves' to highlight their quality and modernity, were exact replicas of American models, but made in Italy. They differed from their American counterparts only in that the Italian models tended to have 'more ornamental ironworks and fewer nickel-plated parts than real American stoves of the same grade.' The upright model sold for around 23 dollars (roughly 125 lire). The demand for ornate products reflected their meaning in the culture. Rural Sicilians did not purchase stoves, pianos, sofas, and bedroom sets for function alone; these were objects of decoration and symbols of status.

Ready-made clothing advertised in daily papers changed local fashions and helped transform rural women into consumers. Like food, housing, and material possessions, clothing was also an important indicator of status and wealth. In 1891 the American consul in Messina, Wallace S. Jones, noted that Germany was replacing England in the cloth industry on the island by supplying a cheaper product: 'The upper classes in Sicily, male and female, devote much time and attention to dress, and essentially thrifty withal, they prefer saving a few cents per yard by buying an inferior article that will look well for one year (they rarely appear two seasons in the same costume) to paying a little more for a first-rate article that would last some four to five years.'[75] By the early twentieth century, residents had incorporated the cultural meanings of clothing into notions of social mobility.

By 1909, fashion columns were appearing in the local papers describing the latest styles from Paris, London, and Rome. By 1910 the women of Sutera were able to order ready-made clothes – dresses, corsets, Parisian veils, and so on – directly from stores in Palermo and Agrigento. If a particular style was not available, they could order a pattern from Butterick.[76] Milan fashion was generally based on Paris fashions. In the first decades of the twentieth century, the fashion industry was targeted by foreign businesses as a potential market. Consul Dunning wrote from Milan: 'It will be seen that the field [of fashion] presents large physical possibilities as to the trade, while everyone in the least familiar with Italy will understand the keen spirit of the feminine population in the hunt for novelties in dress and dress materials. Things new are greatly sought for but with the thrifty spirit peculiar to the country.'[77]

Mass-produced consumer goods blurred regional distinctions. By the end of the nineteenth century, ethnographers were commenting how the 'new generation has let itself be seduced by stuff and clothes made in modern mechanical factories and fashion has invaded and dominated the cities.'[78] In the first decades of the twentieth century, modern fashions regularly appeared in even the most remote hill towns of rural Sicily. When Senator Lorenzoni toured Sicily in 1908, he lamented how rural consumerism had weakened local traditions and customs:

> Sicily has left her isolation and come into contact with the Italian continent, and what is more important, over the last few years, the great land masses of North America and Argentina; she has quit with her old styles, so beautiful and characteristic, appropriate and lasting, but expensive, and has taken on the insipid anti-esthetical modern fashions, extraneous to all traditions in the regions, tastelessly international, but fashionable and a good value.[79]

Remittances and literacy enabled rural women to purchase the cheap, mass-produced manufactured goods that had displaced their own work.

Consumerism and the nationalization of rural Italian women came full circle in the abundant advertising for personal hygiene and pharmaceutical products in the regional papers. Advertisements for laundry soap resonated with textbook lessons on how to wash the family's clothes. Other advertisements exhorted women to buy combs and hair ribbons, lotions to wash away grey hair, creams to erase wrinkles, and makeup to transform themselves into modern, healthy beauties. Testimonials to the power of Bayer Aspirin and tonics to cure all diseases – syphilis, asthma, bronchitis, migraines ... – appeared in nearly every paper.[80] In July 1913 an advertisement for 'Carbone di Balloc' expressed the image of this new woman. The bottle of medicine appeared in the shape of a roadster, with the trademark name emblazoned on its side, running over common diseases. Driving the car was a woman dressed in a simple Grecian gown and wearing a long scarf that streamed out behind her, giving the illusion of great speed. Written in large letters on the scarf was one word: 'Health.' 'Look at this Automobile!!!' screamed the headline. Below the image, the advertisement read: 'Look at this Automobile. Take note of the name (Carbone di Balloc). With this you can eliminate all poisons. Gastritis, Stomach Aches, Digestive Difficulties, and make Constipation disappear.'[81] The image of a woman, representing health, driving the automobile – the ultimate symbol of progress and power – over the common illnesses that plagued every family reflected a woman's civic duty to keep her family healthy using the latest scientific advances.[82] The message was clear: modern commodities would help these rural women fulfil their civic duties as mothers.

Many advertisements were for contractpive devices. In 1908 the *Giornale* was publishing advertisements for 'new English condoms, a dozen for 5 lire. Fine American, 8 Lire, Soft and Strong Italian, 7.5 Lire, Japanese, a dozen for 8 lire.' On the same page, a smaller advertisement appeared offering a 'dischi-antifecondativi' for women.[83] By 1913, advertisements for female contraception were appearing in larger type. Contraceptive devices promised 'easy application at the one time cost of twelve and a half lire.' Contraceptive powders sold for six lire per package of twenty-five. The increased presence of advertisements for condoms after 1910 accompanied the shift to smaller families.

Few rural women actually purchased or regularly used these beauty products. Even so, the marketing and distribution of these goods helped construct a new image of the female consumer in rural regions. By the First World War, the women of Sutera had access to mass consumer culture. These advertisements for beauty creams, furnishings, and clothing created new public and commercial spaces for rural women within a national consumer market. It is unlikely that their new position as consumers actually empowered them as women or fostered a new political identity. All of this does suggest that the economic impact of mass migration on the lives of rural women was linked to new forms of male and female citizenship.[84] When rural Sicilian women entered the consumer culture, it changed the boundaries of their world and allowed them to participate in the growing national and international economy, even though they were neither wage workers nor migrants. The act of consumption radically altered the position of rural women in both local and national communities. The participation of rural Sicilian women in the Italian and global consumer economy reminds us how complicated and often contradictory the process of nation formation must be. In Italy, national markets, like national identities, were built on geographic and gender divisions.

For the men and women of rural Sicily, entry into the imagined political, cultural, and economic communities of the nation came in the wake of mass exodus. An examination of what rural women learned, read, and bought challenges assumptions that they were extraneous to the national community and the emerging consumer economy. The experience of migration led both the migrant men and the women to see themselves as part of much larger national and international communities. How these rural women entered the Italian nation testifies to the multiple communities that make up nations. Clearly, the idea of a nation presupposes certain common characteristics, myths, and historical narratives that on one level erase gender, regional, and class divisions. But the process itself underscores the differences that separate men from women, northerners from southerners, and rural residents from city folk. When the women of Sutera read their newspapers, bought their Singer sewing machines, and memorized their lessons on how to keep their homes clean and raise loyal, healthy Italian children, they entered into the nation of Italians both as women and as southerners. These lessons fostered a sense of belonging to Italy yet at the same time being outside the nation. With their families rooted in Sutera, and separated by an ocean, with American and German goods entering their houses, the women of Sutera moved in and through multiple communities without necessarily leaving their homes.

Conclusion: Gender, Migration, and Globalization

In the late 1950s, Ann Cornelisen moved to a small village in Lucania. Despite the difficulties of daily life in a world where the water ran for two hours each day, electricity was erratic, houses were always cold, and luxuries were few, she came to love the place and the people. When she wrote about her experience, she recalled: 'Life in a Southern Italian village is exclusive of all other life.' The people lived in insular networks circumscribed by their kin and neighbours, as they struggled to survive in an inhospitable world.[1] From the inside, this sense of isolation is strong. Even today in Sutera, it is easy to forget the complicated networks that bind Sutera to Sicily, Italy, and the wider world in the silence and seeming sameness of daily life. Yet the packages that arrive from the United States, England, and Germany each Christmas, the children sent off to study in Palermo and Rome each fall, and the return of emigrants each summer reveal a community tightly connected to other worlds. Family relations stretch across oceans and countries, shaping how rural Sicilians see themselves and one another. In Sutera as in Lucania, women are central to the creation and maintenance of these kinship networks. They send out holiday greetings and presents, pack their children's clothes for university, and greet their brothers, sisters, aunts, and uncles who return each August.

Observers of life in the South have generally described southern Italian women as living in a cloistered world. Over the years, scholars and travellers have extended these women a certain degree of moral authority within the household and in the family, but denied them any political or economic influence. Far from reflecting any sort of objective reality, these descriptions serve to underscore the importance of recognizing one's relationship to historical subjects. Southern Italian women appear in 'shadows' only as a consequence of where we have placed the spotlight. Some scholars have chosen to shine their lights on northern Italian and urban women, others on men, and from these lighted places have turned to consider the women of the South, whom they have left in the shadows. When we fix the light on the women themselves, placing them on centre stage, the shadows shift. In rural Sicily at the turn of the twentieth century, men, absent and present, now move to the margins. In this play the women take the lead roles, as women, workers, citizens, and family members. The history of these women of Sutera reminds us that history is woven from multiple, overlapping stories that are sometimes contradictory. The privileged narrative in any history reflects a scholar's chosen location (social or political history, cultural anthropology, economics, or sociology) and category or categories of analysis (gender, class, or sexuality). Shifting the spotlight not only shifts the light and shadow, allowing us to see the lives of previously invisible actors, but also forces us to draw new conclusions about historical change. The histories of the women of Sutera lead us to new understandings of nation formation and transnational migration as gendered processes, and to a new recognition of how these two processes worked together to define the boundaries of global, local, and national communities.

Over the past few decades there has been a significant shift in the approaches taken to the history of nineteenth and early twentieth-century Italy. Historians of the South are challenging the ruling paradigms of Italian historiography, arguing that the 'Southern Question,' so critical to understanding modern Italy's economic, social, and political development, has distorted the realities of Italy's history. The new scholarship asserts that by accepting the basic premise that the South can only be understood in comparison with the North, the '*meridionalisti*' have succeeded in reducing the South to a problem and in equating the North with modern Italy. A consequence of this approach has been to brand the South as extraneous to Italian history – an unchanging, backward, monolithic world. By adopting an interdisciplinary approach – one that draws from cultural studies, literary theory, social history, and anthropology – the revisionists succeeded in dethroning the 'South as backward' thesis that reigned since the late nineteenth century, and replacing it with a South marked by political, social, and economic diversity. The regional model puts forth a South comprised of a variety of socioeconomic systems formed in response to social, geographic, and cultural factors. These structures have continued to change over time, granting the southern regions their own histories.[2]

The revisionist approach has had a significant impact on histories of the South in a variety of fields. Perhaps the most profound transformation has occurred in economic history. Recent work has led historians to conclude that the latifundia, generally described as conservative, antiquated, inflexible agricultural institutions that had to be reformed along the lines of the northern sharecropping models to be efficient and profitable in a capitalist world, were rational responses to changing conditions in local and international markets. While some estates, mostly in western Sicily, may well have been poorly run, nearly abandoned enterprises, others clearly were not. In her work in the archives of the Barracco estate, Marta Petrusewicz depicted an estate in the midst of change, an estate that fused the traditional with the modern in accordance with its own needs and values. The disappearance of this estate was a consequence of its own push toward modernization. The work of the new southern historians has had an immense impact, pushing scholars to conduct similar reappraisals of the accepted ideas of class formation, social relations, and political power that have shaped the master narrative of modern Italian history.[3]

Without dismissing the importance of these excellent studies, the history of the women of Sutera suggests that we must move gender to centre stage in revising our understanding of the 'Southern Question.' Few of the new studies have challenged the invisibility of Sicilian women and included gender as a meaningful category of analysis. Writing the history of migration from the perspective of the women who remained behind leads to the conclusion that gender is as important as the region in explaining the diversity of social, economic, and political developments in the South. Regional studies grounded in geography, society, and political economy describe a variegated and changing society in which relations of power, wealth, and status constantly shifted in response to internal and external factors. But these studies only tell half the story – that of the men. This history of migration from Sutera shows that Sicilian women also responded to changing economic and political conditions but as women. Their stories suggest that the history of the South was engendered. Men and women both participated in its transformation, and the emergence of new economic systems, class relations, and political arrangements, both local and national, created new ideas of male and female and gendered certain occupations, family roles, and political spaces as masculine or feminine. Sutera offers some evidence for the role that gender played in the transformation of the South, but we clearly need more research. For instance, did other towns experience the increased presence of women in city hall, as is evident in Sutera? If so, what does this tell us about women's incorporation into the state as family representatives? Was this unique to rural women, or to southern women? If it was, can we conclude that southern women contributed to the political transformation of the South?

While a great deal more work needs to be done to understand how gender shaped the history of modern Italy, we can certainly conclude from the histories of the women of Sutera that the process of migration is deeply gendered. Migration integrates men and women in radically different ways. In rural Sicily the act of migration was male, and inextricably linked to men's position as breadwinners. The management of the networks was female. When women migrated, they did so as mothers and wives, as the managers of the household and the family. They did not leave as workers. The history of Sutera's women testifies to the influence of rural women in the creation and maintenance of transnational migration networks. Female participation in the organization and financing of male emigration affected patterns of settlement and return. Certainly, women are not always the ones who remain behind. In the early twenty-first century the act of migration is often female, with women travelling as daughters, mothers, and workers. Yet these patterns of female migration from the Philippines, Sri Lanka, or the Caribbean Islands are also shaped by the interests of the children, husbands, mothers, and fathers who remain behind. No migrant is autonomous. In the stories of these women, gender emerges as a critical tool of analysis in understanding transnational migration.

The recognition that both men and women, as migrants or stay-at-homes, influence patterns of transnational migration has great significance in today's world. When we read about the plight of migrants, we must remember that these men and women are part of much larger networks. Why migrants choose to migrate in the first place, to settle in one country instead of another, to stay or return home, often has more to do with the wives, husbands, mothers, and fathers left behind than with the 'opportunities' available in the new lands. No longer can we see migrants as 'uprooted,' 'transplanted,' or even necessarily evicted from their homelands. The history of migration from Sutera suggests that it is time to abandon these concepts altogether.

Once we accept the notion that migration is a dynamic process that links people and communities together and that transcends political and cultural borders, we cannot avoid placing the household at the centre of any analytic framework. The lives of Sicilian women show that early-twentieth-century migration neither displaced nor transferred communities; rather, it stretched families across oceans and across cultures. In the process, the experience of migration radically altered the lives of those who stayed at home as well as the migrants. From this perspective, the family – which scholars have often seen as a conservative, apolitical, 'female' space – becomes an arguably progressive place that is capable of changing local social relations, politics, and culture.

Mass male emigration repositioned Sutera's women in the political landscape through the family. By encouraging women to use state institutions as tools to keep their families together, to communicate with their husbands and sons in faraway places, and to negotiate overseas financial transactions, emigration created a new, independent relationship between women and the state. Women's ties to the state, mediated through city hall, circumvented party politics. By the 1920s, rural women knew how to use the state to benefit their families, to take large corporations to court, and to ensure that they received their pensions or death benefits. The extension of family networks across the ocean also gave new urgency to education. Schoolhouses provided a new venue for rural women to build ties with the state. These new structural relations linking the women of the South to government agencies reveals a different kind of female politics, one shaped by women's roles as mothers and wives. The state became a tool for maintaining family ties and even for improving the conditions of families. By the end of the First World War, a good Sicilian mother and wife had to be able to negotiate government bureaucracies to get what she could for her family.

By altering the physical relationship between women and the state, transnational migration transformed the very notion of the national community. The experience of migration creates a sense of 'long-distance nationalism' among migrants; it does the same at home.[4] The appearance of rural women in classrooms and government offices and their entry into the reading public integrated them into the nation. Tracing the history of the experiences of the women of Sutera complicates our understanding of nation formation. The making of Italy was actually the making of many Italies. Unification created multiple, overlapping communities distinguished by gender and region. Attempts to instil a sense of common history, culture, and identity both united all Italians and strengthened ideas of difference. All people born within the territorial boundaries of Italy were Italians, yet their position in the nation, their duties and rights, and their identification with national myths varied according to sex and region. In the case of southern Italy, studying transoceanic migration from the location of the women who remained behind further muddles the concept of the nation. We see in Sutera that the idea of a public sense of belonging to the nation accompanied the private experience of entering a global community.

It seems, then, that at the beginning of the twentieth century, migration played a key role in the nationalization of rural Europeans. We are left with the conclusion that citizenship, like migration, is also deeply gendered. Men and women enter into the national body in ways that ascribe to them different kinds of rights and obligations. The women of Sutera were integrated into the nation as consumers, mothers, and wives. We have only begun to explore the connections between family life, shopping, and nation formation, so the lives of Sutera's women perhaps raise many more questions than answers. In particular, the evidence presented here demands that we ask how these women themselves experienced this transformation. We need more studies on how women read the newspapers, fashion columns, and catalogues, and how they saw themselves in relation to the nation. More studies exploring how national identity is formed in relation to local and transnational communities could also shed light on our own world today.

In her essay 'Toward a Feminist Analytics of the Global Economy,' Saskia Sassen writes: 'The current phase of the world economy is characterized by significant discontinuities with the preceding periods and radically new arrangements.' An examination of the weakening of nation-states as physical, economic, and legal entities makes this clear. The rapid flow of capital, the internationalization of corporations, and the transfer of production to other lands have undermined nation-states' exclusive control over economic, legal, and social power. Shifts in the locations of wealth and production have transferred a significant degree of power to local communities (global cities) and supranational bodies (NGOs, etc.). The separation of certain aspects of physical production from social and cultural reproduction has created new economic and political systems that have radically refigured the boundaries of nation-states. Sassen contends that the emergence of global cities as new sites for constructing individual independence, class identification, and legal order has transformed – although by no means vanquished – the world's nation-states.[5] She observes astutely that the new worlds of global finance, work, and legal systems have undermined the ability of nations to control their domestic and foreign affairs. Their autonomy, as defined by their territorial borders and systems of government, has been weakened. In many ways she is absolutely correct. However, it is also important to note that the 'discontinuities' and 'radically new arrangements' she identifies in the late twentieth century are relevant to understanding the late nineteenth century.

Although today's global economy is a very different beast from the world of the Suteresi in 1910 – in large part a consequence of the fluidity of capital and the growth of international financial markets – certain parallels can be drawn. In both cases, labour mobility challenged the power of the nation in 'norming' individuals and communities. National and international communities shaped notions of civic duties, rights, and obligations. As people travel, leaving family members behind, to work in mines and factories or as domestic servants, families and households physically live in a multinational world, subject to the demands of different cultures and value systems. The idea of the global city of today is relevant to the history of Sutera. At the beginning of the twentieth century, Sutera became a global village. Families experienced the same physical dislocation as today's migrants. They too experienced the separation of consumption, production, and reproduction. The global village, like the global city, complicated meanings of work and family and highlighted the importance of local and international communities in the formation of modern nation-states. The history of the women of Sutera show that the rise of the nation as the primary site of legal, economic, and social systems was from its inception linked to both local and international communities. The world of nineteenth-century rural women suggests that the nation's monopoly over labour, economic relations, and legal systems was never as strong as people thought. As Sassen argues for the current world system, gender is central to understanding the processes of globalization. In Sicily in the first decades of the twentieth century, the transformations that accompanied the creation of an international labour force reflected and created ideas of masculinity and femininity at home and abroad. Conceiving of these rural European towns during times of mass migration as global villages focuses our attention on women's changing lives.

Ann Cornelisen described her friends and neighbours in the village as 'women of tremendous strengths, these women of the shadows. One of their strengths, and not the least is their silence, which outsiders have understood as submission.' Appearances, however, are often deceptive. These women have not stood silently by, watching the world move. The lives of the women of Sutera, like those of the women of Lucania, testify to the complicated ways that rural women gave, and still give, meaning to the modern world.

Notes

Introduction: The Women of the South

1 Jane Schneider and Peter Schneider, *Culture and Political Economy in Western Sicily* (New York: Academic Press, 1976), 114–15; Emilio Franzina, *Gli italiani nel mondo: L'emigrazione italiana in America 1492–1942* (Milan: Arnoldo Modadori Editore, 1995), 143–55; also see Donna Gabaccia, *Italy's Many Diasporas* (Seattle: University of Washington Press, 2000), 58–80.

2 Archivio Comunale di Sutera (ACS), 'Risposta dal sindaco al R. ispettorato scolastica della circoscrizione di Caltanissetta, 2 June 1908,' n. 422, cat. IX, cl. 2 fasc. 1; ACS, 'Prospetto dei movimenti avvenuti nella popolazione residente, 1902–1910,' cat. XII. Sex ratios are based on passport records and family reconstructions from Sutera. Ministero degli Affari Esteri (MAE), Commissariato General dell'Emigrazione (CGE), *Annuario statistico della emigrazione italiana* (Rome: Commissariato dell'Emigrazione, 1925), 183.

3 Donna Gabaccia, 'In the Shadows of the Periphery: Italian Women in the Nineteenth Century,' in *Connecting Spheres: Women in the Western World, 1500 to the Present*, ed. Marilyn J. Boxer and Jean H. Quataert (New York: Oxford University Press, 1987), 166–76; Jole Calapso, 'La donna in Sicilia e in Italia: la realtà e la falsa coscienza nella statistica dal 1871 ad oggi,' *Quaderni Siciliani* 2 (March–April 1973), 13–20.

4 For a general discussion of representations of migration, see Russell King, John Connell, and Paul White, eds, *Writing across Worlds: Literature and Migration* (New York: Routledge, 1995). In particular, see Frederica Scarpa, 'Friuliani nel Mondo: The Literature of Italian Emigrant Region,' in ibid., 141–61. Neil Larry Shumsky, in 'Return Migration in Modern Novels,' in ibid., 198–215, notes that in Garibaldi Lapolla's novel *The Grand Gennaro*, 'the United States appeals to people with expansive, aggressive temperaments, the homeland to those with restrained and yielding personalities.'

5 Angelo Mosso, *Vita moderna degli italiani* (Milan: Fratelli Treves, 1906), 13–14; Commissariato dell'Emigrazione, *Bollettino dell'emigrazione* 18 (1910): 53–4; Giuseppe Bruccoleri, *La Sicilia di oggi: appunti economici* (Rome: Athenaeum, 1913), 85–105.

6 Oscar Handlin, *The Uprooted* (Boston: Little Brown, 1951); S.N. Eisenstadt, *The Adaptation of Immigrants* (London: Routledge and Kegan Paul, 1954); William Whyte, *Street Corner Society* (Chicago: University of Chicago Press, 1943); William I. Thomas and Florian Zaniecki, *The Polish Peasant in Europe and America* (Boston: Knopf, 1927); Milton Gordon, *Assimilation in American Life* (New York: Oxford University Press, 1964).

7 Virginia Yans-McLaughlin, *Family and Community: Italian Immigrants in Buffalo, 1880–1930* (Ithaca: Cornell University Press, 1992); John Bodnar, *The Transplanted: A History of Immigrants in Urban America* (Bloomington: Indiana University Press, 1990); John Briggs, *An Italian Passage: Immigrants to Three American Cities* (New Haven: Yale University Press, 1978).

8 Frank Thistlethwaite, 'Migration from Europe Overseas in the Nineteenth and Twentieth Centuries,' in *Population Movement in Modern European History*, ed. Herbert Moller (New York: Macmillan, 1964), 73–92. This article is a reprint of a talk published in the proceedings of the *XIe Congrès International des Sciences Historiques, Stockholm 1960*; John S. MacDonald and L.D. MacDonald, 'Chain Migration, Ethnic Neighborhood Formation, and Social Networks,' *Milbank Memorial Fund Quarterly* 42 (January 1964): 82–97; Samuel L. Baily, 'Chain Migration of Italians to Argentina: Case Studies of the Agnonesi and Sirolesi' *Studi Emigrazione* 19 (1982): 73–91; Donna Gabaccia, *From Sicily to Elizabeth Street: Housing and Social Change among Italian Immigrants, 1880–1930* (Albany: State University of New York Press, 1984); Bodnar, *The Transplanted*; Ewa Morawska, 'The Sociology and Historiography of Immigration,' in *Immigration Reconsidered: History, Sociology, and Politics*, ed. Virginia Yans-McLaughlin (New York: Oxford University Press, 1990), 187–238; Charles Tilly, 'Transplanted Networks,' in ibid., 79–95; Franc Sturino, *Forging the Chain: Italian Migration to North America, 1880–1930* (Toronto: Multicultural History Society of Ontario, 1990).

9 Among the most recent on women and migration are Donna Gabaccia, *From the Other Side: Women, Gender, and Immigrant Life in the United States, 1820–1990* (Bloomington: Indiana University Press, 1994); Miriam Cohen, *Workshop to Office: Two Generations of Italian Women in New York City, 1900–1950* (Ithaca: Cornell University Press, 1992); Elizabeth Ewen, *Immigrant Women in the Land of Dollars: Life and Culture on the Lower East Side, 1890–1925* (New York: Monthly Review Press, 1985); Kathie Friedman-Kasaba, *Memories of Migration: Gender, Ethnicity, and Work in the Lives of Jewish and Italian Women*

in New York, 1870–1924 (Albany: State University of New York, 1996); Hasia Diner, *Erin's Daughters in America: Irish Immigrant Women in the Nineteenth Century* (Baltimore: Johns Hopkins University Press, 1983). For an excellent bibliography of recent work on female migration to the United States, see Donna Gabaccia, ed., *Seeking Common Ground: Multidisciplinary Studies of Immigrant Women in the United States* (Westport, CT: Greenwood Press, 1992). Also see Donna Gabaccia and Franca Iacovetta, 'Women, Work and Protest in the Italian Diaspora: An International Research Agenda,' *Labour/Le Travail* 42 (fall 1998), 161–81. For work focusing on female migration to countries other than the United States, see Donna Gubaccia and Franca Iacovetta, eds, *Women, Gender, and Transnational Lives: Italian Women around the World* (Toronto: University of Toronto Press, 2002), and the special edition 'Le emigrate italiane in prospettiva comparata,' *Altreitalie* 9 (1993).

10 Giovanni Lorenzoni, *Inchiesta parlamentare sulle condizione dei contadini nelle province meridionali e nelle Sicilia*, vol. 6, *Sicilia*, tomo 1, parte 5 (Rome: Tip. Naz. G. Bertero, 1910), 832–3. Gabaccia, *From Sicily*, 57–9.

11 Repatriation rates for Sutera are based on a migrant file that I created from information contained in birth and marriage records, passport lists, ship manifests, and land records. The file contains information on 714 migrants from Sutera. For general rates of repatriation from Italy, see Betty Boyd-Caroli, *Italian Repatriation from the United States, 1900–1914* (New York: Center for Migration Studies, 1973), 9, 12–13.

12 One scholar who has seriously considered women and the role of the homeland in the migration process is Caroline Brettell. See her work, *Men Who Migrate, Women Who Wait: Population and History in a Portuguese Parish* (Princeton: Princeton University Press, 1986). For a discussion on transnationalism, see Gabaccia, *Italy's Many Diasporas*, 11.

13 For a discussion of consumerism and nationalism, see Victoria de Grazia, 'Empowering Women as Citizen Consumers,' in *The Sex of Things: Culture and Consumption in Historical Perspective*, ed. Victoria de Grazia with Ellen Furlough (Berkeley: University of California Press, 1996), 275–86.

14 Rudolph Bell, *Fate and Honor, Family and Village* (Chicago: University of Chicago Press, 1979); William A. Douglass, *Emigration in a South Italian Town: An Anthropological History* (New Brunswick, NJ: Rutgers University Press, 1984); Sydel Silverman, *Three Bells of Civilization: The Life of an Italian Hill Town* (New York: Columbia University Press, 1975).

15 Among recent publications are Matthew Frye-Jacobson, *Different Colors of Whiteness* (Cambridge: Harvard University Press, 1998); also see David Roediger's discussion of the Irish in America in *The Wages of Whiteness: Race and the Making of the American Working Class* (New York: Verso, 1991).

16 Henri Lefebvre, *La production de l'espace*, quoted in *Globallocal: Cultural Production and the Transnational Imaginary*, ed. Rob Wilson and Wimal Dissanayake (Durham: Duke University Press, 1996), 1. In *Italy's Many Diasporas*, 3, Gabaccia also discusses the relationship between local and global communities.

17 Ministero di Agricoltura, Industria e Commercio (MAIC), Direzione Generale della Statistica (DGS), *Censimento della popolazione del regno al 10 febbraio 1901*, II (Rome: Tip. Naz. Bertero, 1903), 276–319.

18 Lucy Riall, *Sicily and the Unification of Italy: Liberal Policy and Local Power, 1859–1866* (Oxford: Clarendon Press, 1998), 17. For an excellent introduction into the historiographical debates over the Southern Question, see Lucy Riall's introduction to *Sicily and the Unification of Italy*; Jane Schneider, 'Introduction: The Dynamics of Neo-orientalism in Italy (1848–1995),' in *Italy's 'Southern Question': Orientalism in One Country*, ed. Jane Schneider (Oxford: Berg, 1998) 1–23; John A. Davis, 'Remapping Italy's Path to the Twentieth Century,' *Journal of Modern History* 66 (June 1994): 291–320, and 'Changing Perspectives on Italy's "Southern Problem,"' in *Italian Regionalism: History, Identity and Politics*, ed. Carl Levy (Oxford: Berg, 1996) 53–68; and Robert Lumley and Jonathan Morris, eds, *The History of the New South: The Mezzogiorno Revisited* (Exeter, U.K.: University of Exeter Press, 1997). Two critical works that have transformed the field are Piero Bevilacqua, *Breve storia dell'Italia meridionale* (Rome: Donzelli, 1992); and Giuseppe Giarrizo, *Mez-zogiorno senza meridonalismo: La Sicilia, lo sviluppo, il potere* (Venice: Marsilio, 1992). An excellent study on the Southern economy is Marta Petrusewicz, *Latifondo: economia morale e vita materiale in una periferia dell'ottocento* (Venice: Marsilio, 1989). Also see Gabriella Gribaudi, *A Eboli: Il mondo merdionale in cent'anni di trasformazioni* (Venice: Marsilio, 1990).

19 The absence of works on women is beginning to be remedied. See Gabriella Gribaudi, *Donne, uomini, famiglie: Napoli nel novecento* (Rome: L'Ancora, 1999).

20 For examples of the assumption of physical integration, see Louise Tilly and Joan Scott, *Women, Work, and Family* (New York: Routledge, 1987). For an exception to the focus on urban women, see Donna Gabaccia, 'In the Shadows of the Periphery: Italian Women in the Nineteenth Century,' in *Connecting Spheres*. For an excellent example of the new scholarship of rural women in the United States, and for a fine bibliographical essay, see Mary Neth, *Preserving the Family Farm: Women, Community, and the Foundations of Agribusiness in the Midwest, 1900–1940* (Baltimore: Johns Hopkins University Press, 1995).

21 Judith Bennett, 'Theoretical Issues, Confronting Continuity,' *Journal of*

Women's History 9, no. 3 (1997): 76; also see Joan Kelly, 'Did Women Have a Renaissance,' in *Women, History and Theory* (Chicago: University of Chicago Press, 1984), 19–47; Joan Landes, *Women and the Public Sphere in the Age of the French Revolution* (Ithaca: Cornell University Press, 1988); Dominique Godineau, *The Women of Paris and Their French Revolution*, trans. Katherine Streip (Berkeley: University of California Press, 1998); Deborah Valenze, *The First Industrial Woman* (New York: Oxford University Press, 1995).

22 Laura Frader and Sonya Rose, 'Introduction,' in *Gender and Class in Modern Europe* (Ithaca: Cornell University Press, 1996), 22; Joan Scott, 'Gender a Useful Category of Analysis,' in *Gender and the Politics of History* (New York: Columbia University Press, 1988), 28–50; Anna Clark, *The Struggle for the Breeches* (Berkeley: University of California Press, 1995); de Grazia with Furlough eds, *The Sex of Things*.

1: Blood, Honour, and Belonging: The World of Rural Sicilians

1 Archivio Comunale di Sutera (ACS), *Atti di matrimonio*, 1889, no. 1.

2 Rudolph Bell, *Fate and Honor, Family and Village* (Chicago: University of Chicago Press, 1979), 67–8. Bell argues that throughout nineteenth-century southern Italy, the future was always precarious. High mortality rates left people grateful for those children who survived to grow old and marry.

3 Sidney Sonnino, *I contadini in Sicilia*, vol. 2 of Leopoldo Franchetti and Sidney Sonnino, *Inchiesta in Sicilia* (1876; reprint, Florence: Vallecchi, 1974), 11.

4 A *frazione* is small settlement under the administration of a larger village. All records are registered with the main village. In 1926 Milocca won its independence, and in the 1930s it changed its name to Milena. I refer to it as Milocca. For an excellent history of Milocca, see Charlotte Gower Chapman, *Milocca: A Sicilian Village* (Cambridge: Schenkman, 1971).

5 Giovanni Lorenzoni, *Inchiesta parlamentare sulle condizione dei contadini nelle province meridionali e nelle Sicilia*, vol. 6, *Sicilia*, tomo 1, parte 3 (Rome: Tip. Naz. G. Bertero, 1910), 486; Gero Difrancesco, *Sutera: I primi anni del '900* (Caltanissetta: Biblioteca Comunale Sutera, 1989), 40. As late as 1907 Sutera was not connected to the main highway between Mussomeli and Aquaviva, to the provincial capital, or to the *frazione* of Milocca.

6 ACS, 'Comune di Sutera: Risposta ai quesiti nella circolare prefettezia 3, ottobre 1901, div 3, #11030, riguardante l'inchiesta per contratto di lavoro,' cat. XI, cl. 2a, fasc, 2a (hereafter cited as Risposta ai quesiti, 1901).

7 Vaccaro, *Sutera e la sua geografia fisica* (Naples: Tip. Gazz. Drit e Gius, 1890), 39.

8 Jane Schneider and Peter Schneider, *Culture and Political Economy in Western Sicily* (New York: Academic Press, 1976), 34–5.

9 ACS, 'Comune di Sutera: Statistica della popolazione del comune sudetto di tutto il 31 dicembre 1893,' cat. XII, cl. 1, fasc. 1; ACS, 'Servizio sanitario: affari diversi 1888–1895,' cat. IV, cl. 1, fasc. 1; Dottore Antonio Vaccaro, *Cenni sulla città di Sutera* (Naples: Tip. dei. Frat Carluccio, 1881), 13–15, 139.

10 Bell, 9–10. Rudolph Bell describes the characteristics associated with villages versus those with towns. After an analysis of various class and architectural differences, he states that 'most villagers are peasants.' My description of Sutera is based on Bell's definitions of village and town.

11 Schneider and Schneider, *Culture,* 34; Biagio Puntero, *Delle condizioni economiche dalla provincia di Caltanissetta* (Caltanissetta: Tip. Ospiz, di Beneficienza, 1905), 17; Luigi Zoda, *La mobilitazione agraria in provincia di Caltanissetta 1918–1919* (Caltanissetta: Tip. Ospiz, di Beneficienza, 1919), 43–9.

12 Leopoldo Franchetti, *Condizioni politiche e amministrative della Sicilia,* vol. 1 of Franchetti and Sonnino, *Inchiesta in Sicilia,* 23–9.

13 Anton Blok, *Mafia in a Sicilian Village* (Oxford: Basil Blackwood, 1974), 46–7; Schneider and Schneider, *Culture,* 34–6.

14 M.I. Finley, Denis Mack Smith, and Christopher Duggan, *History of Sicily* (New York: Viking Press, 1987), 43.

15 Finley et al., *History,* 53.

16 Schneider and Schneider, *Culture,* 33–4.

17 Jane Schneider and Peter Schneider argue that the fourteenth-century enclosures prepared the way for grain production. The pastoral base underlying the estates is what is unique in Sicily and southern Italy and accounts, in part, for the creation of the agricultural village. Schneider and Schneider, *Culture,* 58.

18 Marta Petrusewicz, *Latifondo: Economia morale e vita materiale in una periferia dell'Ottocento* (Venice: Marsilio editori, 1989). In this excellent study of the Barracco estates in Calabria, Marta Petrusewicz makes a compelling case for understanding the *latifondo* system as a flexible, rational, modern, and capitalist enterprise that began to decline at the end of the nineteenth century in the wake of the European agricultural crisis. In her introdution she describes the system as characterized by a high degree of self-sufficency, by a flexible system of capital exchange (production be shifted rapidly from one crop to another), and by the coexistence of multiple labour systems (wages, sharecropping, and mixed contracts). For another study of the flexibility and dynamism of the Sicilian economy, see Salvatore Lupo,

Il giardino degli aranci: il mondo degli agrumi nella storia del Mezzogiorno (Venice: Marsilio editori, 1990).

19 Vaccaro, *Cenni*, 109. For a general history of Sicily in this period see Denis Mack Smith, *A History of Sicily: Medieval Sicily, 800–1713* (New York: Viking Press, 1968).

20 Vaccaro, *Cenni*, 14–15, 65–6.

21 Vaccaro, *Cenni*, 110–11.

22 Schneider and Schneider, *Culture*, 35–6.

23 Vaccaro, *Cenni*, 87; Lorenzoni, *Inchiesta*, parte 3, 218. Only forty-three cities on the island were given the status of demesne. In the seventeenth century the number was the same and there were 248 feudal towns.

24 Vaccaro, *Cenni*, 73–87.

25 Vaccaro, *Cenni*, 89–105.

26 For an excellent discussion of Sicily's political formation, and the importance of the core/periphery relationship, see Paolo Pezzino, *Una certa reciprocità di favori: Mafia e modernizzazione violenta nella Sicilia postunitaria* (Milan: FrancoAngeli, 1990), 40–4.

27 Vaccaro, *Cenni*, 222. According to custom, residents had use rights over the ex-fiefs Milocca, Capraria, Aquilia, and Cimicia, although at times they had to fight for the recognition of these rights from the church, which owned the land. Lorenzoni mentions that Sutera was one of the most successful villages in defending use rights on the common lands.

28 In Sutera the amount of rent varied from 20 to 31 lire per hectare depending on the location and quality of the land. For information on sharecropping contacts, see ACS, 'Risposti ai quesiti contenuti nella circolare prefettezia 3 ottobre 1901, div. 3 #11030 riguardate l'inchiesta pel contratti di lavoro, 1880–1906,' cat. XI, cl. 1a, fasc. 4. For general conditions in the province, see Puntero, *Condizioni economiche*, 69–71.

29 Blok, *Mafia*, 32; Mack Smith, *Modern Sicily*, 279. The *gabellotti* have been well studied in Sicilian historiography. After unification they were associated with the *nouveaux riches*, the new political classes, and the Mafia.

30 Sonnino, 22–9. Two-year contracts varied with the type of land, the harshness of the owner, and the agreeability of the peasant. The distinguishing feature was that the owner would provide seed, to be repaid at the harvest, along with several other stipulations. The other most common contract was a straightforward land-for-grain arrangement.

31 Biagio Puntero, *Condizioni economiche*, 31; Archivio dello Stato-Caltanissetta (ASC), 'Circondario di Caltanissetta: Delle notizie fornite dai comuni in risposto al questionario relativo all'inchiesta sulle condizioni dei contadini febbraio 1908,' Gabinetto.

32 ACS, 'Risposta ai quesiti, 1901'; and Sonnino, 12–29.
33 Difrancesco, 14–15.
34 *Atti della giunta per l'inchiesta agraria e sulle condizioni della classe agricola* vol 13, tomo 1, fasc. 1, Relazione del Commissario Abele Damiani (Rome: Forzani Tip. del Senato, 1884), 56–7 (hereafter cited as *Atti della giunta*).
35 Mack Smith, *Modern Sicily*, 345. The expropriation of feudal lands was required in 1812. However, as Smith points out, aside from turning the fiefs into private property, the law did not clearly specify what else was abolished. For a comprehensive overview of the end of feudalism in Sicily, see Lucy Riall, *Sicily and the Unification of Italy: Liberal Policy and Local Power, 1859–1866* (Oxford: Clarendon Press, 1998), 30–61.
36 Blok, *Mafia*, 39; also see Mack Smith, *Modern Sicily*, 362. In 1824 a law was passed allowing creditors to take possession of lands in payment for outstanding loans. Previously, the aristocracy had been legally protected from any form of repossession.
37 Francesco Romano, *Storia della Sicilia post-unificazione: la Sicilia nell'ultimo ventennio del secolo XIX* (Palermo: Industria Grafica Nazionale, 1958), 125–7. Romano shows that although claims were made that 20, 000 new landholders had been created by the breaking up of the estates and church lands, only twenty-seven out of every hundred parcels of land went to new owners. The other seventy-three went to those who already had land and were increasing their holdings. The largest landholders were buying plots from different estates, not the entire holding; thus they appeared as separate landowners when they were not.
38 Anton Blok, 'Land Reform in a West Sicilian Latifondo Village: The Persistence of a Feudal Structure,' *Anthropological Quarterly* 39 (1966): 1–16; Donna Gabaccia, *From Sicily*, 8–9; Mack Smith, *Modern Sicily*, 362–3.
39 Mack Smith, *Modern Sicily*, 427–8.
40 Francesco De Stefano and Francesco Luigi Oddo, *La Storia della Sicilia* (Bari: ed. Laterza, 1963), 181–3; Mack Smith, *Modern Sicily*, 399–400.
41 Mack Smith, *Modern Sicily*, 456–8.
42 *Atti della giunta*, tomo 1, fasc. 1, 79.
43 Romano, 128; and Mack Smith, *Modern Sicily*, 457–8.
44 *Atti della giunta*, tomo 1, fasc. 1, 57.
45 ASC, *Catasto dei terreni-Sutera.*
46 Romano, 124–5.
47 Vaccaro, *Cenni*, 126–32. This was typical of many local struggles as residents resisted attempts by the aristocracy to enclose lands. The original intent of the 1841 law had been twisted by the landowners, who were able to persuade the king to recognize possession as evidence of ownership. Sutera was

one of the few villages that could actually prove that the land had been illegally acquired. For a further discussion of early land reform attempts, see Mack Smith, *Modern Sicily*, 406–8. Also see Schneider and Schneider, *Culture*, 116–20.

48 Difrancesco, 14. For a general overview of the politics underlying the *Commissariato Civile* see Romano, 279–92; De Stefano and Oddo, 358–72.

49 Difrancesco, 14.

50 ACS, 'Denunzia il esercizio delle miniere Lupa Roccafiacata – San Paolino, 1904,' and 'Denunzia annuale di esercizio degli esercenti aziende soggetti alla legge 19 giugno 1902: Ditta Cav. Ufficiale Salvatore Romano and Ditta Villa Alfonso, 1906,' cat. XV, cl. 1–11. According to these reports by the mining companies, only 3 out of 522 miners were from Sutera. Also see Vaccaro, *Sutera*, 30. Company records indicate that no women worked in the mines, although the law did not prohibit them from doing so.

51 Schneider and Schneider, *Culture*, 123.

52 In an article published shortly after the collapse of the mine in Sutera in 1905, the *Giornale di Sicilia* noted that it had published a warning two years earlier. 'Ancora il disastro di Sutera; nuovi particolari–Le autorità sul luogo. La popolazione affamata reclama giustizia,' *Giornale di Sicilia*, 23–4 September 1905, 3.

53 ACS, 'Memo dal sindaco di Sutera, 13 settembre 1905,' cat. XV, cl. 8a, fasc. 2.

54 'Il disastro di Sutera per franamento del Monte S. Paolino,' *Giornale di Sicilia*, 21–2 September 1905, 2–3.

55 For a description of the mining disaster, see Difrancesco, 29–37. Coverage in the regional paper *Giornale di Sicilia* was extensive in the weeks following the disaster. 'Miniere che minacciano di crollare e di travolgere un paese: Una dimonstrazione di donne,' *Giornale di Sicilia*, 19–20 September 1905, 5; 'Una montagna che comincia a crollare. Sutera minacciata di essere sepolta,' *Giornale di Sicilia*, 20–21 September, 1905, 3; 'Il disastro di Sutera per franamento del Monte S. Paolino,' *Giornale di Sicilia*, 21–2 September 1905, 2–3; 'Ancora il disastro di Sutera; nuovi particolare-Le autorità sul luogo. La popolazione affamata reclama la giustizia.' *Giornale di Sicilia*, 23–4 September 1905, 3.

56 Sonnino, 242. There has been a great deal of debate regarding the relationship between peasant militancy and migration. In Sutera, migration seems to have followed militant action. See chapter 2 for further discussion on protest and emigration.

57 Sonnino, 247. For a description of the different types of associations, see Sonnino, 242–52.

58 *Atti della giunta*, 136–7; Romano, 181–6.

59 Francesco Renda, *I fasci siciliani 1892–1894* (Turin: Einaudi, 1977), 57–66.

60 Romano, 245.

61 Mack Smith, *Modern Sicily*, 537; Renda, *Fasci*, 349–57.

62 Romano, 537.

63 Ibid., 248–52.

64 Renda, *Fasci*, 342, 351, 353.

65 Romano, 432–3.

66 ACS, 'Memo dalla Società Agricoltori Vittorio Emanuele III, Sutera, al sindaco di Sutera, 4 giugno 1902,' cat. XI, cl. 2, fasc. 2.

67 ACS, 'Statuto della società pel miglioramento economico in Sutera,' article 2., cat. XI, cl. 2, fasc. 2a.

68 ACS, 'Statuto della società pel miglioramento economico in Sutera,' article 18, cat. XI, cl. 2, fasc. 2a.

69 ACS, 'Pubblica sicurezza 1900–8,' cat. XV, cl. 5–7.

70 After the First World War, a group of men from Milocca, many of them veterans of the war, occupied the surrounding estates. A local merchant, supported by the socialists, led the occupation. However, class identification was not what defined their political positions. During the occupation a group of people from Sutera took part in a failed attempt to recapture one of the estates, siding with the landowners rather than the workers. The historical animosity between Milocchesi and Suteresi only partially explains this strange alliance. If these estates were occupied by the townspeople of Milocca, Suteresi would be excluded from their fields. Local interests still ruled over class solidarity. ACS, 'Telespressi, 1921' cat. XI, cl. 3, fasc. 1. A series of telegrams and memos relate the various attempts made by the Cassa Rurale di San Paolino and the Cassa Rurale di San Giuseppe and the Banca Popolare to buy the estate; Giovanni Lorenzoni, *Trasformazione e colonizzazione del latifondo siciliano* (Florence: Casa ed. Poligrafia Univ., 1940), 41; Gower Chapman, 4–5.

71 ACS, 'Inchiesta sulle condizioni igeniche e sanitarie dei comuni del regno 1885,' cat. IV, cl. 3, fasc. 1.

72 ACS, 'Inchiesta sulle condizioni igeniche e sanitarie dei comuni del regno 1885,' cat. IV, cl. 3, fasc. 1.

73 Labour patterns among rural women are discussed in chapter 5.

74 Bell, 75.

75 Richard Wall, 'Introduction,' *In Family Forms in Historic Europe*, ed. Richard Wall, Jean Robin, and Peter Laslett (Cambridge: Cambridge University Press, 1983), 1–63; also see Tamara K. Hareven, *Family Time and Industrial Time* (New York: Cambridge University Press, 1982), 154–66, for a similar

discussion concerning the construction of household and family in Manchester, New Hampshire.

76 Wall, 6–7.

77 Edward Banfield, *The Moral Basis of a Backward Society* (New York: The Free Press, 1958). The first Italian critique of Banfield's thesis appeared shortly after publication. Alessandro Pizzorno, 'Familismo amorale e marginalità, ovvero perchè non c'è niente di fare a Montegrano,' *Quaderni di sociologia*, 1960. Also see Bell's critique, pp. 72–3, 77. In her recent work *Donne, uomini, famiglie: Napoli nel novecento* (Naples: Ancora, 1999), Gabriella Gribaudi elegantly illustrates the often contradictory influence that Banfield's hypothesis has had on studies of the southern Italian family. She notes that scholars seeking to discredit Banfield have done so by emphasizing the presence of the patriarchal family and its influence in the Mafia, but ultimately reinforcing the image of the South as an asocial, lawless world. Others have tried to show that the characteristics associated with the southern family are central to Italian families in general. Local studies have shown that the type of family described by Banfield is strongest in those regions with a highly developed civic sense. Yet underlying all of this remains the assumption the family is a regressive institution.

78 Marzio Barbagli and David Kertzer, 'An Introduction to the History of Italian Family Life,' *Journal of Family History* 15 (1990): 357.

79 Gower Chapman, 88.

80 Massimo Livi-Bacci, *A History of Italian Fertility during the Last Two Centuries* (Princeton: Princeton University Press, 1977), 102–6; ACS, *Atti di nascita*, 1880, and *Atti di matrimonio*, 1880–1920.

81 ACS, *Atti di nascita* and *Atti di matrimonio*. According to the comunal birth and marriage records, births in 1880 numbered 131, while the marriages of people born in 1880 numbered 66. These numbers do not account for those who died in infancy and childhood. The late age of marriage for men was also a consequence of military service. Most men did not marry until they had finished their service.

82 ACS, *Atti di matrimonio* 1850–1900.

83 Emma Alaimo, *Proverbi Siciliani* (Florence: Giunti-Martello, 1974), 71. 'La mamma fa la figlia e la vicina la marita' or 'L'amuri di lu stranu è comu l'acqua 'ntra lu panaru.'

84 Gower Chapman, 95. For a general discussion of marriage rituals, see Gower Chapman, 88–114, and Salvatore Salomone-Marino, *Customs and Habits of the Sicilian Peasants*, trans. Rosalie N. Norris (1897; reprint, East Brunswick: Associated University Presses, 1981), 179–90.

85 Salamone-Marino, 179.

86 Giuseppe Pitrè, *La famiglia, la casa, la vita del popolo siciliana* (Palermo: A. Reber, 1913), 33.

87 Gower Chapman, 117–20.

88 Gower Chapman, 89.

89 Gower Chapman, 89.

90 Pitrè, *La famiglia*, 36.

91 Constance Cronin, *Sting of Change: Sicilians in Sicily and Australia* (Chicago: University of Chicago Press, 1970), 56.

92 Gower Chapman, 95–100.

93 Gower Chapman, 106–7.

94 Gower Chapman, 106.

95 ACS, *Foglio di Famiglia.* Each commune was required to register households and record the changes that resulted from marriages, births, deaths, and migration. Although the records in Sutera are far from complete, they roughly correspond to the findings of other scholars working in southern Italy. Marzio Barbagli and David Kertzer, 'An Introduction to the History of Italian Family Life,' *Journal of Family History* 15 (1990): 370–83. Barbagli and Kertzer note that in Puglia, 6 per cent of all households included extended family members.

96 This figure was calculated based on the 1901 census. In Sutera and Milocca the total population of 5, 682 was divided by the total number of families, 1, 498.

97 Cronin, 80–1; Schneider and Schneider, *Culture*, 89. Even today in Sutera it is common for elderly parents to live on their own. However, their houses are usually located close to an adult daughter, who provides them with their meals.

98 ACS, 'Censimento 1911,' cat. XII, cl. 1, fasc. 1; Gower Chapman, 131; Gabaccia, *From Sicily*, 25.

99 Gabaccia, *From Sicily*, 21–3.

100 ASC, *Catasto dei fabbricati-Sutera*, partita 1441.

101 ASC, *Catasto dei fabbricati-Sutera*, partita 1826.

102 Cronin, 47.

103 Cronin, 80.

104 ACS, *Atti di nascita* 1880–1930.

105 Gabaccia, *From Sicily*, 48.

106 Cronin, 80–1.

107 Gower Chapman, 132–3; Gabaccia, *From Sicily*, 48–51.

108 Schneider and Schneider, *Culture*, 93; Gower Chapman, 21, 40; Cronin, 64; Gabaccia, *From Sicily*, 48.

109 Schneider and Schneider, *Culture*, 93.

110 Gower Chapman, 39. Gower Chapman notes that economic necessity had far more to do with gender segregation than specific rules controlling male/female relations.

111 The reconstruction of Giovanni S. and Antonia A.'s lives is based on birth and marriage records in Sutera and on a number of oral interviews with the elderly women I conducted in the summer of 1991 in Sutera. Giovanni S. and Antonia A. were real people who lived and married in Sutera. The daily activities reflect a composite picture of the typical activities of Sicilian men and women. This description is closely modelled on a similar analysis by Donna Gabaccia, *From Sicily*, 37–40.

112 Sonnino, 12.

113 In 1874, water was piped into Sutera from the *corvo* and distributed among 13 fountains. Before the fountains were constructed, most water was collected in the rainy months and stored in large wells. Vaccaro, *Sutera*, 26–9. Onofria V. remembers her mother still going to fetch water in the early 1920s.

114 Gower Chapman, 31–2; Salomone-Marino, 56–7.

115 See Salamone-Marino, 57; Gower Chapman, 131. For a discussion of the problems attached to the concepts of public and private applied to the Mediterranean world, see Renée Hirschon, 'Essential Objects and the Sacred: Interior and Exterior Space in an Urban Greek Locality,' and Lidia Sciama, 'The Problem of Privacy in Mediterranean Anthropology,' in *Women and Space*, ed. Shirley Ardener, 70–111.

116 Gower Chapman, 26.

117 Lorenzoni, *Inchiesta*, parte 4, 463–4.

118 Schneider and Schneider, *Culture*, 89.

119 Gabaccia, *From Sicily*, 37–40.

120 Pitrè, *La famiglia*, 30–1.

121 Schneider and Schneider, *Culture*, 86.

122 Gabaccia, *From Sicily*, 9.

123 Schneider and Schneider, *Culture*, 87–8.

124 Schneider and Schneider, *Culture*, 87; Gabaccia, *From Sicily*, 9.

125 Vaccaro, *Cenni*, 34. Vaccaro was a doctor and considered himself to be a scientist, seeking confirmation of customary beliefs. Throughout his work his faith in the tenets of nineteenth-century liberalism is clearly visible.

126 Vaccaro, *Cenni*, 34–5.

127 Vaccaro, *Cenni*, 36–9. He cites primarily seventeenth- and eighteenth-century sources as evidence of the historical conversion of the Suteresi.

128 Finley et al., 45–6.
129 Vaccaro, *Cenni*, 65–6. Vaccaro qualifies his account of this legend, stating: 'I will not affirm it or reject it; and this is not the place to discuss it.'
130 I heard this story from a number of women. Each one told me that the peasant was her great-great-grandfather.
131 William Douglass, *Emigration from a Southern Italian Town* (New Brunswick, NJ: Rutgers University Press, 1984), 29–31; Bell, 25.
132 Vaccaro, *Cenni*, 23–7.
133 Vaccaro, *Cenni*, 52–4.
134 Vaccaro, *Cenni*, 73–4.
135 Vaccaro, *Cenni*, 134.
136 Vaccaro, *Cenni*, 53.

2: 'Gone to America': Migrating Men and Abandoned Women

1 Information about the migrants from Sutera is derived from a migrant file I created based on information contained in birth and marriage records, passport lists and requests for documentation for a passport, and passenger lists of ships arriving in New York City. The file contains information on 714 people from Sutera.
2 Dino Cinel, *From Italy to San Francisco* (Stanford: Stanford University Press, 1982), 46–52; Robert Foerster, *The Italian Emigration of Our Times* (1919; reprint, New York: Arno Press, 1969), 22–43; Michael Piore, *Birds of Passage* (New York: Cambridge University Press, 1979), 56.
3 ASC, *Catasto dei fabbricati-Sutera*, partita # 2721.
4 Angelo Mosso, *Vita Moderna degli Italiani* (Milan: Fratelli Treves Editori, 1906), 13–14.
5 Mosso, 14.
6 Gaetano Conte, *Dieci Anni in America* (Palermo: tip. G. Spinnato, 1903), 11.
7 Giovanni Lorenzoni, *Inchiesta parlamentare sulle condizione dei contadini nelle province meridionali e nelle Sicilia*, vol. 6, *Sicilia*, tomo 1, parte 5 (Rome: Tip. Naz. G. Bertero, 1910), 758. Southern agriculturists were among the first to speak out against unrestricted immigration in the nineteenth century. However, the Italian state remained neutral on the question of migration. Immigration had become a legally guaranteed right by the end of 1888. There were a few restrictions: shipping agents required government permission to oper-ate in Italy, and the government prohibited any form of contract labour.
8 Lorenzoni, *Inchiesta*, parte 5, 850.
9 Dorothy M. Cula Balancio, 'The Making and Unmaking of a Myth: Italian

American Women and Their Community' (PhD diss., City University of New York, 1985), 88–9. Balancio argues that assumptions about the women who remained behind were used by those opposed to emigration to build propaganda campaigns directed towards men and women, based on fears of dishonor and betrayal. The fears of various critics are nicely summarized by Teti Vito, 'Noti sui comportamenti delle donne sole degli "americani" durante la prima emigrazione in Calabria,' *Studi Emigrazione* 24 (1987): 20–43; also see Commissariato dell'Emigrazione, 'Relazione sui servizi dell'emigrazione per l'anno 1909–1910,' *Bolletino dell'Emigrazione* 18 (1910): 53–4.

10 Commissariato dell'Emigrazione, 'Relazione sui servizi,' 54.

11 Francesco Coletti, 'Classi sociali e delinquenza in Italia 1891–1901,' *Inchiesta parlamentare sulle condizione dei contadini nelle provincie meridionali e nella Sicilia,* vol. 7, tomo 1 (Rome: Bertero, 1910), 26. In this work he shows that between 1890 and 1906 the number of people condemned in the courts declined in southern Italy and the islands, and increased in northern and central Italy. Also see Francesco Coletti, *Dell'emigrazione italiana* (Milan: Ulrico Hoelpi, 1912), 261.

12 In particular, men like Francesco Nitti, Francesco Coletti, and Giustino Fortunato were well known for their writings extolling the economic and moral benefits of immigration.

13 Mosso, 53–4.

14 Betty Boyd-Caroli, *Italian Repatriation from the United States, 1900–1914* (New York: Center for Migration Studies, 1973), 10–11.

15 In particular, see the study by Franchetti and Sonnino in the 1870s, Damiani's survey of agricultural conditions in the 1880s, and the more recent work completed under the direction of Giovanni Lorenzoni. For a general overview of the 'agrarian problem,' see Giovanni Raffiotta, *Storia della Sicilia post-unificazione: la Sicilia nella prima ventennio del secolo XX* (Palermo: Ind. Grafica Nazionale, 1959), 48–53, 141–63. Over the past decade, historians have explored the origins of the Southern Question. In particular, see Giuseppe Giarrizzo, *Mezzogiorno senza meridionalismo: La Sicilia, lo sviluppo, il potere* (Venice: Marsilio editori, 1992), and Marta Petrusewicz, *Come il meridione divenne una questione: rappresentazioni del Sud prima e dopo Quarantotto* (Catanzaro: Rubbettino Editore, 1998). In English, see Robert Lumley and Jonathan Morris, eds., *The New History of the Italian South: The Mezzogiorno Revisted* (Devon: University of Exeter Press, 1997) and Jane Schneider, ed., *Italy's 'Southern Question': Orientalism in One Country* (New York: Berg, 1998).

16 Mosso, 108. For similar arguments, see Carlo Ferraris, 'Il movimento generale dell'emigrazione italiana: suoi caratteri ed effetti,' *Bollettino dell'emigrazione* 5 (1909): 20–36; Bruccoleri, *Oggi in Sicilia*, 97–8; Augusto Bosco,

'L'emigrazione del mezzogiorno,' *Giornale degli Economisti*, 2nd ser., 32 (April 1906): 319–20; Giovanbattista Raja, *Il fenomeno emigratorio siciliano con speciale riguardo al quinquennio 1902–1906* (Palermo: Tip. Imp. Affari Pubblicità, 1908), 78–9.

17 Lorenzoni, *Inchiesta*, parte 5, 860.

18 Coletti, *Dell'emigrazione*, 256–77; Raja, 70–80.

19 Bruccoleri, *Oggi in Sicilia*, 104. Bruccoleri's general analysis is laid out clearly in pages 85–105.

20 Pasquale Villari, 'Discorso sulla emigrazione,' in *Storia politica e istruzione* (Milan: Ulrico Hoelpli, 1917), 372.

21 Mosso, 120–1.

22 Bruccoleri, *Oggi in Sicilia*, 91; Conte, 11.

23 Maria Messina, 'La Mèrica,' in *Piccoli Gorghi* (1911; reprint, Palermo: Sellerio, 1988), 127–37. Trachoma is a contagious eye infection. Anyone with the disease was immediately turned away by the American authorities.

24 Luigi Capuana, *Gli Americani di Rabbato: Racconto* (Palermo: R. Sandrow, 1918), 171.

25 Constance Cronin, *Sting of Change: Sicilians in Sicily and Australia* (Chicago: University of Chicago Press, 1970), 76–8.

26 Charlotte Gower Chapman, *Milocca: A Sicilian Village* (Cambridge: Schenkman, 1971) 111–13.

27 Maria Messina, 'Nonna Lida,' in *Piccoli Gorghi*, 147.

28 Luigi Pirandello, 'L'Altro Figlio,' in *Novelle per un anno*, vol. 1 (Verona: Arnoldo Mondadori Editore, 1956). The gendering of migration is also visible in Italian-American literature, although in a somewhat more complicated form. In relation to the homeland, migrants possess the virility and strength associated with men. In the United States, migrants live in a culture that undermines their claims to the privileges of masculinity – that undermines even their racial claims to whiteness – and that effeminizes the traits linked to 'Italian-American' men. Those traits that are clearly masculine are criminalized. See Matthew Frye Jacobson, *Whiteness of a Different Color* (Cambridge: Harvard University Press, 1998).

For a discussion of migration and literature in southern Italy, see Sebastiano Martelli, 'Emigrazione e America nella letteratura del Sud,' in *Italian Ethnics: Their Languages, Literature and Lives*, vol. 20 *Annual Proceedings of the American Italian Historical Association*, ed. Dominic Candeloro, Fred L. Gardaphe, Paolo A. Giordano (Staten Island: American Historical Association, 1990), 71–8. Martelli argues that migration literature equated the homeland with death and sickness, and contrasts two civilizations, the moribund (southern Italy) with the industrial (urban United States). The peasant culture is a place of nature and of recovery. For a more general discussion of themes in migrant literature, see Russell King, John Connell, and Paul White, eds, *Writing across Worlds: Literature and Migration* (London: Routledge, 1995).

Memoirs and novels on the Italian-American experience include Pietro di Donato, *Christ in Concrete* (New York: Bobbs-Merrill, 1939); Gay Talese, *Unto the Sons* (New York: Knopf, 1992); Leonard Covello, *The Heart Is the Teacher* (New York: McGraw-Hill, 1958); and Angelo Pellegrini, *American Dream: An Immigrant's Quest* (San Francisco: North Point Press, 1986). Pellegrini, *American Dream*, is a memoir modelled on Horatio Alger. For Pellegrini the immigrant dream is 'happiness through self-realization,' and that realization comes through hard work. In describing the Tuscan hills he left behind he writes 'of the peasants who lived there, those who owned enough unencumbered land managed to keep bread on the table; others not so fortunate inherited a marginal existence from their parents. Of those, the ones who had the courage and managed to secure the necessary funds left the region. The more bold and imaginative (my parents among them) went to America.' General works on Italian-American literary criticism include Paolo Giordano and Anthony Julian Tamburri, eds., *Beyond the Margin: Readings in Italian Americana* (Teaneck, NJ: Fairleigh Dickinson University Press, 1998); and Rose Basile Green, *The Italian-American Novel: A Document of the Interaction of Two Cultures* (Teaneck, NJ: Fairleigh Dickinson University Press, 1974); A Kenneth Ciongoli and Jay Parini, eds., *Beyond the Godfather: Italian American Writers on the Real Italian-American Experience* (Hanover: University Press of New England, 1997).

29 Schneider and Schneider, *Culture*, 91.

30 Schneider and Schneider, *Culture*, 91

31 Gower Chapman, 108.

32 ACS, 'Modulo informativo per l'ammissione dei mentecatti al manicomio di Palermo, 1903,' cat. XV, fasc. 1.

33 The connection between sexuality and mental illness is visible in many of the standard textbooks. See for example Dott. Luigi Mongeri, *Patologia speciale delle malattie mentali con sommarie considerazioni medico legali per gli studenti, medici pratici e giuristi* (Milan: Ulrico Hoepli, 1907), 35. Psychiatrists commonly linked female mental illness to reproduction, in particular the onset or cessation of menstruation and pregnancy. See Dott. Lugi Scaba, *Trattato di terapia delle malattie mentali ad suo dei medici e degli studenti* (Turin: Unione Tipografico-editrice, 1900), 21, 27.

34 ACS, 'Modulo Informativo per l'ammissione dei mentecatti al manicomio di Palermo, 1911,' cat. XV, fasc. 1.

35 For a more general discussion about the role of medicine in creating scientific justifications for women's inferior social position, and the connection between physiology and female subordination, see Mary Poovey, '"Scenes of an Indelicate Character": The Medical "Treatment" of Victorian Women,' in *The Making of the Modern Body*, ed. Catherine Gallagher and Thomas Laqueur (Berkeley: University of California Press, 1987), 137–68.

36 Commissariato dell'Emigrazione, 'Relazione sui servizi,' 54.

37 Schneider and Schneider, *Culture*, 86–94. For a broader overview of the Mediterranean conception of honour and its relationship to female sexuality see the essays in J.G. Persitiany, ed., *Honor and Shame: The Values of Mediterranean Society* (Chicago: University of Chicago Press, 1966).

38 Gower Chapman, 40.

39 Gower Chapman, 108.

40 Teti, 13–46.

41 Gower Chapman, 108.

42 Gower Chapman, 108.

43 Schneider and Schneider, *Culture*, 86–91.

44 Schneider and Schneider, *Culture*, 89–91.

45 Cronin, 50–3. Here she relates the story of one man who attempted to explain away the fact that his wife met with her male cousin every morning when he left for work, by telling the townsfolk they were just friends and needed to talk. When no one believed him, his brothers, uncles, and father pressured him to kill his wife. Whenever he walked through the streets the townspeople would jeer, until he finally gave in to their demands. He shot his wife and then turned himself in to the local police. Also see the Schneider and Schneider, *Culture*, 90.

46 Schneider and Schneider, *Culture*, 100–1.

47 Lorenzoni, *Inchiesta*, parte 5, 850.

48 Gower Chapman, 43.

49 Gower Chapman, 42. House nuns were village women who wanted to enter a convent but were either too poor or unable to overcome parental disapproval. Instead they took a vow of chastity, dressed completely in black, attended mass, and confessed daily. Residents who viewed their piety as excessive and hypocritical often ridiculed these religious women.

50 Cataldo Naro, *Momenti e figure della chiesa nissena dell'otto e novecento* (Caltanissetta: Centro Studi Sulla Cooperazione, 'A Cammerata,' 1989), 534–6.

51 Naro, 536 n. 31.

52 'Il marito vendicatore: parte dall'America per uccidere,' *Corriere della Sera*, 22 March 1911, New York edition.

53 Department of Commerce and Labor, Bureau of Statistics, Vol. 30, *Special Consular Reports: Emigration to the United States*, 'From U.S. Consul A.H. Byington, Naples, Italy, February 16, 1904: Causes of Emigration from Naples and throughout the South' (Washington: Government Printing Office, 1904), 91.

54 MAE, CGE, *Annuario statistico della emigrazione italiana 1876–1925* (Rome: Commissariato dell'Emigrazione, 1925) 195 and 204 (hereafter *Annuario statistico*). Before 1895, Sicilians accounted for fewer than 5 per cent of all of the migrants who left Italy to settle in the Americas, Australia, or Africa. By 1910, over 11 per cent of all Italian immigrants came from Sicily alone. Lorenzoni, *Inchiesta*, parte 5, 716. For a general overview of Sicilian migration, see Francesco Renda, *L'emigrazione in Sicilia* (Palermo: Tip. La Cartografica, 1963). Also see L. Arcuri di Marco, 'L'emigrazione siciliana all'estero nel cinquantennio (1876–1925),' *Annali del Mezzogiorno* 6 (1966): 169–232.

55 Lorenzoni, *Inchiesta*, parte 5, 716, 787.

56 Births and deaths are taken from Stefano Somogyi, *Storia demografici dei comuni siciliani dal 1862–1971* (Palermo: Tip. Lux., 1979), 167, 168, 241, 242. The decennial resident and present population is from the national Italian census.

57 This is seen in other villages as well. Samuel L Baily, 'Chain Migration of Italians to Argentina: Case Studies of the Agnonesi and Sirolesi,' *Studi Emigrazione* 19 (1982): 76–7.

58 ACS, 'Prospetto dei movimenti avvenuti nella popolazione residente, 1902–1910,' cat. XII. Mario Tona, a local historian, compiled these figures based on the information in the population registers of the village. Figures from 1901 came from ASC, 'Movimento della popolazione: prospetto trimestrale dell'emigrazione all'estero, 1901,' cat. XII, busta. #3801; ACS, 'Risposto dal sindaco al R. ispettorato scolastico della circoscrizione di Caltanissetta, n. 422, 2 giugno 1908,' cat. IX, cl. 2, fasc. 1.

59 Many villagers who applied for passports never left. The process was easy and cost very little. Most Suteresi were able to waive the required fees by claiming poverty.

60 Foerster, 35.

61 For an explanation of the inherent biases in the sources, see George Calafut, 'An Analysis of Italian Emigration Statistics, 1876–1914,' *Jahrbuch für geschichte, von staat, wirtshchaft und gesellshaft lateinamerikas* 14 (1977): 310–1. Rates of return are discussed in depth at a later point. For a discussion of the problems surrounding migration statistics and possible remedies, see Francesco Coletti, *Dell'emigrazione*, 1–15.

62 ACS, 'Registro delle domande di nulla osta, 1898–1903,' cat. 13, cl. 1–3, fasc. 2. MAIC, 'Notizie sulle condizione industriali della provincia di Caltanis-

setta,' *Annali di Statistica*, fasc. LVI (Rome: Tip. Naz, G. Bertero, 1895), 48–7; ACS, 'Prospetto dei movimenti avvenuti nella popolazione residente,' cat. 12. These figures are based on those compiled by Mario Tona.

63 ACS, 'Inchiesta sulle condizioni igeniche e sanitarie dei comuni del regno 1885,' cat. IV, cl. 3, fasc. 1. More than half the men in Sutera worked as sharecroppers.

64 Biagio Puntero, *L'emigrazione: conferenze tenute nella sala gialla del palazzo municipale in Caltanissetta, la sera 21 maggio 1910* (Caltanissetta: Tip. Ospizio Prof. di Beneficenze, 1911), 4–5. See Rudolph Bell, *Fate and Honor, Family and Village* (Chicago: University of Chicago Press, 1979) 180, for a discussion of the economics of the decision-making process underlying migration.

65 *Giornale di Sicilia*, 10–11 February 1906, 4, 12–13 February 1906, 4, 14–15 February 1906, 4.

66 Raffiotta, 132–3.

67 Raffiotta, 130–4.

68 For a general discussion of migration from Sicily between 1900 and 1906, and the impact of the American political situation, see Coletti, *Dell'emigrazione*, 74, and Lorenzoni, *Inchiesta*, parte 5, 714. Emigration statistics for Sutera were gleaned from ACS, 'Prospetto dei movimenti avvenuti nella popolazione residente,' cat XII, 1901–1910. These figures are based on those compiled by Mario Tona. See also Lorenzoni, *Inchiesta*, parte 5, 787.

69 ACS, 'Memo dal sindaco al R. ispettorato scolastico, 4 settembre 1905,' cat. IX, cl. 2, fasc. 9.

70 ACS, Commissariato dell'Emigrazione, 'Notizie concernenti l'emigrazione italiana,' circolare 203, n. 28 (January 1909); and 'Notizie concernenti l'emigrazione italiana,' circolare 204, n. 10 (April 1909).

71 Piore, 154; Bell, 190.

72 ACS, 'Rappresentanti dei vettori, 1907' cat. 13, cl. 3.

73 Lorenzoni, *Inchiesta*, parte 5, 754.

74 Gower Chapman, 109.

75 Commissariato dell'Emigrazione 'Relazione sui servizi,' 45.

76 Donna Gabaccia, *Militants and Migrants: Rural Sicilians Become American Workers* (New Brunswick, NJ: Rutgers University Press, 1988), 76–81; John Briggs, *An Italian Passage: Immigrants to Three American Cities* (New Haven: Yale University Press, 1978), 9–14.

77 Ages, occupations, and family reconstructions are based on the migrant file.

78 ACS, *Atti di nascita 1880–1930* and *Atti di matrimonio 1880–1930*. The average age of married migrants was thirty-two, and their average age at first marriage was twenty-six. Birth records show that among migrants and their

families, the first child appeared eighteen months after the wedding, on average.

79 ASC, *Lista di leva, classe 1880–1899.*

80 Gero Difrancesco, *Sutera: I primi anni del '900* (Caltanissetta: Biblioteca Comunale Sutera, 1989), 12; Gower Chapman, 62, also notes that none of the *signori* from Milocca had emigrated.

81 ACS, 'Circolare della prefettura di Caltanissetta, 1910,' cat. 13, cl. 3, fasc. 1.

82 ACS, *Atti di nascita 1880.*

83 For a similar analysis, see Gabaccia, *Militants and Migrants,* 79.

84 Gabaccia, *Militants and Migrants,* 80–3.

85 ACS, *Atti di nascita;* ASC, *Catasto dei terreni-Sutera,* partita 4403.

86 J.S. MacDonald, 'Agricultural Organization, Migration and Labor Militancy in Rural Italy,' *Economic History Review,* 2nd ser., 16 (1963): 61–71; for a discussion of the role of the middle peasant, see Eric Wolf, *Peasant Wars of the Twentieth Century* (New York: Harper and Row, 1973).

87 Gabaccia, *Militants and Migrants,* 15.

88 Gabaccia, *Militants and Migrants,* 17–36.

89 The description of these women is taken from 178 migrant files. I have used only those cases where I have the date of marriage, the date of emigration, and the age of the wife.

90 Ministero degli Affari Esteri (MAE), *Norme legislative e regolamentari concernanti la concessione di passaporti per l'estero* (Rome: Tip. Naz. G. Bertero, 1905), 7. According to the immigration laws, a family group was defined as a head of household with his wife and children, and parents if they usually live with him, or as a guardian and his/her charges, or as an older brother with his unmarried younger brother and sisters. According to these regulations, two brothers who decided to leave their wives and emigrate together were not considered a family group.

91 *Annuario statistico,* 193; Renda, *L'emigrazione,* 50.

92 ACS, 'Registro degli emigrati all'estero, 1893–1899,' cat. XIII, cl. 3, fasc. 2.

93 ACS, *Foglio di famiglia.* These records were very sporadic, and in no way should they be considered more than a rough estimate. There were few forms left from the family records prior to the 1930s. I was able to use the records available to see if emigrants had returned or if families had changed their heads of households.

94 *Annuario statistico,* 183.

95 *Annuario statistico,* 183.

96 *Annuario statistico,* 183.

97 Only one unmarried woman and her child requested permission to emigrate. Among women over sixteen, 84 per cent were married.

98 ASC, 'Movimento della popolazione di Sutera,' Prefettura Generale, busta #3799.
99 'From U.S. Consul Byington,' 91.
100 ASC, 'Movimento della popolazione di Sutera,' Prefettura Generale, busta #3799.
101 Lorenzoni, *Inchiesta*, parte 5, 812.
102 Foerster, 35.
103 Boyd-Caroli, 12–13.
104 ACS, *Lista di leva, classe 1880–1899*.
105 Boyd-Caroli, 9.
106 *International Migrations: Statistics* (New York: National Bureau of Economic Research, 1929), 454 and 477; Alberto Beneduce, 'Sul movimento dei rimpatriati dalle americhe,' *Giornale degli Economisti* 3 (September 1910): 240.
107 Interview, Spring 1991.
108 Senate Documents, *Reports of the Immigration Commission*, vol. 1, *Immigrants in Industries, Part 2, Iron and Steel Manufacturing*, S. Doc. #633, 61st Congress, 2nd session (Washington DC: Government Printing Office, 1911), 164.
109 Senate Documents, 'Immigrants in Industries,' part 2, 173, 175.
110 Lorenzoni, *Inchiesta*, parte 3, 21, 75. In 1906 a day labourer earned an average of 1.7 lire a day. On average, agricultural labourers worked between 150 and 200 days each year. Biagio Puntero, *Delle condizione*, 75. Puntero states that a 200 lire profit was considered an excellent year for a sharecropper.
111 Senate Documents, 'Immigrants in Industries,' part 2, 189–231.
112 Senate Documents, 'Immigrants in Industries,' part 2, 187.
113 *Annuario statistico*, 247.
114 MAE, *Norme legislative*, 6.
115 ACS, 'Domanda di nulla osta-Giuseppe C, 1901,' cat. XIII, cl. 3.
116 MAE, *Norme legislative*, 25.
117 ACS, 'Dalla questura di Palermo al sindaco di Sutera,' cat. XIII, cl. 3, fasc. 1.
118 'Evasione e arresto di un detenuto,' *Giornale di Sicilia*, 16–17 February 1906, 4.
119 John Bodnar, *The Transplanted: A History of Immigrants in Urban America* (Bloomington: Indiana University Press, 1987) 38; Donna Gabaccia, *From Sicily to Elizabeth Street: Housing and Social Change among Italian Immigrants, 1880–1930* (Albany: State University of New York Press, 1984), 57–9.
120 Lorenzoni, *Inchiesta*, parte 5, 832–3.

121 Dino Cinel, *The National Integration of Return Migration, 1870–1929* (New York: Cambridge University Press, 1991), 155–6.

122 Cronin, 53.

123 Gower Chapman, 109.

124 Gower Chapman, 37–8; Lorenzoni, *Inchiesta*, parte 4, 463.

125 Giuseppe Pitrè, *La famiglia, la casa, la vita del popolo siciliano* (Palermo: A. Reber, 1913), 36; Cronin, 104.

126 Pitrè, *La famiglia*, 36; Gower Chapman, 98–9.

127 In particular, see the writings of Giuseppe Pitrè and Salomone-Marino on the family. Sonnino and Lorenzoni also note the dominance of the father within the Sicilian family.

128 Pitrè, *La famiglia*, 25; Salomone-Marino, 41–55.

129 Caterina Binetti-Ventura, *Trine e Donne Siciliane* (Milan: Ulrico Hoepli, 1911), 176; Gower Chapman, 36; Salomone-Marino, 42–3.

130 Gower Chapman, 107.

131 Susan Rogers, 'Female Forms of Power and the Myth of Male Dominance: A Model of Female/Male Interaction in Peasant Society,' *American Ethnologist* 2 (November 1975): 727–31.

132 Vaccaro, *Sutera*, 47.

133 Gower Chapman, 38.

134 William Stephens, *The Family in Cross Cultural Perspective* (New York: Holt, Reinhart and Winston, 1963), 290–8; Ernestine Friedl, 'The Position of Women: Appearance and Reality,' in *Gender and Power in Rural Greece*, ed. Jill Dubisch (Princeton, NJ: Princeton University Press, 1986) 42–52; Rogers, 734.

135 Jill Dubisch, Introduction to *Gender and Power in Rural Greece*, 14; Michael Herzfeld, 'Within and Without: The Category of Female in the Ethnography of Modern Greece,' in ibid., 215–33.

136 Michelle Zimbalist Rosaldo, 'Women, Culture and Society: A Theoretical Overview,' in *Women Culture and Society*, ed. Michelle Zimbalist Rosaldo and Louise Lamphere (Stanford: Stanford University Press, 1974), 21.

137 Friedl, 42.

138 Jill Dubisch, 'The Domestic Power of Women in a Greek Island Village,' *Studies in European Society* 1 (1974): 23–33.

139 Pitrè, *La famiglia*, 30–5; Lorenzoni, *Inchiesta*, parte 4, 462–3; Chapman-Gower, 37.

140 Jane Schneider, 'Trousseau as Treasure: Some Contradictions of Late Nineteenth Century Change in Sicily,' in *Beyond the Myths of Culture*, ed. Eric B. Ross (New York: Academic Press, 1980), 326–8.

141 Charles Tilly, 'Transplanted Networks,' in *Immigration Reconsidered: History,*

Sociology, and Politics, ed. Virginia Yans-McLaughlin (New York: Oxford University Press, 1990), 84; Samuel Baily, 'The Village Outward Approach to the Study of Social Networks: A Case Study of the Agnonesi Diaspora Abroad, 1885–1989,' *Studi Emigrazione* 29 (1992): 43–67.

142 ACS, 'Notizie sull'emigrazione, 1900–1928' cat. XIII, cl. 3, fasc. 1. There are numerous memos from the Commissariato dell'Emigrazione and the Prefettura di Caltanissetta relating to emigration.

143 ACS, 'Scuole serale e festive per adulti analfabeti 1905–1906,' cat. XII, cl. 2, fasc. 9.

144 Most Suteresi who emigrated went to Birmingham, Alabama, where they worked in the mines and as truck farmers. Another community was in Pittston, Pennsylvania. A few settled in Buffalo and Chicago. According to local records, nearly 70 per cent of the migrants eventually returned to Sutera.

145 Gower Chapman, 109.

146 New York Library, *Passenger Lists 1900–1910*.

147 Ewa Moroska, 'The Sociology and Historiography of Immigration,' in *Immigration Reconsidered*, ed. Yans-McLaughlin, 194. John S. MacDonald and L.D. MacDonald, 'Chain Migration, Ethnic Neighborhood Formation and Social Networks,' *Milbank Memorial Fund Quarterly* 42 (January 1964): 82–95; Baily, 'Chain Migration,' 73–90; Baily, 'The Village Outward Approach,' 43–67; Tilly, 'Transplanted Networks,' 84–5; Morawska, 187–238.

148 Information about the migrants from Sutera is derived from a database I created. It is based on birth and marriage registers, requests for passports and passport lists from the local archive in Sutera, and passenger lists of ships that sailed into New York's harbour. The file reconstructs the lives of 714 people who left Sutera before the First World War. I have been able to identify family relationships between migrants in approximately 10 per cent of cases.

149 M. Estellie Smith noted that women were also crucial in the construction of new networks in the receiving communities. In her study of a Portuguese community in North America, she noted that women often passed on information about employment, social services, and housing. See M. Estellie Smith, 'Networks and Migration Resettlement: Cherchez la Femme,' *Anthropological Quarterly* 49 (January 1976): 20–7.

150 Lorenzoni, *Inchiesta*, parte 4, 463; Pitrè, *La famiglia*, 33–4.

151 Gower Chapman, 38.

152 Cinel, *National Integration*, 157. Cinel notes that in 1903 a regulatory commission was established to control the cost of overseas fares. By 1906 the price had fallen by 10 per cent on the trip to New York, making it cheaper to sail to New York than to Paris.

153 MAE, *Norme legislative*, p. 58. Between 1880 and the First World War the value of the dollar fluctuated between four and five lire. Dino Cinel, *From Italy*, 4n.

154 Lorenzoni, *Inchiesta*, parte 3, 21, 34–5, 136. On average, day labourers could work between 150 and 200 days out of each year in the interior regions of the island. A day labourer could average 1.9 lire a day hoeing, sowing, and ploughing, and slightly more during the harvest.

155 *Atti della giunta*, 99.

156 ACS, 'Risposte ai quesiti contenuti nella circolare prefettizia 3 ottobre 1901 div. 3 #11030–riguardanti l'inchiesta pel contratti di lavoro,' cat. XI, cl. 2a, fasc. 2a; ACS, 'Patti agrari Sutera, 15 agosto 1911,' cat. XI, cl. 2a, fasc. 2a; ACS, 'Relazione periodica agraria aprile-luglio 1905,' cat. XI, cl. 1a, fasc. 4a. According to these three memos, the average sharecropper in Sutera worked between 1 and 2 *salme* of land, the equivalent of 2 or 3 hectares. In this region, 1 *salma* was generally considered 1.7 hectares. In Sutera the term *salma* was also utilized to measure quantity. One *salma* was the equivalent to 275 litres. In general, every *salma* of land planted with wheat yielded 4 *salme* of grain, while one *salma* of land planted with legumes yielded 3 *salme* at the harvest. About two-thirds of the crop went to the owner and middleman; the sharecropper kept one-third of the total yield. In 1905 a *salma* of grain was worth 65 lire, whereas a *salme* of legumes sold for 32 lire.

157 Lorenzoni, *Inchiesta*, parte 5, 737.

158 Lorenzoni, *Inchiesta*, parte 5, 737; Antonio Mangano, 'The Effect of Emigration upon Italy: "Ci manca la mano d'opera,"' *Charities and the Commons* 20 (4 April 1908): 15.

159 Archivio Comunale di Ficarazzi, 'Al sindaco, June 18, 1937,' cat. XIII, cl. 1.

160 Patrizia Audenino, *Un mestiere per partire: tradizione migratoria, lavoro e comunità in una vallata alpina* (Milan: Franco Angeli, 1990), 152–3.

161 Gower Chapman, 97.

162 Schneider, 'Trousseau as Treasure,' 327.

163 Gower Chapman, 97.

164 Schneider, 'Trousseau,' 343.

165 Lorenzoni, *Inchiesta*, parte 5, 737.

166 Lorenzoni, *Inchiesta*, parte 3, 26.

167 These conclusions are based on a survey of land records. Among house and land records I found 30 entries registered in the names of emigrant wives. This comprises approximately 10 per cent of migrant couples. Based on this sample, I have found that nearly half the land was bought shortly before the husband left. Houses were generally bought with wages earned abroad. The role of women in purchasing property is explored in chapter 4.

168 Lorenzoni, *Inchiesta*, parte 3, 309; Cinel, *National Integration*, 154.

169 Mangano, 'Ci manca la mano d'opera,' 24–5; Cinel, *From Italy*, 94–6; Cinel, *National Integration*, 119.
170 Lorenzoni, *Inchiesta*, parte 5, 834–5.
171 Lorenzoni, *Inchiesta*, parte 3, 279.
172 'From U.S. Consul A.H. Byington, 91.
173 ACS, 'Minuta: 12 ottobre 1915,' cat. XIII, cl. 1, fasc. 1.
174 ACS, 'Dal consulato d'Italia al sindaco, 18 novembre 1915,' cat. XIII, cl. 1, fasc. 1.
175 ACS, 'Dal sindaco al consolare d'Italia, Birmingham, 18 dicembre 1925,' cat. XIII, cl. 3, fasc. 1.
176 ACS, 'Dal consulato d'Italia al sindaco, 1 febbraio 1926,' cat. XIII, cl. 3, fasc. 1.
177 ACS, 'Emigrazione 1902–1906,' cat. XIII, cl. 1–3, fasc. 1.
178 Lorenzoni, *Inchiesta*, parte 3, 279.
179 For an excellent local history of Italians in the southern United States, see Jeff Norrell, *The Italians, From Bisacquino to Birmingham* (Birmingham, AL: Birmingfind Project, n.d.); Dino Cinel, 'Italians in the South: The Alabama Case,' *Italian Americana* 9 (Fall/Winter 1990), 16.

3: Motherhood, Marriage, and Migration

1 Lodovico Frati, *La Donna Italiana secondo i più recenti studi* (Turin: Fratelli Bocca, Editori, 1899), 6–7.
2 For an excellent selection of proverbs regarding women, love, and marriage, see Emma Alaimo, *Proverbi Siciliani* (Florence: Aldo Martello-Giunti Editore, 1974), 63–78. Also see Giuseppe Pitrè, *Nozze Gallenga-Monaci: Donna e Matrimonio, proverbi siciliani inedita* (Palermo: 1903), 7–12.
3 Charlotte Gower Chapman, *Milocca* (Cambridge: Schenkman Publishing Company, 1971), 158–9; Also see Herman Tak, *South Italian Festivals: A Local History of Ritual and Change* (Amsterdam: Amsterdam University Press, 2000), chapters 1 to 4, for an excellent discussion of ritual and religion in rural Italy.
4 Antonio Mangano, 'The Effect of Emigration upon Italy: Threatened Depopulation of the South,' Charities and Commons 20 (1908): 1336. Also see Pasquale Villari, 'L'emigrazione e le sue consequenze in Italia,' Nuova Antologia, 5th series, 127 (January 1907): 36.
5 Antonio Mangano, 'The Effect of Emigration upon Italy: "Ci manca la mano d'opera," "We Lack the Working Hand."' *Charities and Commons* 20 (4 April 1908): 20.

6 Mangano, 'Ci manca la mano d'opera,' 22–3; Augusto Bosco, 'L'emigrazione del mezzogiorno,' *Giornale degli economisti* 32 (April 1906): 327–29, makes a similar argument.

7 Carlo Ferraris, 'Il movimento generale dell'emigrazione italiana: suoi caratteri ed effetti,' *Bollettino dell'emigrazione* 20–7; Francesco Coletti, *Dell'emigrazione italiana* (Milan: Ulrico Hoelpi, 1912), 225–31.

8 Biagio Puntero, *L'emigrazione: conferenze tenute nella sala gialla del palazzo municipale in Caltanissetta. la sera 21 maggio 1910* (Caltanissetta: Tip. Ospizio Prof. di Beneficenze, 1911), 22. For similar sentiments, see Giovanbattista Raja, *Il fenomeno emigratorio siciliano con speciale rigurado al quinquennio 1902–1906* (Palermo: Tip. Imp. Affari Pubblicità, 1908), 73–6; Giuseppe Bruccoleri, *L'emigrazione siciliana: caratteri ed effetti secondo le più recenti inchieste* (Rome: Coop. Tip. Manuzio, 1911), 22–4. Although Bruccoleri admitted that the island's population decline was beneficial, he also argued that emigration contributed to growing mortality rates, and that the exodus of young men posed a serious threat to the armed forces.

9 Puntero, *L'emigrazione*, 22–3.

10 For discussions regarding the relationship between production and reproduction, see E.A. Wrigley, 'Fertility Strategy for the Individual and the Group,' in *Historical Studies of Changing Fertility*, ed. Charles Tilly (Princeton: Princeton University Press, 1978), 135–6. More recent work in historical demography has reinforced the idea that economic growth delays fertility decline. See Michael R. Haines, 'Occupation and Social Class during Fertility Decline: Historical Perspectives,' in *The European Experience of Declining Fertility, 1850–1970*, ed. John R. Gillis, Louise A. Tilly, and David Levine (Cambridge: Blackwell Publishers, 1992), 195.

11 Rudolph Bell, *Fate and Honor, Family and Village* (Chicago: University of Chicago Press, 1979), 54; Jane Schneider and Peter Schneider, 'Going Forward in Reverse Gear: Culture, Economy and Political Economy in the Demographic Transitions of a Rural Sicilian Town,' in *The European Experience of Declining Fertility*, 157–73; Jane Schneider, 'Sex and Respectability in an Age of Fertility Decline: A Sicilian Case Study,' *Social Science and Medicine* 33 (1991): 885–95. For a general discussion regarding birth control, see Angus McLaren, *Reproductive Rituals* (New York: Methuen, 1984). Building on anthropological assumptions about fertility, McLaren argues that long before the 'demographic revolution' of the late nineteenth century western Europeans in rural cultures regulated reproduction. The decline in fertility came about as a result of changing cultural attitudes toward the family, not technological innovation, as so many have argued in the past. See Edward

Shorter and E. Van De Walle, 'The Decline of Non-marital Fertility in Europe, 1880–1940,' *Population Studies* (November 1971): 375–93. For other views on the subject, see John Gillis, Introduction to *European Experience.* Also, Susan Cotts Watkins, *From Provinces into Nations* (Princeton: Princeton University Press, 1991), 56–8.

12 Giuseppe Pitrè, *Usi e costumi del popolo siciliano,* ed. Giuseppe Lisi, 2nd ed. (Bologna: Capelli ed., 1971), 14–39; Rafaelle Castelli, *Credenze e usi popolari siciliani* (Palermo: Tip. Pietro Montana, 1878), 33–5.

13 Antonio Vaccaro, *Sutera e la sua geografia fisica* (Naples: Tip. Gazz. Drit. e Gius., 1890), 63. Also see Vincenzo Borruso, *Practiche abortive e controllo delle nascite in Sicilia* (Palermo: Libri Siciliani, 1966), 25–7 and 72–3.

14 Gower Chapman, 80; Schneider and Schneider, 'Going Forward,' 157–8.

15 John F. May, 'Clarifying Breastfeeding's Role in Contraception,' *Population Today* 20 (May 1992): 9; Barry M. Popkin et al., 'Nutrition, Lactation and Birth Spacing in Filipino Women,' *Demography* 30 (August 1993): 343; Kathy I. Kennedy, 'Contraceptive Efficacy of Lactational Amenorrhoea,' Lancet 339 (25 January 1992): 227–30; Singh Kaushalendra, 'Effects of Breast Feeding after Resumption of Menstruation on Waiting Time to Next Conception,' *Human Biology* 65 (February 1993): 71–86.

16 Gower Chapman, 183–5.

17 Castelli, 34.

18 Popkin et al., 333–52. For a description of diet in nineteenth and twentieth century Italy, see Stefano Somogyi, 'L'alimentazione nell'Italia unita,' in *Storia d'Italia,* vol. 5, *I documenti,* tomo 1 (Turin: Einaudi, 1973), 841–7.

19 Schneider and Schneider, 'Going Forward,' 154.

20 Gower Chapman, 80–1.

21 MAIC, *Censimento 1861,* vol. 1 (Torino, 1863), 128; MAIC, *Censimento della popolazione del Regno al 31 dicembre 1871,* vol. 1 (Rome: Stamperia Reale, 1874), 81; ACS, 'Comune di Sutera: Statistica della popolazione del commune sudetto a tutto il 31, dicembre 1893.' cat. XII, cl. 1.

22

Birth, marriage, and mortality rates, Sutera, 1862–89

	Present pop.*	Birth rate	Marriage rate	Mortality rate**
1862–9	3,725	38	5	37
1870–9	3,897	47	9	31
1880–9	4,424	51	9	33

Source: Stefano Somogyi, *Storia demografici dei comuni siciliani dal 1862–1971* (Palermo: Tip. Lux., 1979), 93, 167, 241. Present population is taken from the decennial census.

A rise in mortality rates in the late 1880s was caused by a measles epidemic that struck the village in 1887 and by the outbreak of influenza that followed.

23 Birth per marriage ratio is strongly influenced by changing age and marriage, mortality, and emigration. Although these factors tend to depress the average, this method provides a more accurate picture of how a community experiences fertility than an analysis of fertility rates alone. For a discussion of birth per marriage ratios, see Bell, 103; and Massimo Livi-Bacci, *A History of Italian Fertility during the Last Two Centuries* (Princeton, NJ: Princeton University Press, 1977), 90–1.

24

Ages of women at first marriage (%)

	Year married			
Age	1860–9	1870–9	1880–9	1890–9
14–19	30	26	29	29
20–24	35	47	38	38
25–29	16	19	16	13
30–34	7	6	8	6
35–44	7	2	7	9
Over 45	5	0	2	5

Source: The ages of women at first marriage were calculated from a total of 909 marriages where both the bride and groom were marrying for the first time, from the *Atti di matrimonio 1860–1899* in the Archivio Comunale di Sutera.

25 Francesco De Stefano and Francesco Luigi Oddo, *La Storia della Sicilia* (Bari: Laterza, 1963), 101–14.

26 Sutera directly benefited from government support of the island's industries. In 1876 the final track was laid connecting the Agrigento rail to the Palermo line, enabling the mines in Sutera to increase production. After 1870 the mines expanded rapidly, and by 1885 at least three working mines were open in the territory of Sutera, two of which were mechanized. Francesco Romano, *Storia della Sicilia post-unficazione: la Sicilia nell'ultimo ventennio del secolo XIX* (Palermo: Industria Grafica Nazionale, 1958), 62–3. Among the more important of the investment companies was the *Società inglese per la fusione dello zolfo,* run by Woodhouse and Ingham Whitaker. Also see Jane Schneider and Peter Schneider, *Culture and Political Economy in Western Sicily* (New York: Academic Press, 1976), 119, and Schneider and Schneider, 'Going Forward,' 156. For a discussion of the development of the railwayys, see Francesco Squarzina, *Produzione e comercio dello zolfo in Sicilia nel secolo XIX* (Turin: ILTE, 1963), 49–50. For the impact these developments had on Sutera, see ACS, 'Questionario per l'inchiesta sulle condizioni igeniche e sanitarie dei comuni del regno, anno 1885,' cat. IV, cl. 3a, fasc. 1. Also see Vaccaro, *Sutera,* 31, and Romano, 46.

27 De Stefano and Oddo, 104–5.

28 Jürg K. Siegenthaler, 'Sicilian Economic Change since 1860,' *Journal of Economic History* 2 (Fall 1973): 378.

29 Antonio Vaccaro, *Cenni sulla città di Sutera* (Naples: Tip. dei. Frat Carluccio, 1881), 136–8. Jane Schneider and Peter Schneider note a similar pattern in Villamura in 'Demographic Transitions,' 250.

30 For a discussion of the connection between fertility and class in Sicily, see Schneider and Schneider, 'Demographic Transitions,' 247, and 'Going Forward,' 147. For a more general discussion of the relationship between reproduction and production, see Susan Cotts Watkins.

31 Vaccaro, *Sutera*, 136.

32 Vaccaro, *Sutera*, 136–9.

33 ACS, *Atti di matrimonio 1860–1879.*

34 Schneider and Schneider, 'Going Forward,' 154. A random survey of 30 per cent of the marriages in Sutera between 1880 and 1910 indicates that local gentry rarely witnessed the death of their first-born.

35 Vaccaro, *Sutera*, 46; ACS, 'l'inchiesta sulle condizioni igeniche e sanitarie anno 1885,' cat. IV, cl. 3, fasc. 1.

36 ACS, *Atti di matrimonio 1884 and 1886.*

37 ACS, *Atti di matrimonio 1870–1879.*

38 Romano, 161.

39 ACS, *Atti di matrimonio 1880–1889.* On average, women who married agricultural workers were twenty-four years old, compared to an average nuptial age of twenty-eight among women who married artisans and twenty-seven among the local gentry.

40 Romano, 183–4; De Stefano and Oddo, 115–18.

41 Schneider and Schneider, 'Going Forward,' 156, 158–9. Jane Schneider and Peter Schneider argue that the decline in capital precipitated the transition from high to low fertility in Sicily.

42 ACS, *Atti di matrimonio 1885–1899.*

43 Schneider and Schneider, 'Going Forward,' 161.

44 Schneider and Schneider, 'Going Forward,' 156.

45 ACS, *Atti di nascita 1906.*

46 ACS, *Atti di nascita 1884–1913* and *Atti di matrimonio 1883 and 1897.*

47 Livi-Bacci, 271.

48 ACS, 'Registro delle domande di nulla osta per ottenere passaporto all'estero, 1902–1904,' cat. XIII, cl. 3, fasc. 2.

49 Schneider and Schneider, 'Demographic Transitions,' 259.

50 ACS, *Atti di nascita 1890–1914.*

51 Livi-Bacci, 69–70; Dino Cinel, *The National Integration of Return Migration,*

1870–1929 (New York: Cambridge University Press, 1991), 65, 250 n 77. Cinel notes that rates of illegitimacy in the South were substantially higher than in the North 'throughout the five decades of mass emigration.' However, he does not provide any evidence that emigration caused these elevated numbers, nor does he show how these rates changed over time.

52 Coletti, *Dell'emigrazione*, 230.

53 MAIC, 'Nati illegitimi riconosciuti da uno o de entrambi i genitori, nati illegittimi non riconosciuti ed esposti; classificati per compartamenti,' *Movimento della popolazione 1901* (Rome: Tip. Nazionale, 1903), XXXII–XXXIII; Direzione Generale della Statistica e del Lavoro Ufficio Centrale di Statistica, *Movimento della popolazione 1913* (Rome: Tip. Ditta Ludovicho Cecchini, 1915), XLII–XLIII.

54 Livi-Bacci, 70–1.

55 Archivio di Sant'Agata, *Registro dei matrimoni di Sant'Agata 1884*; ACS, *Atti di nascita 1887–1906 and Atti di matrimonio 1901*; ASC, *Catasto dei fabbricati-Sutera*, partita #1354. In 1936, Anna divided her house among her six living children.

56 Livi-Bacci, 72, notes that a large proportion of children in other provinces were eventually legitimated.

57 ACS, *Atti di nascita 1880–1889*.

58 ACS, *Atti di nascita 1880*; For an analysis of the governmental and religious institutions designed to care for abandoned children and the politics surrounding unwed mothers, see David I. Kertzer, *Sacrificed for Honor: Italian Infant Abandonment and the Politics of Reproductive Control* (Boston: Beacon Press, 1993).

59 ACS, 'Liquidazione della spesa occorsa per il mantenimento degli esposti nella provincia per l'anno 1906,' and 'Reparto della spesa occorsa per il mantenimento degli esposti nella provincia per l'anno 1913,' cat. II. cl. 3, fasc. 1.

60 ACS, 'Memo dal Enrico Marino al prefetto di Caltanissetta, 1900,' cat. XII, cl. 4.

61 Gower Chapman, 40–1.

62 Pitrè, *La famiglia*, 32.

63 Pitrè, *La famiglia*, 31. 'Cui cu patri e matri è ubbidenti, Campa riccu, filici e cuntenti.'

64 Salvatore Salamone-Marino, *Customs and Habits of the Sicilian Peasants*, trans. Rosalie N. Norris (East Brunswick: Associated University Press, 1981), 45.

65 Sidney Sonnino, *I Contadini in Sicilia*, vol. 2 of Leopoldo Franchetti and Sidney Sonnino, *Inchiesta in Sicilia* (1876; reprint, Florence: Vallecchi, 1974), 274; Salamone-Marino, 44–7.

66 *Atti della giunta per l'inchiesta agraria e sulle condizioni della classe agricola* vol. 13, tomo 1, fasc. 1, Relazione del Commissario Abele Damiani (Rome: Forzani Tip. del Senato, 1884), 121 (hereafter cited as *Atti della giunta*); Archivio Centrale-Roma, 'Memo: Prefettura della Provincia di Caltanissetta al Ministero della Pubblica Istruzione divisione Istruzione primaria e popolare, 20 settembre 1904: Ogg: Istruzione di scuole serali e festive per adulti analfabeti: relazione ed elenco,' 11. Busta 127, fasc. 14.

67 Joan Scott and Louise Tilly, *Women, Work and Family* (Reprint, New York: Routledge, 1989), 210–13. Scott and Tilly framed the transformation of women's domestic roles at the beginning of the twentieth century in terms of the shift from a family-wage economy to a consumer economy. The growing role of the family as a unit of consumption, especially among the urban working class, heightened the importance of the mother's role as household manager and childcare provider. At the same time, her financial contributions to the family's income declined. Married women worked less often in the early twentieth century, but they still sought paid work when necessary. This story of women, work, and family is a useful model for beginning to analyse the economic, political, and social transformations experienced by rural Sicilian women; however, it cannot fully explain the changes experienced by families. The relative importance of married women's domestic, managerial, and financial duties did not follow the same pattern as in the North. Changing economic conditions removed rural Sicilian women from the paid workforce, and this raised the importance of their domestic responsibilities. Only with transoceanic migration did the standard of living among rural Sicilian families rise beyond mere subsistence. Increased cash encouraged families to invest differently in their children and to purchase more material goods. These changes altered women's roles within the family.

68 Gower Chapman, 76–7.

69 Gower Chapman, 79.

70 Giuseppe Pitrè, *La famiglia,* 39–40. The conflation between homeland and mother love is evident in migrant statements such as 'They wanted to give me American citizenship, but I did not accept because of the great love I have for this earth that gave me birth.' Giovanni Lorenzoni, *Inchiesta parlamentare sulle condizione dei contadini nelle province meridionali e nelle Sicilia,* vol. 6, *Sicilia,* tomo 1, parte 3 (Rome: Tip. Naz. G. Bertero, 1910), 310.

71 Gower Chapman, 77.

72 Rosario Baglio 'The Quarrel of the Mother and Daughter,' edited and translated by Charlotte Gower Chapman, in Gower Chapman, *Milocca: A Sicilian Village* (Cambridge: Schenkman, 1971), 239–41. Gower Chapman notes that the eighty-stanza poem, written in dialect, was quite popular in

Milocca. The poem was published by the author and sold at regional fairs for one lira. The phrase 'take a chance' was incorporated into local dialect as 'techiccenza.'

73 Bell, 90–1.

74 Amalia Guglieminetti, 'Il Bisogno d'Amare,' *Giornale di Sicilia*, 14–15 July, 1913, 3.

75 Clarice Tartufari, 'Vaghe Stelle d'Orsa,' *Giornale di Sicilia*, 15–16 March 1913, 3.

76 My ideas about traditional and industrial time are based on the work of Rudolph Bell and Tamara Hareven. Also see E.P. Thompson, 'Time, Work-Discipline, and Industrial Capitalism,' Past and Present 38 (December 1967): 56–97; and Joel Halpern and Richard Wagner, 'Time and Social Structure: A Yugoslavian Case Study,' *Journal of Family History* 93 (1984): 229–43. Also see Herman Tak's *South Italian Festivals* for an excellent study of the effect of migration on ritual time.

77 Halpern and Wagner, 230–4.

78 Halpern and Wagner, 232–4.

79 Pierre Bourdieu, 'The Attitude of the Algerian Peasant toward Time,' *Mediterranean Country Men*, ed. Julian Pitt-Rivers (Westport, CT: Greenwood Press, 1963), 56.

80 Gower Chapman, 11, 21–3.

81 ACS, 'Registro delle domande di nulla osta per ottenere passaporto all'estero, 1900–1902,' cat. XIII, cl. 3, fasc. 2.

82 Vaccaro, *Sutera*, 25; Gower Chapman, 21–2.

83 Gower Chapman, 103. Figures 3.1 to 3.9 are based on information from ACS *Atti di matrimonio, 1880–1920, Atti di nascita, 1880–1920,* and *Atti di morte, 1880–1920,* and the migrant file discussed on page 254, note 1.

84 Gower Chapman, 22.

85 ACS, 'Registro delle domande di nulla osta per ottenere passaporto all'estero, 1900–1902,' cat. XIII, cl. 3, fasc. 2.

86 Gower Chapman, 22.

87 Vaccaro, *Sutera*, 57.

88 ACS, *Atti di nascita 1850*; Vaccaro, *Sutera*, 57.

89 ACS, *Atti di morte 1850*. In their work in Villanova, Jane Schneider and Peter Schneider arrived at similar percentages. See 'Demographic Transitions,' 245–72.

90 Dott. Mario Tono, *Prospetto dei movimenti avvenuti nella popolazione residente di Sutera*, private collection.

91 Gower Chapman, 24.

92 Gower Chapman, 21–4.

93 Vaccaro, *Sutera*, 57; Bell, 40–1.

94 Thompson, 56–97; Tamara K. Hareven, chapter 7.

95 Hareven, 120–53.

96 Senate Documents, 'Iron and Steel Manufacturing,' *Reports of the Immigration Commission: Immigrants in Industries,* vol. 1, part II, 61st Congress, Doc. #633 (Washington: Government Printing Office, 1911), 185–6.

97 *Morton Allen Directory of European Passenger Steamship Arrivals* (Baltimore: Genealogical Publishing Co., 1979).

98 Robert Foerster, *The Italian Emigration of Our Times* (1919; Reprint, New York: Arno Press, 1969), 377.

99 Bell, 61–2.

4: Fulfilling the Dream: Houses, Land, and Work

1 Giovanni Lorenzoni, *Inchiesta parlamentare sulle condizione dei contadini nelle province meridionali e nelle Sicilia,* vol. 6, *Sicilia,* tomo 1, parte 5 (Rome: Tip. Naz. G. Bertero, 5, 818, 832–6.

2 Senate Documents, *Reports of the Immigration Commission,* vol. 1, *Immigrants in Industries, Part 2, Iron and Steel Manufacturing,* S. Doc. #633, 61st Congress, 2nd session (Washington: Government Printing Office, 1911), 232.

3 Giovanbattista Raja, *Il fenomeno emigratorio siciliano con speciale rigurado al quinquennio 1902–1906* (Palermo: Tip. Imp. Affari Pubblicità, 1908) 54–72; Giuseppe Bruccoleri, *La Sicilia,* 94–9; Giuseppe Bruccoleri, *L'emigrazione siciliana: caratteri ed effetti secondo le più recenti inchieste* (Rome: Coop. Tip. Manuzio, 1911), 19–20; Francesco Coletti, *Dell'emigrazione italiana* (Milan: Ulrico Hoelpi, 1912), 253–4; Lorenzoni, *Inchiesta,* parte 5, 852.

4 As Deborah Simonton wrote in her introduction: 'Work is mediated through ideology and concepts of gender, status and power.' Deborah Simonton, *A History of European Women's Work: 1700 to the Present* (London: Routledge, 1998), 2.

5 MAIC, DGS, *Censimento della Popolazione del Regno d'Italia al 31 Dicembre 1881,* vol. 6 (Rome: Tip. Bodoniana, 1884), 699–720. Among Sicilian men, only 21 per cent were property owners. Men and women owned buildings and land separately in roughly equal numbers, however, twice as many men owned buildings and land together.

6 ASC, *Catasto dei terreni-Sutera 1850–1934*; *Catasto dei fabbricati-Sutera 1870–1930.* All information on property ownership in Sutera was taken from these two cadastres.

7 Antonio Vaccaro, *Sutera e la sua geografia fisica* (Naples: Tip. Gazz. Drit. e Gius., 1890), 39.

8 ASC, *Catasto dei fabbricati-Sutera,* partite #2535, 1845; Gero Difrancesco,

Sutera: I primi anni del '900 (Caltanissetta: Biblioteca Comunale Sutera, 1989), 12.

9 ASC, *Catasto dei fabbricati-Sutera*, partite #1082–2129.

10 ACS, *Catasto dei fabbricati-Sutera*, partite #1082–2129; Ida Fazio, 'Trasmissione della proprietà. sussistenza e *status* femminili in Sicilia Capizzi, 1790–1900,' in *Istituto 'Alcide Cervi' Annali 12/1990*, ed. Paula Corti (Imola: Il Mulino, 1992), 183–4.

11 From the 1870s through the 1890s, 502 women appeared in the housing records, and 466 in the land records. However, because the total number of land transactions exceeded the total number of building transactions, female representation in land records seems much lower.

12 Fazio, 181–99.

13 ASC, *Catasto dei fabbricati-Sutera*, partite #1082–2988. Present female population was determined from manuscript census information in the municipal archive of Sutera. cat. XII, cl. 1–3, 1881–1911.

14 ASC, *Catasto dei fabbricati-Sutera*, partite #1680–2755.

15 New York Public Library, 'S.S. *Giorgio*: December 10, 1908,' passenger lists.

16 ASC, *Catasto dei fabbricati-Sutera*, partita #2271.

17 Lorenzoni, *Inchiesta*, parte 5, 820–3.

18 Lorenzoni, *Inchiesta*, parte 5, 817; Raja, 56–60.

19 Coletti, *Dell'emigrazione*, 238–9.

20 Raja, Table 12.

21 Lorenzoni, *Inchiesta*, parte 3, 259, parte 5, 832–3.

22 Lorenzoni, *Inchiesta*, parte 3, 714.

23 ASC, *Catasto dei fabbricati-Sutera*, partite #2130–3555.

24 ASC, *Catasto dei terreni-Sutera*, partita #4596

25 ASC, *Catasto dei terreni-Sutera*, partita #4472.

26 ASC, *Catasto dei terreni-Sutera*, partite #3793, 3891, 4960; Difrancesco, 12.

27 Jane Schneider and Peter Schneider, *Culture and Political Economy in Western Sicily* (New York: Academic Press, 1976), 62; Charlotte Gower Chapman, *Milocca: A Sicilian Village* (Cambridge: Schenkman, 1971), 11, 140–2; Francesco Romano, *Storia della Sicilia post-unificazione: la Sicilia nell'ultimo ventennio del secolo XIX* (Palermo: Industria Grafica Nazionale, 1958), 151–52; Sidney Sonnino, *I Contadini in Sicilia*, vol. 2 of Leopoldo Franchetti and Sidney Sonnino, *Inchiesta in Sicilia* (1876; reprint, Florence: Vallecchi, 1974), 50.

28 ASC, *Catasto dei terreni-Sutera*, partite #3217–5608.

29 Biagio Puntero, *Delle condizioni economiche dalla provincia di Caltanissetta* (Caltanissetta: Tip. Ospiz, di Beneficienza, 1905), 17.

30 ACS, 'Risposta ad un inchiesta 1905–1907'; cat. X1, Lorenzoni, *Inchiesta*, parte 3, 259.

31 Lorenzoni, *Inchiesta*, parte 5, 830.

32 Lorenzoni, *Inchiesta*, parte 3, 259.

33 In 1936 a report tracing the history of rural Sicilian savings banks noted that migration had a significant economic impact on patterns of land ownership. After the First World War, the rural savings banks used the money deposited over the years by emigrants to provide low-interest loans to their members. Interest rates rarely exceeded 6 per cent. These loans enabled villagers to join together to invest in land. In one case, around twenty emigrants banded together to buy land from the monastery near Racalmuto. Sometimes the banks rented the estates to their members. In 1921 the Cassa Agraria, a local cooperative based in Sutera took over the lease of the ex-feudal estate of Toretta. A year later the Banco Popolare, a cooperative society, took out a ten-year lease on the estate of Reina in Mussomeli, owned by the Prince of Trabia. The bank divided the land into smaller lots and rented these out to its members at a fixed rent of 684.75 hectoliters of grain per year for every *salme* of land. Cooperative lending institutions benefited from the remittances sent from overseas; however, financial institutions alone were not enough to force property owners to radically restructure agrarian contracts. Rural economic relationships only began to change when the money was backed by strong protest movements.

In the fall of 1920, Suteran workers on one estate went on strike to protest unfair contracts requiring sharecroppers to pay back seed that had previously been free. The movement quickly spread, and land occupations were staged on other estates. The rural workers urged the government to dissolve the current agricultural contracts and redistribute the land among ex-combatants and rural workers.

For banking and rural protests, see Jürg K Siegenthaler, 'Sicilian Economic Change since 1860,' *Journal of Economic History* 2 (Fall 1973): 395–6; ACS, 'Cassa Agraria prestiti per occupazione dell'ex-feudo Toretta 23/4/1921,' cat. XI, cl. 1, fasc. 1; ACS, 'Risposta a nota #17097, 25/10/1928: Cooperativa con contratti di affittanea agricole collettive, 30 ottobre 1928,' cat. XI, cl. 1, fasc. 1; ACS, 'Informazioni: Al signore direttore dell istituto della cassa nazionale, 5 augusto 1920,' cat. XI, cl. 3, 1920. For information on rural protests in 1920 see Lorenzoni, *Transformazione e colonizzazione del latifondo* (Florence: C. Cifa, 1940), 41; Difrancesco, 20; ACS. 'Dal sindaco di Sutera al prefetto di Caltanissetta, 18 settembre 1920,' cat. XI, cl. 2a, fasc. 1a; ACS, 'Elenco delle associazione agrarie esistenti nel comune, 12/5/1921,' cat. XI, cl. 1, fasc. 1a; ACS, 'Ordine di giorno: circolo de combattenti, 7 novembre 1920,' cat. XI, cl. 1, fasc. 1; ACS, 'Telespresso: Alla Questura di

Caltanissetta, 21 ottobre 1920,' cat. XI, cl. 1, fasc. 1; ACS, 'Telegramma: Occupazioni di terre nella borgata Milocca, risposta a nota 24/12/1920,' cat. XI, cl. 1, fasc. 1; ACS, 'Telegramma: Occupazioni di terra nella borgata Milocca, risposta a nota 24/12/1920,' cat. XI, cl. 1, fasc.1; ACS, 'Concordato agrario reclami del Prof. Scaduto, 28 febbraio 1921,' cat. XI, cl. 1., fasc. 1; Gower Chapman, 4; ACS, 'Concordato agrario reclami del Prof. Scaduto,' cat. XI, cl. 1., fasc. 1, 2.

34 Ettore Taddei and Constantino Ledda, *Contadini Siciliani*, vol. 4, Monografie di Famiglie Agricole (Rome: S.A. Tip. Operaio Romano, 1933), 63.

35 Lorenzoni, *Inchiesta*, parte 5, 834.

36 Lorenzoni, *Inchiesta*, parte 3, 53.

37 ASC, *Catasto dei fabbricati-Sutera*, partite #2130–3555.

38 ASC, *Catasto dei fabbricati-Sutera*, partite #2130–2755.

39 Lorenzoni, *Inchiesta*, parte 3, 833; Gower Chapman, 13–14, 131; For a description of the furnishings commonly found in rural Sicily, see Taddei and Ledda, *Contadini*, 70–4, 97–101.

40 Gower Chapman, 13.

41 Sonnino, 58–9.

42 *Atti della giunta per l'inchiesta agraria e sulle condizioni della classe agricola*, vol. 13, tomo 2, fasc. 4, Relazione del Commissario Abele Damiani (Rome: Forzani Tip. del Senato, 1884), 14–15. Each of the provincial surveys indicates that women did not work in the fields: Lorenzoni, *Inchiesta* parte 4, 462–4; Simona Laudani, 'Trasformazione agricole e condizione femminile in Sicilia,' in *Istituto 'Alcide Cervi' Annali 12/1990* (Imola: Il Mulino, 1992), 113–14.

43 Angelo Mosso, *Vita moderna degli Italiani* (Milan: Fratelli Treves Editori, 1906), 121.

44 For a discussion of the economic benefits of migration on women's work, see Mosso, 115.

45 For an analysis of female labour patterns in Sicily and Italy from the nineteenth to the twentieth centuries, see Jole Calapso, 'La Donna in Sicilia e in Italia: la realtà e la falsa coscienza nella statistica dal 1871 ad oggi,' *Quaderni Siciliani* 2 (March–April 1973),13–20; Donna Gabaccia, 'In the Shadows of the Periphery: Italian Women in the Nineteenth Century,' in *Connecting Spheres: Women in the Western World: 1500 to the Present*, ed. Marilyn J. Boxer and Jean H. Quataert (New York: Oxford University Press), 166–76.

46 MAIC, DGS, *Censimento* 1881, vol. 2 (Rome: Tip. Bodoniana, 1883), 276, 291, 345, 379, 415, 492, 506, and vol. 3 (Rome: Tip. Bodoniana, 1883), 584–93; MAIC, DGS, *Censimento della popolazione del regno d'Italia 1921*, vol. 19 (Rome:

Stabilimento poligrafica per l'amministrazione dello stato, 1927), 238–9; MAIC, DGS, *Censimento 1921*, vol. 11 (Rome: Provveditorato generale dello stato, 1926), 8; Calapso, 14–16.

47 Calapso, 14.

48 MAIC, 'Notizie sulle condizione industriale delle provincia di Palermo,' *Annali di Statistica Industriale*, fasc. XLVIII, 4th ser, n. 69 (Rome: G. Bertero, 1893). In the same series, see Messina, n 89; Caltanissetta, n. 80; Siracusa, n. 81; Girgenti, n. 85; and Trapani, n. 87 (hereafter cited as *Annali di Statistica*).

49 See Louise A. Tilly and Joan W. Scott, *Women Work and Family* (New York: Holt, Rinehart and Winston, 1978), 63–77, for France and England. For a description of women's work in northern Italy, see Anna Bull and Paul Corner, *From Peasant to Entrepreneur* (Providence, RI: Berg Publishers, 1993), 23–30.

50 MAIC, DGS, *Censimento 1901*, vol. 3 (Rome: G. Bertero, 1903), 122; MAIC, DGS, *Censimento 1881*, vol. 3 (Rome: Tip. Bodoniana, 1884), 586–92.

51 ACS, *Atti di matrimonio 1880–1900.*

52 MAIC, DGS, *Censimento 1881*, vol. 4 (Rome: Tip. Bodoniana, 1884), 584–93; MAIC, DGS, *Censimento 1901*, vol. 4 (Rome: G. Bertero, 1904), 162.

53 Calapso, 14–15.

54 MAIC, *Annali di Statistica*, n. 80, 37–9.

55 ACS, 'Dal sindaco alla Società Anonima Cooperativa "Le Industrie Femminili Italiane," 12 ottobre 1904,' cat. XI, cl. 2a, fasc. 3a.

56 Calapso, 14.

57 ACS, *Atti di matrimonio, 1880–99.*

58 ACS, *Atti di matrimonio 1875*; *Atti di nascita 1880–1904.*

59 Lorenzoni, *Inchiesta*, parte 3, 16.

60 Gower Chapman, 32.

61 Binetti-Ventura, 174.

62 Binetti-Ventura, 175.

63 Gower Chapman, 55.

64 ACS, *Atti di matrimonio, 1912*; *Atti di nascita, 1887.*

65 ACS, 'Elenco dei sanitari che esercitano nel comune-1880,' cat. IV, cl. 2, fasc. 1.

66 ACS, *Pubblica salute e igiene 1880–1911*, cat. IV, cl.1–6; also see *Atti di nascita* and *Atti di matrimonio.*

67 Gower Chapman, 51–4.

68 Raja, 61–2; Lorenzoni, *Inchiesta*, parte 3, 21.

69 DGS, 'Le variazioni dei salari agricoli in Italia,' *Annali di Statistica*, vol. 35, 6th ser., 223; Raja, 62.; Lorenzoni, *Inchiesta*, parte 3, 73, 75–86.

70 Lorenzoni, *Inchiesta*, parte 3, 34–5, 84; ACS, 'Memo: Relazione periodica sulle classi agricole e sulla industria agraria, 19 luglio 1890,' cat. XI, cl. 1a, fasc. 4a.

71 Lorenzoni, *Inchiesta*, parte 5, 839, 845; Bruccoleri, *La Sicilia*, 98.

72 'Notizie Statistiche 1905–1907.' From the private library of Dott. Mario Tona of Sutera. This appears to be a response to a survey sent out by Giovanni Lorenzoni. Lorenzoni, *Inchiesta*, parte 3, 73.

73 MAIC, DGS *Censimento* 1901, vol. 3, pp. 272–320; MAIC, DGS, *Censimento della popolazione del regno d'Italia al giugno 1911*, vol. 3 (Rome: Tip. Naz. di G. Bertero, 1914), 331–2. The province of Caltanissetta was comprised of three separate districts. Sutera was one of fifteen villages in the district of Caltanissetta.

74 See sources for Table 4.2, p. 162.

75 Interview, Spring 1991.

76 Bonnie G. Smith, *Changing Lives: Women in European History since 1700* (Lexington, MA: D.C. Heath, 1989), 368–79, provides an excellent survey of the effects of war on European women and the efforts of governments to encourage women to go to work.

77 ACS, 'Premi alle donne lavoratrici dei campi, 17/11/1917,' cat. XI, cl. 1a, fasc. 1a.

78 ACS, 'Premi alle donne, 23/1/1921,' cat. XI, cl. 1a, fasc. 1a.

79 Interview, Summer 1991.

80 Historians have argued that the consequences of industrialization, urbanization, and class formation differed for men and women. See Scott and Tilly, *Women, Work and Family*. Also see the essays in Laura L. Frader and Sonya Rose, eds., *Gender and Class in Modern Europe* (Ithaca: Cornell University Press, 1996). In Sicily, where the industrialization happened far differently than in various northern regions, the gendering of work was perhaps linked more explicitly with the expansion of world markets and the significance of wages, and with the changing ties between local, global, and national economies.

5: Sicilian Women and the Italian State

1 The description of Angelo A. is based on emigration records, birth records, and land records held in the municipal archive of Sutera and the state archive in Caltanissetta. A private collection of photographic plates in Sutera illustrates the concern with appearance exhibited by those emigrants who returned. In many of these photos, migrants are dressed in fancy suits, straw hats, boots, ties, collars, and stiffly starched shirts. Antonio Mangano offers a similar description of the appearance of returning migrants in 'The Effect of Emigration upon Italy: Threatened Depopulation of the South,' *Charities and Commons* 19 (1908): 1, 479.

2 ACS, *Atti di nascita 1874*; also see Gower Chapman, *Milocca*, 25. For a discussion of *campanalismo* and village identity, see Bell, 151–5.

3 Correspondence between migrants and their families back home commonly went through the local government and the Italian consulates. Money orders always went through the Banco di Napoli. See Robert Foerster, *The Italian Emigration of Our Times* (1919; Reprint, New York: Arno Press, 1969), 481; Mark Wyman, *Round-Trip to America: The Immigrants Return to Europe, 1880–1930* (Ithaca: Cornell University Press, 1993), 93–5, for a description of the various official Italian representatives who offered protection, return tickets, and advice to emigrants in the United States. Evidence that migrants used the consulates as a means of communication with family members can be seen in the archives of the Ministry of Foreign Affairs and in local archives. Even the smallest villages, like Sutera, have records of inquiries that mayors received from migrants abroad regarding family members or business affairs.

4 Richard J.B. Bosworth, *Italy and the Wider World* (London: Routledge, 1996), 3–5.

5 ACS, *Atti di matrimonio, 1900*. At the time of her marriage, Rosa was illiterate.

6 At the end of the nineteenth century, European nations began to identify children as a national resource. Motherhood soon became a matter of national concern. The importance of women to the state resided in their capacity to bear children; they weren't seen as productive citizens in their own right. This association, linked to imperialist ambitions and nationalist sentiment, defined the condition of women in European countries in 1900. In Italy the concern was underscored by the fears underlying attitudes toward transoceanic migration, and culminated in fascist policies imposed in the 1920s. See chapters 3 and 4; also see, Augusto Bosco, 'L'emigrazione del mezzogiorno,' *Giornale degli Economisti* 32 (April 1906): 326–7; also see Victoria De Grazia, *How Fascism Ruled Women: Italy 1922–1945* (Berkeley: University of California Press, 1992). For a more general discussion of nationalism and mothers, see Anna Davin, 'Imperialism and Motherhood,' *History Workshop* 5 (Spring 1978): 9–65.

7 Linda Kerber, *No Constitutional Right to Be Ladies* (New York: Hill and Wang, 1998), xxi. I am using John Dickie's definition of the state as defined by society's public institutions. Dickie also notes the contradictory attitudes that colour Italian views of the state. On the one hand, Italians seem to have little faith in the fairness of the state – they 'lack a sense of the state.' On the other hand, Italians in the resistance movement chose to courageously risk their lives for this state. John Dickie, 'Imagined Italies,' in *Italian Cultural Studies: An Introduction*, ed. David Forgacs and Robert Lumley (Oxford: Oxford University Press, 1996), 19–33.

8 Bell, 151–3.

9 ACS, Memo, 'Al Ministero di Agricoltura Industria e Commercio, Ufficio di Lavoro; Statistica mensile dell migrazione periodiche interne nel mese di giugno,' cat. XI, cl 1, fasc. 1, 1902.

10 ACS, *Atti di matrimonio, 1880–1914*. These figures include first marriages and remarriages.

11 Jane Schneider and Peter Schneider, *Culture and Political Economy in Western Sicily* (New York: Academic Press, 1976), 82–5.

12 Charlotte Gower Chapman, *Milocca: A Sicilian Village* (Cambridge: Schenkman, 1971), 8, 156–7.

13 According to Ernesto Ragionieri, only 2.5 per cent of Italians spoke Italian in 1866. Ernesto Ragionieri, 'La storia politica e sociale,' in *Storia dell'Italia: Dall'unita ad oggi*, Vol. 4 (Turin: Giulio Einaudi, 1976), 1714. My ideas of nationalism and the nation-state are strongly influenced by Benedict Anderson, *Imagined Communities: Reflections on the Origin and Spread of Nationalism* (London: Verso, 1983); Ernest Gellner, *Nations and Nationalism* (Ithaca: Cornell University Press, 1983); and Montserrat Guibernau, *Nationalisms: The Nation-State and Nationalism in the Twentieth Century* (Cambridge: Polity Press, 1996).

14 Denis Mack Smith, 'Regionalism,' in *Modern Italy*, ed. Edward R. Tannenbaum and Emiliana P. Noether (New York: New York University Press, 1974), 129; Paolo Pezzino, *Una certa reciprocità di favori* (Milan: FrancoAngeli, 1990), 41; Francesco De Stefano and Francesco Luigi Oddo, *La Storia della Sicilia* (Bari: ed. Laterza, 1963), 85.

15 Gower Chapman, 151–7; Denis Mack Smith, *A History of Sicily: Modern Sicily* (New York: Viking Press, 1968), 445–8.

16 Antonio Vaccaro, *Sutera e la sua geografia fisica* (Naples: Tip. Gazz. Drit. e Gius., 1890), 67.

17 De Stefano and Oddo, 87.

18 Quoted in Giovanni Raffiotta, *Storia della Sicilia post-unificazione*, parte 3 (Palermo: Industria Grafica Nazionale, 1959), 58.

19 Jürg K Siegenthaler, 'Sicilian Economic Change since 1860,' *Journal of Economic History* 2 (Fall 1973): 379–80.

20 For an interesting analysis of the development of local power in the South, see Paolo Pezzino, 'Local Power in Southern Italy,' in Robert Lumley and Jonathan Morris, eds., *The New History of the Italian South: The Mezzogiorno Revisited* (Exeter: University of Exeter Press, 1997), 42–58. See also Mack Smith, *Modern Sicily*, 455; Franchetti, 81–2; Pezzino, 'Local Power,' 42–3. Sicily is an example of how the expansion of the European nation-state – and in the case of Italy, the concomitant rise of capitalist production –

created 'peripheries within its very core.' Eric Wolf, *Europe and the People without History* (Berkeley: University of California Press, 1982), 296. My use of core and periphery is also influenced by Edward W. Soja's analysis in *Post-Modern Geographies* (Bristol: Verso, 1990), 104–12.

21 Mack Smith, *Modern Sicily*, 456.

22 Antonio Vaccaro, *Cenni sulla città di Sutera* (Naples: Tip. dei Fratelli Carluccio, 1881), 135–9.

23 *Atti della giunta per l'inchiesta agraria e sulle condizioni della classe agricola*, vol. 13, tomo 1, fasc. 1, Relazione del Commissario Abele Damiani (Rome: Forzani Tip. del Senato, 1884), 11.

24 Atti della giunta, tomo 2, fasc. 4, 383; Department of Commerce and Labor. Bureau of Statistics. Vol. 30, *Special Consular Reports: Emigration to the United States*, 'From U.S. Consul A.H. Byington, Naples, Italy, February 16, 1904: Causes of Emigration from Naples and throughout the South' (Washington: Government Printing Office, 1904), 91.

25 ASC, *Lista di leva-Sutera*, 1882.

26 ASC, *Lista di leva-Sutera*, 1882–1906; ACS, 'Inchiesta sulle condizioni igeniche e sanitarie dei comuni del regno, anno 1885,' cat. IV, cl. 3a, fasc. 1, 21.

27 Gower Chapman, 155.

28 See Eugen Weber, *Peasants into Frenchmen* (Stanford: Stanford University Press, 1976), 292–302, for a similar description of the effects of national conscription in rural France.

29 Gower Chapman, 19.

30 Gower Chapman, 156.

31 For a general discussion of coverture in British common law, see Mary Lyndon Shanley, *Feminism, Marriage, and the Law in Victorian England* (Princeton: Princeton, University Press, 1989), 8–9. Also see Nicole Arnaud-Duc, 'The Law's Contradictions,' in *A History of Women: Emerging Feminism from Revolution to World War*, ed. Geneviève Fraisse and Michelle Perrot (Cambridge: Belknap Press, 1993), 80–113.

32 Lodovico Frati, *La Donna Italiana secondo i più recenti studi* (Turin: Fratelli Bocca, Editori, 1899), 57.

33 Salvatore Saladino 'Parliamentary Politics in the Liberal Era 1861–1914,' in *Modern Italy*, 28.

34 Gero Difrancesco, *Sutera: I primi anni del '900* (Caltanissetta: Biblioteca Comunale Sutera, 1989), 17.

35 Mack Smith, *Modern Sicily*, 449.

36 Foerster, 100.

37 See chapter 1 for a discussion of the history of *Fasci* in Sutera.

38 Romano, 241.

39 ACS, 'Elenco dei soci della società Vittorio Emanuele III pel miglioramento economico in Sutera, 1901–02,' cat. XI, cl. 2, fasc 2a; and Difrancesco, 49.

40 Jane Schneider and Peter Schneider found a similar situation in Villamura. See Schneider and Schneider, *Culture*, 155–60.

41 Gower Chapman, 4–7.

42 Gower Chapman, 6.

43 Giuseppe Pitrè, *Usi e costumi del popolo siciliano*, ed. Giuseppe Lisi, 2nd ed. (Bologna: Capelli ed., 1971), 14–33.

44 ACS 'Elenchi dei sanitari nel codesto comune 1871–1891,' cat. IV, cl. 2, fasc. 1. According to these lists there was one official midwife, Grazia Ciaccio, who earned a salary of 612 lire a year from the *comune*. Two other women were authorized to practise in the 1890s but were not state employees. According to birth records, these women had been practising for at least a decade.

45 ACS, *Atti di nascita*, 1880–1889. Men accounted for only 1 per cent of the people who appeared to register the birth of a baby, who were not the fathers. I have included only legitimate births, declared by women and men who were not doctors or midwives, and therefore who were not appearing in a professional capacity.

46 Massimo Livi-Bacci, *A History of Italian Fertility during the Last Two Centuries* (Princeton: Princeton University Press, 1977), 294.

47 ACS, *Atti di nascita, 1890–5*.

48 See chapter 1.

49 Ragionieri, 1685–96; Eric Hobsbawm, *Age of Empire* (New York: Vintage, 1989), 149–50; Weber, *Peasants into Frenchmen*, chaps 17 and 18; Gaetano Bonetta, *Istruzione e società nella Sicilia dell'ottocento* (Palermo: Sellerio, 1981), 56; Alberto Asor Rosa, 'La Cultura,' in *Storia d'Italia*, vol. 4, *Dall'Unità ad oggi*, 2 (Turin: Einaudi, 1975), 900–9.

50 Ministero di Agricoltura, Industria e Commercio (MAIC), Direzione Generale della Statistica (DGS), *Censimento della popolazione del regno al 10 febbraio 1901*, II (Rome: Tip. Naz. Bertero, 1903), 276–319.

51 Tracy Koon, *Believe, Fight and Obey* (Chapel Hill: University of North Carolina Press, 1985), 35–7.

52 Bonetta, *Istruzione*, 58. Article 344 of the Casati law stipulated that the towns were responsible for all educational expenses. According to Article 345, the state would provide an annual stipend in those cases where a town was too poor to fund an elementary school. However, no money was allocated in the national budget for elementary education.

53 *Atti della giunta*, tomo 1, fasc. 1, 121.

54 Koon, 37.

55 Bonetta, *Istruzione*, 285.

56 Vaccaro, *Sutera*, 54.

57 Bonetta, *Istruzione*, 55–9. Also see Edward R. Tannenbaum, 'Education,' in *Modern Italy*, ed. Edward R. Tannenbaum and Emiliana P. Noether (New York: New York University Press, 1974), 235; Giovanni Lorenzoni, *Inchiesta parlamentare sulle condizioni dei contadini nelle provincie meridionali e nella Sicilia*, VI (Rome: Tip. Naz. G. Bertero, 1910), tomo 1, parte 3, 541; *Atti della giunta*, XIII, tomo 1, fasc. 1, 121.

58 Ministero della Pubblica Istruzione, *Bollettino ufficiale del ministero dell'istruzione pubblica*, Supplemento al No. 42, anno XXVII, II (Rome: 19 October, 1900), XII.

59 See John Briggs, *An Italian Passage: Immigrants to Three American Cities* (New Haven: Yale University Press, 1978), 37–64, for a thorough description of the social and economic conditions that influenced schooling in southern Italy at the turn of the century.

60 Lorenzoni, *Inchiesta*, VI, tomo 1, parte 3, 257.

61 ACS, 'Memo da N. Ingrao al Sig. Sindaco: Oggetto scuole serale e festive per adulti analfabeti 1905–1906, 18 settembre, 1905,' cat. IX, cl. 2, fasc. 9.

62 ACS; 'Memo: Dal Sindaco al Circolo Agricolo Operaio, 1886,' cat. IX, cl. 2, fasc. 9; Lorenzoni, Inchiesta, VI, tomo 1, parte 2, 714.

63 ACS, 'Obbligati alla scuola: 1901–02, gennaio 1902,' cat. IX, cl. 1, fasc. 1.

64 ACS 'Dalla maestro della borgata al sindaco di Sutera: Oggetto prestabilamento degli esami finali, 11/6/1889,' cat. IX, cl. 2a, fasc. 2a; Professor Ingrao from Sutera also wrote to the provincial authorities. ACS, 'Maestro N. Ingrao: Oggetto provvedimenti per gli esami finali, luglio 1889,' cat. IX, cl 2a, fasc. 2a.

65 Atti della giunta, XIII, tomo 1, fasc. 1, 127. For an excellent survey of women and education, see the collection of essays edited by Simonetta Soldani, *L'educazione delle donne: Scuole e modelli di vita femminile nell'Italia dell'Ottocento* (Milan: Franco Angeli Libri, 1989).

66 ACS, 'Memo dalla Provveditore R. prefettura della provincia di Caltanissetta al Sindaco di Sutera, 22 novembre, 1897,' cat. IX, cl.2, fasc. 1.

67 Elvira Mancuso, *Sulle condizione della donna borghese in Sicila: appunti e riflessione* (Caltanissetta: Tip. dell'Omnibus, 1907), 5. Mancuso suggests that the background of these teachers is one of the reasons for the inadequate quality of middle-class female education: 'No matter how well run a normal school, in the education of its teachers, it cannot replace the civil and moral basis provided by a well-to-do family.'

68 Lorenzoni, *Inchiesta*, parte III, 314.

69 ACS, 'Istruzione di scuole rurale e festivi per adulti analfabeti, 16 luglio 1905,' cat. IX, cl. 2, fasc. 9. Atti della giunta, XIII, tomo 1. fasc. 1, 121.

70 ACS, 'Scuola Serale 1895,' cat. IX, cl. 2, fasc. 9. As late as 1905, Rava commented that the weekend schools failed to meet the needs of rural residents. Agricultural workers did not want to spend their one full day at home in the classroom, and rural women were too busy on Sundays to attend. V. Rava, 'Le scuole serali e festive nell'anno scolastico 1904–05,' *Bollettino Ufficiale del Ministero dell'Istruzione Pubblica*, 34 (23 August 1906): 2,400.

71 Ministero Pubblica Istruzione, Istruzione Primaria e Normale, 1905, 'Dal R. Prefettura della Provincia di Caltanissetta al Ministero della Pubblica Istruzione divisione Istruzione Primaria e Popolare. 20 Settembre 1904, Ogg: Istituzione di Scuole Serali e Festive per Adulti Analfabeti. Relazione ed Elenco, 13.' Busta 127, Provincia di Caltanisetta., fasc. 14.

72 MAIC, DGS, *Censimento della popolozione del regno al 31 dicembre 1901*, II (Rome: Tip. Naz. G. Bertero, 1903).

73 *Atti della giunta*, tomo 1, fasc 1, 130.

74 ACS, 'Memo: Oggetto istruzione di scuole rurali e festive per adulti analfabeti, 1905,' cat. IX, cl. 2, fasc. 9. According to one report from the mayor to the district superintendent, the illiteracy rate among adults was around 70 per cent.

75 Mack Smith, *Modern Italy*, 459. For an excellent discussion on dialects and language in the process of nation building, see Eugen Weber, chap. 6.

76 ACS, *Atti di nascita*, 1900–1910.

77 ACS, 'Memo dal sindaco al consolato d'Italia, 12 ottobre 1915.'

78 ACS, 'Dal sindaco al questura di Napoli, 1907,' cat. XV, cl. 8a.

79 ACS, 'Dal sindaco al questura di Napoli, 1907,' cat. XV, cl. 8a.

80 ACS, 'Invio domanda di passaporto per l'estero a nome di Onofria R, giugno 12 1914,' cat. XIII, cl. 3, fasc. 1; ACS, 'Documenti necessari per ottenere indeminità spettanti ad operaio da famiglie di operai morti sul lavoro all'estero, 28 ottobre 1904,' cat. XIII, cl. 3, fasc. 1.

81 See chapter 2 for a discussion of rural attitudes toward the church and the ambiguous position of women living alone.

82 Cataldo Naro, *Momenti e figure della chiesa nissena dell'otto e novecento* (Caltanissetta: Centro Studi Sulla Cooperazione 'A Cammerata,' 1989), 534–5.

83 MAE, Commissariato Generale dell'Emigrazione, 'Commissione Arbitrale d'Emigrazione della Provincia di Caltanissetta 1906–1913,' busta 10, fasc. 122; and 'Commissione Arbitrale di Palermo,' busta 29, fasc. 111.

84 Miriam Cohen, *From Workshop to Office*, 110; Linda Gordon, *Heroes of Their*

Own Lives: The Politics and History of Family Violence in Boston, 1800–1960 (New York: Viking Press, 1988), chaps 8 and 9. For a first-hand account, see Marie Hall Ets, *Rosa: The Life of an Italian Immigrant* (Minneapolis: University of Minnesota Press, 1970).

85 Weber, 327. Throughout this chapter on education, Weber clearly illustrates how rural residents in France began to attend school when classroom lessons proved useful in meeting the needs and demands of a changing world.

86 Lorenzoni, *Inchiesta*, parte 3, 531: also see Briggs, 55–8, and Coletti, *Dell'emigrazione*, 257–61.

87 Lorenzoni, *Inchiesta*, parte 3, 531.

88 Francesco Paolo Minnetti, 'Scuole rurali, festive e di complemento,' in *I Diritti della Scuola*, 'La Scuola in azione,' Anno IX, Roma, 9 February 1908, n. 18, 271. Also see Briggs, 57.

89 ACS, 'Pubblica istruzione 1900–1907,' cat. IX, cl. 2., fasc. 1.

90 Lorenzoni, *Inchiesta*, parte 3, 543.

91 Ministero Pubblica Istruzione, Istruzione Primaria e Normale, 1905, 'Dal R. Prefettura della Provincia di Caltanissetta al Ministero della Pubblica Istruzione divisione Istruzione Primaria e Popolare. 20 Settembre 1904, Ogg: Istituzione di Scuole Serali e Festive per Adulti Analfabeti. Relazione ed Elenco,' 13. Busta 127, Provincia di Caltanisetta., fasc. 14.

92 Wyman, 158–9.

93 Antonio Mangano, 'The Effect of Emigration upon Italy: '"Ci manca la mano d'opera"; "We Lack the Working Hand,"' *Charities and Commons* 20 (4 April 1908): 17.

94 Senate Documents, *Reports of the Immigration Commission*, vol. 1, *Immigrants in Industries, Part 2, Iron and Steel Manufacturing*, S. Doc. #633, 61st Congress, 2nd session (Washington: Government Printing Office, 1911), 188.

95 Lorenzoni, *Inchiesta*, parte 3, 531–2; for similar observations, see Foerster, 460–1, and Briggs, 55–6. Migrants who permanently settled overseas also believed in the importance of education. See Briggs, 191–244.

96 Foerster, 460.

97 Ministero Pubblica Istruzione, Istruzione Primaria e Normale, 1905, 'Dal R. Prefettura della Provincia di Caltanissetta al Ministero della Pubblica Istruzione divisione Istruzione Primaria e Popolare. 20 Settembre 1904, Ogg: Istituzione di Scuole Serali e Festive per Adulti Analfabeti. Relazione ed Elenco,' cat. XI, busta 127, Provincia di Caltanisetta., fasc. 14.

98 Archivio della Scuola Elementare a Sutera (ASES), 'Elenchi degli iscritti, abbandoni e promossi dal 1900–1914.'

99 ACS, 'Iscritte nelle scuole femminile 1904–1905,' cat. IX. cl.1, fasc. 9; ACS, 'Iscritte nelle scuole femminile 1906–1907,' cat. IX. cl.1, fasc. 9.

100 ACS, 'Memo dal Prefettura: Provveditorato agli studi scuola Rabato, 12 novembre 1909,' cat. IX, cl. 11, fasc. 1.

101 ACS, 'Iscritte nelle scuole femminile 1901–1902,' cat. IX, cl. 1, fasc. 9; ACS, 'Iscritte nelle scuole femminile 1906–1907,' cat. IX, cl. 1, fasc. 9.

102 ACS, 'Scuole seriale e festivi 1904–1909,' compiled from various memos.

103 Lorenzoni, *Inchiesta*, parte 3, 540–3.

104 MAIC, DGS, *Censimento della popolazione del regno al 31 dicembre 1901*, II (Rome: Tip. Naz. di G. Bertero, 1903), 277; MAIC, DGS, *Censimento della popolazione del regno d'Italia al giugno 1911*, II (Rome: G. Bertero, 1914), 568.

105 Interview, summer 1991.

106 Francesco Gazzetti, *Manuale di agricoltura ad uso della scuola popolare e complementare e d'ogni famiglia d'agricoltori* (Turin: Presso le ditte Paravia e Tarizzo, 1885), 3.

107 Ildebrando Bencivenni, *Il libro completo per gli alunni e le alunne della 1a classe elementare* (sezione superiore), 22nd ed. (Turin: Tip. del Maestro Elementare Italiano, 1880), 53.

108 Francesco Paulo Minnetti, 'Per le scuole ruralie per le scuole serali e festivi: Note ed appunti,' in *I Diritti della Scuola*, 'La Scuola in Azione,' 14 (15 January, 1905), 175.

109 Franceso Paolo Minnetti, 'Scuole rurali, festive e di complemento,' in *I Diritti della Scuola*, 'La Scuola in Azione,' 18 (Rome, 9 February 1908), 271–2.

110 Weber, 314–36.

6: Beyond Sutera: Sicilian Women Join the Nation

1 Ada Bagnoli, *La scuola popolare e la sua influenza nella preparazione della donna alla vita domestica e civile* (n.p., 1920), 97–8.

2 John Dickie, 'Imagined Italies,' in *Italian Cultural Studies: An Introduction*, ed. David Forgacs and Robert Lumley (Oxford: Oxford University Press, 1996), 20

3 Dickie, 20–1; Benedict Anderson, *Imagined Communities: Reflections on the Origins and Spread of Nationalism* (London: Verso, 1983), 15–16.

4 Dickie, 22–3; Anderson, 16.

5 Adrian Lyttelton notes that Italian regionalism is limited by the history of strong city-states, which were never fully incorporated into regional states. In addition, the economic, social, and political differences that marked the

world of the cities and the surrounding countryside 'complicated and modified regional loyalties.' The history of Italian regionalism accounts for the absence of clearly identified regional political movements, although there were strong regional factions within national politics. This history also accounts for the strength of local allegiances. See Adrian Lyttelton, 'Nation, Region and City,' in *Italian Regionalism: History, Identity and Politics*, ed. Carl Levy (Washington: Berg: 1996), 33–52.

6 For an excellent history of early attempts to map the nation, see Silvana Patriarca, *Numbers and Nationhood: Writing Statistics in Nineteenth-Century Italy* (Cambridge: Cambridge University Press, 1996).

7 Charlotte Gower Chapman, *Milocca: A Sicilian Village* (Cambridge: Schenkman Publishing, 1971), 152–3.

8 Bernard P. Dauenhauer, *Citizenship in a Fragile World* (Lanham, MD: Rowman and Littlefield, 1996), 191.

9 This understanding of the Piedmontese leaders is part of Antonio Gramsci's identification of the Unification of Italy as a passive revolution – a revolution that could not claim popular support, and where a weak middle-class was incapable of uniting the people. Antonio Gramsci, *Prison Notebooks*, trans. Quintin Hoare and Geoffrey Nowell Smith (New York: International Publishers, 1985), 104–15.

10 Denis Mack Smith, *Modern Italy: A Political History* (Ann Arbor: University of Michigan Press, 1997), 62–3.

11 Quoted in John Dickie, 'Imagined Italies;' Nelson Moe, '"Altro Che Italia!" Il sud dei piemontesi (1860–1),' *Meridiana* 15 (1992): 53–89.

12 Quoted in Gabriella Gribaudi, 'Images of the South,' *Italian Cultural Studies: An Introduction*, ed. David Forgacs and Robert Lumley (Oxford: Oxford University Press, 1996), 73. See Benedetto Croce, *History of the Kingdom of Naples*, trans. F. Frenaye (Chicago: University of Chicago Press, 1970), 73.

13 Gabriella Gribaudi eloquently traces the exclusion of the South in the symbolic formation of Italy in her essay 'Images of the South,' in *Italian Cultural Studies: An Introduction*, ed. David Forgacs and Robert Lumley (Oxford: Oxford University Press, 1996), 73. She astutely notes that the exclusion of the southern provinces extended well into the twentieth century and the founding of the Italian Republic. Post 1945, Italy constructed itself out of the resistance, and so located its founding myths in the northern experience. The South, subject to Allied invasions in 1943, did not participate in the northern resistance movement against German occupation between 1943 and 1945.

14 Mack Smith, *Modern Italy*, 78–9; Denis Mack Smith, *A History of Sicily: Modern Sicily after 1713* (New York: Viking Press, 1968), 445–61; Lucy Riall, *Sicily and*

the Unification of Italy: Liberal Policy and Local Power, 1859–1866 (Oxford: Clarendon Press, 1998), 156–78.

15 Frederico De Roberto, '*I Viceré*,' in *Frederico de Roberto: I grandi romanzi* ed. Sergio Campailla (Rome: Grandi Tascabili Economici Newton, 1994), 673; Alberto Asor Rosa, in 'La Cultura,' in *Storia d'Italia*, vol. 4, *Dall'Unità ad oggi* 2 (Turin: Giulio Einaudi editore, 1975), 835, also quotes De Roberto as evidence of the growing sense that Unification had not changed a thing with respect to the old government systems and structures of power.

16 Francesco Saverio Nitti, 'Napoli e la questione meridionale,' in *La questione meridionale*, III, ed. Manlio Rossi Doria (Rome-Bari: Laterza, 1978), 16.

17 Gaetano Bonetta, *Istruzione e società nella Sicilia dell'ottocento* (Palermo: Sellerio, 1981), 285, 290–1; Francesco Bettini, *I programmi di studio per le scuole elementari dal 1860 al 1945* (Brescia: 'La Scuola' Editrice, 1953), 40. For a general discussion of linguistic unity and national identity, see Weber, *Peasants*, 303–38; and Susan Watkins, *From Provinces to Nations* (Princeton: Princeton University Press, 1991), 114–21.

18 Bettini, *I programmi*, 34; Geltrude Malagoli, *Un Vezzo di Perle: Alle giovinette della scuola popolare* (Rocca San Casciano: Licinio Cappelli, 1913), 26–31.

19 Tullio di Mauro notes that even in the 1990s, there exists a 'deep instinctive conviction that those who speak differently from others can be suspected of not being good citizens, good Catholics, etc.' See Tullio de Mauro, 'Linguistic Variety and Linguistic Minorities,' in *Italian Cultural Studies: An Introduction*, ed. David Forgacs and Robert Lumley (Oxford: Oxford University Press, 1996), 88.

20 Gower Chapman, 152–3.

21 Giovanni Scavia, *L'uomo e l'universo* (Turin: Tip. Scolastica-Seb Franco e Figli e Comp., 1861), 61. The first Italian textbooks appeared in the beginning of the nineteenth century. In 1836 a draft of L.A. Parravicini's book, *Giannetto*, won first prize in a contest offered by La Società Fiorentina, and was published in 1838. More than fifty editions of *Giannetto* were eventually published, and this work became the model for textbooks well into the twentieth century. The chapters were divided into *L'uomo I suoi bisogni e I suoi doveri*, *Nozioni di Geografia*, *Esempi domestici sui doveri*, and *Esempi di morale domestica*. The readings explored the central ideas of civic duty, science, literature, and arithmetic through stories that traced the familial and school life of Giannetto, a young boy growing up in the North. In the 1880s and 1890s the number of textbooks published expanded rapidly, but most were still based on Parravicini's model. Until the end of the nineteenth century, teachers were permitted to select their own texts. By 1905 teachers were being required to submit suggestions to a provincial committee for approval. The

committee approved books on a three-year basis. See L.A. Parravicini, *Giannetto* (Bologna: Angelo Gordoni, 1838). For more information on the distribution of textbooks, see Ministero della Pubblica Istruzione, 'Alla scelta dei libri di testo,' *I Diritti della scuola* 21 (Rome, 5 March 1905), 163.

22 Ministero della Pubblica Istruzione, 'Indice della materie-programmi e istruzione per le scuole elementari,' *Bollettino Ufficiale del Ministero dell'Istruzione pubblica, Supplemento al N 9*, I (Rome, 2 March 1904), 481; Ministero della Pubblica Istruzione, *Bollettino Ufficiale del Ministero dell'istruzione pubblica, Supplemento al No. 42*, II (Rome, 19 October 1900), XII. For a general overview of the politics of female education, see Simonetta Soldani, ed., *L'educazione delle donne: Scuole e modelli di vita femminile nell'Italia dell'Ottocento* (Milan: Franco Angeli, 1989). The utilization of public schools to spread specific values and beliefs is obviously not unique to Italy. The French school system was especially adept at instilling the same values through classroom texts and curriculum development. Linda L. Clark, *Schooling the Daughters of Marianne: Textbooks and the Socialization of Girls in Modern French Primary Schools* (Albany: State University of New York Press, 1984), 26–59.

23 'Programmi didattici per il corso elementare,' *La Scuola in Azione*, VI, n. 2 (Rome: 22 October 1904), 112.

24 Ministero della Pubblica Istruzione, 'Indice della materie-programmi e istruzione per le scuole elementari,' *Bollettino Ufficiale del Ministero dell'Istruzione pubblica, Supplemento al N 9*, I (Rome, 2 March 1904), 543.

25 Giuseppina Rezzo, *Letture morali e civili, ad uso della 2a e 3a Classe Rurale* (Turin: Stamperia Reale G BN. Paravia e. C., 1910), 214–16.

26 Malagoli, 50.

27 Luigi Natoli, *In Cammino ... letture educative per le scuole elementari urbane maschili e femminili* (Palermo: Remo Sandron, 1911), 156–7. Similar descriptions appear in A. Perugini, *Casa mia! Patria mia! Compimento al sillabario* (Milan: Antonio Vallardi, 1919), 44–5.

28 Richard J.B. Bosworth, *Italy and the Wider World* (London: Routledge, 1996), 4–5.

29 Scavia, *L'uomo*, 89–90. This conception of the state was often associated with Giuseppe Mazzini and the Italian Unification. A number of textbooks and pedagogical works reminded their readers that Mazzini, the father of the Italian state, had first equated the nation with the family.

30 Ildebrando Bencivenni, *Il libro completo per gli alunni e le alunne della 3 cl elementare* (Turin: Tip ed. del maestro elementare italiano, 1880), 18.

31 Guido Fabiani, *Casa mia! Patria mia! Libro di lettura per la 3a classe elementare femminile* (Milan: Antonio Vallardi, 1903), 120–1, 147. Another excellent

example of the gendered construction of citizenship can be found in Luigi Natoli's *In Cammino ... letture educative per le scuole elementare urbane maschili e femminili* (Palermo: Remo Sandron, 1905), 155–61.

32 Ermelinda Fornari, *Le Fanciulle per bene: Galateo per le fanciulle ad uso delle scuole elementari femminile* (Palermo: Remo Sandron, ed, 1888), 126.

33 Ministero della Pubblica Istruzione, 'Appunti pedogogici,' in *Bollettino Ufficiale del Ministero dell'Istruzione Pubblica* (Rome: Tip. detta L. Cecchini, 1905), 483.

34 Luigi Natoli, *In Cammino* (1905), 161.

35 Geltrude Malagoli, *Un vezzo di perle: alle giovinette della scuola popolare* (Rocca San Casciano: Licinio Cappelli, ed, 1913), 14.

36 Ermelinda Fornari, *Le fanciulle per bene: Galateo per le fanciulle ad uso delle scuole elementari femminile* (Palermo: Remo Sandron, ed, 1880), 125.

37 Malagoli, *Un vezzo,* 89–90.

38 Rezzo, 12.

39 Francesco Paolo Minnetti, 'Programmi didattici per il corso elementare,' *Le Scuole in Azione* anno VI, n. 2 (Rome: 22 October 1904), 22. Fabiani, 24, 99–100.

40 Gherardo Ferreri, *Sulla soglia della scuola: La donna e l'anafabetismo italiano* (Rome: Tip. del Campidoglio Eredi D'Antonis, 1911), 43, 110–34; also see Scavia, *L'uomo,* 10–32; Ministero della Pubblica Istruzione, *Istruzioni e programmi per l'insegnamento delle primi nozioni di agricoltura, del lavoro manuale educativo, dei lavori donneschi, dell'igiene e dell'economia domestica nelle scuole elementari approvati con R Decreto 10 aprile, 1899* (Rome: Tipografia ditta Ludovico Cecchini, 1899), cxcvi, 38.

41 Angelo Mosso, 'Il passato e l'avvenire della educazione fisica,' *Nuova Antologia* 62, series 4 (1896): 156.

42 Clark, *Schooling,* chaps 3 and 5. Linda Clark suggests that some students and teachers opposed the glorification of domestic work and ridiculed the moral messages of thrift, hard work, modesty, and obedience that permeated classroom lessons. By the First World War, these messages blatantly contradicted the reality of women's experience. Married women often did not have the luxury of staying home and caring for their children. While examinations and notebooks suggest that most students accepted the basic principles underlying elementary school curriculum, it does not appear that they necessarily changed their behaviour based on what they learned at school. These contradictions were not as obvious in rural Sicily at the beginning of the twentieth century.

43 Emma Alaimo, *Proverbi Siciliani* (Florence: Aldo Martello-Giunti ed, 1974), 63–78.

44 Robert Lumley, 'Peculiarities of the Italian Newspaper,' 200–1. In the years after Unification the number of local dailies and weeklies in circulation across the island rose rapidly, although many of them folded after only a few years. Between 1862 and 1863 at least fourteen new newspapers appeared on the streets. Most of these claimed to represent a distinct political position, and all appealed to an educated urban elite interested in politics, literature, and culture. Only a few of the papers managed to remain in circulation for any significant time. For a general history of Sicilian journalism, see Luigi Chibbaro, *Storia del giornalismo in Sicilia*, Collana di Monografie sui Problemi della Stampa (Rome: Centro Studi, 1957). For a history of Italian journalism, see Valerio Castronovo, *La Stamp italiana dall'unità al fascismo* (Bari: Laterza, 1970).

45 Gower Chapman, 20.

46 Gower Chapman, 20. The regional character of Italian journalism has led many cultural historians and journalists to question whether there exists an Italy created in print, especially in light of the comparatively low number of readers. By the mid-twentieth century, Italian readership, as measured by total circulation, lagged well behind that of Great Britain, France, and the United States. In 1952 there were only 107 newspapers for every 1,000 Italians, as compared to 615 papers in Great Britain. Even within Italy, readership rates varied greatly from province to province, and there are still far fewer papers in circulation per person in the South than in the North. For the early part of the twentieth century, these 'particularities' of the Italian newspaper industry have been explained by high illiteracy rates, the strength of local dialects, and the slowness of urbanization. Explanations for the continued low number of readers during the second half of the century have proved more challenging. Some critics have pointed to the obscure, highly stylized language favoured by many Italian journalists as one explanation for poor circulation, while others have blamed the readers. Tullio de Mauro suggested that despite greater familiarity with Italian, people still felt alienated from their national language. Milly Buonanno has argued that low readership reflects the exclusion of women from public life. Women, she notes, comprise the vast majority of the reported non-readers. While all of this may be true, it is equally important to remember that at the beginning of the twentieth century newspaper circulation increased sharply, and by the First World War the residents of even the most remote villages were seeing dailies and weeklies on a regular basis. Estimating readership is made more complicated by the fact that many people read one newspaper. Even today in the town hall of Sutera, one newspaper often makes its way through a number of different readers before the doors close at two o'clock and the

rightful owner takes it home. Female readership in particular is difficult to gauge based on the number of papers sold. Most women borrowed a paper from a neighbour or relative. Women of Sutera today remember sitting outside sewing and listening to someone read from the paper. Although few southerners bought their own individual papers, it cannot be concluded that they did not read papers. For a summary of all of these positions see Robert Lumley, 'Peculiarities of the Italian Newspaper,' in *Italian Cultural Studies: An Introduction*, ed. David Forgacs and Robert Lumley (Oxford: Oxford University Press, 1996), 204. For an excellent discussion of Italian journalism, see William E. Porter, *The Italian Journalist* (Ann Arbor: University of Michigan Press, 1983), and I. Weiss, *Il potere di carta: Il giornalismo ieri e oggi* (Turin: Cane and Durando, 1965).

47 David Forgacs, ed., *An Antonio Gramsci Reader: Selected Writings, 1916–1935* (New York: Schocken Books, 1988), 365–6.

48 Alberto Abruzzese e Ilena Panico, 'Giornale e giornalismo,' in *Letteratura italiana* V II, *Produzione e consumo* (Turin: Einaudi, 1983), 781.

49 Gower Chapman, 153.

50 Clarice Tartufari, 'Vaghe Stelle dell'Orsa,' *Giornale di Sicilia* (15–16 March 1913), 3; Carola Prosperi, 'Una Lezione d'Umilità,' *Giornale di Sicilia* (24–5 February 1913), 2.

51 Giornale di Sicilia, 'Ricordi patriottici per una eroina: Festa al nord (Perugia)' (6–7 September 1910), n. 247, 3. I would also like to thank Rosanna De Longis, at the Biblioteca di Storia Moderna e Contemporanea in Rome, for her information on Colomba Antonietti. For a discussion of women on the battle field in the American Civil War, see LeeAnn Whites, *The Civil War as a Crisis in Gender: Augusta, Georgia, 1860–1890* (Athens: University of Georgia Press, 1995), 39–40.

52 'Da Calabria Giolosa Ionica' *Giornale di Sicilia* (13–14 December 1909), 4.

53 'La tragedie dell'Adulterio,' *Giornale di Sicilia* (7–8 September 1910), 3; 'Arresto per Adulterio,' *Giornale di Sicilia* (13–14 March 1913), 5.

54 'Il Matrimonio di Due Donne,' *Giornale di Sicilia* (10–11 February 1906), 1.

55 'La Leader della Suffragette Inglesi' *Giornale di Sicilia* (6–7 March 1913), 3. A satirist for *Avanti!*, Guido Podrecca was an active member of the early congresses of the Italian Socialist Party, and a supporter for female suffrage.

56 Department of Commerce and Labor, 'Italy – Progress in Trade,' *Bureau of Manufactures Monthly Consular and Trade Reports – November, 1905*, no. 302 (Washington: Government Printing Office, 1905), 121; Department of Commerce and Labor, *Bureau of Manufacturers Monthly Consular and Trade Reports–October 1907*, no. 325 (Washington: Government Printing Office, 1907), 210.

57 Department of Commerce and Labor, Bureau of Statistics, *Marketing Goods in Foreign Countries*, Special Consular Reports, vol. 34 (Washington: Government Printing Office, 1905), 9; Department of Commerce and Labor, 'Italy: Trade for the Year 1907 (Sept. 1908),' *Bureau of Manufacturers Consular Reports – Annual Series*, No. 6 (Washington: Government Printing Office, 1908), 5.

58 Ministero d'Agricoltura, Industria e Commercio, division industria e commercio, 'Stati Uniti: Il commercio estero degli Stati Uniti nell'anno fiscale 1 luglio 1901–30 Giugno 1902, specie riguardi con l'Italia,' *Bollettino di Notizie Commerciali*, no. 45 November 1902, serie III, vol. 19 (Rome: Tip. Naz. di G. Bertero, 1902), 3, 057.

59 Department of Commerce and Labor, Bureau of Manufacturers, *Monthly Consular and Trade Reports*, September 1905, no. 300 (Washington: Government Printing Office, 1905), 173–4; ibid., November 1905, no. 302, 126.

60 David Forgacs, 'Cultural Consumption, 1940s–1990s,' in *Italian Cultural Studies*, 276–9. In this article Forgacs outlines the history of cultural consumption, dating the great transformation in the late 1950s. I am not arguing with his analysis – certainly the late 1950s did see important changes in what people bought and access to radio, cinema, books, television, and sports. Forgacs is also correct in pointing out the regional distinctions that marked patterns of consumption. However, it would be a mistake to dismiss the importance of the earlier period between 1900 and the Second World War, when there was a significant shift in the presence of material goods in rural homes. While rural Italians did not spend their afternoons browsing through department stores, they did begin to fill their houses with furniture, purchase new clothes, and change the material standards of their lives.

61 Ufficio Conservatorio dei Beni Immobiliare, Caltanissetta, vol. 641, #527, 1915 and vol. 1215.1, #10273, 1920. Direzione Generale della Statistica e del Lavoro, *Annuario Statistico Italiano*, Seconda Serie, vol. II – 1912 (Rome: Tip. Naz. de G. Bertero, 1913), 135–7.

62 Leonard Covello, *The Heart Is the Teacher* (New York: McGraw-Hill, 1958), 36.

63 *Reports from the Consuls of the United States*, No. 128, May 1891 (Washington: Government Printing Office, 1891), 132; Department of Commerce and Labor, Bureau of Statistics, *Marketing Goods in Foreign Countries*, Special Consular Reports, vol. 34 (Washington: Government Printing Office, 1905), 9.

64 Department of Commerce and Labor, 'Italy: Trade for the Year 1907 (Sept. 1908),' *Bureau of Manufacturers Consular Reports – Annual Series*, No. 6 (Washington: Government Printing Office, 1908), 44.

65 Department of Commerce and Labor, Bureau of Manufacturers, *Monthly Consular and Trade Reports*, January 1909, no. 340 (Washington: Government Printing Office, 1909), 38.

66 For a discussion of mail order catalogues as a means of change, see Thomas J. Schlereth, 'Country Stores, County Fairs, and Mail-Order Catalogues: Consumption in Rural America,' in *Consuming Visions: Accumulation and Display of Goods in America, 1880–1920*, ed. Simon Bonner (New York: W.W. Norton, 1989), 339–75. For a discussion of consumerism in rural America, see Mary Neth, *Preserving the Family Farm: Women, Community and the Foundation of Agribusiness in the Midwest, 1900–1940* (Baltimore: Johns Hopkins University Press, 1995).

67 Department of Commerce and Labor, Bureau of Manufacturers, *Monthly Consular and Trade Reports*, January 1909, no. 340, 38. Department of Commerce and Labor, Bureau of Statistics, *Marketing Goods in Foreign Countries*, Special Consular Reports, vol. 34, 9.

68 Chibbaro, *Storia del Giornalismo in Sicilia*, 27.

69 These descriptions are taken from advertisements that appeared in *Giornale di Sicilia* between 1908 and 1910. Many of the clothing and health and beauty ads appeared on a regular basis.

70 Letter from Fru Pardi, April 2000.

71 See advertisements in *Giornale di Sicilia* (1–29 March 1911, 1–29 March 1913, 1–29 March 1925). For a discussion of how migrants spent their money see *Inchiesta*, VI, tomo 1, parte 3, 832–3. For information on the cultural worth of material possessions, see Gower Chapman, 19, 131.

72 Herman Tak, *South Italian Festivals: A Local History of Ritual and Change* (Amsterdam: Amsterdam University Press, 2000), 153.

73 Department of Commerce and Labor, 59th Congress, First Session, House of Representatives, Doc. 940, *Commercial Relations of the United States with Foreign Countries during the year 1905* (Washington: Government Printing Office, 1906), 189; Department of Commerce and Labor, Bureau of Manufacturers, *Commercial Relations of the United States with Foreign Countries, 1909* (Washington: Government Printing Office, 1911), 182.

74 Department of Commerce and Labor, Bureau of Foreign and Domestic Commerce: Special Consular Reports – No. 55, *Foreign Trade in Musical Instruments* (Washington: Government Printing Office, 1912), 39.

75 *Reports from the Consuls of the United States*, No. 128, May 1891, 148.

76 Advertisement, *Giornale di Sicilia* (13–14 December 1909), 6.

77 Department of Commerce and Labor, Bureau of Manufacturers, *Monthly Consular and Trade Reports* – May, 1906, no. 308 (Washington: Government Printing Office, 1906), 107–8.

78 Salvatore Salamone-Marino, *Customs and Habits of the Sicilian Peasants*, trans. Rosalie N. Norris (1897; reprint, East Brunswick: Associated University Presses, 1981), 241.

79 *Inchiesta*, VI, tomo 1, parte 3, 53.

80 Shampoos, lotions, and medicines were advertised in *Giornale di Sicilia* continually from 1909 to 1925. Aspirin was advertised in *Giornale di Sicilia*, (1–2 March 1925), 6.

81 *Giornale di Sicilia* (8–9 July 1913), Anno LIII, n. 283, 6.

82 Stuart Ewen, *Captains of Consciousness: Advertising and the Social Roots of the Consumer Culture* (New York: McGraw-Hill, 1976), 5.

83 *Giornale di Sicilia* (7–8 January 1908), n. 8, 5.

84 Victoria de Grazia, 'Empowering Women as Citizen Consumers,' in *The Sex of Things: Gender and Consumption in Historical Perspective*, ed. Victoria de Grazia with Ellen Furlough (Berkeley: University of California Press, 1996), 275–7.

Conclusion: Gender, Migration, and Globalization

1 Ann Cornelisen, *Women of the Shadows: A Study of the Wives and Mothers of Southern Italy* (New York: Vintage Books, 1977), 3.

2 For a general overview of the new historiography, see Robert Lumley and Jonathan Morris, eds., *The New History of the Italian South: The Mezzogiorno Revisited* (Exter: University of Exeter Press, 1997), and Jane Schneider, ed., *Italy's 'Southern Question': Orientalism in One Country* (New York: Berg, 1998). For an excellent discussion of how the South became a question, see Marta Petrusewicz, *Come il meridione divenne una questione: rappresentazioni del sud prima e dopo il quarantotto* (Catanzaro: Rubbettino, 1998).

3 Some of the most important works on the southern economy include Giuseppe Giarrizzo, *Mezzogiorno senza meridionalismo: La Sicilia, lo sviluppo, il potere* (Venice: Marsilio ed, 1992); Marta Petrusewicz, *Latifondo: economia morale e vita materiale in una periferia dell'Ottocento* (Venice: Marsilio, 1989), recently translated into English by Judith C. Green as *Latifundium: Moral Economy and Material Life in a European Periphery* (Ann Arbor: University of Michigan Press, 1996); and Paolo Pezzino, *Una Certa Reciprocità di favori: Mafia e modernizzazione nella Sicilia postunitaria* (Milan: FrancoAngeli, 1990). Also see Paolo Macry, *Ottocento. Famiglie, élite e patrimoni a Napoli* (Turin: Einaudi, 1988), and Gabriella Gribaudi, *A Eboli. Il mondo meridionale in cent'anni di trasformazioni* (Venice: Marsilio, 1990).

4 Although I have not had a chance to read the forthcoming book on Haitian migration by Nina Glik Schiller and Georges Eugen Fouron, *Georges Woke Up*

Laughing: Long-Distance Nationalism and the Search for Home (Durham: Duke University Press, 2001), it would appear that they explore this idea from the perspective of the emigrant. I believe that their title, 'long-distance nationalism,' is an excellent description of the relationship between migrants, their families, and the nation.

5 Saskia Sassen, *Globalization and Its Discontents: Essays on the New Mobility of People and Money* (New York: New Press, 1998), 81.

Selected Bibliography

Archival Sources

Archivio Centrale dello Stato, Roma: Gabinetto, Inchieste Parlamentari
Archivio Comunale di Ficarazzi: Archivio Storico
Archivio Comunale di Sutera (ACS): Atti di Nascita
  Atti di Matrimonio
  Atti di Morte
  Foglio di Famiglia
  Lista di Leva
  Archivio Storico
Archivio dello Stato di Caltanissetta (ASC): Catasto dei Fabbricati
  Catasto dei Terreni
Archivio dello Stato Palermo: Gabinetto
Archivio Storico del Ministero degli Affari Esteri, Roma: Commissiariato Generale Dell' Emigrazione, Archivio Generale
Ufficio Conservatorio dei Beni Immobiliare, Caltanissetta

Contemporary Newspapers and Periodicals

Giornale di Sicilia (Palermo)
I diritti della scuola (Rome)
Le scuole in azione (Supplement to *I diritti della Scuola*)
Nuova antologia
Giornale degli economisti

Government Publications

Italy

Atti della giunta per l'inchiesta agraria e sulle condizioni della classe agricola. Vol. 13. Tomo I and II. Relazione del Commissario Abele Damiani. Rome: Forzani Tip. del Senato, 1884.

Direzione Generale della Statistica e del Lavoro. Ufficio Centrale di Statistica. *Movimento della popolazione 1913.* Rome: Tip. Ditta Ludovicho Cecchini, 1915.

– *Annuario Statistico Italiano.* Seconda Serie. Vol. 2. *1912.* Rome: Tip. Naz. di G. Bertero, 1913.

Inchiesta parlamentare sulle condizioni dei contadini nelle province meridionali e nella Sicila. Vol. 6. *Sicilia.* Tomo 1. Rome: Tip. Naz. di G. Bertero, 1910.

Istituto Centrale di Statistica. *Comuni e loro popolazione ai censimenti da 1861 al 1951.* Rome: Azienda Benventana Tipografia Editoriale, 1960.

Ministero degli Affari Esteri. *Norme legislative e regolamentari concernanti la concessione di passaporti per l'estero.* Rome: Tip. Naz. G. Bertero, 1905.

– Commissariato Generale dell'Emigrazione. *Annuario statistico della emigrazione italiana 1876–1925.* Rome: Commissariato dell'Emigrazione, 1925.

– *Bollettino dell'Emigrazione.* Rome: Tip. Naz. G. Bertero, 1904, 1910.

Ministero di Agricoltura, Industria e Commercio. *Annali di Statistica.* Rome. Tip. Naz. di G. Bertero, 1893, 1895, 1896.

– *Movimento della popolazione 1901.* Rome: Tip. Nazionale, 1903.

– Direzione Generale della Statistica. *Censimento della popolazione del regno al 31 dicembre 1861.* Vol 1. Turin: Tipografia letteraria d'Italia, 1863.

– *Censimento della popolazione del regno al 31 dicembre 1871.* Vol. 1. Rome: Stamperia Reale, 1874.

– *Censimento della popolazione del regno d'Italia al 31 dicembre 1881.* 4 vols. Rome: Tipografica Bodoniana, 1882–1884.

– *Censimento della popolazione del regno d'Italia al 10 febbraio 1901.* 3 vols. Rome: Tip. Naz. di G. Bertero, 1902–1903.

– *Censimento della popolazione del regno d'Italia al giugno 1911.* 3 vols. Rome: Tip. Naz. Di G. Bertero, 1914.

– *Censimento della popolazione del regno d'Italia 1921.* Vol. 11. Rome: Provveditorato generale dello stato, 1926.

– *Censimento della popolazione del regno d'Italia 1921.* Vol. 19. Rome: Stabilimento poligrafica per l'amministrazione dello stato, 1927.

– Divisione Industria e Commercio. *Bollettino di Notizie Commerciali,* No. 45. Serie 3. Vol. 19. Rome: Tip. Naz. Di G. Bertero, 1902.

Ministero della Pubblica Istruzione. *Istruzione primaria e popolare in Italia con speciale riguardo all'anno scolastico 1907–1908.* Rome: Tip. Operario Romana Cooperativa, 1910.

– *Istruzioni e programmi per l'insegnamento delle primi nozioni di agricoltura, del lavoro manuale educativo, dei lavori donneschi, dell'igiene e dell'economia domestica nelle scuole elementari approvati con R Decreto 10 aprile, 1899.* Rome. Tipografia ditta Ludovico Cecchini, 1899.

– *Bollettino ufficiale del ministero dell'istruzione pubblica.* Rome. Tipografia ditta Ludovico Cecchini, 1905.

United States

Department of Commerce and Labor. *Reports from the Consuls of the United States,* No. 128, May 1891. Washington: Government Printing Office, 1891.

– Bureau of Foreign and Domestic Commerce. *Foreign Trade in Musical Instruments.* Special Consular Reports. No. 55. Washington: Government Printing Office, 1912.

– Bureau of Manufactures. *Commercial Relations of the United States with Foreign Countries, 1909.* Washington: Government Printing Office, 1911.

– Bureau of Manufactures. *Consular Reports Annual Series,* No. 6. Washington: Government Printing Office, 1908.

– Bureau of Manufactures. *Monthly Consular and Trade Reports.* Nos. 300–344. Washington: Government Printing Office, 1905–1909.

– Bureau of Statistics. *Special Consular Reports: Marketing Goods in Foreign Countries.* Vol. 34. Washington: Government Printing Office, 1905.

– *Special Consular Reports: Emigration to the United States.* Vol. 30. Washington: Government Printing Office, 1904.

U.S. Congress. House. *Department of Commerce and Labor Commercial Relations of the United States with Foreign Countries during the year 1905.* 59th Cong. 1st. sess. H. Doc. 940. Washington: Government Printing Office, 1906.

– Senate. *Reports of the Immigration Commission.* Vol. 1, 78. *Immigrants in Industries, Part 2: Iron and Steel Manufacturing.* 61st Cong. 2nd sess. S. Doc. 633. Washington: Government Printing Office, 1911.

– *Reports of the Immigration Commission.* Vol. 12. *Emigrant Conditions in Europe: Italy.* 61st Congress. 3rd Session. S. Doc. 748. Washington: Government Printing Office, 1911.

Books and Articles

Ardener, Shirley, ed. *Women and Space: Ground Rules and Social Maps.* Providence, RI: Berg, 1993.

Alaimo, Emma. *Proverbi Siciliani.* Florence: Giunti-Martello, 1974.

Anderson, Benedict. *Imagined Communities: Reflections on the Origin and Spread of Nationalism.* London: Verso Editions, 1983.

Audenino, Patrizia. *Un mestiere per partire: tradizione migratoria. lavoro e comunità in una vallata alpina.* Milan: Franco Angeli, 1990.

Aymard, Maurice, and Giuseppe Giarrizzo, eds. *La Sicilia. Storia d'Italia. Le regioni dall'unità ad oggi.* Turin: Einaudi. 1987.

Baily, Samuel L. 'Chain Migration of Italians to Argentina: Case Studies of the Agnonesi and Sirolesi.' *Studi Emigrazione* 19 (1982): 73–91.

– 'The Future of Italian-American Studies: An Historian's Approach to Research in the Coming Decade.' *Italian-Americans: New Perspectives in Italian Immigration and Ethnicity.* Edited by Lydio Tomasi. New York: Center for Migration Studies, 1985.

– 'The Village Outward Approach to the Study of Social Networks: A Case Study of the Agnonesi Diaspora Abroad, 1885–1989.' *Studi Emigrazione* 29 (1992): 43–67.

Baily, Samuel L., and Franco Ramella, eds., *One Family Two Worlds, An Italian Family's Correspondence across the Atlantic.* Translated by John Lenaghan. New Brunswick, NJ: Rutgers University Press, 1988.

Balancio, Dorothy M. Cula. 'The Making and Unmaking of a Myth: Italian American Women and Their Community.' PhD diss., City University of New York, 1985.

Barbagli, Marzio, and David Kertzer. 'An Introduction to the History of Italian Family Life.' *Journal of Family History* 15 (1990): 370–83.

Bell, Rudolph. *Fate and Honor: Family and Village.* Chicago: University of Chicago Press, 1979.

Bencivenni, Ildebrando. *Il libro completo per gli alunni e le alunne della 1a classe* elementare (sezione superiore). 22nd ed. Turin: Tip. del Maestro Elementare Italiano, 1880.

Beneduce, Alberto. 'Sul movimento dei rimpatriati dalle americhe.' *Giornale degli Economisti* 3 (September 1910): 225–58.

Bennett, Judith. 'Theoretical Issues, Confronting Continuity.' *Journal of Women's History* 9, no. 3 (1997): 73–94.

Bettini, Francesco. *I programmi di studio per le scuole elementari dal 1860 al 1945.* Brescia: 'La Scuola' Editrice, 1953.

Bevilacqua, Piero. *Breve storia dell'Italia meridionale.* Rome: Donzelli, 1992.

Binetti-Ventura, Caterina. *Trine e Donne Siciliane.* Milan: Ulrico Hoepli, 1911.

Birnbaum. Lucia Chiavola. *Liberazione della Donna, Feminism in Italy.* Middletown, CT: Wesleyan University Press, 1986.

Blok, Anton. 'Land Reform in a West Sicilian Latifondo Village: The Persistence of a Feudal Structure.' *Anthropological Quarterly* 39 (1966): 1–16.

– *Mafia in a Sicilian Village.* Oxford: Basil Blackwood, 1974.

Bodnar, John. *The Transplanted: A History of Immigrants in Urban America.* Bloomington: Indiana University Press, 1987.

Bonetta, Gaetano. *Istruzione e società nella Sicilia dell'ottocento.* Palermo: Sellerio, 1981.

Bonner, Simon, ed. *Consuming Visions: Accumulation and Display of Goods in America, 1880–1920.* New York: W.W. Norton, 1989.

Borruso, Vincenzo. *Practiche abortive e controllo delle nascite in Sicilia.* Palermo: Libri Siciliani, 1966.

Bosco, Augusto. 'L'emigrazione del mezzogiorno.' *Giornale degli Economisti* 32 (April 1906): 313–30.

Bosworth, Richard. *Italy and the Wider World.* London: Routledge, 1996.

Boyd-Caroli, Betty. *Italian Repatriation from the United States. 1900–1914.* New York: Center for Migration Studies, 1973.

Boyd-Caroli, Betty, Robert F. Harney, and Lydio F. Tomasi, eds. *The Italian Imigrant Woman in North America.* Toronto: Multicultural History Society of Ontario, 1978.

Brettell, Caroline. *The Men Who Migrate and The Women Who Wait: Population and History in a Portuguese Parish.* Princeton: Princeton University Press, 1986.

Briggs, John. *An Italian Passage: Immigrants to Three American Cities.* New Haven: Yale University Press, 1978.

Bruccoleri, Giuseppe. *L'emigrazione siciliana: caratteri ed effetti secondo le più recenti inchieste.* Rome: Coop. Tip. Manuzio, 1911.

– *La Sicilia di oggi: appunti economici.* Rome: Athenaeum, 1913.

Bull, Anna, and Paul Corner. *From Peasant to Entrepreneur.* Providence, RI: Berg Publishers, 1993.

Cafagna, Luciano. 'The Industrial Revolution in Italy, 1830–1914.' In *The Emergence of Industrial Societies.* Vol. 4. Edited by Carlo M. Cipolla. New York: Harper and Row, 1976.

Caico, Louise. *Sicilian Days and Ways.* London: John Long, 1910.

Calapso, Jole. 'La Donna in Sicilia e in Italia: la realtà e la falsa coscienza nella statistica dal 1871 ad oggi.' *Quaderni Siciliani* 2 (March–April 1973): 13–20.

Calfut, George. 'An Analysis of Italian Emigration Statistics. 1876–1914.' *Jahrbuch für Geschichte: von Staat, Wirtschaft und Gesellschaft Lateinamerikas* 14 (1977): 310–31.

Candeloro, Dominic, Fred L. Gardaphe, Paolo A. Giordano, eds. *Italian Ethnics: Their Languages, Literature and Lives.* Vol. 20. *Annual Proceedings of the American Italian Historical Association.* Staten Island: American Historical Association, 1990.

Capuana, Luigi. *Gli Americani di Rabbato: Racconto.* Palermo: R. Sandrow, 1918.

Castelli, Rafaelle. *Credenze e usi popolari siciliani.* Palermo: Tip. Pietro Montana, 1878.

Castronovo, Valerio. *La Stamp italiana dall'unità al fascismo.* Bari: Laterza, 1970.

Cerase, Francesco P. 'Expectations and Reality: A Case Study of Return Migration from the United States to Southern Italy.' *International Migration Review* 8 (1974): 245–62.

Chapman, Charlotte Gower. *Milocca: A Sicilian Village.* Cambridge: Schenkman, 1971.

Chibbaro, Luigi. *Storia del giornalismo in Sicilia.* Rome: Collana di Monografie sui Problemi della Stampa, Centro Studi, 1957.

Cinel, Dino. *From Italy to San Francisco.* Stanford: Stanford University Press, 1982.

– 'Italians in the South: The Alabama Case.' *Italian Americana* 9 (Fall/Winter 1990): 7–24.

– *The National Integration of Return Migration. 1870–1929.* New York: Cambridge University Press, 1991.

Ciongoli, A Kenneth, and Jay Parini, eds.. *Beyond the Godfather: Italian American Writers on the Real Italian American Experience.* Hanover: University Press of New England, 1997.

Clark, Anna. *The Struggle for the Breeches.* Berkeley: University of California Press, 1995.

Clark, Linda. *Schooling the Daughters of Marianne: Textbooks and the Socialization of Girls in Modern French Primary Schools.* Albany: State University of New York Press, 1984.

Cohen Miriam. *Workshop to Office: Two Generations of Italian Women in New York City, 1900–1950.* Ithaca: Cornell University Press, 1992.

Coletti, Francesco. 'Classi sociali e delinquenza in Italia 1891–1901.' Vol 7. Tomo I. *Inchiesta parlamentare sulle condizione dei contadini nelle provincie meridionali e nella Sicilia.* Rome: Bertero, 1910.

– *Dell'emigrazione italiana.* Milan: Ulrico Hoelpi, 1912.

Conte, Gaetano. *Dieci Anni in America.* Palermo: Tip. G. Spinnato, 1903.

Cornelisen, Ann. *Women of the Shadows: A Study of the Wives and Mothers of Southern Italy.* New York: Vintage Books, 1977.

Covello, Leonard. *The Heart Is the Teacher.* New York: McGraw-Hill, 1958.

Croce, Benedetto. *History of the Kingdom of Naples.* Trans. F. Frenaye. Chicago: University of Chicago Press, 1970.

Cronin, Constance. *Sting of Change: Sicilians in Sicily and Australia.* Chicago: University of Chicago Press, 1970.

Dauenhauer, Bernard P. *Citizenship in a Fragile World.* Lanham, MD: Rowman and Littlefield, 1996.

Davin, Anna. 'Imperialism and Motherhood.' *History Workshop* 5 (Spring 1978): 9–65.

Davis, John A., ed. *Gramsci and Italy's Passive Revolution.* London: Croom Helm, 1979.

– 'Remapping Italy's Path to the Twentieth Century.' *Journal of Modern History* 66 (June 1994): 291–320.

De Giorgio, Michela, *Le italiane dall'unità a oggi: modelli culturali e comportamenti sociali.* Rome-Bari: Editori Laterza, 1992.

De Grazia, Victoria. *How Fascism Ruled Women: Italy, 1922–1945.* Berkeley: University of California Press, 1992.

De Grazia, Victoria, and Ellen Furlough, eds. *The Sex of Things: Culture and Consumption in Historical Perspective.* Berkeley: University of California Press, 1996.

De Stefano, Francesco, and Francesco Luigi Oddo. *La Storia della Sicilia.* Bari: Laterza, 1963.

Di Donato, Pietro. *Christ in Concrete.* New York: Bobbs-Merrill, 1939.

Di Marco, Arcuri Luigi. 'L'emigrazione siciliana all'estero nel cinquantennio 1876–1925.' *Annali del Mezzogiorno* 6 (1966): 169–232.

Difrancesco, Gero. *Sutera: I primi anni del '900.* Caltanissetta: Biblioteca Comunale Sutera, 1989.

Diner, Hasia. *Erin's Daughters in America: Irish Immigrant Women in the Nineteenth Century.* Baltimore: Johns Hopkins University Press, 1983.

Douglass, William. *Emigration from a Southern Italian Town.* New Brunswick, NJ: Rutgers University Press, 1984.

Doumanis, Nicholas. *Italy.* London: Arnold, 2001.

Dubisch, Jill, ed. *Gender and Power in Rural Greece.* Princeton: Princeton University Press, 1986.

Dwyer, Daisy, and Judith Bruce, eds. *A Home Divided: Women and Income in the Third World.* Stanford: Stanford University Press, 1988.

Eisenstadt, S.N. *The Adaptation of Immigrants.* London: Routledge and Kegan Paul, 1954.

Ets, Marie Hall. *Rosa. The Life of an Italian Immigrant.* Minneapolis: University of Minnesota Press, 1970.

Ewen, Elizabeth. *Immigrant Women in the Land of Dollars: Life and Culture on the Lower East Side, 1890–1925.* New York: Monthly Review Press, 1985.

Ewen, Stuart. *Captains of Consciousness: Advertising and the Social Roots of the Consumer Culture.* New York: McGraw-Hill, 1976.

Fabiani, Guido. *Casa mia! Patria mia! Libro di lettura per la 3a classe elementare femminile.* Milan: Antonio Vallardi, 1903.

Fazio, Ida. 'Trasmissione della proprietà. Sussistenza e *status* femminili in Sicilia Capizzi, 1790–1900.' In *Istituto 'Alcide Cervi' Annali 12/1990.* Edited by Paula Corti. Imola: Il Mulino. 1992.

Ferraris, Carlo. 'Il movimento generale dell'emigrazione italiana: suoi caratteri ed effetti.' *Bollettino dell'Emigrazione* 5 (1909): 3–42.

Ferreri, Gherardo. *Sulla soglia della scuola: La donna e l'anafabetismo italiano.* Rome: Tip. Del Campidoglio Eredi D'Antonis, 1911

Finley, M.I., Denis Mack Smith, and Christopher Duggan. *History of Sicily.* New York: Viking Press, 1987.

Foerster, Robert. *The Italian Emigration of Our Times.* 1919; Reprint, New York: Arno Press, 1969.

Forgacs, David. *An Antonio Gramsci Reader: Selected Writings, 1916–1935.* New York: Schocken Books, 1988.

Forgacs, David, and Robert Lumley, eds. *Italian Cultural Studies: An Introduction.* Oxford: Oxford University Press, 1996.

Fornari, Ermelinda. *Le Fanciulle per bene: Galateo per le fanciulle ad uso delle scuole elementari femminile.* Palermo: Remo Sandron, 1888.

Frader, Laura, and Sonya Rose, eds. *Gender and Class in Modern Europe.* Ithaca: Cornell University Press, 1996.

Fraisse, Geneviève, and Michelle Perrot, eds. *A History of Women: Emerging Feminism from Revolution to World War.* Cambridge, MA: Belknap Press, 1993.

Franchetti, Leopoldo. *Inchiesta in Sicilia.* 1876: Reprint, Florence: Vallecchi, 1974.

Franzina, Emilio. *Gli italiani nel mondo: L'emigrazione italiana in America 1492–1942.* Milan: Arnoldo Modadori Editore, 1995.

Frati, Lodovico. *La Donna Italiana secondo i più recenti studi.* Turin: Fratelli Bocca, 1899.

Friedl, Ernestine. 'The Position of Women: Appearance and Reality.' In *Gender and Power in Rural Greece.* Edited by Jill Dubisch. Princeton: Princeton University Press, 1986.

Friedlander, Dov. 'Demographic Response and Socioeconomic Structure: Population Process in England and Wales in the 19th Century.' *Demography* 20 (1983): 249–72.

Friedman-Kasaba, Kathie. *Memories of Migration: Gender, Ethnicity, and Work in the Lives of Jewish and Italian Women in New York, 1870–1924.* Albany: State University of New York Press, 1996.

Frye-Jacobson, Matthew. *Different Colors of Whiteness.* Cambridge: Harvard University Press, 1998.

Gabaccia. Donna. *From Sicily to Elizabeth Street: Housing and Social Change among Italian Immigrants, 1880–1930.* Albany: State University of New York Press, 1984.

– 'In the Shadows of the Periphery: Italian Women in the Nineteenth Century.' In *Connecting Spheres: Women in the Western World: 1500 to the Present.* Edited by

Marilyn J. Boxer and Jean H. Quataert. New York: Oxford University Press, 1987.

– *Militants and Migrants: Rural Sicilians Become American Workers.* New Brunswick, NJ: Rutgers University Press, 1988.

– *Italy's Many Diasporas.* Seattle: University of Washington Press, 2000.

Gabaccia, Donna, ed. *Seeking Common Ground: Multidisciplinary Studies of Immigrant Women in the United States.* Westport, CT: Greenwood Press, 1992.

Gabaccia, Donna, and Franca Iacovetta. 'Women, Work and Protest in the Italian Diaspora: An International Research Agenda.' *Labour/Le Travail* 42 (Fall 1998): 161–81

Gabaccia, Donna, and Franca Iacovetta, eds. *Women, Gender, and Transnational Lives: Italian Women around the World.* Toronto: University of Toronto Press, 2002.

Galasso, Giuseppe, and Rosario Romeo. *Storia del Mezzogiorno.* Vol. 15. Rome: Edizioni del Sole, 1986.

Gallagher, Catherine, and Thomas Laquer, eds. *The Making of the Modern Body.* Berkeley: University of California Press, 1987.

Gandalfo, Romolo. 'Del alto molise al centro de Buenos Aires: las mujeres agnonesas y la primera emigracion transatlantica 1870–1900.' *Estudio Migratorios Latinoamericanos* 7 (1992): 71–98.

Gazzetti, Francesco. *Manuale di agricoltura ad uso della scuola popolare e complementare ed'ogni famiglia d'agricoltori.* Turin: Presso le ditte Paravia e Tarizzo, 1885.

Gellner, Ernest. *Nations and Nationalism.* Ithaca: Cornell University Press, 1983.

Giarrizzo, Giuseppe. *Mezzogiorno senza meridionalismo: La Sicilia, lo sviluppo, il potere.* Venice, Marsilio, 1992.

Gibson, Mary. *Prostitution and the State in Italy, 1860–1915.* New Brunswick, NJ: Rutgers University Press, 1986.

Gilkey, George R. 'The United States and Italy: Migration and Repatriation.' *Journal of Developing Areas* 2 (1967): 23–35.

Giordano, Paolo, and Anthony Julian Tamburri eds. *Beyond the Margin: Readings in Italian Americana.* Teaneck, NJ: Fairleigh Dickinson University Press, 1998.

Godineau, Dominique. *The Women of Paris and their French Revolution.* Translated by Katherine Streip. Berkeley: University of California Press, 1998.

Gordon, Linda. *Heros of Their Own Lives: The Politics and History of Family Violence in Boston, 1800–1960.* New York: Viking Press, 1988.

Gordon, Milton. *Assimilation in American Life.* New York: Oxford University Press, 1964.

Gramsci, Antonio. *Prison Notebooks.* Translated by Quintin Hoare and Geoffrey Nowell Smith. New York: International Publishers, 1985.

– *La questione meridionale.* Edited by Franco De Felice and Valentino Parlato. Rome: Editori Riuniti, 1982.

Green, Rose Basile. *The Italian-American Novel: A Document of the Interaction of Two Cultures.* Teaneck, NJ: Fairleigh Dickinson University Press, 1974.

Gribaudi, Gabriella. *A Eboli, il mondo meridionale in cent' anni di trasformazioni.* Venice: Marsilio, 1990.

– *Donne, uomini, famiglie: Napoli nel novecento.* Rome: L'Ancora, 1999.

Guibernau, Montserrat. *Nationalisms: The Nation-State and Nationalism in the Twentieth Century.* Cambridge: Polity Press, 1996.

Guttantag, Marcia, and Paul Secord. *Too Many Women: The Sex Ratio Question.* Beverly Hills, CA: Sage, 1983.

Habbakkuk. H.G. 'Family Structure and Economic Change in Nineteenth-Century Europe.' *Journal of Economic History* 15 (1955): 1–12.

Haines, Michael R. 'Occupation and Social Class during Fertility Decline: Historical Perspectives.' In *The European Experience of Declining Fertility, 1850–1970.* Edited by John R. Gillis, Louise A. Tilly, and David Levine. Cambridge: Blackwell Publishers, 1992.

Halpern, Joel, and Richard Wagner. 'Time and Social Structure: A Yugoslavian Case Study.' *Journal of Family History* 93 (1984): 229–43.

Handlin, Oscar. *The Uprooted.* Boston: Little Brown, 1951.

Hareven, Tamara K. *Family Time and Industrial Time.* New York. Cambridge University Press, 1982.

Herzfeld, Michael. 'Within and Without: The Category of Female in the Ethnography of Modern Greece.' In *Gender and Power in Rural Greece.* Edited by Jill Dubisch. Princeton: Princeton University Press, 1986.

Hilowitz, Jane. *Economic Development and Social Change in Sicily.* Cambridge: Schenkman, 1976.

Hobsbawm, Eric. *Age of Empire.* New York: Vintage, 1989.

Katznelson, Ira, and Aristide R. Zolberg, eds. *Working-Class Formation: Nineteenth-Century Patterns in Western Europe and the United States.* Princeton: Princeton University Press, 1986.

Kaushalendra, Singh. 'Effects of Breast Feeding after Resumption of Menstruation on Waiting Time to Next Conception.' *Human Biology* 65 (February 1993): 71–86.

Kelly, Joan. *Women, History and Theory.* Chicago: University of Chicago Press, 1984.

Kennedy, Kathy I. 'Contraceptive Efficacy of Lactational Amenorrhoea.' *Lancet* 339 (25 January 1992): 227–30.

Kerber, Linda. *No Constitutional Right to Be Ladies.* New York: Hill and Wang, 1998.

Kertzer, David I. *Sacrificed for Honor: Italian Infant Abandonment and the Politics of Reproductive Control.* Boston: Beacon Press, 1993.

Koon, Tracy. *Believe, Fight and Obey.* Chapel Hill: University of North Carolina Press, 1985.

King, Russell, John Connell, and Paul White, eds. *Writing across Worlds: Literature and Migration.* New York: Routledge, 1995.

Landes, Joan. *Women and the Public Sphere in the Age of the French Revolution.* Ithaca: Cornell University Press, 1988.

Laslett, Peter, and Richard Wall, eds. *Household and Family in Past Time.* Cambridge: Cambridge University Press, 1972.

Laudani, Simona. 'Trasformazione agricole e condizione femminile in Sicilia.' *Istituto 'Alcide Cervi' Annali 12/1990.* Edited by Paula Corti. Imola: Il Mulino, 1992.

Levy, Carl ed. *Italian Regionalism: History, Identity and Politics.* Oxford: Berg, 1996.

Livi-Bacci, Massimo. *A History of Italian Fertility during the Last Two Centuries.* Princeton: Princeton University Press, 1977.

Lorenzoni, Giovanni. *Trasformazione e colonizzazione del latifondo siciliano.* Florence: Casa ed. Poligrafia Univ., 1940.

Lumley Robert, and Jonathan Morris, eds. *The History of the New South: The Mezzogiorno Revisited.* Exeter: University of Exeter Press, 1997.

Lupo, Salvatore. *Il giardino degli aranci: il mondo degli agrumi nella storia del mezzogiorno.* Venice: Marsilio Editore, 1990.

MacDonald, John S. 'Agricultural Organization: Migration and Labor Militancy in Rural Italy.' *Economic History Review,* 2nd ser., 16 (1963): 61–75.

MacDonald, John S., and L.D. MacDonald. 'Chain Migration. Ethnic Neighborhood Formation and Social Networks.' *Milbank Memorial Fund Quarterly* 42 (January 1964): 82–97.

Mack Smith, Denis. *A History of Sicily: Modern Sicily.* New York: Doset Press, 1968.

– *Modern Italy: A Political History.* Ann Arbor: University of Michigan Press, 1997.

Macry, Paolo. *Ottocento: Famiglie, élite e patrimoni a Napoli.* Turin: Einaudi, 1988.

Malagoli, Geltrude. *Un Vezzo di Perle: Alle giovinette della scuola popolare.* Rocca San Casciano: Licinio Cappelli, 1913.

Mancuso, Elvira. 'The Effect of Emigration upon Italy: "Ci manca la mano d'opera," "We lack the working hand."' *Charities and the Commons* 20 (4 April 1908): 13–25.

– 'The Effect of Emigration upon Italy: Hard lives of Peasants the Reason for Emigration, Misery, Misery, Misery!' *Charities and Commons* 19 (February 1908): 1475–86.

– 'The Effect of Emigration upon Italy: A Social and Industrial Revolution Necessary.' *Charities and Commons* 20 (6 June 1908): 323–35.

– *Perchè non si deve emigrare.* Rome: Edizione del 'Diritto del Lavoro,' 1928.

– *Sulla condizione della donna borghese in Sicilia: appunti e riflessione.* Caltanissetta: Tip. dell'omnibus, 1907.

Mangano, Antonio. 'The Effect of Emigration upon Italy: Threatened Depopulation of the South.' *Charities and Commons* 19 (1908): 1329–39.

– 'The Effect of Emigration upon Italy: Torritto and San Demetrio, Christopher Columbus the Second, A Greek Colony in Southern Italy.' *Charities and Commons* 20 (2 May 1908): 167–79.

May, John F. 'Clarifying Breastfeeding's Role in Contraception.' *Population Today* 20 (May 1992): 20.

McLaren, Angus. *Reproductive Rituals.* New York: Methuen, 1984.

Messina, Maria. *Piccoli Gorghi.* 1911; Reprint, Palermo: Sellerio, 1988.

Miller, Kerby. *Emigrants and Exiles.* Oxford: Oxford University Press, 1985.

Mondschean, Thomas H. 'Estimating the Probability of Emigration from Individual-Specific Data: The Case of Italy in the Early Twentieth Century.' *International Migration Review* 20 (Spring 1988): 69–80.

Mongeri, Luigi. *Patologia speciale delle malattie mentali con sommari considerazioni medico legali per gli studenti, medici pratici e giuristi.* Milan: Ulrico Hoepli, 1907.

Morawska, Ewa. 'The Sociology and Historiography of Immigration.' In *Immigration Reconsidered: History, Sociology, and Politics.* Edited by Virginia Yans-McLaughlin. New York: Oxford University Press, 1990.

Mormino, Gary Ross. *Immigrants on the Hill.* Urbana: University of Illinois Press, 1986.

Mormino, Gary Ross, and George Pozzetta. *The Immigrant World of Ybor City: Italians and Their Latin Neighbors in Tampa, 1885–1985.* Urbana: University of Illinois Press, 1987.

Mosso, Angelo. *Vita Moderna degli Italiani.* Milan: Fratelli Treves Editori, 1906.

Naro, Cataldo. *Momenti e figure della chiesa nissena dell'otto e novecento.* Caltanissetta: Centro Studi Sulla Cooperazione 'A Cammerata,' 1989.

Natoli, Luigi. *In Cammino ... letture educative per le scuole elementare urbane maschili e femminili.* Palermo: Remo Sandron, 1905.

– *In Cammino ... letture educative per le scuole elementari urbane maschili e femminili.* Palermo: Remo Sandron, 1911.

Neth, Mary. *Preserving the Family Farm: Women, Community, and the Foundations of Agribusiness in the Midwest, 1900–1940.* Baltimore: Johns Hopkins University Press, 1995.

Nicastro, Cettina. *La terra chiama-studi di emigranti.* Sutera: Comitato Comunale per L'Emigrazione e L'Immigrazione, 1992.

Nitti, Francesco Saverio. 'Napoli e la questione meridionale.' *La questione meridionale.* Edited by Manlio Rossi Doria. Rome-Bari: Laterza, 1978.

Noether. Emiliana. 'The Silent Half: Le Contadine del Sud, before World War One.' *The Italian Immigrant Women in North America.* eds. Betty Caroli, Robert F. Haney, and Lyda F. Tomasi. Toronto: Multicultural History Society of Ontario, 1978.

Norrell, Jeff. *The Italians: From Bisacquino to Birmingham.* Birmingham, AL: Birmingfind Project, n.d.

Parravicini, L.A. *Giannetto.* Bologna: Angelo Gordoni, 1838.

Patriarca, Silvana. *Numbers and Nationhood: Writing Statistics in Nineteenth-Century Italy.* Cambridge: Cambridge University Press, 1996.

Pellegrini , Angelo. *American Dream: An Immigrant's Quest.* San Francisco: North Point Press, 1986.

Persitany, J.G. ed. *Honor and Shame: The Values of Mediterranean Society.* Chicago: University of Chicago Press. 1966.

Perugini, A. *Casa mia! Patria mia! Compimento al sillabario.* Milan: Antonio Vallardi, 1919.

Petrusewicz, Marta, *Come il meridione divenne una questione Rappresentazioni del sud prima e dopo il Quarantotto.* Catanzaro: Rubbettino Editore, 1998.

– *Latifundium: Moral Economy and Material Life in a European Periphery.* Translated by Judith C. Green. Ann Arbor: University of Michigan Press, 1996.

Pezzino, Paolo. *Una certa reciprocità di favori.* Milan: FrancoAngeli, 1990.

Piore, Michael. *Birds of Passage.* New York: Cambridge University Press, 1979.

Pirandello, Luigi. *Novelle per un anno.* Vol. 1. Verona: Arnoldo Mondadori Editore, 1956.

Pitrè, Giuseppe. *La famiglia, la casa, la vita del popolo siciliano.* Palermo: A. Reber, 1913.

– *Nozze Gallenga-Monaci: Donna e Matrimonio, proverbi siciliani inedita.* Palermo: n.p., 1903.

– *Usi e costumi del popolo siciliano.* Edited by Giuseppe Lisi. 2nd ed. Bologna: Capelli ed., 1971.

Pitt-Rivers, Julian, ed. *Mediterranean Country Men.* Westport, CT: Greenwood Press, 1963.

Popkin, Barry M., David K. Guilkey, John S. Atkin, Linda S. Adain, J. Richard Adry, and William Flieger. 'Nutrition, Lactation and Birth Spacing in Filipino Women.' *Demography* 30 (August 1993): 333–52.

Porter, William E. *The Italian Journalist.* Ann Arbor: University of Michigan Press, 1983.

Pozzetta, George, ed. *Emigration and Immigration: The Old World Confronts the New.* New York: Garland Publishers, 1991.

– ed. *Immigrant Family Patterns: Demography, Fertility, Housing, Kinship and Urban Life.* New York: Garland Publishers, 1991.

Puntero, Biagio. *Delle condizioni economiche dalla provincia di Caltanissetta.* Caltanissetta: Tip. Ospiz. di Beneficienza, 1905.

– *L'emigrazione: conferenze tenute nella sala gialla del palazzo municipale in Caltanissetta. la sera 21 maggio 1910.* Caltanissetta: Tip. Ospizio Prof. Di Beneficenze, 1911

Raffiotta, Giovanni. *Storia della Sicilia post-unificazione: la Sicilia nella prima ventennio del secolo XX.* Palermo: Ind. Grafica Nazionale, 1959.

Raja, Giovanbattista. *Il fenomeno emigratorio siciliano con speciale rigurado al quinquennio, 1902–1906.* Palermo: Tip. Imp. Affari Pubblicità, 1908.

Renda, Francesco. *L'emigrazione in Sicilia.* Palermo: Tip. La Cartografica, 1963.

– *I fasci siciliani 1892–1894.* Turin: Einaudi, 1977.

Revelli. Nuto. *L'anello forte: la donna – storie di vita contadine.* Turin: Giuglio Einaudi, 1985.

Rezzo, Giuseppina. *Letture morali e civili, ad uso della 2a e 3a Classe Rurale.* Turin: Stamperia Reale G BN. Paravia e. C., 1910.

Riall, Lucy. *Sicily and the Unification of Italy: Liberal Policy and Local Power, 1859–1866.* Oxford: Clarendon Press, 1998.

Roediger David. *The Wages of Whiteness: Race and the Making of the American Working Class.* New York: Verso, 1991.

Rogers, Susan. 'Female Forms of Power and the Myth of Male Dominance: A Model of Female/Male Interaction in Peasant Society.' *American Ethnologist* 2 (November 1975): 727–56.

Romano, Francesco. *Storia della Sicilia post-unficazione: la Sicilia nell'ultimo ventennio del secolo XIX.* Palermo: Industria Grafica Nazionale, 1958.

Rosaldo, Michelle Zimbalist, and Louise Lamphere, eds. *Women Culture and Society.* Stanford: Stanford University Press, 1974.

Rösener, Werner. *The Peasantry of Europe.* Oxford: Blackwell Publishers, 1994.

Ross, Ellen. 'Survival Networks: Women's Neighbourhood Sharing in London before World War I.' *History Workshop* 15 (Spring 1983): 4–27.

– *Love and Toil.* New York: Oxford University Press, 1993.

Rotberg, Robert, and Theodore K. Rabb. eds. *Population and Economy: Population and History from the Traditional to the Modern World.* New York: Cambridge University Press, 1986.

Salamone-Marino, Salvatore. *Customs and Habits of the Sicilian Peasants.* Translated by Rosalie N. Norris. East Brunswick, NJ: Associated University Press, 1981.

Sassen, Saskia. *Globalization and Its Discontents: Essays on the New Mobility of People and Money.* New York: New Press, 1998.

Scabia, Luigi. *Trattato di terapia delle malattie mentali ad suo dei medici e degli studenti.* Turin: Unione Tipografico-editrice, 1900.

Scavia, Giovanni. *L'uomo e l'universo.* Turin: Tip Scolastica-Seb Franco e Figli, 1861.

Schneider, Arnd. 'Presente e passato in un paese del Sud.' *Nuove Effemeridi* 1 (1988): 76–9.

Schneider, Jane. 'Family Patrimonies and Economic Behavior in Western Sicily.' *Anthropological Quarterly* 42 (1969): 109–25.

– 'Sex and Respectability in an Age of Fertility Decline: A Sicilian Case Study.' *Social Science and Medicine* 33 (1991): 885–95.

– 'Trousseau as Treasure: Some Contradictions of Late Nineteenth Century Change in Sicily.' *Beyond the Myths of Culture.* Edited by Eric B. Ross. New York: Academic Press. Inc., 1980.

– 'Of Vigilance and Virgins: Honor, Shame, and Access to Resources in Mediterranean Societies.' *Ethnology* 10 (January 1971): 1–24.

Schneider, Jane, ed. *Italy's Southern Question: Orientalism in One Country.* Oxford: Berg, 1998.

Schneider, Jane, and Peter Schneider. *Culture and Political Economy in Western Sicily.* New York: Academic Press, 1976.

– 'Demographic Transitions in a Sicilian Rural Town.' *Journal of Family History* 9 (Fall 1984): 245–72.

– 'Going Forward in Reverse Gear: Culture, Economy, and Political Economy in the Demographic Transitions of a Rural Sicilian Town.' In *The European Experience of Declining Fertility, 1850–1970.* Edited by John R. Gillis, Louise A. Tilly, and David Levine. Cambridge: Blackwell Publishers, 1992.

Scott, Joan. 'Gender, a Useful Category of Analysis.' *Gender and the Politics of History.* New York: Columbia University Press, 1988.

Shanley, Mary Lyndon. *Feminism, Marriage, and the Law in Victorian England.* Princeton: Princeton University Press, 1989.

Siegenthaler, Jürg K. 'Sicilian Economic Change Since 1860.' *Journal of Economic History* 2 (Fall 1973): 363–415.

Simonton, Deborah. *A History of European Women's Work, 1700 to the Present.* London: Routledge, 1998.

Sivamurthy. M. *Growth and Structure of Human Population in the Presence of Migration.* London: Academic Press, 1982.

Smith, Bonnie G. *Changing Lives: Women in European History since 1700.* Lexington, MA: D.C. Heath, 1989.

Smith, Estellie M. 'Networks and Migration Resettlement: Cherchez la Femme.' *Anthropological Quarterly* 49 (January 1976): 20–7.

Soja, Edward W. *Post-Modern Geographies.* Bristol: Verso, 1990.

Soldani, Simonetta. *L'educazione delle donne: Scuole e modelli di vita femminile nell'Italia dell'Ottocento.* Milan: Franco Angeli Libri, 1989.

Somogyi, Stefano. *Bilanci demografici dei Communi Siciliani dal 1861 al 1961.* Palermo: Università di Palermo, Istituto di Scienze Demografiche, 1971.

– *Storia demografici dei comuni siciliani dal 1862–1971.* Palermo: Tip. Lux., 1979.

Sonnino, Sidney. *Inchiesta in Sicilia.* 1876; Reprint, Florence: Vallecchi, 1974.

Squarzina, Francesco. *Produzione e comercio dello zolfo in Sicilia nel secolo XIX.* Turin: ILTE, 1963.

Stephens,William. *The Family in Cross Cultural Perspective.* New York: Holt Rinehart and Winston, 1963.

Sturino, Franc. *Forging the Chain: Italian Migration to North America, 1880–1930.* Toronto: Multicultural History Society of Ontario, 1990.

Taddei, Ettore, and Constantino Ledda. *Contadini Siciliani.* Vol. 4. Monografie di Famiglie Agricole. Rome: S.A. Tip. Operaio Romano, 1933.

Tak, Herman. *South Italian Festivals: A Local History of Ritual and Change.* Amsterdam: Amsterdam University Press, 2000.

Talese, Gay. *Unto the Sons.* New York: Knopf, 1992.

Tannenbaum, Edward R., and Emiliana P. Noether. *Modern Italy.* New York: New York University Press, 1974.

Teti, Vito. 'Noti sui comportamenti delle donne sole degli "americani" durante la prima emigrazione in Calabria.' *Studi Emigrazione* 24 (1987): 13–46.

Thistlethwaite, Frank. 'Migration from Europe Overseas in the Nineteenth and Twentieth Centuries.' *Population Movement in Modern European History*, edited by Herbert Moller. New York: Macmillan, 1964.

Thomas, William I., and Florian Zaniecki. *The Polish Peasant in Europe and America.* Boston: Knopf, 1927.

Thompson, E.P. *The Making of the English Working Class.* New York: Vintage, 1966.

– 'Time, Work-Discipline, and Industrial Capitalism.' *Past and Present* 38 (December 1967): 56–97.

Tilly, Charles. 'Transplanted Networks.' In *Immigration Reconsidered: History, Sociology, and Politics.* Edited by Virginia Yans-McLaughlin. New York: Oxford University Press, 1990.

Tilly, Charles, ed. *Historical Studies of Changing Fertility.* Princeton: Princeton University Press, 1978.

Tilly, Charles, Louise Tilly, and Richard Tilly. *The Rebellious Century, 1830–1930.* Cambridge: Harvard University Press, 1975.

Tilly, Louise A., and Joan W. Scott. *Women Work and Family.* New York: Holt Rinehart and Winston, 1978.

Traina, Salvatore. *L'operaio alla scuola serale. Libro di lettura per le scuole popolari.* Palermo: Ufficio Tipografico di Michele Amenta, 1882.

Vaccaro, Antonio. *Cenni sulla città di Sutera.* Naples: Tip. dei. Frat Carluccio, 1881.

– *Sutera e la sua geografia fisica.* Naples: Tip. Gazz. Drit. e Gius., 1890.

Valenze, Deborah. *The First Industrial Woman.* New York: Oxford University Press, 1995.

Villari, Pasquale. 'Discorso sulla emigrazione.' *Storia politica e istruzione.* Milan: Ulrico Hoelpli, 1917.

– 'L'emigrazione e le sue consequenze in Italia.' *Nuova Antologia* 127 (January 1907): 33–56.

Wall Richard, Jean Robin, and Peter Laslett, eds. *Family Forms in Historic Europe.* Cambridge: Cambridge University Press, 1983.

Wallerstein, Immanuel. *The Modern World System I, Capitalist Agriculture and the Origins of the European World-Economy in the Sixteenth Century.* New York: Academic Press, 1974.

Watkins, Susan Cotts. *From Provinces into Nations: The Demographic Integration of Western Europe. 1870–1960.* Princeton: Princeton University Press, 1991.

Weber, Eugen. *Peasants into Frenchmen.* Stanford: Stanford University Press, 1976.

Weiss, I. *Il potere di carta: Il giornalismo ieri e oggi.* Turin: Cane e Durando, 1965.

Whyte, William. *Street Corner Society.* Chicago: University of Chicago Press, 1943.

Wilson, Rob, and Wimal Dissanayake, eds. *Globallocal: Cultural Production and the Transnational Imaginary.* Durham: Duke University Press. 1996.

Wolf, Eric. *Europe and the People without History.* Berkeley: University of California Press, 1982.

– *Peasant Wars of the Twentieth Century.* New York: Harper and Row, 1973.

Wyman, Mark. *Round-Trip to America: The Immigrants Return to Europe, 1880–1930.* Ithaca: Cornell University Press, 1993.

Yans-McLaughlin, Virginia. *Family and Community: Italian Immigrants in Buffalo, 1880–1930.* Ithaca: Cornell University Press, 1977.

– Introduction to *Immigration Reconsidered: History, Sociology, and Politics.* Edited by Virginia Yans-McLaughlin. New York: Oxford University Press, 1990.

Zamagni, Vera. *Della periferia al centro: la seconda renascita economica dell'Italia (1861–1990).* Bologna: Il Mulino, 1990).

Zoda, Luigi. *La mobilitazione agraria in provincia di Caltanissetta, 1918–1919.* Caltanissetta: Tip. Ospiz. di Beneficienza, 1919.

Index

STUDIES IN GENDER AND HISTORY

General editors: Franca Iacovetta and Karen Dubinsky

1 Suzanne Morton, *Ideal Surroundings: Domestic Life in a Working-Class Suburb in the 1920s*
2 Joan Sangster, *Earning Respect: The Lives of Working Women in Small-Town Ontario, 1920–1960*
3 Carolyn Strange, *Toronto's Girl Problem: The Perils and Pleasures of the City, 1880–1930*
4 Sara Z. Burke, *Seeking the Highest Good: Social Service and Gender at the University of Toronto, 1888–1937*
5 Lynne Marks, *Revivals and Roller Rinks: Religion, Leisure, and Identity in Late-Nineteenth-Century Small-Town Ontario*
6 Cecilia Morgan, *Public Men and Virtuous Women: The Gendered Languages of Religion and Politics in Upper Canada, 1791–1850*
7 Mary Louise Adams, *The Trouble with Normal: Postwar Youth and the Making of Heterosexuality*
8 Linda Kealey, *Enlisting Women for the Cause: Women, Labour, and the Left in Canada, 1890–1920*
9 Christina Burr, *Spreading the Light: Work and Labour Reform in Late-Nineteenth-Century Toronto*
10 Mona Gleason, *Normalizing the Ideal: Psychology, Schooling, and the Family in Postwar Canada*
11 Deborah Gorham, *Vera Brittain: A Feminist Life*
12 Marlene Epp, *Women without Men: Mennonite Refugees of the Second World War*
13 Shirley Tillotson, *The Public at Play: Gender and the Politics of Recreation in Post-War Ontario*
14 Veronica Strong-Boag and Carole Gerson, *Paddling Her Own Canoe: The Times and Texts of E. Pauline Johnson (Tekahionwake)*
15 Stephen Heathorn, *For Home, Country, and Race: Constructing Gender, Class, and Englishness in the Elementary School, 1880–1914*
16 Valerie J. Korinek, *Roughing It in the Suburbs: Reading* Chatelaine *Magazine in the Fifties and Sixties*
17 Adele Perry, *On the Edge of Empire: Gender, Race, and the Making of British Columbia, 1849–1871*
18 Robert A. Campbell, *Sit Down and Drink Your Beer: Regulating Vancouver's Beer Parlours, 1925–1954*
19 Wendy Mitchinson, *Giving Birth in Canada, 1900–1950*

20 Roberta Hamilton, *Setting the Agenda: Jean Royce and the Shaping of Queen's University*

21 Donna Gabaccia and Franca Iacovetta, eds., *Women, Gender, and Transnational Lives: Italian Workers of the World*

22 Linda Reeder, *Widows in White: Migration and the Transformation of Rural Italian Women, Sicily, 1880–1920*

www.ingramcontent.com/pod-product-compliance
Lightning Source LLC
LaVergne TN
LVHW040757070826
844660LV00025B/1174

* 9 7 8 0 8 0 2 0 8 5 2 5 2 *